CENTURY 21® 10e
Computer Skills and Applications

Lessons 1–90

Jack P. Hoggatt, Ed. D.

*Assistant Dean and Director of Center for Advising,
Development, and Enrichment*
University of Wisconsin - Eau Claire
Eau Claire, Wisconsin

Jon A. Shank, Ed. D.

Professor of Education, Emeritus
Robert Morris University
Moon Township, Pennsylvania

James R. Smith, Jr., Ed. D.

Assistant Teaching Professor
North Carolina State University
Morrisville, North Carolina

SOUTH-WESTERN
CENGAGE Learning·

Australia • Brazil • Japan • Korea • Mexico • Singapore • Spain • United Kingdom • United States

Century 21® Computer Skills and Applications, Tenth Edition
Jack P. Hoggatt, Jon A. Shank, **James R. Smith, Jr.**

SVP Global Product Management, Research, School & Professional: Frank Menchaca

Sr. Development Editor: Dave Lafferty

Development Consulting Editor: Jean Findley, LEAP Publishing Services Inc.

Sr. Product Marketing Manager: Leah Klein

Sr. Content Project Manager: Martha Conway

Sr. Media Editor: Sally Nieman

Sr. Website Project Manager: Ed Stubenrauch

Manufacturing Planner: Kevin Kluck

Production Service: PreMediaGlobal

Copyeditor: Gary Morris

Sr. Art Director: Michelle Kunkler

Internal and Cover Designer: Grannan Design LTD.

Cover Images: © Fancy/Alamy; © imagebroker/Alamy; © Jack Hollingsworth/Getty Images, Inc.; © quavondo/iStockphoto

Key reach images: © Cengage Learning, Cengage Learning/Bill Smith Group/Sam Kolich

Teamwork photo: © Chad Baker/Ryan McVay/Getty Images, Inc.

Rights Acquisition Specialist, Image and Text: Deanna Ettinger

Photo Researcher: Josh Garvin, Bill Smith Group

Text Permissions Researcher: Jennifer Wagner, PreMediaGlobal

ISBN-13: 978-1-111-57175-7
ISBN-10: 1-111-57175-9

Cengage Learning
200 First Stamford Place, 4th Floor
Stamford, CT 06902
USA

Cengage Learning is a leading provider of customized learning solutions with office locations around the globe, including Singapore, the United Kingdom, Australia, Mexico, Brazil, and Japan. Locate your local office at: **www.cengage.com/global**

Cengage Learning products are represented in Canada by Nelson Education, Ltd.

For your course and learning solutions, visit **www.cengage.com/school**

Visit our company website at **www.cengage.com**

Printed in the United States of America
7 8 9 10 11 12   21 20 19 18 17

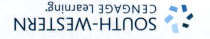

Century 21

Computer Skills and Applications, 10e

Provide your students with the **best in computing education** from the proven business education leader—now stronger than ever! This Tenth Edition of *Century 21 Computer Skills and Applications* helps students prepare for a lifetime of keyboarding and computer success with innovative solutions updated to reflect today's business challenges. Trust the leader who has taught more than 90 million people to type—bringing 100 years of publishing experience and a century of innovations together in a complete line of computing solutions.

The Right Approach, with the Right Coverage

- ▶ A cleaner look with a new internal design
- ▶ Streamlined and more focused units of instruction
- ▶ Emphasis on Ribbon Path (Tab/Group/Command) enables students to quickly navigate the software.

Home/Slides/New Slide/ Layout/Title and Content/ Insert Table

Increased emphasis on introductory **computer basics**.

The **Application Guide Activities** prepare students for the lessons that follow.

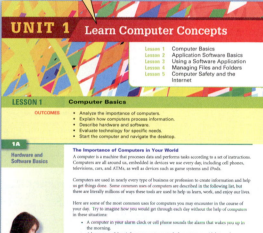

Learning Outcomes mapped to lesson activities.

Short generic drills support **Microsoft Office** versions.

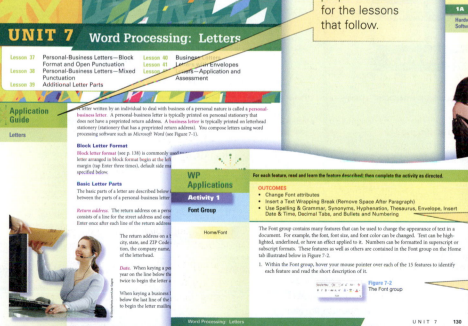

Integrated Learning for Stronger Results

Academic and Career Connections

Complete the following exercises that introduce various topics that involve academic themes and careers.

Grammar and Writing: Abbreviations and Word Usage

MicroType 6

• References/Communication Skills/Abbreviations
• References/Communication Skills/Word Usage
• CheckPro/Communication Skills 7
• CheckPro/Word Choice 7

1. Open *MicroType 6* and use this feature path for review: References/Communication Skills/Abbreviations.
2. Click *Rules* and review the rules of using abbreviations.
3. Then, under *Abbreviations*, click *Posttest*.
4. Follow the instructions to complete the posttest.
5. Repeat this process for Word Usage.

Optional Activities:
1. Go to this path: CheckPro/Communication Skills 7.
2. Complete the activities as directed.
3. Go to this path: CheckPro/Word Choice 7.
4. Key the Apply lines, and choose the correct word.

Communication: Reading

Open the document *df u09 communications*. Read the document carefully, and then close the file. Create a new presentation and apply a design theme of your choice. Insert a title slide and key the title **Habitat for Humanity**. Key your name as the subtitle. Insert a slide for each of the following questions. Key the question on the slide. Below the question, key your answer in a complete sentence. Select an appropriate slide layout, and apply formatting of your choice.

1. Who founded the organization Habitat for Humanity International?
2. What motivated the founder to start the organization?
3. What is the basic mission of Habitat for Humanity?
4. Habitat is not a giveaway program. When Habitat works on a home, what are the partner family's financial obligations? What other obligation does the family have?
5. Habitat for Humanity operates at the grassroots level. What does this mean?
6. Save the presentation as *u09 communications*.

Math Skills: Markups and Discounts

1. Will is a pharmacist who operates a small drugstore. In order to achieve a targeted level of gross profits (sales revenue minus product costs) to cover his fixed expenses—such as rent, utilities, and payroll—he needs to determine how much he should mark up his products. For example, if he expects to sell $2.5 million of products (based on cost) and he needs to produce gross profits of $500,000 to cover fixed expenses, how much does he have to mark up his products, on average, to achieve that target?
2. Will's drugstore has just signed up to participate in a health-care discount program. Although he does not know yet exactly how many customers will sign up to be club members, he expects that purchases on average will earn a 4 percent discount. How much will that reduce the store's projected sales revenue?
3. To make up for the discounts, how much would Will now have to mark up his of $500,000 in gross profits?

New end-of-unit projects for Academic and Career preparation provide the connection to Common Core integration. The coverage of Career Clusters and the *NEW* School and Community activities emphasize critical thinking.

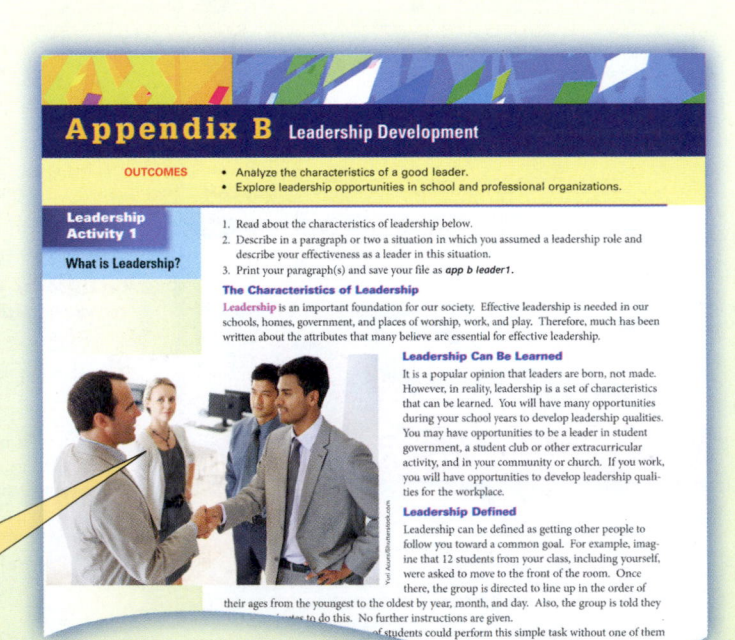

Appendix B Leadership Development

OUTCOMES
• Analyze the characteristics of a good leader.
• Explore leadership opportunities in school and professional organizations.

Leadership Activity 1

What is Leadership?

1. Read about the characteristics of leadership below.
2. Describe in a paragraph or two a situation in which you assumed a leadership role and describe your effectiveness as a leader in this situation.
3. Print your paragraph(s) and save your file as *app b leader1*.

The Characteristics of Leadership

Leadership is an important foundation for our society. Effective leadership is needed in our schools, homes, government, and places of worship, work, and play. Therefore, much has been written about the attributes that many believe are essential for effective leadership.

Leadership Can Be Learned

It is a popular opinion that leaders are born, not made. However, in reality, leadership is a set of characteristics that can be learned. You will have many opportunities during your school years to develop leadership qualities. You may have opportunities to be a leader in student government, a student club or other extracurricular activity, and in your community or church. If you work, you will have opportunities to develop leadership qualities for the workplace.

Leadership Defined

Leadership can be defined as getting other people to follow you toward a common goal. For example, imagine that 12 students from your class, including yourself, were asked to move to a situation in which you assumed a leadership role and their ages from the youngest by year, month, and day. Also, the group is told they to do this. No further instructions are given.

of students could perform this simple task without one of them one who assumes that role? If so, would you do

Leadership skills are *key* to personal and business success, and students can develop these skills using the material found in the **New Leadership Appendix** as well as the teamwork and Winning Edge activities.

Digital Citizenship and Ethics The rules governing appropriate and courteous behavior while you are online are called **netiquette**. Think of netiquette as online manners—the way you should behave as you surf the Web or correspond via e-mail, text messaging, and chats.

You might already know some netiquette rules. For example, you should not send e-mails or text messages in all caps because it implies shouting. Long and wordy postings on discussion groups and should be avoided because readers may of hearing the tone of your voice or seeing your facial expressions. Don't flood your messages or cute pictures you've found online. And don't start **flame wars**—hostile trouble rather than discuss issues.

The addition of **21ˢᵗ Century Skills** and **Digital Citizenship** add interesting and relevant topics for classroom discussion.

21st Century Skills: Media Literacy Think about the various ways you receive information. In addition to classroom lectures and studies, you might watch a television show, listen to a radio broadcast, browse the Web, or read a magazine. As you process the information you receive daily, you form impressions and make interpretations and judgments. Consciously—or subconsciously—the many messages you process every day influence the decisions you make and have a significant impact on the way you live your life.

Think Critically
1. Think of an advertisement you have recently seen or heard. Where did you see or hear the ad? What was being opinion of the advertiser? Would you make a purchase based on the ad? of clothing or shoes or a favorite food or

A Proven Approach for Mastering Keyboarding Skills

Triple control guidelines for timed writings and skill building include three factors—syllabic intensity, average word length, and percentage of high–frequency words—for the most accurate evaluation of students' keying skills.

Tested and proven pedagogy provides sound new key learning, skill building, model document illustrations, and triple-controlled timed writings to ensure that assessments are reliable and consistent.

LA all letters used

Computer Applications and Beyond!

Core computer application skills are taught and reinforced so that students are prepared for life! Instead of teaching students the entire application, the critical components are emphasized and mastered.

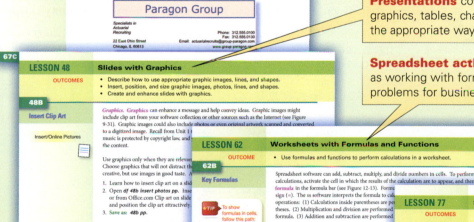

Word processing skill is enhanced by the model documents provided for letters, tables, reports, and special documents.

Presentations coverage includes creating slides, graphics, tables, charts, and slide shows—and learning the appropriate way to present.

Spreadsheet activities include basic functions as well as working with formulas and charts to help resolve numeric problems for business, education, and personal use.

Database coverage includes adding/deleting records and fields, sorting, and reports.

LESSON 67 — Documents with Shapes and Text Boxes

OUTCOME
- Insert and modify shapes and text boxes to enhance the content of documents and make them attractive and easy to read.

67B — Letterhead

1. Open a new document. Using the information below, create a header that serves as letterhead on the company stationery. Use Verdana 36-pt. font within a text box to display the company name and colors similar to those shown below. You decide all other format features.
2. Save as: *67b letterhead*.

Paragon Group
Specialists in
Actuarial
Recruiting
22 East Ohio Street
Chicago, IL 60613
Phone: 312.555.0100
Fax: 312.555.0130
Email: actuarialrecruits@group-paragon.com
www.group-paragon.com

67C

LESSON 48 — Slides with Graphics

OUTCOMES
- Describe how to use appropriate graphic images, lines, and shapes.
- Insert, position, and size graphic images, photos, lines, and shapes.
- Create and enhance slides with graphics.

48B — Insert Clip Art

Insert/Online Pictures

Graphics. Graphics can enhance a message and help convey ideas. Graphic images might include clip art from your software collection or other sources such as the Internet (see Figure 9-31). Graphic images could also include photos or even original artwork scanned and converted to a digitized image. Recall from Unit 1 that music is protected by copyright law, and the content.

Use graphics only when they are relevant. Choose graphics that will not distract. Be creative, but use images in good taste. A

1. Learn how to insert clip art on a slide.
2. Open *df 48b insert photos pp*. Insert or from Office.com Clip art on slide and position the clip art attractively.
3. Save as: *48b pp*.

Figure 9-31 Sample clip art

LESSON 62 — Worksheets with Formulas and Functions

OUTCOME
- Use formulas and functions to perform calculations in a worksheet.

62B — Key Formulas

Spreadsheet software can add, subtract, multiply, and divide numbers in cells. To perform calculations, activate the cell in which the results of the calculation are to appear, and then key a **formula** in the formula bar (see Figure 12-13). Formu sign (=). The ss software interprets the formula to ca operations: (1) Calculations inside parentheses are pe theses. (2) Multiplication and division are performed formula. (3) Addition and subtraction are performed

TIP — To show formulas in cells, follow this path:

Formulas/Formula Auditing/Show Formulas

TIP — To show the answer, click Show Formulas to deselect it.

Figure 12-13 Formulas

LESSON 77 — Sorts, Filters, and Queries

OUTCOMES
- Learn to create single and multiple data sorts.
- Learn to create filters.
- Learn to create queries.

77B — Sort Information for Franklin HS FBLA

Home/Sort & Filter/Select Type of Sort or Filter

1. Review the Sort feature in the Application Guide (p. 298); learn how to create sorts.
2. Open the *FHS FBLA Members* table file.
3. Perform the following sorts.

Single Sorts – *Ascending* Order
1. Last Name
2. ZIP Code

Single Sorts – *Descending* Order
1. Last Name
2. ZIP Code

4. Print the single sort by Last Name in Descending order.
5. Save and close the database.

77C

1. Open *df 77c Softwa*

Digital Solutions Take You Beyond the Book!

For supporting software that is motivating, teaches new keys, checks documents for speed and accuracy, and is built for student success, **MicroType™ 6** and **MicroType 6 with CheckPro™** are your ideal solutions.

◄ **MicroType 6 includes touch-typing instruction** for alphabetic and numeric keyboarding and the numeric keypad.

◄ **MicroType 6 with CheckPro** checks keystrokes and formatting in Microsoft Word and Excel, providing the most comprehensive teaching and learning tool.

MicroType 6
with CheckPro
Alphabetic Keyboarding
Lesson 1

If you only need new-key learning and skill building, then MicroType 6 is your solution. With either solution, textbook marginal references will indicate the appropriate points for incorporating the software. Skill building lessons can be used throughout the course to continue to build those essential productivity skills.

An **Interactive eBook** provides students with an interactive, online-only version of the printed textbook to be used at school or at home with indexing, highlighting, and quick navigation.

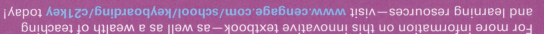

Visit Us Online!

For more information on this innovative textbook—as well as a wealth of teaching and learning resources—visit **www.cengage.com/school/keyboarding/c21key** today!

► Data Files
► Web Links
► Assessments/Tests
► Flashcards
► Solutions Files
► Lesson Plans
► PowerPoint® Presentations
► **And much more!**

PREFACE

The tenth edition of *Century 21® Computer Skills and Applications* provides a high degree of flexibility for moving between traditional and new content areas. This flexibility permits the structuring of courses to meet the needs of students, school districts, and the community.

The tenth edition presents choices in word processing, database, spreadsheet, and presentation software features. It offers units on computer concepts, using Help, and Personal Information Management (PIM). Additionally, one unit is a business simulation for real-world practice. A new appendix on leadership development provides activities on leadership topics that can be taught as a unit or distributed throughout the course.

New special features highlight 21st Century Skills and themes for Digital Citizenship. New end-of-unit activities include Academic and Career Connections, Language Arts, Math, Career Clusters, School and Community, and The Winning Edge for student organizations' competitive events.

For this edition, South-Western/Cengage Learning surveyed business teachers, employed content reviewers, and met with focus groups to determine the needs of today's keyboarding students and instructors. The features of *Century 21 Computer Skills and Applications, 10th Edition*, address those needs.

The *Century 21* family includes a full range of high-quality supplementary items to enhance your courses, including a website at www.cengage.com/school/keyboarding/c21key. Thank you for choosing *Century 21*. Whether you are a new instructor, new to *Century 21*, or simply updating your *C21* materials, we know that you will find this edition an exciting solution for your classes.

How to Use this Book

There are a number of ways that the many available digital and print resources can be used in a classroom/lab.

Student Edition

The **student text** (ISBN 9781111571757) provides features designed to meet your instructional needs. Each software unit opens with an **Application Guide** that introduces concepts and shows thumbnail model documents. Some guides have activities for reinforcement. Within each unit, a series of lessons provides plenty of hands-on activities.

Each lesson begins with a list of learning outcomes and warm-up drills that prepare students for lesson activities. Lessons contain computer applications for learning and applying skills and documents to format. Tips in the margins provide helpful hints, and data files assist with the completion of longer activities.

Most units end with an Application and Assessment lesson. The end-of-unit materials include **Academic and Career Connections**, grammar and language activities, math activities, **Career Cluster** projects; **School and Community** projects, and **Winning Edge** competitive events practice.

Certain activities are identified as suitable for **teamwork** projects. Special features within a unit include **21st Century Skills** and **Digital Citizenship**. These two features cover topics such as media literacy, personal responsibility and initiative, plagiarism, and identity theft, along with questions for critical thinking and discussion.

Between conceptual/software units, Input Skill Development units containing skill building and timed writings provide opportunities for students to improve their keying techniques and productivity. The book ends with a business simulation unit and a comprehensive Assessment unit.

Resources

In addition to the textbook, the complete instructional program includes a **Wrap-around Instructor's Edition** (ISBN 9781111580063).

The IRCD contains a digital **manual** with solutions and teaching tips, a **Spanish Language supplement**, lesson plans, *PowerPoint* presentations to present formats and software features, teaching suggestions, printable rubrics, end-of-unit answers, and tests.

Also available is Cognero web-based assessment with testing and questions and a **PC Keyboard Wall Chart** (ISBN 9781111581305).

MicroType 6™ is the software that teaches and reinforces keyboarding skills. See www.cengage.com/school/keyboarding/microtype for more information.

There are also available **e-Book versions** of the text; call for more information on these (800-354-9706). A **website** (www.cengage.com/school/keyboarding/c21key) provides many of the same resources from the instructor DVD.

About the Authors

Dr. Jon A. Shank is a Professor Emeritus of Education at Robert Morris University in Moon Township, Pennsylvania. For more than 20 years, he served as Dean of the School of Applied Sciences and Education at Robert Morris. Most recently, Dr. Shank taught keyboarding and software methods courses to undergraduate and graduate students who were studying to become business education teachers. Dr. Shank holds memberships in regional, state, and national business education organizations. He has received many honors during his career, including Outstanding Post-Secondary Business Educator in Pennsylvania.

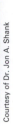

Courtesy of Dr. Jon A. Shank

Dr. Jack P. Hoggatt is Assistant Dean of Student Affairs and CADE Director for the University of Wisconsin-Eau Claire. He has taught courses in Business Writing, Advanced Business Communications, and the communication component of the university's Masters in Business Administration (MBA) program. Dr. Hoggatt has held offices in several professional organizations, including president of the Wisconsin Business Education Association. He has served as an advisor to local and state business organizations and has been named the Outstanding Post-Secondary Business Educator for Wisconsin.

Courtesy of Dr. Jack P. Hoggatt

Dr. James R. Smith, Jr. is a Teaching Assistant Professor in the Department of Curriculum, Instruction, and Counselor Education at North Carolina State University. He has been a secondary business and marketing teacher, a North Carolina State Consultant for Business and Information Technology, and a local school system Career and Technical Education Administrator. Currently he is the undergraduate and graduate program coordinator for the business and marketing teacher education program at North Carolina State University. Dr. Smith has held offices in professional organizations, and he has received the Outstanding Leadership Award from the National Association of Supervisors of Business Education and the Outstanding Career and Technical Educator from the North Carolina Career and Technical Education Association—Business Education Division. Dr. Smith is active with his church and community organizations.

Courtesy of Dr. James R. Smith, Jr.

Note from the Authors

This text will serve as a solid foundation upon which you can build your course to meet the varying needs of your students. It contains an appropriate balance between new-key learning, building input skill, and formatting frequently used documents using features from various software application packages. Each software application is presented in the breadth and depth needed for students to be able to use their software competencies, as well as their keyboarding skills and formatting knowledge, to enhance their productivity as they continue their education, carry out their personal affairs, and enter the workplace. The unit activities, including the variety of end-of-unit activities, provide teachers with many opportunities to connect computer skills and applications to other curricular goals valued by administrators, other teachers, and the community.

Reviewers

Robin M. Albrecht
Osbourn High School
Manassas, VA

Diana Davis
Deep Creek High School
Chesapeake, VA

Tanya Evans
Hattiesburg High School
Hattiesburg, MS

Diane Harrington
Sault Area High School and Career Center
Sault Ste. Marie, MI

Shellie Hughes
Cherokee High School South
Marlton, NJ

Karen Bean May
Blinn College
Brenham, TX

Jerre L. McManama, Jr.
Roncalli High School
Indianapolis, IN

Susan Munk
Rockland School District 382
Rockland, ID

Beverly Nix
Carver Junior High School
Spartanburg, SC

Linda H. Robinson
Winter Haven High School
Winter Haven, FL

Laurel Stevenson
Holly Hill School
Holly Hill, FL

CONTENTS

Unit 1   **Learn Computer Concepts**   **1**

1   Computer Basics   **1**
2   Application Software Basics   **12**
3   Using a Software Application   **15**
Digital Citizenship and Ethics   19
4   Managing Files and Folders   **19**
5   Computer Safety and the Internet   **24**
21st Century Skills: *Leadership*   29
Academic and Career Connections   30
Introducing Career Clusters   31
The Winning Edge   32
School and Community   32

Unit 2   **Alphabetic Keys**   **33**

6   Home Keys (fdsa jkl;)   **33**
7   Review Home Keys (fdsa jkl;)   **38**
8   New Keys: h and e   **40**
9   New Keys: i and r   **42**
10   Review   **44**
11   New Keys: o and t   **47**
12   New Keys: n and g   **49**
13   New Keys: Left Shift and Period (.)   **51**
14   Review   **53**
15   New Keys: u and c   **55**
16   New Keys: w and Right Shift   **57**
17   New Keys: b and y   **59**
18   Review   **61**
19   New Keys: m and x   **63**
20   New Keys: p and v   **65**
21   New Keys: q and Comma (,)   **67**
22   Review   **69**
23   New Keys: z and Colon (:)   **71**
24   New Keys: Caps Lock and Question Mark (?)   **74**
25   New Keys: Backspace, Quotation Mark ("), and Tab   **76**
21st Century Skills: *Initiative and Self-Direction*   79
26   New Keys: Apostrophe (') and Hyphen (-)   **80**
Digital Citizenship and Ethics   82
Academic and Career Connections   84
Career Clusters   85
The Winning Edge   86
School and Community   86

Unit 3   **Enhance Input Skills**   **87**

27   Input Skill Development   **87**
28   Input Skill Development   **90**

Unit 4   **Help**   **93**

29   Help Basics   **93**
Digital Citizenship and Ethics   94
21st Century Skills: *Access and Evaluate Information*   96
30   Special Features   **97**
Academic and Career Connections   101
Career Clusters   102
The Winning Edge   103
School and Community   103

Unit 5   **E-Mail and Personal Information Management**   **104**

Application Guide   **104**
21st Century Skills: *Communicate Clearly*   110
31   Format E-mail Messages   **111**
32   Create and Format E-mail Messages   **112**
33   Create and Format E-mail Messages   **114**
34   Calendaring, Contacts, Tasks, and Notes   **114**
Digital Citizenship and Ethics   118
Academic and Career Connections   119
Career Clusters   120
The Winning Edge   121
School and Community   121

Unit 6   **Enhance Input Skills**   **122**

35   Input Skill Development   **122**
36   Input Skill Development   **125**

Unit 7   **Word Processing: Letters**   **128**

Application Guide   **128**
WP Applications   **130**
37   Personal-Business Letters—Block Format and Open Punctuation   **137**
Digital Citizenship and Ethics   139
38   Personal-Business Letters—Mixed Punctuation   **140**
39   Additional Letter Parts   **142**
40   Business Letters   **146**
41   Letters with Envelopes   **148**
21st Century Skills: *Entrepreneurial Literacy*   148
42   Letters—Application and Assessment   **151**
Academic and Career Connections   154
Career Clusters   155
The Winning Edge   156
School and Community   156

Contents

Unit 8 Word Processing: Tables 157

Application Guide 157
WP Applications 159
Digital Citizenship and Ethics 165
43 Tables—Basic Features 166
21st Century Skills: *Information, Communications, and Technology (ICT) Literacy* 168
44 Table Layout Features 170
45 Table Design Features 171
46 Tables—Application and Assessment 174
Academic and Career Connections 177
Career Clusters 179
The Winning Edge 180

Unit 9 Presentations—Slide Shows 181

Application Guide 181
47 Text Slides 187
48 Slides with Graphics 191
49 Tables, Graphs, and Charts 196
50 Create and Deliver a Presentation 200
Digital Citizenship and Ethics 204
51 Slide Show Assessment 205
21st Century Skills: *Media Literacy* 206
Academic and Career Connections 207
Career Clusters 208
The Winning Edge 209
School and Community 209

Unit 10 Enhance Input Skills 210

52 Input Skill Development 210
53 Input Skill Development 212

Unit 11 Word Processing: Reports 215

Application Guide 215
WP Applications 219
Digital Citizenship and Ethics 223
54 Unbound Reports with Styles 224
55 Unbound Reports with Documentation 225
21st Century Skills: *Make Judgments and Decisions* 228
56 MLA Reports with Textual Citations 229
57 MLA Reports with Documentation 230
58 Report Application and Assessment 232
Academic and Career Connections 234
Career Clusters 235
The Winning Edge 236
School and Community 236

Unit 12 Spreadsheet: Learn Spreadsheet Essentials 237

Application Guide 237
SS Applications 237
Digital Citizenship and Ethics 238
59 Worksheets 240
60 Edit Worksheets 242
61 Format Worksheets 245
62 Worksheets with Formulas and Functions 249
63 Worksheets with Charts 252
64 Worksheet Application and Assessment 254
21st Century Skills: *Productivity and Accountability* 255
Academic and Career Connections 256
Career Clusters 257
The Winning Edge 258
School and Community 258

Unit 13 Word Processing: Special Documents 259

Application Guides 259
WP Applications 261
65 Templates—Memos and Agendas 265
66 Templates—Meeting Minutes, Certificates, and Invitations 268
Digital Citizenship and Ethics 270
67 Documents with Shapes and Text Boxes 271
68 Flyers with Graphics 272
69 Employment Resumes 274
70 Employment Letters and Forms 278
71 Mail Merge 282
72 Special Documents Application and Assessment 285
21st Century Skills: *Creativity and Innovation* 287
Academic and Career Connections 288
Career Clusters 289
The Winning Edge 290
School and Community 290

Unit 14 Learn Database 291

DB Applications 291
Digital Citizenship and Ethics 300
73 Adding Records to an Existing Database 301
21st Century Skills: *Use and Manage Information* 303
74 Creating a Database and Table 308
75 Adding Records to Update a Database 311
76 Editing Records, Adding Fields, and Deleting Records 313
77 Sorts, Filters, and Queries 317
78 Database Application Assessment 319
Academic and Career Connections 324
Career Clusters 325
The Winning Edge 326
School and Community 326

Unit 15 **Enhance Input Skills** **327**

79 Input Skill Development 327
80 Input Skill Development 329

Unit 16 **HPJ Communication Specialists:**
An Integrated Project **332**

81–85 HPJ Communication Specialists:
An Integrated Project 337

Unit 17 **Assessment** **350**

86 Assess E-mail, PIM, Help, and Input Skills 350
87 Assess Word Processing
(Letters and Tables) Skills 354

88 Assess Presentation and Input Skills 356
89 Assess Word Processing (Reports)
and Spreadsheet Skills 359
90 Assess Word Processing (Special Documents)
and Database Skills 362

Appendices

A Numeric Keys and Numeric Keypad 365
B Leadership Development 382
C Reference Guide 388

Glossary G1
Index I1

Software Skill	Page No.
Computer Basics **Units 1 & 4**	
Close Button	15
Computer Ethics	27
Computer Safety and Security	28
Copying and Moving Files and Folders	21
Desktop	9
Document Views	17
Files and Folders	19
Help	93
Internet	24
Menu Bar	13
New Document	15
Open Document	15
Print	17
Renaming and Deleting Files and Folders	23
Save/Save As	18
Search the Web	25
Shut Down	11
Start Button	12
Task Bar	10
Tool Bar, Ribbon	13
Window (Maximize, Minimize)	14
E-mail and PIM **Unit 5**	
Attach File	105
Calendar	107
Categorize/E-mail Tags	106
Contacts	108
E-mail	105
Find a Contact	106
Manage E-mail	114
Notes	110
Tasks	109
Word Processing **Units 2, 7, 8, 11, & 13**	
Adjusting Column Width and Row Height in Tables	163
AutoCorrect	45
Bold	46

Software Skill	Page No.
Bullets and Numbering	134
Centering Tables	161
Clip Art and Pictures	264
Cover Page	223
Cut, Copy, Paste	54, 223
Decimal Tab	135
Envelopes	133
Fonts	130
Format Painter	161
Hyphenation	131
Indentations	220
Insert	45, 220
Insert Date and Time	132
Insert Footnote	222
Insert/Delete Rows and Columns in Tables	162
Italic	46
Line and Page Breaks	220
Line and Paragraph Spacing	70, 219
Mail Merge	282
Margins	70
Merge and Split Cells in Tables	162
Overtype	45
Page Break	219
Page Numbers	220
Portrait/Landscape Orientation	163
Print Preview and Print	62
Remove Space after Paragraph	133
Select Text	54
Selecting and Formatting Table Cell Content	160
Shading and Borders in Tables	164
Shapes	263
Show/Hide ¶	135
Sort Tables	165
Spelling and Grammar	131
Styles	221
Table Styles	164
Tables	157
Tabs	79
Templates (Memo, Agenda, Meeting Minutes, Certificates, Invitations)	261
Text Boxes	262
Text Inserted from File	222

Software Skill	Page No.
Text Wrapping Break	133
Thesaurus	131
Underline	46
Undo/Redo	62
Vertical Alignment	163
Zoom	62
Presentations **Unit 9**	
Bulleted List Slide	188
Design Theme	182
Notes Page	185
Outline View	185
Slide Layouts	183
Slide Show	185
Slide Sorter View	185
Slides with Graphics	191
Slides with Tables, Graphs (Bar, Line), and Charts (Pie)	196
Slides	181
Title and Content Layout	188
Title Slide	188
View Options	185
Spreadsheets **Unit 12**	
Cells, Columns, and Rows	239
Chart Layout and Styles	253
Chart Type	252
Charts (Column, Bar, Line, and Pie)	252
Cut, Copy, and Move	244
Cell Content and Format—Clear and Delete	243
Cell Content—Format	247
Cell Content—Select and Edit	242

Software Skill	Page No.
Format Numbers	246
Formulas	249
Functions (SUM, AVERAGE, COUNT, MAX, MIN)	250
Gridlines and Column and Row Headings—View and Print	241
Labels and Values	241
Move Around in a Worksheet	240
Range of Cells—Select	243
Rows and Columns—Insert and Delete	245
Worksheet Window	239
Worksheets and Workbooks	238
Database **Unit 14**	
Add Records	303
Data Type (Number, Text, Currency, Date and Time)	294
Datasheet View	293
Design View	293
Fields	292
Filter	300
Forms	295
Move in Tables and Forms	313
Print a Table	305
Queries	295
Records	295
Reports and Report Wizard	297
Sorts (Multiple)	299
Sorts (Primary and Secondary)	298
Tables	292

FEATURES

Unique Unit Features	Pages
21st Century Skills	29, 79, 96, 110, 148, 168, 206, 228, 255, 287, 303
Academic and Career Connections	30, 84, 101, 119, 154, 177, 207, 234, 256, 288, 324
Application Guide	104, 128, 157, 181, 215, 237, 259, 291
Career Clusters	31, 85, 102, 120, 155, 179, 208, 235, 257, 289, 325
Communications	30, 84, 101, 119, 154, 177, 207, 234, 256, 288, 324
Digital Citizenship and Ethics	19, 82, 94, 118, 139, 165, 204, 223, 238, 270, 300
Math Skills	31, 84, 101, 119, 154, 178, 207, 234, 256, 288, 324
MicroType 6	30, 37, 39, 41, 43, 44, 48, 50, 52, 53, 56, 58, 60, 61, 64, 66, 68, 69, 73, 75, 78, 81, 84, 89, 92, 101, 119, 124, 127, 154, 177, 207, 234, 256, 288, 324, 367, 370, 372, 374
School and Community	32, 86, 103, 121, 156, 178, 209, 236, 258, 290, 326
TEAMWORK	94, 139, 165, 203, 223, 270, 287, 300
Timed Writings	73, 88, 89, 91, 92, 123, 124, 126, 127, 211, 213, 214, 328, 331, 353, 358, 367, 370, 374
WinningEdge	32, 86, 103, 121, 156, 180, 209, 236, 258, 290, 326

UNIT 1 Learn Computer Concepts

Lesson 1   Computer Basics
Lesson 2   Application Software Basics
Lesson 3   Using a Software Application
Lesson 4   Managing Files and Folders
Lesson 5   Computer Safety and the Internet

LESSON 1   Computer Basics

OUTCOMES

- Analyze the importance of computers.
- Explain how computers process information.
- Describe hardware and software.
- Evaluate technology for specific needs.
- Start the computer and navigate the desktop.

1A

Hardware and Software Basics

The Importance of Computers in Your World

A computer is a machine that processes data and performs tasks according to a set of instructions. Computers are all around us, embedded in devices we use every day, including cell phones, televisions, cars, and ATMs, as well as devices such as game systems and iPods.

Computers are used in nearly every type of business or profession to create information and help us get things done. Some common uses of computers are described in the following list, but there are literally millions of ways these tools are used to help us learn, work, and enjoy our lives.

Here are some of the most common uses for computers you may encounter in the course of your day. Try to imagine how you would get through each day without the help of computers in these situations:

- A computer in your alarm clock or cell phone sounds the alarm that wakes you up in the morning.
- A large, powerful mainframe computer controls the vast power grid that sends power to light and heat your home, as well as the water systems that bring you fresh water for your shower.

- A microchip computer in the microwave oven, stove, or coffee maker helps monitor the temperature while cooking your breakfast.
- Computers control the traffic lights that regulate the flow of traffic at busy intersections on your way to school.
- Computers regulate the heating and cooling systems in your home and school, keeping the buildings comfortable.

© Supri Suharjoto/Shutterstock.com

directly in front of the chair. The front edge should be even with the edge of the table or desk.

Place the monitor for easy viewing. Some experts maintain that the top of the screen should be at or slightly below eye level. Others recommend placing the monitor even lower. Set it a comfortable distance from your eyes—at least an arm's length away.

Position the monitor to avoid glare (an antiglare filter can help). Close blinds or pull shades as needed. Adjust the brightness and contrast controls, if necessary, for readability. Keep the screen clean with a soft, lint-free cloth and (unless your instructor tells you otherwise) a nonalcohol, nonabrasive cleaning solution or glass cleaner.

If you cannot adjust your equipment and the desk or table is too high, try adjusting your chair. If that does not work, you can sit on a cushion, a coat, or even a stack of books.

Use a straight-backed chair that will not yield when you lean back. The chair should support your lower back (try putting a rolled-up towel or sweater behind you if it does not). The back of your knees should not be pressed against the chair. Use a seat that allows you to keep your feet flat on the floor, or use a footrest. Even a box or a backpack will do.

Position the mouse next to and at the same height as the keyboard and as close to the body as possible. Research has not shown conclusively that one type of pointing device (mouse, trackball, touch pad, stylus, joystick, etc.) is better than another. Whatever you use, make sure your arms, hands, and fingers are relaxed. If you change to a new device, evaluate it carefully first and work up gradually to using it all the time.

Arrange your work material so you can see it easily and maintain good posture. Some experts recommend positioning whatever you look at most often (the monitor or paper material) directly in front of you so you do not have to turn your head to the side while keying.

Exercise And Take Breaks

Exercise your neck, shoulders, arms, wrists, and fingers before beginning to key each day and often during the workday. Neck, shoulder, wrist, and other exercises appear at the Cornell University ergonomics website listed below.

Take a short break at least once an hour. Rest your eyes from time to time as you work by focusing on an object at least 20 feet away. Blink frequently.

Use Good Posture And Proper Techniques

Sit erect and as far back in the seat as possible. Your forearms should be parallel to the slant of the keyboard, your wrists and forearms low, but not touching or resting on any surface. Your arms should be near the side of your body in a relaxed position. Your shoulders should not be raised, but should be in a natural posture.

Keep your fingers curved and upright over the home keys. Strike each key lightly using the finger*tip*. Grasp the mouse loosely. Make a conscious effort to relax your hands and shoulders while keying.

For more information on mouse and keyboard use and CTS/RSI, visit the following Internet sites:

- http://kidshealth.org/kid/ (search for *ergonomics*)
- http://www.tifaq.org
- http://ergonomics.ucla.edu/
- http://www.office-ergo.com
- http://ergo.human.cornell.edu/

© InstinctDesign/Shutterstock.com

Ergonomic Keyboards

Ergonomic keyboards (see illustration at left) are designed to improve hand posture and make keying more comfortable. Generally they have a split design with left and right banks of keys and the ability to tilt or rotate the keyboard for comfort. More research is needed to determine just how effective ergonomic keyboards are in preventing RSI injuries and carpal tunnel syndrome.

- Microcomputers are used to operate the cell phones and the wireless network you use to communicate with others.
- Mainframe computers, network servers, and routers are used to host and deliver the vast network that makes up the Internet and World Wide Web. (You will learn more about networks and the Internet in Lesson 5 of this unit.)
- Personal computers (PCs) in your school and in offices around the world are used to create and manipulate information and documents.
- Computers are used to control and operate televisions, game systems, MP3 players, and other entertainment devices.

Figure 1-1 Each of these devices uses a type of computer to process data

Think about the ways computers impact your life each day. Make a list of each time you have used a computer or a device that includes a microprocessor today.

How Computers Process Information

Most of our time in this text will be spent learning about how to use personal computers (PCs) and laptop computers to key data and create various types of documents. To work with data, all computers have five basic functions: input, processing, output, distribution, and storage. See Figure 1-2 for an illustration of this process. **Input** is the raw data you enter into the computer. Input data can include anything from letters and numbers you key to photos you scan, music you download, or videos you record. When you use the mouse (more later in this lesson about this tool) or the keyboard, you are giving instructions, or input, to your computer. That's why the mouse and keyboard are referred to as input devices. Whatever input you enter, the computer converts the data into a program language that enables the computer to process it. To be used by the computer, the data is converted into bits and bytes, which are coded combinations of just two digits—0s and 1s. That's why computers and other electronic devices are often called digital devices.

Repetitive stress injury (RSI) is a result of repeated movement of a particular part of the body. It is also known as repetitive motion injury, musculoskeletal disorder, cumulative trauma disorder, and by a host of other names. A familiar example of RSI is "tennis elbow." RSI is the number-one occupational illness, costing employers more than $80 billion a year in health-care fees and lost wages.

Of concern to keyboard and mouse users is the form of RSI called carpal tunnel syndrome (CTS). CTS is an inflammatory disease that develops gradually and affects the wrists, hands, and forearms. Blood vessels, tendons, and nerves pass into the hand through the carpal tunnel (see illustration below). If any of these structures enlarge, or the walls of the tunnel narrow, the median nerve is pinched and CTS symptoms may result.

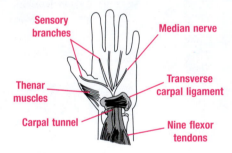

Sensory branches
Median nerve
Thenar muscles
Transverse carpal ligament
Carpal tunnel
Nine flexor tendons

Palm view of left hand

Symptoms Of RSI/CTS

CTS symptoms include numbness in the hand; tingling or burning in the hand, wrist, or elbow; severe pain in the forearm, elbow, or shoulder; and difficulty in gripping objects. Symptoms usually appear during sleeping hours, probably because many people sleep with their wrists flexed.

If not properly treated, the pressure on the median nerve, which controls the thumb, forefinger, middle finger, and half the ring finger, causes severe pain. The pain can radiate into the forearm, elbow, or shoulder. There are many kinds of treatment, ranging from simply resting to surgery. Left untreated, CTS can result in permanent damage or paralysis.

The good news is that 99 percent of people with carpal tunnel syndrome recover completely. Computer users can avoid reinjuring themselves by taking the precautions discussed later in this article.

Causes Of RSI/CTS

RSI/CTS often develops in workers whose physical routine is unvaried. Common occupational factors include (1) using awkward posture, (2) using poor techniques, (3) performing tasks with wrists bent (see below), (4) using improper equipment, (5) working at a rapid pace, (6) not taking rest breaks, and (7) not doing exercises that promote graceful motion and good techniques.

RSI/CTS is not limited to workers or adults. Keying school assignments, playing computer or video games, and surfing the Internet are increasing the incidence of RSI/CTS in younger people.

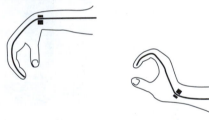

Improper wrist positions for keystroking

CTS is frequently a health concern for people who use a computer keyboard or mouse. The risk of developing CTS is less for those who use proper furniture or equipment, keyboarding techniques, posture, and/or muscle-stretching exercises than for those who do not.

Reducing The Risk Of RSI/CTS

By taking the following precautions, keyboard and mouse users can reduce the risk of developing RSI/CTS and can keep it from recurring. Experts stress that good computer habits like these are very important in avoiding RSI/CTS. They can also help you avoid back, neck, and shoulder pain, and eyestrain.

Arrange The Work Area

Arrange your equipment in a way that is natural and comfortable for you. Position the keyboard at elbow height and

Describe ways in which you have input data into a computer in the past several days. This could include any type of device, from a PC to a cell phone or game controller.

A **bit** is the most basic unit of data stored or processed by a computer, and it must be either a 1 or a 0, which basically correspond to an On or Off state in the computer's electronic circuits. A **byte** is typically composed of a group of 8 bits. A megabyte is approximately one million bytes, and a gigabyte is a little over a billion bytes.

Every piece of information you use in a computer is merely a coded group of 0s and 1s—for example, the coded format for the letter A in bits is 01000001.

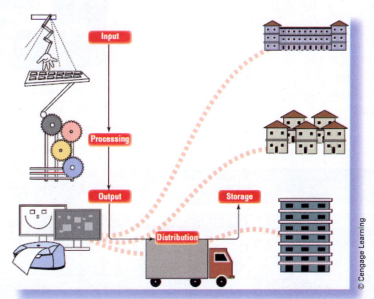

Once data is converted into bytes, the data can be **processed**, which means the computer is doing something to manipulate the data. The instructions that tell the computer what to do with the data are called **software**.

After the computer processes the data, it displays the completed work as **output**. The output may be displayed on a screen, printed on a report, played over speakers as sound, or sent via a network link to another computer.

Figure 1-2 The five steps of information processing

Next, **distribution** enables the computer to share information with computers and other users, typically across a network. Networks enable you to distribute data in ways such as sending e-mail, texting, or posting a picture to a website. You will learn more about different types of networks and how the Internet works in Lesson 5 of this unit.

There are two basic types of computer memory for storing data. **RAM**, which stands for **random-access memory**, is used for temporary **storage** while the computer is processing the data. You can think of RAM in the same way as your own short-term memory. All data stored in RAM is lost once the computer is shut off.

The second type of memory is **ROM**, which stands for **read-only memory**. This is long-term memory that resides in the computer and is used for programs that run when the computer is started up; it cannot be easily accessed or changed.

You can save the data the computer has processed on a storage device. This enables you to keep the data for use at a later time. Storage devices that provide a more permanent home for the information you want to keep and use again include media such as DVDs, thumb drives, and a computer's hard drive, as shown in Figure 1-3.

The numbered parts are found on most computers. The location of some parts will vary.

1. **CPU (Central Processing Unit):** Internal operating unit or "brain" of computer.
2. **CD-ROM drive:** Reads data from and writes data to a CD.
3. **Monitor:** Displays text and graphics on a screen.
4. **Mouse:** Used to input commands.
5. **Keyboard:** An arrangement of letter, figure, symbol, control, function, and editing keys and a numeric keypad.

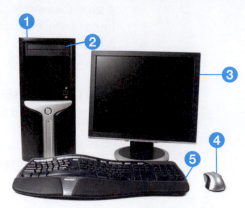

© Dmitry Melnikov/Shutterstock.com

KEYBOARD ARRANGEMENT

© PixAchi/Shutterstock.com

1. **Alphanumeric keys:** Letters, numbers, and symbols.
2. **Numeric keypad:** Keys at the right side of the keyboard used to enter numeric copy and perform calculations.
3. **Function (F) keys:** Used to execute commands, sometimes with other keys. Commands vary with software.
4. **Arrow keys:** Move insertion point up, down, left, or right.
5. ESC **(Escape):** Closes a software menu or dialog box.
6. TAB: Moves the insertion point to a preset position.
7. CAPS LOCK: Used to make all capital letters.
8. SHIFT: Makes capital letters and symbols shown at tops of number keys.
9. CTRL **(Control):** With other key(s), executes commands. Commands may vary with software.
10. ALT **(Alternate):** With other key(s), executes commands. Commands may vary with software.
11. **Space Bar:** Inserts a space in text.
12. ENTER **(**RETURN**):** Moves insertion point to margin and down to next line. Also used to execute commands.
13. DELETE: Removes text to the right of insertion point.
14. NUM LOCK: Activates/deactivates numeric keypad.
15. INSERT: Activates insert or typeover.
16. BACKSPACE: Deletes text to the left of insertion point.

Figure 1-3 DVDs and a computer hard drive are two common types of data storage devices

Hardware Basics

Hardware is computer equipment, the physical components of the device. Hardware is the mechanism that carries out the software instructions.

For a personal computer or laptop, hardware includes the central processing unit (CPU) as well as the monitor, keyboard, mouse, printer, and other peripherals, as shown in Figure 1-4. **Peripheral** is the name used for a piece of hardware that works with the CPU.

Wireless network router

Mouse

Monitor

USB cable

Hard disk drive

Central processing unit inside case

CDs and DVDs

USB or thumb drive

Figure 1-4 Common components of a desktop PC

Take a look at the computers in your school's lab. Make a list of the components in the computers you see and use.

Many of the key components of the computer are located inside the laptop or the casing of the PC. This includes the CPU, which processes data; and what is commonly referred to as the motherboard, which is where the CPU and other internal components are attached, as shown in Figure 1-5.

The hard drive is also located inside the computer case. This device looks similar to a CD or DVD and is used for long-term storage inside the computer.

Other drives such as CD-ROM drives or DVD drives may be located in the case and open up to allow insertion of the CD or DVD into the computer for input, output, and storage such as playing or recording music, videos, or games.

Cables are used to connect the computer to power outlets and peripheral devices such as a keyboard, mouse, printer, wireless network router, or external speakers.

Figure 1-5 Many internal components of the computer are attached to the motherboard

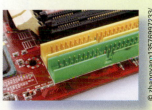

Douglas H. Ruckert
8503 Kirby Drive
Houston TX 77054-8220
(713) 555-0121
dougr@suresend.com

SUMMARY

Strong communication and telephone skills; excellent keyboarding, computer, and Internet skills; and good organizational and interpersonal skills.

EDUCATION

Will graduate from Eisenhower Technical High School in June 2014 with a high school diploma and information technology emphasis. Grade point average is 3.75.

RELEVANT SKILLS AND COURSES

Proficient with most recent versions of Windows and Office, including Word, Excel, Access, PowerPoint, and Publisher.

Excelled in the following courses: Computer Applications, Business Communications, and Information Technology.

MAJOR ACCOMPLISHMENTS

Future Business Leaders of America: Member for four years, vice president for one year. Won second place in Public Speaking at District Competition; competed (same event) at state level.

Varsity soccer: Lettered three years and served as captain during senior year.

Recognition: Named one of Eisenhower's Top Ten Community Service Providers at end of junior year.

WORK EXPERIENCE

Hinton's Family Restaurant, Server (2012-present): Served customers in culturally diverse area, oriented new part-time employees, and resolved routine customer service issues.

Tuma's Landscape and Garden Center, Sales (2010-2012): Assisted customers with plant selection and responsible for stocking and arranging display areas.

COMMUNITY SERVICE

First Methodist Church Vacation Bible School teacher assistant (2012-2013).

Race for the Cure publicity committee (2013).

ETHS Senior Citizens Breakfast server (2011-2014).

United Youth Camp student helper (2013).

REFERENCES

Will be furnished upon request.

Electronic Resume (Resume 1)

Douglas H. Ruckert

8503 Kirby Drive
Houston TX 77054-8220
(713) 555-0121
dougr@suresend.com

Objective:	To use my computer, Internet, communication, and interpersonal skills in a challenging customer service position.
Education:	Will graduate from Eisenhower Technical High School in June 2014 with a high school diploma and business technology emphasis. Grade point average is 3.75.

Relevant Skills and Courses:

- Proficient with most recent versions of Windows and Office, including Word, Excel, Access, PowerPoint, and FrontPage.

- Excelled in the following courses: Keyboarding, Computer Applications, Business Communications, and Information Technology.

Major Accomplishments:

- Future Business Leaders of America: Member for four years, vice president for one year. Won second place in Public Speaking at the District Competition; competed (same event) at state level.

- Varsity soccer: Lettered three years and served as captain during senior year.

- Recognition: Named one of Eisenhower's Top Ten Community Service Providers at end of junior year.

Work Experience:	Hinton's Family Restaurant, Server (2012-present): Served customers in culturally diverse area, oriented new part-time employees, and resolved routine customer service issues.
	Tuma's Landscape and Garden Center, Sales (2010-2011): Assisted customers with plant selection and responsible for stocking and arranging display areas.
References:	Will be furnished upon request.

Print Resume (Resume 2)

Application for Employment   **An Equal Opportunity Employer**
Regency Insurance Company

PERSONAL INFORMATION

NAME (LAST FIRST) Ruckert, Douglas H.	SOCIAL SECURITY NO. 368-56-2890	CURRENT DATE 5/11/2014	PHONE NUMBER (713) 555-0121
ADDRESS (NUMBER, STREET, CITY, STATE, ZIP CODE) 8503 Kirby Dr, Houston, TX 77054-8220		U.S. CITIZEN ☑ Yes ☐ No	DATE YOU CAN START 6/10/2012

ARE YOU EMPLOYED NOW? ☑ Yes ☐ No	IF YES, MAY WE INQUIRE OF YOUR PRESENT EMPLOYER? ☑ Yes ☐ No	IF YES, GIVE NAME AND NUMBER OF PERSON TO CALL James Veloski, Manager (713) 555-0149
POSITION DESIRED Customer Service	SALARY DESIRED Open	STATE HOW YOU LEARNED OF POSITION From Ms. Anne D. Salgado Eisenhower Information Technology Instructor

HAVE YOU EVER BEEN CONVICTED OF A FELONY?
☐ Yes ☑ No   IF YES, EXPLAIN.

EDUCATION

	NAME AND LOCATION OF SCHOOL	YEARS ATTENDED	DID YOU GRADUATE?	SUBJECTS STUDIED
COLLEGE				
HIGH SCHOOL	Eisenhower Technical High School Houston, TX	2010 to 2014	Will graduate 06/2014	Information Technology
GRADE SCHOOL				
OTHER				

SUBJECTS OF SPECIAL STUDY/RESEARCH WORK OR SPECIAL TRAINING/SKILLS DIRECTLY RELATED TO POSITION DESIRED

Windows and Office Suite, including Word, Excel, Access, PowerPoint, and Publisher

Office Procedures course with telephone training and interpersonal skills role playing

FORMER EMPLOYERS (LIST LAST POSITION FIRST)

FROM - TO (MTH & YEAR)	NAME AND ADDRESS	SALARY	POSITION	REASON FOR LEAVING
9/2012 to present	Hinton's Family Restaurant, 1204 S. Wayside Avenue, Houston, TX 77023-8841	Minimum wage plus tips	Server	Want full-time position in my field
6/2010 to 9/2012	Tuma's Landscape and Garden Center 10155 East Freeway, Houston, TX 77029-4619	Minimum wage	Sales	Employed at Hinton's

REFERENCES (LIST THREE PERSONS NOT RELATED TO YOU, WHOM YOU HAVE KNOWN AT LEAST ONE YEAR)

NAME	BUSINESS ADDRESS	PHONE NUMBER	TITLE	YEARS KNOWN
Ms. Anne D. Salgado	Eisenhower Technical High School, 100 N. Cavalcade, Houston, TX 77009-2651	(713) 555-0134	Information Technology Instructor	Four
Mr. James R. Veloski	Hinton's Family Restaurant, 1204 S. Wayside Avenue, Houston, TX 77023-8841	(713) 555-0149	Manager	Two
Mrs. Helen T. Landis	Tuma's Landscape and Garden Center, 10155 East Freeway, Houston, TX 77029-4619	(713) 555-0181	Owner	Three

I UNDERSTAND THAT I SHALL NOT BECOME AN EMPLOYEE UNTIL I HAVE SIGNED AN EMPLOYMENT AGREEMENT WITH THE FINAL APPROVAL OF THE EMPLOYER AND THAT SUCH EMPLOYMENT WILL BE SUBJECT TO VERIFICATION OF PREVIOUS EMPLOYMENT DATA PROVIDED IN THIS APPLICATION, ANY RELATED DOCUMENTS, OR DATA SHEET. I KNOW THAT A REPORT MAY BE MADE THAT WILL INCLUDE INFORMATION CONCERNING ANY FACTOR THE EMPLOYER MIGHT FIND

RELEVANT TO THE POSITION FOR WHICH I AM APPLYING, AND THAT I CAN MAKE A WRITTEN REQUEST FOR ADDITIONAL INFORMATION AS TO THE NATURE AND SCOPE OF THE REPORT IF ONE IS MADE.

Douglas H. Ruckert
SIGNATURE OF APPLICANT

Employment Application Form

8503 Kirby Drive
Houston, TX 77054-8220
May 10, 2014

Ms. Jenna St. John
Personnel Director
Regency Insurance Company
219 West Greene Road
Houston, TX 77067-4219

Dear Ms. St. John:

Ms. Anne D. Salgado, my business technology instructor, informed me of the customer service position with your company that will be available June 15. She speaks very highly of your organization. After learning more about the position, I am confident that I am qualified and would like to be considered for the position.

As indicated on the enclosed resume, I am currently completing my senior year at Eisenhower Technical High School. All of my elective courses have been computer and business-related courses. I have completed the advanced computer application class where we integrated word processing, spreadsheet, database, presentation, and Web page documents by using the latest suite software. I have also taken an office technology course that included practice in using the telephone and applying interpersonal skills.

My work experience and school activities have given me the opportunity to work with people to achieve group goals. Participating in FBLA has given me an appreciation of the business world.

An opportunity to interview with you for this position will be greatly appreciated. You can call me at (713) 555-0121 or e-mail me at dougr@suresend.com to arrange an interview.

Sincerely,

Douglas H. Ruckert

Enclosure

Employment Application Letter

Desktop computers also have separate screens to provide larger, high-resolution viewing of information. Other peripheral output devices include printers, speakers, projectors, and other types of whiteboards or flat screens.

USB ports and other types of data ports allow external storage devices such as USB or thumb drives to be plugged into the computer. These small storage drives enable you to store and conveniently transfer several gigabytes of data without a network connection. Larger external hard drives used for data backup and additional storage may also be connected through the USB port, as shown in Figure 1-6.

For a PC, the mouse and keyboard are the most common input devices. The keyboard enables you to key text and manipulate it, while the mouse lets you move the cursor, arrow, or other types of icons around the screen to point and select text or other objects.

On laptop computers, pointing devices such as touch pads or rubber nubs are used instead of a mouse. Many computers and handheld devices allow you to select icons or text by touching the computer screen.

We will practice using the mouse and other pointing devices later in this lesson.

Other common input devices, as shown in Figure 1-7, include microphones for speaking or recording voice data, tablets for recording written notes, joysticks for playing games, digital cameras, and scanners for scanning photos and documents into the computer.

Figure 1-7 Common input devices

Software Basics

The instructions used to tell the computer what to do with data are called software. **Software**, such as that used for word processing, is a set of step-by-step instructions for the computer, written by computer programmers in a programming language such as BASIC, Pascal, or C. **Operating Systems** (**OSs**) such as Microsoft Windows 8, Macintosh OS X, and GNU/Linux are one important kind of software. Operating system software provides the user interface between you and the computer, a set of instructions that controls how you interact with the computer hardware and manages the various devices and data used by the computer.

[Company/Department Name]

Agenda

[Date]

[Time]

Type of Meeting: **[Description of meeting]**

Meeting Facilitator: **[Name of meeting facilitator]**

Invitees: **[List of invitees]**

I. Call to order

II. Roll call

III. Approval of minutes from last meeting

IV. Open issues

    a) **[Description of open issue]**

    b) **[Description of open issue]**

    c) **[Description of open issue]**

V. New business

    a) **[Description of new business]**

    b) **[Description of new business]**

    c) **[Description of new business]**

VI. Adjournment

VII.

Agenda

		TRAVEL ITINERARY FOR LISA PEROTTA	
		222 Pine View Drive	
		Coraopolis, PA 15108	
		(412) 555-1320	
		perotta@fastnet.com	
		Pittsburgh, PA to Santa Ana, CA—April 18-22, 20--	

Date	Time	Activity	Comments
Tuesday April 18	3:30 p.m. (ET)	Depart **Pittsburgh International Airport** (PIT) for Santa Ana, CA Airport (SNA) on **USEast Flight 146**. *Arrival time is 5:01 p.m.(PT)*.	The flight is non-stop on an Airbus A319, and you are assigned seat 22E.
	5:30 p.m. (PT)	Reservation with **Star Car Rental** (714-555-0190). Return by 12 noon (PT) on April 22.	Confirmation No.: 33-345. Telephone: 714-555-1030.
	6:00 p.m. (PT)	Reservations at the Hannah Hotel, 421 Race Avenue, Santa Ana for April 18 to April 22 for a single, non-smoking room at $145 plus tax. Telephone: 714-555-0200.	Confirmation No.: 632A-04/18. Check-in after 6 p.m. is guaranteed. Check out by 11 a.m.
Saturday April 22	1:25 p.m. (PT)	Depart **Santa Ana Airport** (SNA) for Pittsburgh International Airport (PIT) on **USEast Flight 148**. *Arrival time is 8:52 p.m. (ET)*.	The flight is non-stop on an Airbus A319, and you are assigned seat 16A.
Travel Agency Contact Information—Agent is Mary Grecco; 444 Grant Street, Pittsburgh, PA 15219; Telephone: 412-555-0087; Fax: 412-555-0088; E-Mail: greccom@netway.com			

Itinerary

[Company/Department Name]

Meeting Minutes

[Date]

I. <u>Call to order</u>

    [Name of Meeting Facilitator] called to order the regular meeting of the **[Organization/Committee Name]** at **[time of meeting]** on **[date of meeting]** in **[Location of Meeting]**.

II. <u>Roll call</u>

    [Name of Organization Secretary] conducted a roll call. The following persons were present: **[List of Attendees]**

III. <u>Approval of minutes from last meeting</u>

    [Name of Organization Secretary] read the minutes from the last meeting. The minutes were approved as read.

IV. <u>Open issues</u>

    a) **[Open issue/summary of discussion]**

    b) **[Open issue/summary of discussion]**

    c) **[Open issue/summary of discussion]**

V. <u>New business</u>

    a) **[New business/summary of discussion]**

    b) **[New business/summary of discussion]**

    c) **[New business/summary of discussion]**

VI. <u>Adjournment</u>

    [Name of Meeting Facilitator] adjourned the meeting at **[time meeting ended]**.

Minutes submitted by: **[Name]**

Meeting Minutes

News Release

For Release: Immediate

Contact: Heidi Zemack

    CLEVELAND, OH, May 25, 20--. Science teachers from school districts in six counties are eligible for this year's Teacher Excellence awards funded by The Society for Environmental Engineers.

    Nominations can be submitted through Friday, July 31, by students, parents, residents, and other educators. Nomination forms are available from the participating school districts or on the Society's website at http://www.tsee.webhost.com.

    An anonymous committee reviews the nominations and selects ten finalists. From that group, seven "teachers of distinction" and three award winners are selected. The top award winner receives $5,000, the second receives $2,500, and the third receives $1,500. Each teacher of distinction receives $500. The teachers of distinction and the award winners will be announced on September 5 at a dinner at the Cleveland Inn.

    School districts participating in the program include those in these counties: Cuyahoga, Lorain, Medina, Summit, Lake, and Geauga.

###

News Release

The operating system is the most critical piece of software. It is used to start or boot the computer, and it also controls how other software interacts with the computer hardware, allocating space in RAM for each program to operate. If conflicts occur between two programs in RAM, they may crash, causing them to stop working until they are closed or the computer is restarted.

The operating system is also used to store and organize data files. You will learn more about navigating and using the Windows operating system in Lessons 2 and 4 of this unit.

What operating system software have you used in the past? Write down the different names and versions of operating systems you have used.

Figure 1-8 *Windows* is one of the most widely used operating systems

Application software provides instructions for accomplishing a specific type of task, such as creating a word processing document, sending e-mail, or finding information on the Web. Application software can be used as a stand-alone program dedicated to one specific task, such as editing photos or videos, or it may contain several different applications, such as an office applications suite. Office suites such as Microsoft Office are some of the most commonly used commercial software products in business. Accordingly, most of the hands-on applications in this book will use the Microsoft Office Suite.

Different types of application software include productivity programs such as *Microsoft Word, Microsoft Excel, Microsoft Access*, and *Microsoft PowerPoint*. Word processing software such as *Word* is used to create and edit documents and reports. Spreadsheet software such as *Excel* is used to analyze data with mathematical operations, sorting, filtering, and charts.

Presentation software such as *PowerPoint* is used to create animated presentation graphics used with public speaking or other types of graphic media presentations. Database software such as *Access* is used to input, store, organize, and analyze large amounts of data.

Other popular productivity software includes multimedia programs such as *Adobe Photoshop, Adobe Acrobat*, and *Adobe Flash*. *Photoshop* is used to edit and enhance photos and other types of graphics. *Acrobat* is used to read and work with documents from many different formats and display the documents on the Web. *Flash* is used to create animations for use on the Web and in software applications.

1. What application software have you used in the past? Write down the names and versions of the ones you have used.
2. Which application software was the most enjoyable for you to use?
3. Have you used any application software to help you with homework assignments in the past? If so, describe which application it was and what you did with it.

Communications programs such as *Microsoft Internet Explorer* or *Microsoft Outlook* are used to communicate on the Web. *Internet Explorer* and other Web browsers such as *Google Chrome* help you get online and search for websites and information on the Internet. Programs such as *Microsoft Outlook* help you manage your schedule and your contact information and enable you to create and send e-mail messages. In Unit 5, you'll learn more about Personal Information Management software and e-mail.

Report Documentation

Good report writing includes proof that the reported statements are sound. The process is called **documenting.**

Most school reports are documented in the body and in a list. A reference in the body shows the source of a quotation or paraphrase. A list shows all references alphabetically.

In the report body, references may be noted (1) in parentheses in the copy (textual citations or parenthetical documentation); (2) by a superscript in the copy, listed on a separate page (endnotes); or (3) by a superscript in the copy, listed at the bottom of the text page (footnotes). A list may contain only the sources noted in the body (REFERENCES or Works Cited) or include related materials (BIBLIOGRAPHY).

Two popular documenting styles are shown: *Century 21* and MLA (Modern Language Association).

Century 21

Examples are listed in this order: (1) textual citation, (2) endnote/footnote, and (3) References/Bibliography page.

Book, One Author

(Schaeffer, 1997, 1)

[1]Robert K. Schaeffer, *Understanding Globalization*, (Lanham, MD: Rowman & Littlefield Publishers, Inc., 1997), p. 1.

Schaeffer, Robert K. *Understanding Globalization* (Lanham, MD: Rowman & Littlefield Publishers, Inc., 1997).

Book, Two or Three Authors

(Prince and Jackson, 1997, 35)

[2]Nancy Prince and Jeanie Jackson, *Exploring Theater* (Minneapolis/St. Paul: West Publishing Company, 1997), p. 35.

Prince, Nancy, and Jeanie Jackson. *Exploring Theater*. Minneapolis/St. Paul: West Publishing Company, 1997.

Book, Four or More Authors

(Gwartney, et al., 2014, 9)

[3]James D. Gwartney, et al., *Economics: Private and Public Choice* (Cincinnati: South-Western, Cengage Learning, 2014), p. 9.

Gwartney, James D., et al. *Economics: Private and Public Choice*. Cincinnati: South-Western, Cengage Learning, 2014.

Encyclopedia or Reference Book

(*Encyclopedia Americana*, 2008, Vol. 25, p. 637)

[4]*Encyclopedia Americana*, Vol, 25 (Danbury, CT: Grolier Incorporated, 2008), p. 637.

Encyclopedia Americana, Vol. 25. "Statue of Liberty." Danbury, CT: Grolier Incorporated, 2008.

Journal or Magazine Article

(Harris, 1993, 755)

[5]Richard G. Harris, "Globalization, Trade, and Income," *Canadian Journal of Economics*, November 1993, p. 755.

Harris, Richard G. "Globalization, Trade, and Income." *Canadian Journal of Economics*, November 1993, 755–776.

Website

(Railton, 2014)

[6]Stephen Railton, "Your Mark Twain," http://www.etext.lib.virginia.edu/railton/sc_as_mt/yourmt13.html (September 24, 2014).

Railton, Stephen. "Your Mark Twain." http://www.etext.lib.virginia.edu/railton/sc_as_mt/yourmt13.html (24 September 2014).

Modern Language Association

Examples include reference (1) in parenthetical documentation and (2) on Works Cited page.

Book, One Author

(Schaeffer 1)

Schaeffer, Robert K. *Understanding Globalization*. Lanham, MD: Rowman & Littlefield, 1997.

Book, Two or Three Authors

(Prince and Jackson 35)

Prince, Nancy, and Jeanie Jackson. *Exploring Theater*. Minneapolis/St. Paul: West Publishing, 1997.

Book, Four or More Authors or Editors

(Gwartney et al. 9)

Gwartney, James D., et al. *Economics: Private and Public Choice*. Cincinnati: South-Western, Cengage Learning, 2014.

Encyclopedia or Reference Book

(*Encyclopedia Americana* 637)

Encyclopedia Americana. "Statue of Liberty." Danbury, CT: Grolier, 2008.

Journal or Magazine Article

(Harris 755)

Harris, Richard G. "Globalization, Trade, and Income," *Canadian Journal of Economics*. Nov. 1993: 755–776.

Website

(Railton)

Railton, Stephen. *Your Mark Twain Page*. (24 Sept. 2014) http://www.etext.lib.virginia.edu/railton/sc_as_mt/yourmt13.html.

Figure 1-9 Entertainment programs such as this game often come preloaded on your computer

There are a wide variety of educational and entertainment programs that provide games, multimedia, and interactive learning software for users of all interests and age levels. Entertainment programs may be purchased to use on your local computer or can be played online with users across the Internet. Educational programs provide opportunities for millions of students and adults to learn topics from foreign languages to basic math skills.

Online applications (or **online apps**) provide another way to accomplish specific tasks such as finding directions, browsing multimedia content, sending e-mail, or creating office documents such as presentations and spreadsheets.

Online apps are available on the Web and are viewed from within your Web browser. The software for the application is stored on the host server rather than on your local computer, and the data you input to the online app is also sent to the server for processing. We will explore more about using online apps in Lesson 5 of this unit.

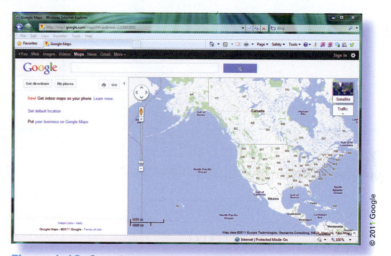

Figure 1-10 Google maps is an example of an online app

Another type of software is called **system utilities**, or **utility software**. This kind of software helps you maintain your computer and perform other routine tasks associated with file maintenance.

Many system utilities are typically contained within operating system software to help you manage your files, but people also use third-party utilities such as antivirus software, file compression software, backup utilities, and data recovery applications in addition to the utilities that come with their computer operating system.

Many people use software called shareware or freeware that can be downloaded from the Internet. **Shareware** is copyrighted commercial software that you can use on a trial basis before deciding to purchase it. **Freeware** is commercial or privately developed software you can download and use for free. Public-domain programs are available from the software author without charge, but freeware and public-domain software may not be as reliable as commercially developed software.

Some freeware is also called **open-source software**, which means the software code is available for users to develop their own applications and to distribute it according to the terms of a license.

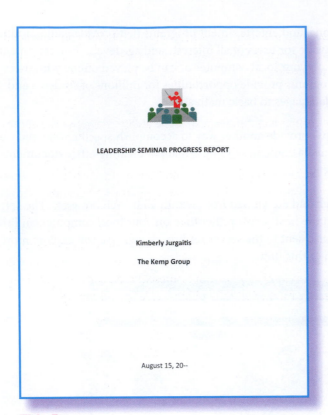

Title Page

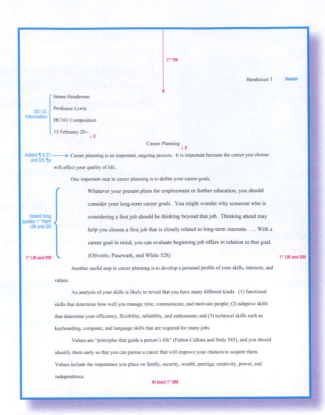

MLA Report, page 1

MLA Report, page 2

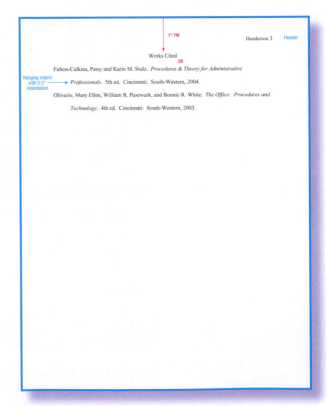

Works Cited Page for MLA Report

GNU/Linux is the most widely known example of open source software. Before you download any software from the Internet, do some research and make sure it is safe to use. There are many trustworthy sites that rate and review software.

Choosing the Right Technology

One of the most important skills to learn as a computer user is the ability to choose the appropriate technology for a given task.

For example, you might be asked to create a multimedia presentation for an upcoming meeting with the staff in your business or organization. The first decisions you must make involve evaluating both the hardware and software you use for these specific needs.

Should you use a digital camera or your smartphone to capture pictures for the presentation—or would you be better served by purchasing images you find from an online search? Should you create the presentation using a word processing application or presentation software? Do you need to use a separate multimedia application to edit the photos, videos, and music?

Figure 1-11 Evaluating technology for specific needs requires careful analysis

Evaluating and choosing the right technology is also important when you're making purchase decisions for your own needs or for your business.

When buying computer hardware and other digital devices, you have to consider several factors, including:

- Your budget.
- What applications you will use with the hardware.
- System requirements for the applications you want to use.

When purchasing software applications, the same basic considerations apply:

- Your budget.
- What you will do with the software.
- System requirements for the software and how well they match the hardware you have.

For example, there are many types of software available that can be used for writing. Some are very basic, allowing you simply to key and save your words. Others provide extensive options for formatting and output. If you just want to take notes in class, you might choose a simple freeware program. But if you need to produce a fancy color brochure or newsletter, you may need to buy a more expensive software package.

If you choose to use shareware, freeware, or open-source software, be sure to download the software from a reliable source to avoid harming your computer system. Also, be sure not to download pirated software that has been copied or distributed illegally.

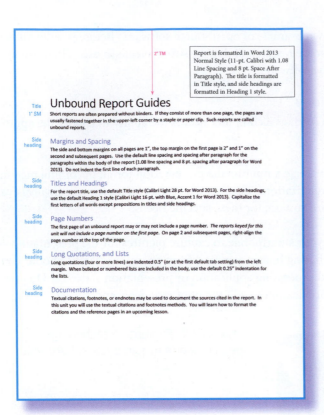

Report is formatted in Word 2013 Normal Style (11-pt. Calibri with 1.08 Line Spacing and 8 pt. Space After Paragraph). The title is formatted in Title style, and side headings are formatted in Heading 1 style.

Title
1" SM

Unbound Report Guides

Short reports are often prepared without binders. If they consist of more than one page, the pages are usually fastened together in the upper-left corner by a staple or paper clip. Such reports are called unbound reports.

Side heading
Margins and Spacing

The side and bottom margins on all pages are 1", the top margin on the first page is 2" and 1" on the second and subsequent pages. Use the default line spacing and spacing after paragraph for the paragraphs within the body of the report (1.08 line spacing and 8 pt. spacing after paragraph for Word 2013). Do not indent the first line of each paragraph.

Side heading
Titles and Headings

For the report title, use the default Title style (Calibri 28 pt. for Word 2013). For the side headings, use the default Heading 1 style (Calibri Light 16 pt. with Blue, Accent 1 for Word 2013). Capitalize the first letters of all words except prepositions in titles and side headings.

Side heading
Page Numbers

The first page of an unbound report may or may not include a page number. *The reports keyed for this unit will not include a page number on the first page.* On page 2 and subsequent pages, right-align the page number at the top of the page.

Side heading
Long Quotations, and Lists

Long quotations (four or more lines) are indented 0.5" (or at the first default tab setting) from the left margin. When bulleted or numbered lists are included in the body, use the default 0.25" indentation for the lists.

Side heading
Documentation

Textual citations, footnotes, or endnotes may be used to document the sources cited in the report. In this unit you will use the textual citations and footnotes methods. You will learn how to format the citations and the reference pages in an upcoming lesson.

Unbound Report

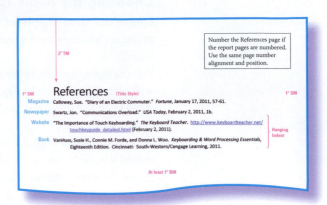

Number the References page if the report pages are numbered. Use the same page number alignment and position.

1" SM   **2" TM**   **1" SM**

References   (Title Style)

Magazine Calloway, Sue. "Diary of an Electric Commuter." *Fortune*, January 17, 2011, 57-61.

Newspaper Swartz, Jon. "Communications Overload." *USA Today*, February 2, 2011, 1b.

Website "The Importance of Touch Keyboarding." *The Keyboard Teacher.* http://www.keyboardteacher.net/ touchkeyguide_detailed.html (February 2, 2011).

Book VanHuss, Susie H., Connie M. Forde, and Donna L. Woo. *Keyboarding & Word Processing Essentials,* Eighteenth Edition. Cincinnati: South-Western/Cengage Learning, 2011.

Hanging Indent

At least 1" BM

References Page

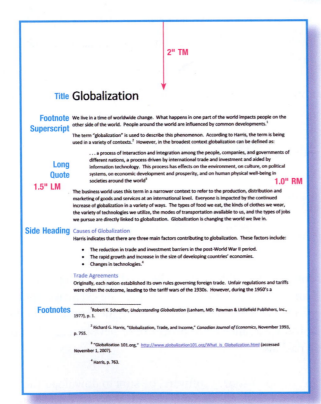

2" TM

Title # Globalization

Footnote Superscript We live in a time of worldwide change. What happens in one part of the world impacts people on the other side of the world. People around the world are influenced by common developments.[1]

The term "globalization" is used to describe this phenomenon. According to Harris, the term is being used in a variety of contexts.[2] However, in the broadest context globalization can be defined as:

Long Quote
1.5" LM . . . a process of interaction and integration among the people, companies, and governments of different nations, a process driven by international trade and investment and aided by information technology. This process has effects on the environment, on culture, on political systems, on economic development and prosperity, and on human physical well-being in societies around the world[3]   **1.0" RM**

The business world uses this term in a narrower context to refer to the production, distribution and marketing of goods and services at an international level. Everyone is impacted by the continued increase of globalization in a variety of ways. The types of food we eat, the kinds of clothes we wear, the variety of technologies we utilize, the modes of transportation available to us, and the types of jobs we pursue are directly linked to globalization. Globalization is changing the world we live in.

Side Heading Causes of Globalization

Harris indicates that there are three main factors contributing to globalization. These factors include:

- The reduction in trade and investment barriers in the post-World War II period.
- The rapid growth and increase in the size of developing countries' economies.
- Changes in technologies.[4]

Trade Agreements

Originally, each nation established its own rules governing foreign trade. Unfair regulations and tariffs were often the outcome, leading to the tariff wars of the 1930s. However, during the 1950's a

_____
Footnotes [1]Robert K. Schaeffer, *Understanding Globalization* (Lanham, MD: Rowman & Littlefield Publishers, Inc., 1977), p. 1.

[2] Richard G. Harris, "Globalization, Trade, and Income," *Canadian Journal of Economics*, November 1993, p. 755.

[3] "Globalization 101.org," http://www.globalization101.org/What_is_Globalization.html (accessed November 1, 2007).

[4] Harris, p. 763.

Bound Report with Long Quotation and Footnotes

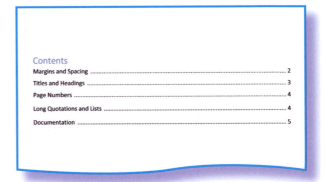

Contents

Margins and Spacing 2

Titles and Headings 3

Page Numbers 4

Long Quotations and Lists 4

Documentation 5

Table of Contents

Downloading or distributing pirated software is ethically wrong and is also a violation of copyright law. We will discuss computer ethics and appropriate use in more detail in Lesson 5 of this unit.

Figure 1-12 Software piracy is ethically wrong and illegal

1. Describe the five steps computers use to process information.
2. List the names of the peripheral equipment you use with your computer.
3. Describe the key considerations you should use in making a technology purchase.

1B

Starting Your Computer

Now we'll begin working with computer hardware and software. Start your computer by following the steps in the next activity.

1. Turn on the power.
   - You may need to flip a switch or press a button on the CPU or press a button or key on the keyboard.
   - You may also have to turn on the monitor separately.
   - Your computer may take a few moments to power up.
   - The computer will execute a series of automatic steps that will load the operating system. The operating system—*Windows 8,* for example—is the program that manages other programs on the computer. It will prepare the computer to receive your instructions and run software.
2. When you have successfully started your computer, you are greeted with a screen that shows the time and a picture. To get past it with a touch-screen device, swipe upward with your finger from the bottom edge of the screen. If you have a keyboard, hit any key.
3. Next, you'll see a mosaic of Live Tiles, each representing an application. The Start Screen is the main screen on your monitor for beginning work with the computer. The start screen may look similar to Figure 1-13 below.

Figure 1-13 The Start Screen

Envelope Guides

Return Address

Use block style, SS, and Initial Caps or ALL CAPS. If not using the Envelopes feature, begin as near to the top and left edge of the envelope as possible—TM and LM about 0.25".

Receiver's Delivery Address

Use block style, SS, and Initial Caps. If desired, use ALL CAPS instead of initial caps and omit the punctuation. Place city name, two-letter state abbreviation, and ZIP Code +4 on last address line. One space precedes the ZIP Code.

If not using the Envelopes feature, tab over 2.5" for the small envelope and 4" for the large envelope. Insert hard returns to place the first line about 2" from the top.

Mailing Notations

Key mailing and addressee notations in ALL CAPS.

Key mailing notations, such as SPECIAL DELIVERY and REGISTERED, below the stamp and at least three lines above the envelope address.

Key addressee notations, such as HOLD FOR ARRIVAL or PERSONAL, a DS below the return address and about three spaces from the left edge of the envelope.

If an attention line is used, key it as the first line of the envelope address.

Standard Abbreviations

Use USPS standard abbreviations for states (see list below) and street suffix names, such as AVE and BLVD. Never abbreviate the name of a city or country.

International Addresses

Omit postal (ZIP) codes from the last line of addresses outside the U.S. Show only the name of the country on the last line. Examples:

```
Mr. Hiram Sanders
2121 Clearwater St.
Ottawa, Onkia  OB1
CANADA
```

```
Ms. Inge D. Fischer
Hartmannstrasse 7
4209 Bonn 5
FEDERAL REPUBLIC OF GERMANY
```

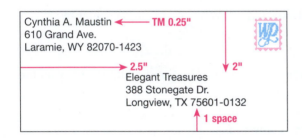

Folding Procedures

Small Envelopes (Nos. 6¾, 6¼)

1. With page face up, fold bottom up to 0.5" from top.
2. Fold right third to left.
3. Fold left third to 0.5" from last crease.
4. Insert last creased edge first.

Large Envelopes (Nos. 10, 9, 7¾)

1. With page face up, fold slightly less than one-third of sheet up toward top.
2. Fold down top of sheet to within 0.5" of bottom fold.
3. Insert last creased edge first.

Window Envelopes (Letter)

1. With page face down, top toward you, fold upper third down.
2. Fold lower third up so address is showing.
3. Insert sheet into envelope with last crease at bottom.
4. Check that address shows through window.

State and Territory Abbreviations

Alabama	AL	Illinois	IL	Nebraska	NE	South Carolina	SC
Alaska	AK	Indiana	IN	Nevada	NV	South Dakota	SD
Arizona	AZ	Iowa	IA	New Hampshire	NH	Tennessee	TN
Arkansas	AR	Kansas	KS	New Jersey	NJ	Texas	TX
California	CA	Kentucky	KY	New Mexico	NM	Utah	UT
Colorado	CO	Louisiana	LA	New York	NY	Vermont	VT
Connecticut	CT	Maine	ME	North Carolina	NC	Virgin Islands	VI
Delaware	DE	Maryland	MD	North Dakota	ND	Virginia	VA
District of Columbia	DC	Massachusetts	MA	Ohio	OH	Washington	WA
Florida	FL	Michigan	MI	Oklahoma	OK	West Virginia	WV
Georgia	GA	Minnesota	MN	Oregon	OR	Wisconsin	WI
Guam	GU	Mississippi	MS	Pennsylvania	PA	Wyoming	WY
Hawaii	HI	Missouri	MO	Puerto Rico	PR		
Idaho	ID	Montana	MT	Rhode Island	RI		

The Start Screen is your home base. You can open applications or "apps," websites, contacts, and folders. The contents are tiles representing all of the apps installed. You can glance at the tiles to get the latest headlines, updates, and information.

Tiles can be static or dynamic. With Live tiles you will be able to preview information about the associated application. For instance, if you have a Stock Market app that you use to keep track of stocks you will notice that without having to open the app you will be able to get a glimpse of the latest market information. The same applies to emails, messages, games and other apps that make use of this feature.

Ways to get to the Start Screen:
- With touch, swipe the right edge of your screen, and then tap the Start charm.
- With a mouse, move the pointer into the lower-left corner. When Start appears, click the corner.
- With a keyboard, press the Windows logo key

Charm Bar

The Charm Bar is a universal toolbar in Windows 8 that can be accessed from anywhere no matter what you are doing or what application you are running.

Figure 1-14 The Charm Bar

There are two ways to access the Charm Bar. The first is by moving the cursor with your mouse or swipe to the bottom right corner of the screen which will cause the bar to appear on the right. You can also use the Windows logo key + C shortcut on your keyboard.

There are five key elements for Windows 8 in the Charm Bar, they are as follows: *Search*, *Share*, *Start*, *Devices* and *Settings*. Let's take a look at each of these elements in detail.

- The **Search** charm allows you to search for a particular keyword in the screen you are in. Search charm's behavior changes depending on the application that is currently active. For example, if you are in the Start Screen, then the Search charm will search for files, apps, or settings. Or if you are in the News app, it will search for a particular news story.
- The **Share** charm allows you to share information from a particular app with family, friends, classmates, and colleagues. Just like the Search charm, the Share charm's function will change depending on the app you are running. The default sharing method is email, but once you install apps for Twitter, Facebook and other social platforms, sharing will be easy.
- The **Start** charm allows you to access the contents of the Start Screen. The Start screen is like the Home screen on other touch devices with the exception that the icons are tiles and they are dynamic.
- The **Devices** charm is where all your computer's device information and settings reside. This is also the place where you can send the contents of the screen you are looking at to another device. For example, if you have another monitor attached to your computer, you can select it to display the contents there or if you are in the Maps app, you can select a printer to print the document.
- The **Settings** charm allows you access to settings for the network, volume, screen brightness, notifications, power, and language.

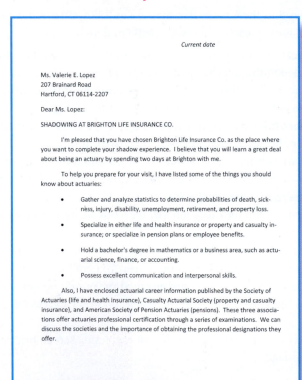

Approximately 2" TM or Center Vertically

Begin Dateline, Complimentary Close, Writer's name and title at same tab at or near the center.

Date — September 15, 20—↓1

Mailing notation — FACSIMILE ↓1

Attention line in letter address — Attention Training and Development Department ↓1
Science Technologies ↓1
3368 Bay Path Road ↓1
Miami, FL 33160-3368 ↓1

Remove space after paragraph—use Shift Enter to insert Line Break after first three lines.

Salutation — Ladies and Gentlemen: ↓1

Subject line — MODIFIED BLOCK FORMAT ↓1

Body — This letter is arranged in modified block format. In this letter format the date and closing lines (complimentary close, name of the writer, and the writer's title) begin at or near horizontalcenter. In block format all letter parts begin at the left margin. ↓1

Default or 1.25" LM and RM — Mixed punctuation (a colon after the salutation and a comma after the complimentary close) is used in this example. Open punctuation (no mark after the salutation or complimentary close)may be used with the modified block format if you prefer. ↓1

The first line of each paragraph may be blocked as shown here or indented one-half inch. If paragraphs are indented, the optional subject line may be indented or centered. If paragraphs are blocked at the left margin, the subject line is blocked, too. ↓1

Complimentary close — Sincerely, ↓2

Writer
Writer's title — Derek Alan ↓1
Manager ↓1

Remove space after paragraph—use Shift Enter to insert Line Break after name.

Reference initials — DA:xx ↓1

Enclosure notation — Enclosure ↓1

Copy notation — c   Kimberly Rodriquez-Duarte ↓1

Postscript — A block format letter is enclosed so that you can compare the two formats. As you can see, either format presents an attractive appearance.

At least 1" BM

Letter in Modified Block Format with Postscript

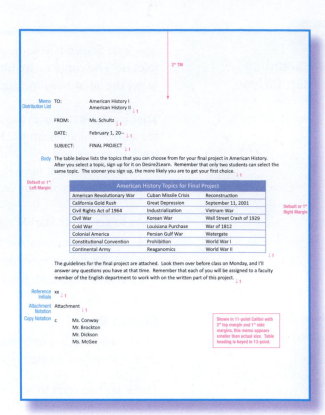

2" TM

Memo Distribution List — TO: American History I
                              American History II ↓1

FROM: Ms. Schultz ↓1

DATE: February 1, 20— ↓1

SUBJECT: FINAL PROJECT ↓1

Body — The table below lists the topics that you can choose from for your final project in American History. After you select a topic, sign up for it on Desire2Learn. Remember that only two students can select the same topic. The sooner you sign up, the more likely you are to get your first choice. ↓1

Default or 1" Left Margin

American History Topics for Final Project		
American Revolutionary War	Cuban Missile Crisis	Reconstruction
California Gold Rush	Great Depression	September 11, 2001
Civil Rights Act of 1964	Industrialization	Vietnam War
Civil War	Korean War	Wall Street Crash of 1929
Cold War	Louisiana Purchase	War of 1812
Colonial America	Persian Gulf War	Watergate
Constitutional Convention	Prohibition	World War I
Continental Army	Reaganomics	World War II

Default or 1" Right Margin

The guidelines for the final project are attached. Look them over before class on Monday, and I'll answer any questions you have at that time. Remember that each of you will be assigned to a faculty member of the English department to work with on the written part of this project. ↓1

Reference Initials — xx ↓1

Attachment Notation — Attachment ↓1

Copy Notation — c   Ms. Conway
                    Mr. Brockton
                    Mr. Dickson
                    Ms. McGee

Shown in 11-point Calibri with 2" top margin and 1" side margins, this memo appears smaller than actual size. Table heading is keyed in 13-point.

Memo with Special Features

Current date

Ms. Valerie E. Lopez
207 Brainard Road
Hartford, CT 06114-2207

Dear Ms. Lopez:

SHADOWING AT BRIGHTON LIFE INSURANCE CO.

I'm pleased that you have chosen Brighton Life Insurance Co. as the place where you want to complete your shadow experience. I believe that you will learn a great deal about being an actuary by spending two days at Brighton with me.

To help you prepare for your visit, I have listed some of the things you should know about actuaries:

- Gather and analyze statistics to determine probabilities of death, sickness, injury, disability, unemployment, retirement, and property loss.

- Specialize in either life and health insurance or property and casualty insurance; or specialize in pension plans or employee benefits.

- Hold a bachelor's degree in mathematics or a business area, such as actuarial science, finance, or accounting.

- Possess excellent communication and interpersonal skills.

Also, I have enclosed actuarial career information published by the Society of Actuaries (life and health insurance), Casualty Actuarial Society (property and casualty insurance), and American Society of Pension Actuaries (pensions). These three associations offer actuaries professional certification through a series of examinations. We can discuss the societies and the importance of obtaining the professional designations they offer.

Letter in Modified Block Format with Paragraph Indentations and List

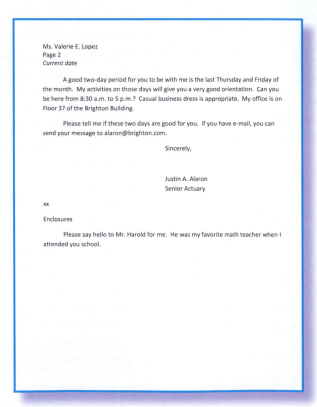

Ms. Valerie E. Lopez
Page 2
Current date

A good two-day period for you to be with me is the last Thursday and Friday of the month. My activities on those days will give you a very good orientation. Can you be here from 8:30 a.m. to 5 p.m.? Casual business dress is appropriate. My office is on Floor 37 of the Brighton Building.

Please tell me if these two days are good for you. If you have e-mail, you can send your message to alaron@brighton.com.

Sincerely,

Justin A. Alaron
Senior Actuary

xx

Enclosures

Please say hello to Mr. Harold for me. He was my favorite math teacher when I attended you school.

Letter (p. 2) Showing Second-Page Heading

1D

Mouse Skills

Right mouse button

Left mouse button

Mouse wheel

© ZoneFatal/Shutterstock.com

Figure 1-15 Parts of the mouse

A mouse is a tool for getting around the desktop—it lets you move the cursor or arrow around the screen to point to and select text or other objects. The same mouse actions are used in any software, though the results may vary depending on the software and version.

Here are the basic ways to use a mouse:

- **Point**. Move the mouse (roll it on the work surface) so that the **pointer** (the arrow that represents the mouse's position on the screen) points to an item.
- **Click**. Tap the left mouse button once and let go.
- **Double-click**. Tap the left mouse button twice quickly and let go.
- **Right-click**. Tap the right mouse button once and let go.
- **Drag**. Press and hold down the left mouse button and move the pointer.

The mouse wheel can be used to either click or scroll up and down the screen.

1E

Navigating the Start Screen Tiles

1. Make sure the Start Screen is showing on your screen.
2. Move your mouse arrow/pointer or swipe around the start screen. Practice moving faster or more slowly through the tiles. Notice the feel for the speed and direction you have to move to achieve a particular movement on the start screen.
3. Notice the tiles on your Start Screen. Some tiles are static like the email or calendar. Some tiles are dynamic like the Weather tile indicating the current weather conditions in your area.
4. Open the Charm Menu.
   - Tap or click the search charm. Review the apps available on your computer. Key "Email" in the search box and enter. Notice the Email application appears on the left. Tap or click Email to open your email.
   - Tap or click the devices charm. Review the devices that are connected to your computer. You may see a printer, additional screen, scanner, etc. on your list of devices.
   - Tap or click the Start charm to return to your Start Menu.
5. Tap or click your Internet browser. Notice that your browser opens immediately.
6. Explore other tiles on your Start screen to see the information and apps available when your start your computer.

1F

Turning Off the Computer

After you have practiced with the mouse, follow the steps in the next activity to turn off your computer.

1. Close any desktop apps you have open—this will prompt you to save your work.
2. Open the Settings charm.
3. Tap or click Power, and then tap or click Shut Down.
4. After the computer has shut down, turn off the power switch on the monitor and any other peripheral devices.

Power Button

Figure 1-16 Change PC Settings Menu

Interoffice Memo

At 2" (3 returns down)

```
TO:        Maria Gutierrez, Secretary  ↓1

FROM:      Jackson Phipps, President  ↓1

DATE:      Current Date  ↓1

SUBJECT:   Next FBLA Meeting  ↓1
```

Our next Future Business Leaders of America meeting is scheduled for this Friday at 6:30 p.m. in SSS 400F. Please put up the posters to remind members. ↓1

Default or 1" SM

Based on the attendance at the last meeting, you should have 45 copies of the attached agenda and the minutes to distribute. We will be going over five more competitive event descriptions at the meeting. You can make copies of the descriptions from the FBLA-PBL National Site (www.fbla.org). The events that we will be covering at this meeting are: ↓1

```
Future Business Leaders
Entrepreneurship
Electronic Career Portfolio
Word Processing 1
Business Communication  ↓1
```

Hold down the Shift key when you return after the first four items in this list to avoid extra space between lines.

Thank you again for all the time and effort you devote to our organization. You set a great example for other FBLA members at Jefferson High School to follow. ↓1

xx ↓1
Attachment

Shown in 11-point Calibri with 2" top margin and 1" side margins, this memo appears smaller than actual size.

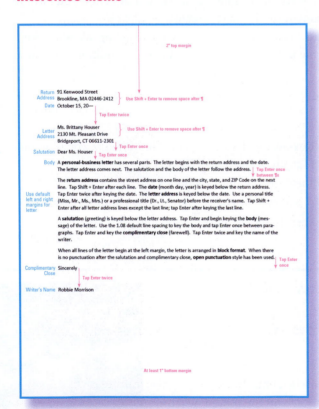

Personal-Business Letter in Block Format with Open Punctuation

2" top margin

```
Return Address    91 Kenwood Street
                  Brookline, MA 02446-2412    Use Shift + Enter to remove space after ¶
Date              October 15, 20—
                                              Tap Enter twice

Letter Address    Ms. Brittany Houser         Use Shift + Enter to remove space after ¶
                  2130 Mt. Pleasant Drive
                  Bridgeport, CT 06611-2301    Tap Enter once
Salutation        Dear Ms. Houser             Tap Enter once
```

Body A **personal-business letter** has several parts. The letter begins with the return address and the date. The letter address comes next. The salutation and the body of the letter follow the address. | Tap Enter once between ¶s

The **return address** contains the street address on one line and the city, state, and ZIP Code on the next line. Tap Shift + Enter after each line. The **date** (month day, year) is keyed below the return address. Tap Enter twice after keying the date. The **letter address** is keyed below the date. Use a personal title (Miss, Mr., Ms., Mrs.) or a professional title (Dr., Lt., Senator) before the receiver's name. Tap Shift + Enter after all letter address lines except the last line; tap Enter after keying the last line.

Use default left and right margins for letter

A **salutation** (greeting) is keyed below the letter address. Tap Enter and begin keying the **body** (message) of the letter. Use the 1.08 default line spacing to key the body and tap Enter once between paragraphs. Tap Enter and key the **complimentary close** (farewell). Tap Enter twice and key the name of the writer.

When all lines of the letter begin at the left margin, the letter is arranged in **block format**. When there is no punctuation after the salutation and complimentary close, **open punctuation** style has been used. | Tap Enter once

```
Complimentary     Sincerely
Close
                                  Tap Enter twice
Writer's Name     Robbie Morrison
```

At least 1" bottom margin

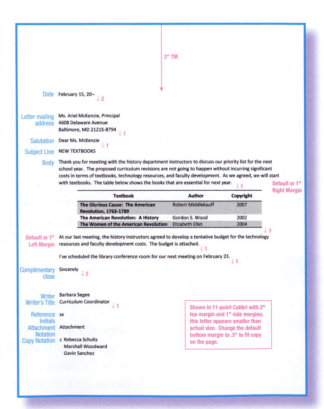

Business Letter in Block Format with Special Features

2" TM

```
Date              February 15, 20—   ↓2

Letter mailing    Ms. Ariel McKenzie, Principal
address           4608 Delaware Avenue
                  Baltimore, MD 21215-8794   ↓1
Salutation        Dear Ms. McKenzie   ↓1
Subject Line      NEW TEXTBOOKS
```

Body Thank you for meeting with the history department instructors to discuss our priority list for the next school year. The proposed curriculum revisions are not going to happen without incurring significant costs in terms of textbooks, technology resources, and faculty development. As we agreed, we will start with textbooks. The table below shows the books that are essential for next year. ↓1

Default or 1" Right Margin

Textbook	Author	Copyright
The Glorious Cause: The American Revolution, 1763-1789	Robert Middlekauff	2007
The American Revolution: A History	Gordon S. Wood	2002
The Women of the American Revolution	Elizabeth Ellet	2004

↓1

Default or 1" Left Margin

At our last meeting, the history instructors agreed to develop a tentative budget for the technology resources and faculty development costs. The budget is attached. ↓1

I've scheduled the library conference room for our next meeting on February 23. ↓1

```
Complimentary     Sincerely   ↓2
close

Writer            Barbara Segee
Writer's Title    Curriculum Coordinator   ↓1

Reference         xx
Initials
Attachment        Attachment
Notation
Copy Notation     c  Rebecca Schultz
                     Marshall Woodward
                     Gavin Sanchez
```

Shown in 11-point Calibri with 2" top margin and 1" side margins, this letter appears smaller than actual size. Change the default bottom margin to .5" to fit copy on the page.

If you want to change the default setting, complete the following steps:

1. Open the Search charm; tap or click "Settings" on the right, enter "power", and then tap or click "Power options" on the left.

2. Do one of the following:

   - If you are using a desktop or tablet, tap or click "Choose what the power buttons do" and under Power button settings, Choose "When I press the power button"—both for when it is running on battery power and when it is plugged into a receptacle select (Sleep, Do nothing, Hibernate, Shut down), and then click or tap "Save changes."

   - If you are using a laptop, tap or click Choose "What closing the lid does"—both for when it is running on battery power and when it is plugged into a receptacle select (Sleep, Do nothing, Hibernate, Shut down), and then click or tap "Save changes." Then, tap or click "Save changes."

LESSON 2   Application Software Basics

OUTCOMES

- Start software.
- Use menus or ribbons and toolbars.
- Maximize, minimize, restore, and resize windows.
- Close a document and exit software.

2A

Starting Applications

Your computer gives you several different ways of starting applications, depending on the operating system and version. Here are two of the most commonly used ways:

- From the Start Screen, display the Charm Bar. Tap or click the Search charm. Key the name of the application you wish to open in the search box.
- If you have saved a shortcut to the app on the desktop, tap or click the application's icon.

Figure 1-17 Search for Apps

Applications software is displayed in a window on the monitor. The features of all windows are the same. At the top is the title bar. The title bar displays the name of the file you are working on and, for some programs, the name of the software (such as *Microsoft Word*).

Proofreaders' marks are used to mark corrections in keyed or printed text that contains problems and/or errors. As a keyboard user, you should be able to read these marks accurately when revising or editing a rough draft. You also should be able to write these symbols to correct the rough drafts that you and others key. The most-used proofreaders' marks are shown below.

Mark	Meaning
‖	Align copy; also, make these items parallel
¶	Begin a new paragraph
Cap ≡	Capitalize
⌒	Close up
ℓ	Delete
<#	Delete space
No ¶	Do not begin a new paragraph
∧	Insert
⋀	Insert comma
⊙	Insert period
⌄⌄	Insert quotation marks
#>	Insert space
⌄	Insert apostrophe
stet	Let it stand; ignore correction
lc	Lowercase
⊔	Move down; lower
⊏	Move left
⊐	Move right
⊓	Move up; raise
osp	Spell out
∼ tr	Transpose
—	Underline or italic

E-Mail Format And Software Features

E-mail format varies slightly, depending on the software used to create and send it.

E-mail Heading

Most e-mail software includes these features:

Attachment: line for attaching files to an e-mail message

Bcc: line for sending copy of a message to someone without the receiver knowing

Cc: line for sending copy of a message to additional receivers

Date: month, day, and year message is sent; often includes precise time of transmittal; usually is inserted automatically

From: name and/or e-mail address of sender; usually is inserted automatically

Subject: line for very brief description of message content

To: line for name and/or e-mail address of receiver

E-mail Body

The message box on the e-mail screen may contain these elements or only the message paragraphs (SS with DS between paragraphs).
• Informal salutation and/or receiver's name (a DS above the message)
• Informal closing (e.g., "Regards," "Thanks") and/or the sender's name (a DS below the message). Additional identification (e.g., telephone number) may be included.

Special E-mail Features

Several e-mail features make communicating through e-mail fast and efficient.

Address list/book: collection of names and e-mail addresses of correspondents from which an address can be entered on the To: line by selecting it, instead of keying it.

Distribution list: series of names and/or e-mail addresses, separated by commas, on the To: line.

Forward: feature that allows an e-mail user to send a copy of a received e-mail message to others.

Recipient list (Group): feature that allows an e-mail user to send mail to a group of recipients by selecting the name of the group (e.g., All Teachers).

Reply: feature used to respond to an incoming message.

Reply all: feature used to respond to all copy recipients as well as the sender of an incoming message.

Signature: feature for storing and inserting the closing lines of messages (e.g., informal closing, sender's name, telephone number, address, fax number).

If you haven't yet saved the document with a filename, the title bar will say something like *Document* or *unmodified*, along with the name of the software. Under the title bar, you may see a menu bar and one or more toolbars or button bars. These bars allow you to choose commands in your software. We'll talk more about them in the next section.

1. Start your computer.
2. Open *Microsoft Word*, a word processing software package.

2B

Using Menus

Most software gives you several different ways to choose commands. As you work with a program, you will find the ways that are easiest for you. A **menu bar** typically appears at the top of your application window, just under the title bar, as shown in Figure 1-18.

Figure 1-18 Menu bar

Like a menu in a restaurant, a menu bar offers you choices. From the menu bar, you can open a document, spell-check it, and so on.

To open a menu and see its options, click the menu name in the menu bar. For example, to open the File menu, click File. For some software, you have to hold the mouse button down to keep the menu displayed. To choose a command, click it (Windows) or drag down to it (Macintosh).

In some software, you can also open menus by pressing Alt plus the underlined letter in the menu name. For example, Alt + F opens the File menu. Menu names vary a little but are much the same across application software.

Newer versions of Microsoft Office applications (*Office 2010* and *Office 2013*) no longer include menus as part of the software. Users choose commands using toolbars, which we will look at next.

1. If menus are available in your version of *Word*, practice opening some menus by clicking them and seeing which commands are available.
2. For example, click File, Insert, or Page Layout.

2C

Working with Toolbars

Toolbars let you choose commands quickly and easily. Most applications have toolbars, and some applications use different names for them, such as button bars; but all toolbars are similar. They consist of icons or buttons that represent commands—some of the same commands found on menus. The Standard toolbar contains icons for basic, often-used commands, such as saving and printing. Toolbars also exist for specific tasks, such as formatting text or creating tables. In most software, pointing to a toolbar icon displays the name of the command. Clicking the icon executes the command.

In newer versions of Microsoft Office applications (*Office 2010* and *Office 2013*), toolbar icons are arranged on what is called the **Ribbon**. The Ribbon provides a convenient way to organize toolbar icons according to the type of task you're currently doing. Each set of icons is displayed in a **tab** that includes icons for commands relating to a particular feature.

For example, if you're working in a *Word* document and want to insert a picture or other item into the document, you click the Insert tab. *Word* then displays all the toolbar icons available for commands having to do with inserting an object into a document, as shown in Figure 1-19.

Confusing Words

accept (vb) to receive; to approve; to take

except (prep/vb) with the exclusion of; leave out

affect (vb) to produce a change in or have an effect on

effect (n) result; something produced by an agent or a cause

buy (n/vb) to purchase; to acquire; a bargain

by (prep/adv) close to; via; according to; close at hand

choose (vb) to select; to decide

chose (vb) past tense of "choose"

cite (vb) use as support; commend; summon

sight (n/vb) ability to see; something seen; a device to improve aim

site (n) location

complement (n) something that fills, completes, or makes perfect

compliment (n/vb) a formal expression of respect or admiration; to pay respect or admiration

do (vb) to bring about; to carry out

due (adj) owed or owing as a debt; having reached the date for payment

farther (adv) greater distance

further (adv) additional; in greater depth; to greater extent

for (prep/conj) indicates purpose on behalf of; because of

four (n) two plus two in number

hear (vb) to gain knowledge of by the ear

here (adv) in or at this place; at or on this point; in this case

hole (n) opening in or through something

whole (adj/n) having all its proper parts; a complete amount

hour (n) the 24th part of a day; a particular time

our (adj) possessive form of "we"; of or relating to us

knew (vb) past tense of "know"; understood; recognized truth or nature of

new (adj) novel; fresh; existing for a short time

know (vb) to be aware of the truth or nature of; to have an understanding of

no (adv/adj/n) not in any respect or degree; not so; indicates denial or refusal

lessen (vb) to cause to decrease; to make less

lesson (n) something to be learned; period of instruction; a class period

lie (n/vb) an untrue or inaccurate statement; to tell an untrue story; to rest or recline

lye (n) a strong alkaline substance or solution

one (adj/pron) a single unit or thing

won (vb) past tense of win; gained a victory as in a game or contest; got by effort or work

passed (vb) past tense of "pass"; already occurred; moved by; gave an item to someone

past (adv/adj/prep/n) gone or elapsed; time gone by

personal (adj) of, relating to, or affecting a person; done in person

personnel (n) a staff or persons making up a workforce in an organization

plain (adj/n) with little decoration; a large flat area of land

plane (n) an airplane or hydroplane

pole (n) a long, slender, rounded piece of wood or other material

poll (n) a survey of people to analyze public opinion

principal (n/adj) a chief or leader; capital (money) amount placed at interest; of or relating to the most important thing or matter or persons

principle (n) a central rule, law, or doctrine

right (adj) factual; true; correct

rite (n) customary form of ceremony; ritual

write (v) to form letters or symbols; to compose and set down in words, numbers, or symbols

some (n/adv) unknown or unspecified unit or thing; to a degree or extent

sum (n/vb) total; to find a total; to summarize

stationary (adj) fixed in a position, course, or mode; unchanging in condition

stationery (n) paper and envelopes used for processing personal and business documents

than (conj/prep) used in comparisons to show differences between items

then (n/adv) that time; at that time; next

to (prep/adj) indicates action, relation, distance, direction

too (adv) besides; also; to excessive degree

two (n/adj) one plus one

vary (vb) change; make different; diverge

very (adv/adj) real; mere; truly; to high degree

waist (n) narrowed part of the body between chest and hips; middle of something

waste (n/vb/adj) useless things; rubbish; spend or use carelessly; nonproductive

weak (adj) lacking strength, skill, or proficiency

week (n) a series of seven days; Monday through Sunday

wear (vb/n) to bear or have on the person; diminish by use; clothing

where (adv/conj/n) at, in, or to what degree; what place, source, or cause

your (adj) of or relating to you as possessor

you're (contraction) you are

In many cases, the tabs and icons displayed on the Ribbon will change to anticipate the kinds of commands you may want to use based on the task you're currently doing.

1. Click the Review tab and then click the Spelling & Grammar icon. The spell check will run, giving you any results for misspelled words. If you have a blank document on your screen, the spell check will complete immediately. Click OK.

Figure 1-19 Toolbar icons displayed on the Insert tab of the Ribbon

2D

Working with Application Windows

Scroll bar

Empty area – click here to move larger increments

Scroll bar arrow

Scroll bar double-arrows — click to move by a whole page

Figure 1-20 The scroll bar

The title bar contains buttons that allow you to resize and close the window. If the window contains more material than you can see at once, **scroll bars** may appear at the right and/or bottom, as shown in Figure 1-20. Clicking a scroll bar arrow moves the document in small increments. Clicking the empty area of a scroll bar moves the document in larger increments. Dragging the bar portion of a scroll bar moves the document exactly as much and as fast as you want.

At the right end of the title or menu bar are the Minimize, Maximize, and Close buttons, as shown in Figure 1-21. Clicking the **Minimize button** reduces a window to a button on the taskbar. This is useful when you want to **multitask** (perform more than one task at a time) and do not want to exit a program. To restore the window, click the button for the program on the taskbar.

Clicking the **Maximize button** enlarges a window to take up almost the entire screen. Many people like to maximize application documents to have more room to work.

After you have maximized a window, the **Restore Down button** will replace the Maximize button. Clicking this button restores the window to a smaller size.

Clicking the **Close button** closes a window.

Restore down

Minimize

Close

Figure 1-21 Windows control buttons

To move a window, drag it by the title bar. To resize a window, move the mouse pointer to a side or corner of the window. The pointer will become a double-headed arrow (↔). Drag until the window is the size you want.

When more than one window is displayed at a time, clicking a window makes it the **active window**— the one you can work in. The other window(s) will have a gray title bar to indicate that it is **inactive**.

1. Practice clicking different parts of the scroll bar to navigate the window. Click and drag the scroll bar down to move down in the document.
2. Click in the open area above the scroll bar to move up in the document.
3. Click the down arrow to move down in the document.
4. Click the double-headed up arrow until you reach the top of the document.
5. Click the Restore Down button.
6. Click the Maximize button.
7. Click and drag the edge of the window to resize it.

Basic Grammar Guides

Use a singular verb

1. With a singular subject.

   Dr. Cho was to give the lecture, but he is ill.

2. With indefinite pronouns (*each, every, any, either, neither, one,* etc.)

   Each of these girls has an important role in the class play.
   Neither of them is well enough to start the game.

3. With singular subjects linked by *or* or *nor*; but if one subject is singular and the other is plural, the verb agrees with the nearer subject.

   Neither Ms. Moss nor Mr. Katz was invited to speak.
   Either the manager or his assistants are to participate.

4. With a collective noun (*class, committee, family, team,* etc.) if the collective noun acts as a unit.

   The committee has completed its study and filed a report.
   The jury has returned to the courtroom to give its verdict.

5. With the pronouns *all* and *some* (as well as fractions and percentages) when used as subjects if their modifiers are singular. Use a plural verb if their modifiers are plural.

   Some of the new paint is already cracking and peeling.
   All of the workers are to be paid for the special holiday.
   Historically, about 40 percent has voted.

6. When *number* is used as the subject and is preceded by *the*; use a plural verb if *number* is the subject and is preceded by *a*.

   The number of voters has increased again this year.
   A number of workers are on vacation this week.

Use a plural verb

1. With a plural subject.

   The players were all here, and they were getting restless.

2. With a compound subject joined by *and*.

   Mrs. Samoa and her son are to be on a local talk show.

Negative forms of verbs

1. Use the plural verb *do not* or *don't* with pronoun subjects *I, we, you,* and *they* as well as with plural nouns.

   I do not find this report believable; you don't either.

2. Use the singular verb *does not* or *doesn't* with pronouns *he, she,* and *it* as well as with singular nouns.

   Though she doesn't accept the board's offer, the board doesn't have to offer more.

Pronoun agreement with antecedents

1. A personal pronoun (*I, we, you, he, she, it, their,* etc.) agrees in person (first, second, or third) with the noun or other pronoun it represents.

   We can win the game if we all give each play our best effort.
   You may play softball after you finish your homework.
   Andrea said that she will drive her car to the shopping mall.

2. A personal pronoun agrees in gender (feminine, masculine, or neuter) with the noun or other pronoun it represents.

   Each winner will get a corsage as she receives her award.
   Mr. Kimoto will give his talk after the announcements.
   The small boat lost its way in the dense fog.

3. A personal pronoun agrees in number (singular or plural) with the noun or other pronoun it represents.

   Celine drove her new car to Del Rio, Texas, last week.
   The club officers made careful plans for their next meeting.

4. A personal pronoun that represents a collective noun (*team, committee, family,* etc.) may be singular or plural, depending on the meaning of the collective noun.

   Our women's soccer team played its fifth game today.
   The vice squad took their positions in the square.

Commonly confused pronouns

it's (contraction): it is; it has
its (pronoun): possessive form of *it*
It's good to get your e-mail; it's been a long time.
The puppy wagged its tail in welcome.

their (pronoun): possessive form of *they*
there (adverb/pronoun): at or in that place; sometimes used to introduce a sentence
they're (contraction): they are
The hikers all wore their parkas.
Will they be there during our presentation?
They're likely to be late because of rush-hour traffic.

who's (contraction): who is; who has
whose (pronoun): possessive form of *who*
Who's seen the movie? Who's going now?
I chose the one whose skills are best.

Closing a Document and Exiting Software

When you're finished working with a document, there are several ways you can close the document and exit a software application. You can:

- Click the Close button on the windows control buttons located at the top right of the window (in Macintosh applications this button is located at the top left of the window).
- In *Microsoft Word*, click File, Close to close the document.
- In *Microsoft Word*, click File, Exit (or Quit) to close both the document and the software application.
- Use the keyboard shortcut to close a document, which is Ctrl + W.
- Use the keyboard shortcut to close a program, which is Alt + F4.

If you have not yet saved the document, or have not saved recent changes you made to the document, the application will show a dialog box that asks you if you want to save changes. Clicking *Yes* will save the most current changes to the document. Clicking *No* will close the document without saving your work. Be certain that you have saved any work you want to keep in the document before you decide to close it.

Now, close the current document and exit *Word* by clicking File, Exit. If prompted to save your changes, click *No*.

LESSON 3
Using a Software Application

OUTCOMES

- Open a new or existing document.
- Work with documents.
- Change the document display.
- Print a document.
- Save files.

3A

Opening a New or Existing Document

When working with documents in this book, you will sometimes be asked to open a new document, and other times you will be asked to open a data file. Data files include existing information that gives you a head start on completing the work in a document.

The data filenames in this book will use the following naming convention: *df 3a activity1*, where *df* stands for Data File, *3a* or a similar abbreviation stands for the lesson name and number (in this case, Lesson 3A), followed by the activity number.

To open a new, blank document:

1. Open *Word*.
2. Click File, New, as shown in Figure 1-22. Then click Blank Document.
3. Click File, Open. Follow your instructor's directions to choose the folder on your computer or network where your data files are stored.
4. Click the data file named *df 3a activity1*, as shown in Figure 1-23.
5. Click Open. The data file opens on screen.

Figure 1-22 Opening a new file

Punctuation Guides (continued)

Use an exclamation point

1. After emphatic interjections.

   Wow!   Hey there!   What a day!

2. After sentences that are clearly exclamatory.

   "I won't go!" she said with determination.
   How good it was to see you in New Orleans last week!

Use a hyphen

1. To join parts of compound words expressing the numbers twenty-one through ninety-nine.

   Thirty-five delegates attended the national convention.

2. To join compound adjectives preceding a noun they modify as a unit.

   End-of-term grades will be posted on the classroom door.

3. After each word or figure in a series of words or figures that modify the same noun (suspended hyphenation).

   Meeting planners made first-, second-, and third-class reservations.

4. To spell out a word.

   The sign read, "For your c-o-n-v-i-e-n-c-e." Of course, the correct word is c-o-n-v-e-n-i-e-n-c-e.

5. To form certain compound nouns.

   WGAL-TV   spin-off   teacher-counselor   AFL-CIO

Use italic

To indicate titles of books, plays, movies, magazines, and newspapers. (Titles may be keyed in ALL CAPS or underlined.)

   A review of *Runaway Jury* appeared in *The New York Times*.

Use parentheses

1. To enclose parenthetical or explanatory matter and added information.

   Amendments to the bylaws (Exhibit A) are enclosed.

2. To enclose identifying letters or figures in a series.

   Check these factors: (1) period of time, (2) rate of pay, and (3) nature of duties.

3. To enclose figures that follow spelled-out amounts to give added clarity or emphasis.

   The total award is fifteen hundred dollars ($1,500).

Use a question mark

At the end of a sentence that is a direct question. But use a period after requests in the form of a question (whenever the expected answer is action, not words).

   What has been the impact of the Information Superhighway?
   Will you complete the enclosed form and return it to me.

Use quotation marks

1. To enclose direct quotations.

   Professor Dye asked, "Are you spending the summer in Europe?"
   Was it Emerson who said, "To have a friend is to be one"?

2. To enclose titles of articles, poems, songs, television programs, and unpublished works, such as theses and dissertations.

   "Talk of the Town" in the *New Yorker*   "Fog" by Sandburg
   "Survivor" in prime time   "Memory" from *Cats*

3. To enclose special words or phrases or coined words (words not in dictionary usage).

   The words "phony" and "braggart" describe him, according to coworkers.
   The presenter annoyed the audience with phrases like "uh" and "you know."

Use a semicolon

1. To separate two or more independent clauses in a compound sentence when the conjunction is omitted.

   Being critical is easy; being constructive is not so easy.

2. To separate independent clauses when they are joined by a conjunctive adverb, such as *consequently* or *therefore*.

   I work mornings; therefore, I prefer an afternoon interview.

3. To separate a series of phrases or clauses (especially if they contain commas) that are introduced by a colon.

   Al spoke in these cities: Denver, CO; Erie, PA; and Troy, NY.

4. To precede an abbreviation or word that introduces an explanatory statement.

   She organized her work; for example, naming folders and files to indicate degrees or urgency.

Use an underline

To call attention to words or phrases (or use quotation marks or italic).

   Take the presenter's advice: Stand up, speak up, and then sit down.
   Students often confuse its and it's.

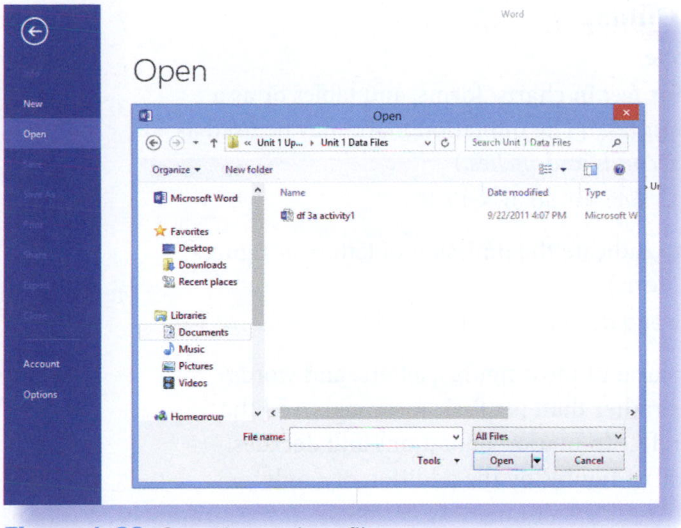

Figure 1-23 Opening a data file

Once a document is open, you can begin working with it by selecting and formatting text.

To select a word or text, use the mouse to place the insertion point at the beginning of the word, then click and drag over the word until it is highlighted. The insertion point is shaped like an I-beam when you move the mouse around in a document. The flashing curor is a single line that indicates the position where you can begin keying text.

You can also select a word by moving the cursor to the beginning of the word and pressing Ctrl + Shift + Right Arrow. Another way to select a word is to double-click the word.

1. In **df 3a activity1**, select the word *Location* and make it boldface by clicking the Bold icon in the Font group of the Home tab on the Ribbon (or use the keyboard shortcut, Ctrl + B).
2. Format the words *Price* and *Floor plan* in bold. Your document should look similar to Figure 1-24.
3. In the third line of the document, delete the word "within."

Considerations when looking for a new home:

Location Choose the best location for your needs.

Price Make sure the price fits within your budget.

Floor plan Find a floor plan with enough space.

Figure 1-24 Selecting and formatting text in a document

Punctuation Guides

Use an apostrophe

1. As a symbol for *feet* in charts, forms, and tables or as a symbol for *minutes*. (The quotation mark may be used as a symbol for *seconds* and *inches*.)

   12' x 16'   3' 54"   8' 6" x 10' 8"

2. As a symbol to indicate the omission of letters or figures (as in contractions).

   can't   do's and don'ts   Class of '14

3. To form the plural of most figures, letters, and words used as words rather than for their meaning: Add the apostrophe and *s*. In market quotations and decades, form the plural of figures by the addition of *s* only.

   7's   ten's   ABC's   Century 4s   1960s

4. To show possession: Add the apostrophe and *s* to (a) a singular noun and (b) a plural noun that does not end in *s*.

   a woman's watch   men's shoes   girl's bicycle

   Add the apostrophe and *s* to a proper name of one syllable that ends in *s*.

   Bess's Cafeteria   James's hat   Jones's bill

   Add the apostrophe only after (a) plural nouns ending in *s* and (b) a proper name of more than one syllable that ends in *s* or *z*.

   girls' camp   Adams' home   Martinez' report

   Add the apostrophe (and *s*) after the last noun in a series to indicate joint or common possession by two or more persons; however, add the possessive to each of the nouns to show separate possession by two or more persons.

   Lewis and Clark's expedition
   the secretary's and the treasurer's reports

Use a colon

1. To introduce a listing.

   These poets are my favorites: Shelley, Keats, and Frost.

2. To introduce a question or a long direct quotation.

   The question is this: Did you study for the test?

3. Between hours and minutes expressed in figures.

   10:15 a.m.   4:30 p.m.   12:00 midnight

Use a comma (or commas)

1. After (a) introductory phrases or clauses and (b) words in a series.

   When you finish keying the report, please give it to Mr. Kent.
   We will play the Mets, Expos, and Cubs in our next home stand.

2. To set off short direct quotations.

   Mrs. Ramirez replied, "No, the report is not finished."

3. Before and after (a) appositives—words that come together and refer to the same person, thing, or idea—and (b) words of direct address.

   Colette, the assistant manager, will chair the next meeting.
   Please call me, Erika, if I can be of further assistance.

4. To set off nonrestrictive clauses (not necessary to meaning of sentence), but not restrictive clauses (necessary to meaning).

   Your report, which deals with that issue, raised many questions.
   The man who organized the conference is my teacher.

5. To separate the day from the year in dates and the city from the state in addresses.

   July 4, 2005   St. Joseph, Missouri   Moose Point, AK

6. To separate two or more parallel adjectives (adjectives that modify the noun separately and that could be separated by the word *and* instead of the comma).

   The big, loud bully was ejected after he pushed the coach.
   The big, powerful car zoomed past the cheering crowd.
   Cynthia played a black lacquered grand piano at her concert.
   A small red fox squeezed through the fence to avoid the hounds.

7. To separate (a) unrelated groups of figures that occur together and (b) whole numbers into groups of three digits each. (Omit commas from years and page, policy, room, serial, and telephone numbers.)

   By the year 2015, 1,200 more local students will be enrolled.
   The supplies listed on Invoice #274068 are for Room 1953.

Use a dash

Create a dash by keying two hyphens or one em-dash.

1. For emphasis.

   The skater—in a clown costume—dazzled with fancy footwork.

2. To indicate a change of thought.

   We may tour the Orient—but I'm getting ahead of my story.

3. To emphasize the name of an author when it follows a direct quotation.

   "All the world's a stage. . . ."—Shakespeare

4. To set off expressions that break off or interrupt speech.

   "Jay, don't get too close to the—." I spoke too late.
   "Today—er—uh," the anxious presenter began.

3C

Changing the Document Display

When working with a document in *Word*, it is sometimes helpful to change the document display, either by zooming in or out, or by changing the document view.

The tools for changing the document display are located at the right side of the status bar, which is at the bottom of the document window. See Figure 1-25.

Figure 1-25 Document Views on bottom status bar

You can change the size of the document text by clicking the plus or minus signs at either end of the zoom control. Zoom in to increase the size of the document by either clicking the plus sign or dragging the zoom control indicator to the right. Zoom out to decrease the size of the document by either clicking the minus sign or dragging the zoom control indicator to the left.

You can also choose one of the following document views:

- Print Layout view shows the document as it will look when printed.
- Read Mode view minimizes toolbars and presents the document in a full-screen view to improve readability.
- Web Layout View shows the document as it will appear if viewed as a Web page.

The most commonly used view, and the one we will use most often in this book, is Print Layout, because it gives the most accurate view of what your printed document will look like.

1. In *df 3a activity1*, change the document zoom to 120%.
2. Now change the document zoom to 70% and note the difference in the display.
3. Change the document zoom back to 100%.
4. Click each of the different document views and note the differences in each view.

3D

Printing a Document

After you have keyed text into a document, edited the document, and applied formatting, you may want to print the document.

You can print the document by clicking File and Print. After you click the File tab, you can see the Backstage view (versions of Microsoft Office 2010 or newer). Backstage view shows you all the file management available for your document, including opening, closing, saving, and printing the document, as well as, viewing the document properties and more advanced features such as document sharing and permissions.

The Backstage view of Print options allows you to select the printer, number of copies, specify pages to print, among other options, as shown in Figure 1-26.

Capitalization Guides

Capitalize

1. The first word of every sentence and complete quotation. Do not capitalize (a) fragments of quotations or (b) a quotation resumed within a sentence.

   Crazy Horse said, "I will return to you in stone."
   Gandhi's teaching inspired "nonviolent revolutions."
   "It is . . . fitting and proper," Lincoln said, "that we . . . do this."

2. The first word after a colon if that word begins a complete sentence.

   Remember: Keep the action in your fingers.
   These sizes were in stock: small, medium, and extra large.

3. First, last, and all other words in titles except articles, conjunctions, or prepositions of four or fewer letters.
   The Beak of the Finch   *Raleigh News and Observer*
   "The Phantom of the Opera"

4. An official title when it precedes a name or when used elsewhere if it is a title of distinction.

   In what year did Juan Carlos become King of Spain?
   Masami Chou, our class president, met Senator Thurmond.

5. Personal titles and names of people and places.

   Did you see Mrs. Watts and Gloria while in Miami?

6. All proper nouns and their derivatives.

   Mexico   Mexican border   Uganda   Ugandan economy

7. Days of the week, months of the year, holidays, periods of history, and historic events.

Friday	July	Labor Day
Middle Ages	Vietnam War	Woodstock

8. Geographic regions, localities, and names.

the East Coast	Upper Peninsula Michigan
Ohio River	the Deep South

9. Street, avenue, company, etc., when used with a proper noun.

Fifth Avenue	Wall Street	Monsanto Company

10. Names of organizations, clubs, and buildings.

National Hockey League	Four-H Club
Biltmore House	Omni Hotel

11. A noun preceding a figure except for common nouns, such as line, page, and sentence.

    Review Rules 1 to 18 in Chapter 5, page 149.

12. Seasons of the year only when they are personified.

    the soft kiss of Spring   the icy fingers of Winter

Number Expression Guides

Use words for

1. Numbers from one to ten except when used with numbers above ten, which are keyed as figures. Common business practice is to use figures for all numbers except those that begin a sentence.

   Did you visit all eight websites, or only four?
   Buy 15 textbooks and 8 workbooks.

2. A number beginning a sentence.

   Twelve of the new shrubs have died; 48 are doing well.

3. The shorter of two numbers used together.

   fifty 45-cent stamps   150 twenty-cent stamps

4. Isolated fractions or indefinite numbers in a sentence.

   Nearly seventy members voted, which is almost one-fourth.

5. Names of small-numbered streets and avenues (ten and under).

   The theater is at the corner of Third Avenue and 54th Street.

Use figures for

1. Dates and times except in very formal writing.

   The flight will arrive at 9:48 a.m. on March 14.
   The ceremony took place the fifth of June at eleven o'clock.

2. A series of fractions and/or mixed numbers.

   Key 1/4, 1/2, 5/6, and 7 3/4.

3. Numbers following nouns.

   Case 1849 is reviewed in Volume 5, page 9.

4. Measures, weights, and dimensions.

   6 feet 9 inches   7 pounds 4 ounces
   8.5 inches by 11 inches

5. Definite numbers used with percent (%), but use words for indefinite percentages.

   The late fee is 15 percent of the overdue payment.
   The brothers put in nearly fifty percent of the start-up capital.

6. House numbers except house number *One*.

   My home is at 8 Rose Lane; my office is at One Rose Plaza.

7. Amounts of money except when spelled for emphasis (as in legal documents). Even amounts are keyed without the decimal. Large amounts (a million or more) are keyed as shown.

$17.75	75 cents	$775	seven hundred dollars ($700)
$7,500	$7 million	$7.2 million	$7 billion

Figure 1-26 Backstage view of Print options

1. In *df 3a activity1*, click the File tab.
2. Click Print.
3. Choose the printer your instructor tells you to use (and ask your instructor for permission to print).
4. Select 1 for the number of copies to print, if it is not already selected.
5. Click Print.

3E

Saving a Document

After working with a document, you can save your work so that it will be available for later use. Saving is quick and easy—simply click the File tab and click, Save As. You can then determine whether to save the document on your Computer or the SkyDrive. (If you choose SkyDrive, you will need to set up an account and sign in to do so.) Select Computer and choose Recent Folders, Documents, Desktop, or Browse to determine where your document will be saved. Then give the document a descriptive name. See Figure 1-27.

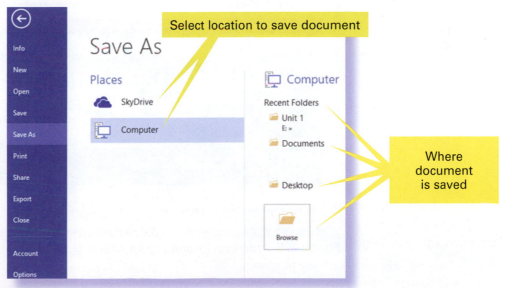

Figure 1-27 Saving documents

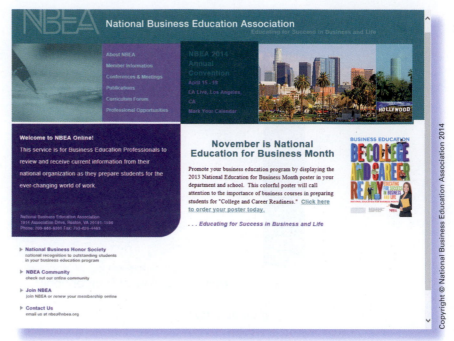

Figure B-4 National Business Education Association (www.nbea.org)

If you are an architect in the Cleveland, Ohio, area, you may want to join The American Institute of Architects (national level) (see Figure B-5 below). You could also be a member of the American Institute of Architects Ohio (state level) and/or the American Institute of Architects Cleveland (local level).

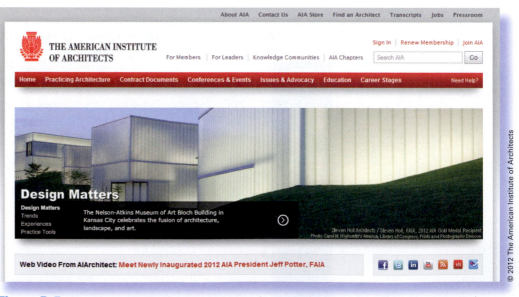

Figure B-5 American Institute of Architects (www.aia.org)

After saving the document the first time, you can click the Save icon on the Quick Access Toolbar or press Ctrl + S to save frequently and avoid losing any of your work.

1. In *df 3a activity1*, click the File tab.
2. Click Save As.
3. In the Save As dialog box, go to the location where your instructor tells you to save your document.
4. Click the File Name text box, and key *3e activity1* as the new filename for the document as shown in Figure 1-28.
5. Click Save.
6. Close *3e activity1* as well as the blank document you created earlier in this lesson; then exit *Word*.

Digital Citizenship and Ethics

A computer is a very powerful tool that has many uses. Unfortunately, all people do not use the computer for good and moral purposes. In other words, computer usage has ethical dimensions that should concern all of us. Use a search engine to research computer ethics, and then write a paragraph describing what you have learned about computer ethics. Print at least one page from a website that is a good resource for this activity.

© wavebreakmedia ltd/Shutterstock.com

Think Critically

1. Evaluate the sources of the information you found—is the information reliable?
2. Describe the ways your use of the computer each day can have an impact on others.
3. Describe three ways use of the Internet and Web can have a positive impact on the lives of your friends, family, and colleagues each day.

LESSON 4   Managing Files and Folders

OUTCOMES
- Navigate files and folders.
- Copy and move files and folders.
- Rename and delete files and folders.

4A

Navigating Files and Folders

Setting up a logical and easy-to-use file management system will help you organize files efficiently and find them quickly and easily. You can manage files with your file management program, *File Explorer*. This feature may be somewhat different on your computer, depending on your *Windows* version and setup.

Figure B-3 Rotary International (www.rotary.org)

Leadership Activity 5

Professional Association Research

1. Read the information about leadership opportunities in professional associations below, and review the web pages in Figures B-4 and B-5.
2. Identify a profession you want to learn more about. Search the Internet to find associations related to the profession you choose. Look for national, regional, state, and local associations.
3. Explore the website to learn how the organization provides leadership opportunities for its members. Write a paragraph or two describing your findings.
4. Save your file as *app b leader5*. Print your file and one or more pages from the website to support your description.

Leadership Opportunities in Professional Associations

Nearly every profession has an association to serve its members. Many professions have national, regional, state, and local associations. Each provides services to the profession and the members of the association. The associations, regardless of level, also provide opportunities for members to assume leadership positions.

For example, if you are a business education teacher in the Eastern Region of Illinois, there are several professional associations you might want to join. You could join the National Business Education Association (national level) (see Figure B-4 below), the North-Central Business Education Association (regional level), the Illinois Business Education Association (state level), and/or the Eastern Illinois Business Education Association (local level).

Good file organization begins with giving your files and folders names that are logical, relevant, and easy to understand. For example, you might create a folder for your English assignments called *English*. In this folder, you might have a journal that you add to each day (called *Journal*); monthly compositions (e.g., *Comp 10-9*, *Comp 3-10*); and occasional essays (such as *EssaySports* or *EssayEthics*). A system like this would make finding files simple.

You can use *File Explorer* (formerly *Windows Explorer*) to see how files and folders are organized on your computer. Use the Ribbon for common tasks, such as copying and moving, creating new folders, emailing and zipping items, and changing the view. The tabs change to show extra tasks that apply to the selected items. For example, if you select **Computer** in the navigation pane, the ribbon show different than if would if you select a folder in your **Music** library. Use the navigation pane to access the locations of your folders and files. To browse your PC's drives and the folders in them, expand the **Computer**. You can use the Preview pane to see the contents of a file, such as an Office document, without opening it in an application. To use the preview pane, tap or click the View tab and then tap or click Preview pane. It will appear in the far right of your screen. See Figure 1-28.

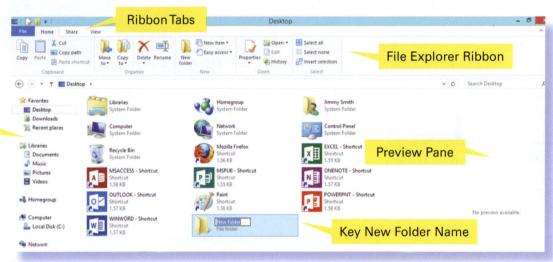

Figure 1-28 File Explorer Panel

By default, you have three tabs across the top of the Ribbon—Home, Share, and View. The Home tab contains functions like copy, Paste, Move to, Delete, Rename, New Folder, Properties, and more. Tapping or clicking on the Share tab will let you email a file or folder, put it into a zip file, or even burn it to a disk. The View tab manages what File Explorer looks like—this is where you can turn on the preview pane, choose your icon view, and set how Windows sorts your icons in the File Explorer window.

Quick Access Toolbar

The quick access toolbar is a small set of buttons in the title bar of File Explorer, containing a few of the functions inside the ribbon—See Figure 1-29. There, you can put some of your most-used functions for super-quick access. You can customize the toolbar with the small arrow button at the end of it, which will let you put any combination of the Undo, Redo, Delete, New Folder, Properties, and Rename buttons on the top left of the toolbar.

computer subjects commonly completed in high school. Students who do well at the local level advance to the regional level. Those who do well at the regional level advance to the state level, and likewise those who do well at the state level can compete at the national level. Students who are successful in these competitions bring favorable recognition to themselves, their teachers, and their schools.

Figure B-1 FBLA-PBL Home Page

Leadership Activity 4

Service Organization Research

1. There are several organizations for service- and community-minded individuals. Among these are Kiwanis International and Rotary International, both of which sponsor organizations for high school students. Review the home page from each of their websites in Figures B-2 and B-3 below to get an overview of each service organization.

2. Explore the website of Kiwanis International or Rotary International to learn how the organization provides leadership opportunities for high school students. Write a paragraph or two describing your findings.

3. Save your file as *app b leader4*. Print your file and one or more pages from the website to support your description.

Figure B-2 Kiwanis International (www.kiwanis.org)

Figure 1-29 Quick Access Toolbar

You will want to create folders to store files. You can do so using File Explorer. In addition to putting files in your folders, you can create folders within folders to further organize the contents.

In File Explorer, select the drive or folder that will contain the new folder. Tap or click the Home tab, and then tap or click New folder. Key the name of the new folder. See Figure 1-28.

1. From the Start Menu, open your Charm Bar. Tap or click the Share charm.
2. Key File Explorer in the search box and enter. Tap or click File Explorer on the left.
3. Click the arrow beside the drive or folder in the navigation pane to expand the contents for viewing. Click again and the contents are hidden.
4. Tap or click a folder (icon or name) in the Navigation Pane. All its content (Files and/or folders) will be displayed in the right pane.
5. Tap or click a folder in the right pane to display its contents.
6. Practice steps 3 through 5 with various folders.
7. In the Navigation Pane, tap or click Desktop (you may need to scroll up a little to find it).
8. Tap or click New Folder. A new folder call New Folder will appear in the right pane of the window with the name highlighted.
9. Key a name for the folder (**Century 21**) and tap enter.
10. Create another new folder and call it **Compositions**.

Copying and Moving Files and Folders

NOTE
The easiest way to arrange two windows side by side is to use Snap. Just drag the title bar of a window all the way to the left or right side of the screen until you see the outline of the window cover that half of the screen. Repeat this step with the other window on the other side of the screen to arrange the two windows side by side.

With *File Explorer*, you can move or copy files or folders in a number of few different ways.

- Select the items you want to copy or move, tap or click the Home tab, and tap or click Copy to copy them or Cut to move them. Then open the new location and tap or click Paste.
- Open two *File Explorer* windows side by side, and then drag items from one window to the other. (To open a new File Explorer window, tap or click the File tab, and then choose Open new window.)
- Select the file you want to copy or move, tap or click the Home tab. In the Organize section of the *File Explorer* ribbon, tap or click the drop down box for Move to or Copy to and select where you want to move or copy the file or folder. If you do not see the location displayed, tap or click Choose location for options. Select the location and tap or click Move or Copy.
- Press and hold or right-click the item you want to copy or move; choose Cut or Copy on the shortcut menu, press and hold or right-click the new location, and then choose Paste on the shortcut menu.
- Use the keyboard shortcut Ctrl + C to copy or Ctrl + X to cut, and then browse to the new location and press Ctrl + V to paste.

7. *A successful leader can be trusted and is loyal to his or her followers.* Trust is the single most important factor in building personal and professional relationships. Trust implies accountability, predictability, and reliability. More than anything else, followers want to believe in and trust their leaders. Only then will people follow them. Trust must be earned day by day. It calls for consistency. Some of the ways a leader can betray trust include breaking promises, gossiping, withholding information, or lying.

8. *A successful leader delegates tasks.* The question leaders must ask themselves is whether a task can be done by someone else. If so, it should probably be delegated. Good leaders focus on performing tasks that no one can do as well. Oftentimes these tasks relate to long-term planning and strategic thinking.

9. *A successful leader makes decisions.* Successful leaders do not agonize over a decision because they're afraid of making a mistake. They know mistakes are likely to happen, and they are willing to live with the consequences of their decisions. Also, leaders do not second-guess decisions they have already made. Rather, effective leaders focus their attention on doing the best thing in the present moment and planning for a better future.

10. *A successful leader is friendly, teachable, and can control his or her ego.* Leaders put empathy ahead of authority. Leaders are not arrogant or egotistical. They are friendly with all kinds of people regardless of their position or status. Successful leaders don't have fragile egos. They recognize that no single person can have all of the correct answers all of the time and that they can always learn from others. Leaders don't let their egos get in the way.

These attributes of leadership apply in all settings. They apply while attending school, playing with friends, participating in sports or other extracurricular activities, working with others, governing others, and being a family and community member.

Leadership Activity 3

Research FBLA

1. Read the information below about leadership opportunities through school student organizations.
2. Access the FBLA-PBL website (see Figure B-1) to locate information about FBLA and how it is organized to serve middle school, high school, and college/university students and alumni.
3. On the FBLA-PBL website or, if you prefer, on your state's FBLA-PBL website, explore how FBLA provides leadership opportunities for high school students. Write a paragraph or two describing your findings.
4. Save your file as *app b leader3*. Print your file and print one or more pages from the website that support your findings.

Leadership Opportunities Through Student Organizations

One school organization that is popular with students who study business and computers is FBLA. FBLA stands for Future Business Leaders of America. It exists primarily to provide students with opportunities to learn and apply leadership and competitive skills. Members of FBLA have opportunities to become leaders by holding office at the local, regional, state, and national levels. In addition, you will have many opportunities to use leadership skills while serving on committees and participating in activities. FBLA sponsors numerous conferences to help students develop specific leadership skills.

Another aspect of participating in FBLA is the opportunity to take part in competitions at the local, regional, state, and national levels. These competitions are centered around business and

When you are moving or copying multiple files or folders, selecting (tapping or clicking) several items at once can save time. This can be achieved in one of two methods:

- To select consecutive items, click the first item, hold down the Shift key, and tap or click the last item.
- To select items in different places, hold down the Ctrl key while you click each item.

You can arrange the icons in a window by name, type, size, date modified, or by other attributes. Tap or click the View tab. Under Current view, tap or click Group by to expand the list of attributes by which you can arrange files and folders. See Figure 1-30.

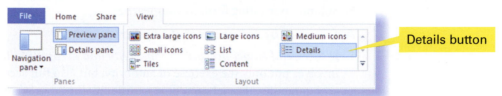

Figure 1-30 Arranging folders and files

You can also group folders and files by attributes such as the file size and the date the file was last modified. Tap or click the View tab. Under Layout, tap or click Details. See Figure 1-31.

Figure 1-31 Grouping folders and files

1. Open two *File Explorer* windows side by side. In one window, locate and click the drive or folder from which you retrieve data files for this text. The files will be displayed in the right pane.
2. In the other window, scroll in the navigation pane until you can see the *Compositions* folder you created in Activity 4A.
3. Hold down Ctrl and drag one of your data files to the *Compositions* folder.
4. Select a block of data files to copy by selecting the first file and pressing Shift as you select the last file. Hold down Ctrl and drag the files to the *Compositions* folder.
5. Select several separate data files to copy by pressing Ctrl as you select each file. Hold down Ctrl and drag these files to the *Compositions* folder.
6. Close the *File Explorer* window for the drive or folder housing the data files for this text (tap or click the X at the upper right of the window). Oops! We put a keyboarding file in the *Compositions* folder. Now we will use the *Move to* command to move the files to the Century 21 folder.
7. Select the first file from the *Compositions* window. Tap or click the *Move to* button (see the Home tab) and tap or click *Choose location*.
8. Select the *Century 21* folder and tap or click *Move*.
9. Select a group of files in the *Compositions* window and copy them to the *Century 21* folder using the Copy to button. Do not worry if the files are not neatly arranged. You will organize them next.
10. Open the *Century 21* folder to see if all the files you copied are there.
11. In the *Century 21* window, click the View tab and group the folders and files by name.
12. With no tiles selected, note (between the window and the task bar) how many files the *Century 21* window contains and the total file size.
13. Select one file. What does the window tell you about it? What does it tell you about a group of selected files?
14. Click the View tab, display or arrange the folders and files by their details.
15. Click the View tab, group the files by the date they were modified. When might this view be useful?

Leadership Activity 2

A Classmate as a Leader

1. Think of a student in your school whom you consider to be an effective leader. It doesn't matter whether he or she is a leader of a student club, in athletics, in student government, or in the community. What matters is that you believe this person is an effective leader.
2. Open *df app b leader2* and print the file.
3. As you read each of the ten attributes of a successful leader below, use the four-point scale to rate that student you consider to be a leader. If desired, use the space at the bottom to explain your ratings.
4. Write any additional comments you have in the space provided on the rating form.
5. Submit your rating form to your teacher.

Attributes of a Successful Leader

1. *A successful leader accepts responsibility and accountability for results.* True leadership involves not only the exercise of authority, but also full acceptance of responsibility and accountability. Leaders accept responsibility for those whom they lead. The leader is accountable for everything that occurs, even the errors. Don't fault others; just accept the blame when things go wrong. On the other hand, good leaders always share credit for their successes. Leaders always try to exhibit an attitude of sharing, except when things go wrong.

2. *A successful leader has self-discipline and good character and is committed to personal development.* The best leaders commit themselves to a life of ongoing personal development. An effective leader understands his or her own shortcomings and seeks improvement from within. The great leaders also give others the opportunity and encouragement to develop. The best leaders love to read. Most subscribe to a lot of different magazines, many of which are outside their area of expertise or current knowledge. They also read books about strategies for leading and biographies or autobiographies about respected leaders.

mangostock/Shutterstock.com

3. *A successful leader is a great communicator.* What separates many great leaders from others is that they have truly mastered the art of listening. They ask questions, and they really listen to the answers. They have learned the power of silence and remember the wise saying, "You can't learn with your mouth open!" Leaders follow up verbal communications with written communications to lessen misunderstandings.

4. *A successful leader has great people skills.* Leaders are open enough so that everyone around them can get to know and trust them. Great leaders have a genuine concern for those whom they lead. People expect their leader to safeguard their future.

5. *A successful leader builds momentum and takes action.* To be appointed or elected to a leadership position is not sufficient to make you a leader. You must, after being appointed or elected, take charge and begin leading. Leaders must have strong personal energy to get a project up and running. They must also maintain that energy to see the projects through to completion. Remember, effective leaders perform for results, not recognition.

6. *A successful leader sets high standards and expectations.* Leaders expect excellence of themselves and the people they lead, because they realize that for the most part leaders get what they expect. If they have low expectations, they are likely to get low performance. Conversely, if they have high expectations, they are likely to get high performance.

Renaming and Deleting Files and Folders

You can rename a file or folder in one of these ways:

- In *File Explorer*, select the file or folder; tap or click the Home tab. Then tap or click Rename and key the new name.
- Right-click the file or folder, choose Rename, key the new name, and tap Enter.

In the filename **Lesson1.docx**, the docx **extension** indicates that the file is a Microsoft Word document. When you rename a file, be sure to include the extension that is recognized by your software program, or you may not be able to open the file.

You can select and delete several files and folders at once, just as you selected several items to move or copy. If you delete a folder, you automatically delete any files and folders inside it. Here are two ways to delete a file or folder:

- In *File Explorer*, select the file or folder, tap or click the Home tab. Then tap or click Delete.
- Right-click the file or folder and choose Delete.

When you delete a file or folder, it is moved to the Recycle Bin, where it is stored temporarily. The Recycle Bin allows you to restore files or folders that you might have accidentally deleted. Occasionally, you should empty the Recycle Bin to free up storage space with folders and files you no longer need. See Figure 1-32.

Figure 1-32 Recycle Bin Tools

1. Right-click the *Century 21* folder on the desktop, choose Rename, key **Keyboarding**, and tap Enter.
2. Open *File Explorer*. Tap or click the *Compositions* folder. Choose Rename from the Organize menu, key **English**, and tap Enter.
3. In the *Keyboarding* window, right-click a file, choose Delete.
4. Select several files in the *Keyboarding* window, choose Delete from the Organize menu.
5. Assume there was one file you did not mean to delete from the Keyboarding window. Tap or click the Recycle Bin icon to open the Recycle Bin window.
6. Select one of the files you just deleted by tapping or clicking the file. Tap or click Restore the selected items button as shown in Figure 1-32.
7. Close the Recycle Bin window. Tap or click the *Keyboarding* folder. It should contain the file you just restored.
8. Close the *Keyboarding* window and delete the *Keyboarding* and *English* folders.

Appendix B   Leadership Development

OUTCOMES
- Analyze the characteristics of a good leader.
- Explore leadership opportunities in school and professional organizations.

Leadership Activity 1

What is Leadership?

1. Read about the characteristics of leadership below.
2. Describe in a paragraph or two a situation in which you assumed a leadership role and describe your effectiveness as a leader in this situation.
3. Print your paragraph(s) and save your file as *app b leader1*.

The Characteristics of Leadership

Leadership is an important foundation for our society. Effective leadership is needed in our schools, homes, government, and places of worship, work, and play. Therefore, much has been written about the attributes that many believe are essential for effective leadership.

Yuri Acurs/Shutterstock.com

Leadership Can Be Learned

It is a popular opinion that leaders are born, not made. However, in reality, leadership is a set of characteristics that can be learned. You will have many opportunities during your school years to develop leadership qualities. You may have opportunities to be a leader in student government, a student club or other extracurricular activity, and in your community or church. If you work, you will have opportunities to develop leadership qualities for the workplace.

Leadership Defined

Leadership can be defined as getting other people to follow you toward a common goal. For example, imagine that 12 students from your class, including yourself, were asked to move to the front of the room. Once there, the group is directed to line up in the order of their ages from the youngest to the oldest by year, month, and day. Also, the group is told they have five minutes to do this. No further instructions are given.

Consider whether this group of students could perform this simple task without one of them assuming a leadership role. Would you be the one who assumes that role? If so, would you do so immediately or would you wait to see if someone else was willing to step forward to lead the group?

If you assumed the role as leader, would you show any signs of frustration if you could not get others to follow your directions? If you did not assume leadership responsibilities, would you resent being "bossed" around by someone who assumed those responsibilities? Or would you willingly follow the leader's directions and help the group meet its goal? If so, you would be demonstrating an equally important set of qualities—being a good follower or team player.

LESSON 5   Computer Safety and the Internet

OUTCOMES

- Connect with the Internet.
- Describe uses of the Internet.
- Explore websites with a browser.
- Identify the features of search engines and social networks.
- Search for information and explain how to perform transactions via the Web.

- Describe threats to computers and networks.
- Discuss computer crime and legal and ethical issues such as copyright law and fair use.
- Identify netiquette as well as ethical and legal practices of conducting business such as safeguarding confidential information.

5A

Connecting with the Internet

When two or more computers are connected either by a cable or wireless connection, the computers are part of a **network**. The two basic categories of networks are **local area networks** (**LANs**) and **wide area networks** (**WANs**). The network of computers at your school or the wireless network at your home or local coffee shop is a LAN. A network of computers across a city is a WAN.

The most well-known and certainly most used network is the global network of computers called the **Internet**, which connects millions of networks and computers around the world. The Internet connects local networks and computers with distant networks and computers through **routers**, which direct information, and **servers**, which house vast databases of information.

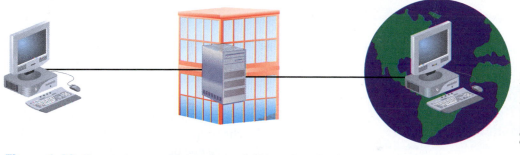

© Cengage Learning

Figure 1-33 Computers connected to a LAN and to the Internet

Billions of people around the world use the Internet to find information, conduct business, purchase goods, and communicate via e-mail and social networking sites such as Facebook and Twitter. The Internet is the global network of computers that is comprised of various servers and their links. The **World Wide Web** is the system of sites, documents, and content hosted on Internet servers that can be viewed graphically because it has been formatted with a set of graphic codes called **HTML**, which stands for Hypertext Markup Language.

There are several different ways you can connect to the Internet. The most common include:

- using your desktop or laptop computer, which is connected to a network via a cable or wireless connection.
- using your cell phone and a wireless cellular network.
- using a gaming or other entertainment device.

LESSON 10   Division & Math Calculations

OUTCOMES
- Learn division on numeric keypad.
- Learn to complete math calculations on numeric keypad.

10A
Keypad Review

Calculate the totals for the following problems.

A	B	C	D	E	F
20	92	872	613		
65	−43	−115	+716	438	704.9
39	+20	+178	−690	× 4.8	× 5.03
124	69	935	639	2,102.4	3,545.65

10B
Division

1. Locate / (division key) on the numeric keypad.
2. Practice tapping the / key a few times as you watch the middle finger move up to the / and back to the 5 key.
3. With eyes on copy, key the data in Drills 1–2.
4. Verify your answer with those shown.

Drill 1

A	B	C	D	E
51.17	42	179	106	91
6/307	10/420	5/895	7/742	9/819

Drill 2

A	B	C	D	E
32.25	75.52	229.13	96.42	159.04
12/387	66/4,984	32/7,332	52/5,014	56/8,906

10C
Math Calculations

Use the numeric keypad to solve the following math problems.

1. Ken opened a checking account with $100. He wrote checks for $12.88, $15.67, $8.37, and $5.25. He made one deposit of $26.80 and had a service charge of $1.75. What is his current balance?
2. Jan purchased six tickets for the Utah Jazz basketball game. Four of the tickets cost $29.50; the other two cost $35.00. The service charge for each ticket was $1.50. What was the total cost of the six tickets?
3. Four friends went out for dinner. The cost of the dinner came to $47.88. They left a 15 percent tip and split the cost of the dinner equally among them. How much did each person have to pay?
4. Jay filled his car up with gas. The odometer reading was 45,688 miles. Jay drove to New York to see a Yankees game. When he got there he filled the car up again. It took 15.7 gallons. The odometer now read 45,933. How many miles per gallon did Jay get?
5. Mary bowled six games this week. Her scores were 138, 151, 198, 147, 156, and 173. What was her average for those six games?
6. There are 800 points available in the history class. Roberto wants an A in the class. To get an A, he needs to achieve 95 percent or better. What is the minimum number of points he will need to earn the A?

After you have established a connection to the Internet on your computer via an **Internet service provider** (ISP) such as Comcast, AT&T, or Verizon, you need a software application called a **browser** to be able to view Web pages. Browsers allow your computer to see online documents and websites created with HTML. Some of the most commonly used browsers include *Microsoft Internet Explorer, Firefox,* and *Google Chrome.*

One of the newer uses of the Internet is **cloud computing**. With cloud computing, your software and files are stored on remote computers, and you access them through the Internet. One advantage to cloud computing is that you can access your files from anywhere, on any computer.

One of the most common uses of the Internet is connecting with friends, family, and colleagues via a **social network** such as Facebook or Twitter, or a **blog**, which is a type of Web page dedicated to frequent updates on a particular topic. Social networking sites typically offer users a personal page to post information about themselves as well as frequent updates on what's going on with their lives. These sites also offer ways to advertise products and connect to customers by providing information about a business, service, or organization, and have become key ways to conduct business online, which is sometimes called **e-commerce**.

Social networking sites also offer fast and easy **instant messaging** or **chat** services.

To use a browser, you open the application as you would any other software package and then key the website address, or **URL** (uniform resource locator), into the address box. For example, to search for information or websites using Google, key www.google.com. The .com portion of the address is known as the **domain**. Commonly used domains include .com for business, .gov for government sites, .edu for education sites, .org for noncommercial sites, and .ca, .fr, .uk, and other similar domains for different countries.

Google is the most popular search engine on the Web, and it can be used to search the entire Internet for specific data or information. Other popular search engines include Microsoft Bing and Yahoo search.

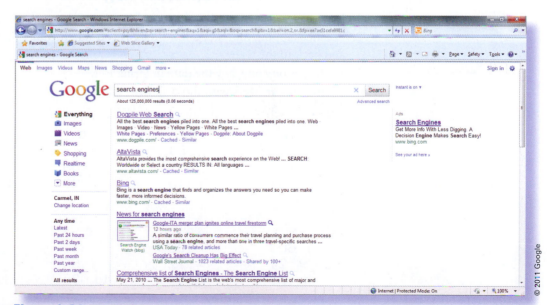

Figure 1-34 Find information or shop for products using search engines

Learn Reach to – (Minus Key)

1. Locate – (minus key) on the numeric keypad above the + (plus key).
2. Practice tapping the – key a few times as you watch the little finger move up to the – and back to the +.
3. With eyes on copy, key the data in Drills 1–3.
4. Verify your answers with those shown below the column.
5. Tap Esc on the main keyboard to clear the calculator; then key numbers in the next column.

Drill 1

A	B	C	D	E	F
27	50	893	798	523	401
−14	−26	−406	−235	−178	−300
13	24	487	563	345	101

Drill 2

A	B	C	D	E	F
84	56	996	829	759	83.6
−17	−38	−476	−514	−420	−41.5
67	18	520	315	339	42.1

Drill 3

A	B	C	D	E	F
99	89	505	807	978	63.4
−16	−10	−264	−234	−220	+37.5
−23	− 8	− 45	− 65	+461	− 8.9
−33	−17	− 87	−104	+309	−46.5
− 9	−24	−156	− 57	−218	+70.1
18	30	−47	347	1,310	115.6

Learn Reach to * (Multiplication Key)

1. Locate the * (multiplication key) on the numeric keypad above the 9.
2. Practice tapping the * key a few times as you watch your ring finger move up to the * key and back to the 6 key.
3. With eyes on copy, key the data in Drills 1–2.
4. Verify your answers with those shown.

Drill 1

A	B	C	D	E
28	54	43	145	68.8
×13	×60	×89	×271	×19.3
364	3,240	3,827	39,295	1,327.84

Drill 2

A	B	C	D	E
603	109	837	468	219
× 24	× 72	× 55	× 90	× 34
14,472	7,848	46,035	42,120	7,446

Use **keyword search** techniques to quickly find the information you need online. One commonly used source for finding information on the Web is Wikipedia, a free online encyclopedia created by the contributions of millions of users.

Wikipedia is a growing and ever-changing storehouse of excellent information, but, as with all data you find online, be sure to double-check the source and accuracy of the information you find. Just because the information is on the Internet, you cannot always assume that it is true or 100 percent accurate. Often, search sites and sites such as Wikipedia are just the starting point for your research. It pays to go directly to the original source of data whenever possible.

For example, after gathering information on the Hubble Space Telescope from Wikipedia, you might also go directly to the NASA home page and find information about the telescope there.

Figure 1-35 Use sites such as Wikipedia to help you find information

Billions of people use the Web every day to solve real-life problems and perform transactions. You can use the Web to get a news or weather update, find directions to a location, find a business phone number, and shop for millions of items.

Buying items online has become one of the most convenient ways to shop, because the search capabilities of the Web enable you to find exactly what you need without going from one store to the next. The downside of online shopping is not having personal interaction with a salesperson who can answer questions immediately, not being able to see and hold the item you're buying, and also the risks of transmitting credit card information across the network. For this reason, it's important to know you are buying from a secure site before submitting any credit card or personal information and agreeing to a transaction.

1. Click Start, All Programs, Internet Explorer.
2. Key www.google.com in the address bar.
3. Key the words you want to search for—in this case, key **search engines** and then click Search.
4. A list of various search engines appears. To narrow the search results, add more keywords in the search box. In this case, add the word **local** after search engines, and then click Search.
5. Click one of the links provided to see what the resulting website looks like.
6. Key www.wikipedia.org in the address bar and tap Enter.

Drills 2–4

Calculate the totals for each problem and check your answers.

Drill 2

A	B	C	D	E	F	G
411	552	663	571	514	481	963
144	255	366	482	425	672	852
414	525	636	539	563	953	471
969	1,332	1,665	1,592	1,502	2,106	2,286

Drill 3

A	B	C	D	E	F	G
471	582	693	303	939	396	417
41	802	963	220	822	285	508
14	825	936	101	717	174	639
526	2,209	2,592	624	2,478	855	1,564

Drill 4

A	B	C	D	E	F	G
75	128	167	102	853	549	180
189	34	258	368	264	367	475
3	591	349	549	971	102	396
267	753	774	1,019	2,088	1,018	1,051

Learn Reach to . (Decimal)

1. Learn the ring-finger reach to the decimal point (.) located below the 3.
2. Calculate the totals for each problem in Drill 5.
3. Repeat Drills 2–5 to increase your input speed.

Drill 5

A	B	C	D	E	F	G
1.30	2.58	23.87	90.37	16.89	47.01	59.28
4.17	6.90	14.65	4.25	3.25	28.36	1.76
5.47	9.48	38.52	94.62	20.14	75.37	61.04

LESSON 9

Subtraction & Multiplication

OUTCOMES

- Learn subtraction on numeric keypad.
- Learn multiplication on numeric keypad.

9A

Keypad Review

Calculate the totals for the following problems.

A	B	C	D	E	F
17	49	672	513	371	109
+83	+60	+415	+724	+564	+357
+52	+93	+808	+690	+289	+620
152	202	1,895	1,927	1,224	1,086

7. On the Wikipedia home page, key **Hubble telescope** in the search box and then click the arrow icon, as shown in Figure 1-35.

8. Read some of the information on the resulting Hubble Space Telescope page in Wikipedia; then key www.mapquest.com in the address bar and tap Enter.

9. At the Mapquest home page, key **Indianapolis Motor Speedway** in the Search For box and then click Get Map. A map showing the address and location of the famous Speedway is shown.

10. Next, key www.weather.com in the address bar and tap Enter.

11. At the Weather.com home page, key your home town in the search box and then click Find Weather. The weather forecast for your area appears.

5B

Computer Ethics and Netiquette

Figure 1-36 Spam is unwanted mail that needs to be cleared from your inbox

Computers, the Internet, and the Web are powerful tools that help people solve problems and find information every day. But these powerful tools can also be used for unethical and illegal purposes as well. Mobile devices and computers can be used to download pirated software, games, music, or videos as well as inappropriate images or information.

Working in a shared environment such as the Internet or any computer network means having respect for other users of the network. Much of your computer time will be spent as part of an online environment, communicating with others and sharing information in multiple ways—on the Web and with other mobile devices—but some people ignore simple rules of common courtesy when they communicate online. These rules are often referred to as **netiquette**.

Some guidelines for good behavior when using the Internet, e-mail, social networking, blogs, texting, and chatting include the following.

- Don't "shout" at people in any form of e-mail, text, chat, or social network message by avoiding text in ALL CAPS.
- Use courteous and respectful language in all text and online messages—it's always wise to reread a message to check the tone and content before you click Send.
- Don't get involved in **cyberbullying**—using online communications to harass or upset someone by sending hateful, humiliating, or threatening messages or photos.
- Avoid sending or forwarding unsolicited messages such as promotions for businesses, ads, or chain letters—such unwanted messages are often referred to as **spam.**
- Check with recipients before sending large attachments over 1 MB, thus avoiding long downloads and clogging up their inbox.
- Respect the privacy of other people's e-mail, social network, cell phone, and text message accounts—avoid viewing these accounts or logging in as another person to view or send messages.

Remember that just because material has been posted on the Internet does not make it free to download and reuse.

Web page content such as photographs, documents, clip art images, videos, music, and other scanned and downloadable content is protected by **copyright law**. This means that you must seek **permission** from the owner or author of the content before reusing it for your personal website, business, or school project. In some cases, you may need to pay a fee for use of the material—in other cases a **credit line** listing the source may be all that's required for appropriate use.

Numeric Keypad Keys 1/2/3

OUTCOMES

• Learn reachstrokes for **1**, **2**, and **3** on numeric keypad.

8A

Keypad Review

Calculate the totals for the problems below.

A	B	C	D	E	F	G
45	74	740	996	704	990	477
56	85	850	885	805	880	588
67	96	960	774	906	770	699
168	255	2,550	2,655	2,415	2,640	1,764

8B

New Keys: 1, 2, and 3

Learn Reach to 1

1. Locate 1 (below 4) on the numeric keypad.
2. Watch your index finger move down to 1 and back to 4 a few times.
3. Key 14 a few times as you watch the finger.
4. With eyes on copy, key the data in Drills 1A and 1B.

Drill 1A	Drill 1B
144	114
141	414
414	141
699	669

Learn Reach to 2

1. Learn the middle-finger reach to 2 (below 5) as directed in steps 1–3 above.
2. With eyes on copy, key the data in Drills 1C and 1D.

Drill 1C	Drill 1D
525	252
252	552
225	525
1,002	1,329

Learn Reach to 3

1. Learn the ring-finger reach to 3 (below 6) as directed above.
2. With eyes on copy, key the data in Drills 1E–1G.

Drill 1E	Drill 1F	Drill 1G
353	636	120
363	366	285
336	636	396
1,052	1,638	801

Some material may be used without permission if it falls under the doctrine of **fair use**, which means that you are quoting only a small amount of content for a purpose such as research or criticism, not for profit. Some material may also be used without permission if it is part of the **public domain**—generally content that's more than 75 years old.

In any case, copyright law is complex, so it's always best to check with the owner or author of the content and seek permission before use. Always avoid **plagiarism,** which is using someone else's work without credit or portraying it as your own.

Another aspect of ethical conduct online is protecting the **confidentiality** of business information pertaining to a project, service, or product. When you're working on a project, be careful not to send confidential information to those who are not involved in the work or should not see the information. Again, just because information is available on e-mail or a website does not mean it should be sent or made available to the general public.

1. Go online and research some recent examples of inappropriate or criminal uses of the Internet. For each case you find, describe what harm may have come to those who were affected by the inappropriate or unethical behavior.
2. Find examples of credit lines used on websites, in books, magazines, or other types of media such as videos, games, or music. List at least three credit lines and the content they define.
3. List any examples of spam e-mail or text messages you have received. In what way did these messages affect your privacy, time, or usage of the computer or device?
4. Go online and use search techniques to find high-profile examples of plagiarism. Why do you think the people in these examples used material without permission?

5C

Online Safety and Computer Security

Figure 1-37 Keep your computer secure to protect personal and confidential information

© bioraven /Shutterstock.com

When you log on to the Internet, you expose your computer to a vast network of other computers and computer users from around the world. Because your online connection is open to both send and receive data, your computer and the software you use can be exposed to various kinds of attack from malicious users.

Some attacks can come in the form of a **computer virus,** which is a set of computer code or a program that can be sent to your computer via a downloaded file that you open on your machine. Other types of attacks include **Trojan horses** and **malware.** These are also types of programs or code that can load on your machine and cause damage to your software, your network connections, or your data.

Installing and using **antivirus software** on your machine is the best way to protect your system from attack. This commercial software can be purchased at retail stores or downloaded from trusted online stores. Another key component of protecting your system is backing up your data frequently. Most antivirus software includes a prescheduled **backup** feature that prompts you to store data in a safe place on a regular schedule.

Using the Internet to shop, communicate, and transfer data has many benefits, but it also can expose you to users who may attempt to use your personal information for criminal activity.

Identity theft can occur when someone obtains personal information such as a person's Social Security number, bank account information, personal data, and job information. When identity theft occurs, the malicious user may attempt to make large purchases using the victim's information or may portray himself as the victim for other purposes, perhaps even impersonating the victim online.

Learn Reach to 9

1. Learn the ring-finger reach to 9 (above 6) as directed above.
2. With eyes on copy, key the data in Drills 1E and 1F.

Drill 1E	Drill 1F
696	969
969	966
999	696
2,664	2,631

Drills 2–5

1. Calculate the totals for each problem in Drills 2–5. Check your answers with those shown.
2. Repeat Drills 2–5 to increase your input speed.

Drill 2

A	B	C	D	E	F
774	885	996	745	475	754
474	585	696	854	584	846
747	858	969	965	695	956
1,995	2,328	2,661	2,564	1,754	2,556

Drill 3

A	B	C	D	E	F
470	580	690	770	707	407
740	850	960	880	808	508
705	805	906	990	909	609
1,915	2,235	2,556	2,640	2,424	1,524

Drill 4

A	B	C	D	E	F
456	407	508	609	804	905
789	408	509	704	805	906
654	409	607	705	806	907
987	410	608	706	904	908
2,886	1,634	2,232	2,724	3,319	3,626

Drill 5

A	B	C	D	E	F
8	786	4	804	76	86
795	69	705	45	556	564
78	575	59	6	5	78
60	4	446	556	666	504
941	1,434	1,214	1,411	1,303	1,232

★ TIP
A strong password has these characteristics:

- at least eight characters long
- contains no complete real words or names
- contains a combination of uppercase letters, lowercase letters, numbers, and symbols

Online **scams** are financial offers or bogus sweepstakes designed to solicit personal information, persuade the victim to give money, or sell something illegal.

To avoid identity theft and other computer crimes, shop only at secure, reputable online businesses. Avoid giving your personal and financial information to others online, and use strong passwords on all financial and cell phone logins. Shredding personal paper documents, account statements, and receipts is also a good idea.

Computer safety also refers to your physical safety and well-being when using the device. To avoid repetitive stress injuries such as carpal tunnel syndrome or pain in your back, shoulders, or neck, use proper **ergonomics** when using the computer. This means sitting up straight in a comfortable chair with proper support for your back. Both feet should be on the floor, and hands should be held slightly raised from the keyboard. (You will learn more about proper ergonomics in Unit 2.)

Also, make sure the computer has proper ventilation to avoid overheating, and keep all food and drinks away from it. And remember to shut off the power to the computer before opening the device or installing new components to avoid the risk of electrical shock.

1. Make a list of examples of recent malware attacks over cell phones and the Internet. Describe the damages these attacks have caused.
2. Describe the difference between spam, identity theft, and malware attacks. Which of these do you think can be the most harmful? Which is the least harmful?
3. What kind of security precautions do you take when using your phone or computer each day? How do you think you can use your devices more securely?

www.cengage.com/school/
keyboarding/c21key

21st Century Skills: Leadership

Complete Leadership Activity 1 as directed on page 382 after reading about the characteristics of leadership in Appendix B. Consider these attributes of a successful leader, and write your responses to the questions below in the form of a paragraph.

- A successful leader accepts responsibility and accountability for results.
- A successful leader has self-discipline, good character, and is committed to personal development.
- A successful leader is a great communicator.
- A successful leader has great people skills.

Think Critically

1. What attributes of a successful leader apply to ethical and appropriate computer use?
2. How does use of netiquette demonstrate leadership qualities?
3. Describe ways in which you have demonstrated leadership abilities when using the computer, the Internet, or a mobile device such as a cell phone.
4. Write your responses in paragraph form and give the page to your instructor.

© Golden Pixels LLC/Shutterstock.com

Drill 5

A	B	C	D	E	F
45	404	404	406	450	650
55	405	505	506	540	560
65	406	606	606	405	605
165	1,215	1,515	1,518	1,395	1,815

Drill 6

A	B	C	D	E	F
40	606	444	554	646	456
50	505	445	555	656	654
60	404	446	556	666	504
150	1,515	1,335	1,665	1,968	1,614

LESSON 7 — Numeric Keypad Keys 7/8/9

OUTCOMES
- Learn reachstrokes for **7**, **8**, and **9** on numeric keypad.

7A

Home-Key Review

Calculate the totals for the problems presented below.

A	B	C	D	E	F
4	44	400	404	440	450
5	55	500	505	550	560
6	66	600	606	660	456
15	165	1,500	1,515	1,650	1,466

7B

New Keys: 7, 8, and 9

Learn Reach to 7

1. Locate 7 (above 4) on the numeric keypad.
2. Watch your index finger move up to 7 and back to 4 a few times without tapping keys.
3. Practice tapping 74 a few times as you watch the finger.
4. With eyes on copy, key the data in Drills 1A and 1B.

Drill 1A	Drill 1B
474	747
747	477
777	474
1,998	1,698

Learn Reach to 8

1. Learn the middle-finger reach to 8 (above 5) as directed in steps 1–3 above.
2. With eyes on copy, key the data in Drills 1C and 1D.

Drill 1C	Drill 1D
585	858
858	588
888	585
2,331	2,031

Academic and Career Connections

Complete the following exercises that introduce various topics that involve academic themes and careers.

Grammar/Writing: Capitalization

MicroType 6

- References/Communication Skills/Capitalization
- CheckPro/Communication Skills 1
- CheckPro/Word Choice 1

1. Go to *MicroType 6* and use this feature path for review: References/Communication Skills/Capitalization.
2. Click *Rules* and review the rules of using capitalization.
3. Then, under *Capitalization*, click *Posttest*.
4. Follow the instructions to complete the posttest.

Optional Activities:

1. Go to this path: CheckPro/Communication Skills 1.
2. Complete the activities as directed.
3. Go to this path: CheckPro/Word Choice 1.
4. Key the Apply lines and choose the correct word.

Communications: Composition

1. Read the following article about lost e-mail messages and data security.

How would you feel if you logged on to your e-mail account only to find that all of your messages and your contacts had disappeared? That's exactly what happened to thousands of users of Google's Gmail service. All of their saved messages and contact information simply disappeared.

Of course, Google apologized for the disruption in service and quickly found an answer for what went wrong. The e-mails were lost because of a problem with a software update the company was installing on all of its computer servers.

How was Google able to find and restore those millions of lost messages? Google, like many other online businesses, stores all of its data in huge warehouses filled with computers in sites around the world. These data centers house more than one backup copy of every message ever sent on Gmail.

But how was Google able to retrieve all the e-mails and contacts successfully? The company still relies on what many may consider outdated technology—Google stores all of its backup data on tape.

The blog Data Center Knowledge confirms that tape is still a safe way to back up data, even if it may seem strange to save "virtual" messages on a hard-copy tape:

"Even today, tape has two significant advantages over other media: cost and portability. Unfortunately, these two advantages outweigh the more significant (logically speaking) disadvantages of tape media: fragility, replacement rate, failure rate, vulnerability to theft, and unencrypted data storage."

2. Write a two-paragraph response to this article, describing your concerns as well as ideas for how you might protect the safety of your e-mail messages and other data.
3. If requested, give the response you have written to your instructor.

6B

Access the Calculator

Follow the instructions given below to access the calculator on your computer.

1. Click Start.
2. Click All Programs.
3. Click Accessories.
4. Click Calculator.
5. Activate the Num (number) Lock located above the 7 on the numeric keypad.

Courtesy of Jack P. Hoggatt

6C

New Keys: 4, 5, 6, and 0 (Home Keys)

TIP Tap each key with a quick, sharp stroke with the *tip* of the finger; release the key quickly. Keep the fingers curved and upright.

Tap the 0 with the side of the right thumb, similar to the way you tap the Space Bar.

Use the calculator to complete the drills.

1. Enter each number: Key the number and enter it by tapping the + key with the little finger of the right hand.
2. After entering each number in the column, verify your answer with the answer shown below the column.
3. Tap Esc on the main keyboard to clear the calculator; then key the numbers in the next column.
4. Repeat steps 1–3 for Drills 1–6.

Drill 1

A	B	C	D	E	F
4	5	6	4	5	6
4	5	6	4	5	6
8	10	12	8	10	12

Drill 2

A	B	C	D	E	F
44	55	66	44	55	66
44	55	66	44	55	66
88	110	132	88	110	132

Drill 3

A	B	C	D	E	F
44	45	54	44	55	66
55	56	46	45	54	65
66	64	65	46	56	64
165	165	165	135	165	195

Drill 4

A	B	C	D	E	F
40	50	60	400	500	600
50	60	40	506	604	405
60	40	50	650	460	504
150	150	150	1,556	1,564	1,509

1. Katherine has saved $750 to buy a new computer and office application software for her school work. If she has any money left over from the computer purchase, she would also like to buy a new cell phone. She has shopped online and at local electronics stores and found that the best options are the following:
    a. Basic laptop computer: $539
    b. Desktop computer: $700
    c. Slim tablet computer (must be docked to a desktop computer for full functionality): $499
    d. Office application software suite: $150
    e. Fully loaded smartphone with games, text messaging, Internet, and music downloads: $250
    f. Normal cell phone with basic phone service and text messaging: $100

2. Which combination of computer, software, and phone will best fit Katherine's needs and still remain within her budget? Is it possible for her to buy all three items for $750?

3. Katherine's friend Emilio tells her that he has heard of an electronics store that is offering a special limited-time $50 discount for purchasing a basic laptop and a normal cell phone with basic phone service. Will this enable Katherine to purchase everything she wants to meet her needs?

Introducing Career Clusters

Architecture icon: Each Career Cluster has its own icon, such as this one for Architecture and Construction. Icons are shown throughout this text.

There are many different career opportunities available to you once you graduate from high school. Some careers require no additional education, while others require many years of additional education.

The career exploration activities in this text will help you understand the requirements for some of the careers in which you may have an interest. Begin your exploration by completing the following steps.

1. Access www.careertech.org.
2. Complete the Career Clusters Interest Survey. Your instructor will provide you with a copy of the survey and the Sixteen Career Clusters pages that follow the Interest Survey.
3. Obtain a folder for your Career Exploration Portfolio from your instructor, write your name and class period on it, pace your completed Interest Survey and descriptions of the career clusters in the folder, and file the folder as instructed.

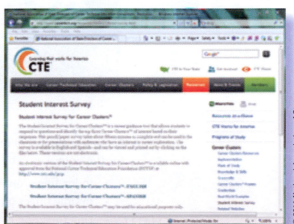

Figure 1-38 Interest Survey Activity

Key each ¶ once. DS between ¶s. Key a 1' timed writing on each ¶.

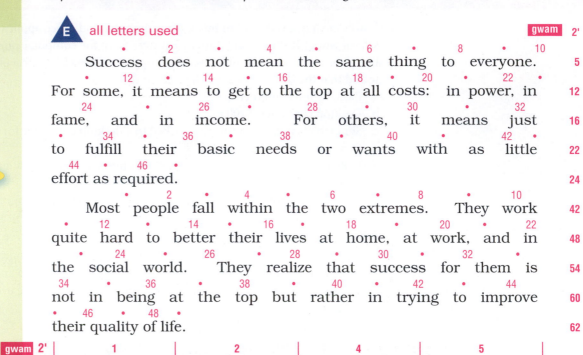

E all letters used   gwam 2'

| . | 2 | . | 4 | . | 6 | . | 8 | . | 10 |

Success does not mean the same thing to everyone.   5

| .   12 | .   14 | .   16 | .   18 | .   20 | .   22 | . |

For some, it means to get to the top at all costs: in power, in   12

| 24 | .   26 | .   28 | .   30 | .   32 |

fame, and in income.   For others, it means just   16

| .   34 | .   36 | .   38 | .   40 | .   42 | . |

to fulfill their basic needs or wants with as little   22

| 44 | .   46 | . |

effort as required.   24

| .   2 | .   4 | .   6 | .   8 | .   10 |

Most people fall within the two extremes.   They work   42

| .   12 | .   14 | .   16 | .   18 | .   20 | .   22 |

quite hard to better their lives at home, at work, and in   48

| .   24 | .   26 | .   28 | .   30 | .   32 | . |

the social world.   They realize that success for them is   54

| 34 | .   36 | .   38 | .   40 | .   42 | .   44 |

not in being at the top but rather in trying to improve   60

| .   46 | .   48 | . |

their quality of life.   62

gwam 2' | 1 | 2 | 4 | 5 |

MicroType 6

Use MicroType Numeric Lesson 5 for additional practice.

LESSON 6   Numeric Keypad Keys 4/5/6/0

OUTCOMES

- Learn reachstrokes for **4**, **5**, **6**, and **0** on numeric keypad.

6A

Numeric Keypad Operating Position

Position yourself at the keyboard as shown below. Sit in front of the keyboard with the book at the right—body erect, both feet on the floor.

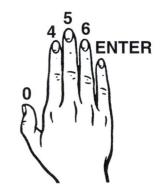

Curve the fingers of the right hand and place them on the numeric keypad. Use the little finger for the Enter key. To key the numbers, place the :

- index finger on **4**
- middle finger on **5**
- ring finger on **6**
- thumb on **0**

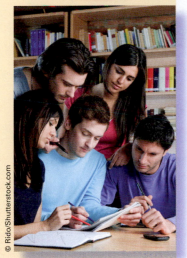

© Rido/Shutterstock.com

A Career Technical Student Organization (CTSO), such as Business Professionals of America and Future Business Leaders of America-Phi Beta Lambda, offer a variety of individual and group programs and activities that help you prepare for life after high school. These organizations promote career training and preparation through educational programs as well as events at the regional, state, and national levels. Members of a student organization:

- meet students from other schools around the country who have similar interests and goals.
- are part of a motivated and positive group that encourages them to explore new ways of thinking and strengthens teamwork skills.
- participate in competitive events that build confidence and communication skills.

Business Professionals of America (BPA)

BPA is a national organization for students interested in careers in business management, office administration, information technology, and other related careers. It offers the Workplace Skills Assessment Program (WSAP), a series of conferences in which students showcase their workplace skills through participation in various competitive events. Go to www.bpa.org for more information.

Future Business Leaders of America-Phi Beta Lambda (FBLA-PBL)

FBLA-PBL is a nationwide business education association for students preparing for a career in business. Its membership also consists of educators, administrators, and business professionals. Through its National Awards Program, students demonstrate their business knowledge in a variety of competitive events. Go to www.fbla-pbl.org for more information.

Think Critically

1. How can joining a CTSO help you identify a career that interests you?
2. Why would an employer want to hire a worker who is or was a member of a CTSO?
3. How could being a member of a CTSO help you in your academic pursuits?

School and Community

Volunteering in your school and your community is an important part of developing your leadership and professional skills. Volunteer work can be anything as simple as helping to clean up your neighborhood streets, to helping work in a political campaign on election day. Often, volunteering your time and talents to a worthy cause is more important than any financial contribution you can make, and it pays off by developing your skills and giving you the good feeling of having helped others.

1. Get started with volunteer work by researching volunteer opportunities at your school or in your community. Find at least one opportunity at school and in the community. Which opportunities appeal to you?
2. State three ways the opportunities you have selected will help other people.
3. Write a brief statement describing how the opportunities you have found might help improve your career skills or contribute to your resume and help improve your chances for success when applying for a job. If requested, give the statement to your instructor.

5B

New Keys: 6 and 2

Key each line twice. If time permits, rekey lines 7–9.

6 *Right index* finger

2 *Left ring* finger

Learn 6

1 j 6 j 6|jj 66 jj 66|j6j j6j|66j 66j|6j6 6j6|6j; 6j

2 There were 66 entries. All 66 competed yesterday.

3 He said 76 trombones. I said that is not correct.

Learn 2

4 s 2 s 2|ss 22 ss 22|s2s s2s|22s 22s|2s2 2s2|2s; 2s

5 Of the 222 items, Charlton labeled 22 incorrectly.

6 The 22 girls may play 2 games against the 22 boys.

Combine 6 and 2

7 Monique has gone 262 miles; she has 26 more to go.

8 March 26, August 26, and October 26 are the dates.

9 Just 26 more days before Gilberto is 26 years old.

5C

Practice: Keying Numbers

TIP Keep your forearms parallel to the slant of the keyboard.

Key each line twice.

Straight copy

1 Jose moved from 724 Park Lane to 810 State Street.

2 Marcos was 3 minutes and 56 seconds behind Carlos.

Script

3 Call me at 195.438.9057 on Saturday, September 26.

4 The dates of the games are October 19, 20, and 23.

Rough draft

5 Mrs. kendall siad the practice will be June 30.

6 Flihgt Nos. 3875 leave at 6:45 a.m. on Octobre 13.

UNIT 2 — Alphabetic Keys

Lesson 6   Home Keys (fdsa jkl;)
Lesson 7   Review
Lesson 8   h and e
Lesson 9   i and r
Lesson 10   Review
Lesson 11   o and t
Lesson 12   n and g
Lesson 13   Left Shift and Period (.)
Lesson 14   Review
Lesson 15   u and c
Lesson 16   w and Right Shift

Lesson 17   b and y
Lesson 18   Review
Lesson 19   m and x
Lesson 20   p and v
Lesson 21   q and Comma (,)
Lesson 22   Review
Lesson 23   z and Colon (:)
Lesson 24   Caps Lock and Question Mark (?)
Lesson 25   Backspace, Quotation Mark ("), and Tab
Lesson 26   Apostrophe (') and Hyphen (-)

LESSON 6 — Home Keys (fdsa jkl;)

OUTCOMES

- Learn home keys (**fdsa jkl;**).
- Learn the **Space Bar** and **Enter** keys.

6A

Work-Area Arrangement

Arrange your work area as shown in Figure 2-1.

- Keyboard directly in front of chair
- Front edge of keyboard even with edge of desk
- Monitor placed for easy viewing
- Book at right of monitor

© Cengage Learning

Figure 2-1 Work-area arrangement

4C

Practice: Tab Key

TIP Click the Show/Hide ¶ button to see the *Tab* characters on your screen.

Key each line twice SS. DS between sets of lines.

1 5 tab→   10 tab→   394 tab→   781 tab→   908

2 9 tab→   45 tab→   703 tab→   185 tab→   731

3 4 tab→   81 tab→   930 tab→   507 tab→   405

4 7 tab→   30 tab→   585 tab→   914 tab→   341

5 3 tab→   79 tab→   485 tab→   180 tab→   789

4D

Practice: Keying Technique

TIP Keep your wrists low, but not resting on the keyboard.

MicroType 6

Use *MicroType* Numeric Keyboarding Lesson 4 for additional practice.

Key each line twice. Key 1' timings on lines 2, 4, and 6.

Letter response

1 milk milk|extra extra|pink pink|wage wage|oil oil;

2 Edward saw a deserted cat on a crate in my garage.

Word response

3 burn burn|hand hand|duck duck|rock rock|mend mend;

4 The eight signs are down by the lake by the docks.

Combination response

5 with only|they join|half safe|born free|goal rates

6 Dave sat on the airy lanai and gazed at the puppy.

LESSON 5   New Keys: 6 and 2

OUTCOMES

- Learn reach technique for **6** and **2**.
- Improve skill at keying copy with numbers.

5A

Warmup

Key each line twice.

Alphabet 1 Wade Javey quickly found extra maps in the gazebo.

Spacing 2 am to|is an|by it|of us|an oak|is to pay|it is due

Easy 3 I am to pay the six men if they do the work right.

gwam 1' | 1 | 2 | 3 | 4 | 5 | 6 | 7 | 8 | 9 | 10 |

Keying Position

The features of correct keying position are shown in Figure 2-2 and listed below.

- Fingers curved and upright over home keys
- Wrists low, but not touching keyboard
- Forearms parallel to slant of keyboard
- Body erect, sitting back in chair
- Feet on floor for balance
- Eyes on copy

Figure 2-2 Keying position at computer

Home-Key Position

The keys where you place your fingers to begin keying are called the **home keys**. The home keys are f d s a for the left hand and j k l ; for the right hand.

1. Find the home keys on the keyboard illustration shown below in Figure 2-3.
2. Locate and place your fingers on the home keys on your keyboard with your fingers well curved and upright (not slanting).
3. Remove your fingers from the keyboard; then place them in home-key position again, curving and holding them lightly on the keys.

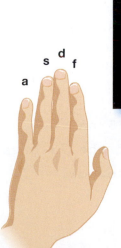

Left Fingers   Right Fingers

Figure 2-3 Home-key position

LESSON 4

New Keys: 7 and 3

OUTCOMES

- Learn reach technique for **7** and **3**.
- Improve skill at keying copy with numbers.

4A

Warmup

Key each line twice.

Alphabet	1	Kevin can fix the unique jade owl as my big prize.
Punctuation	2	Al, did you use these words: vie, zeal, and aqua?
Easy	3	The small ornament on their door is an ivory duck.
gwam	1'	1 | 2 | 3 | 4 | 5 | 6 | 7 | 8 | 9 | 10 |

4B

New Keys: 7 and 3

Key each line twice. If time permits, rekey lines 7–9.

Learn 7

1 j 7 j 7|jj 77 jj 77|j7j j7j|77j 77j|7j7 7j7|7j 7j;

2 Of the 77 computers, 7 are connected to a printer.

3 The highest score on the March 7 exam was only 77.

Learn 3

4 d 3 d 3|dd 33 dd 33|d3d d3d|33d 33d|3d3 3d3|3d 3d;

5 Dr. Ho used only 33 of the original 333 questions.

6 She scheduled quizzes on January 3 and on April 3.

Combine 7 and 3

7 Melanie scored only 73 on the July 3 exam, not 77.

8 Sandra answered 37 of the 73 questions in an hour.

9 Jessie bowled 73, Mike bowled 77, and I bowled 73.

7 *Right index* finger

3 *Left middle* finger

Keystroking and Space Bar

1. Read the hints and study the illustrations below.
2. Place your fingers in home-key position as directed in 6C.
3. Key the line beneath the illustrations. Tap the Space Bar once at the point of each arrow.
4. Review proper position at the keyboard (6B); key the line again.

TECHNIQUE HINTS

Keystroking: Tap each key with the tip of the finger. Keep your fingers curved as shown in Figure 2-4.

Figure 2-4 Keying technique

Spacing: Tap the Space Bar with the right thumb, as shown in Figure 2-5; use a quick down-and-in motion (toward the palm). Avoid pauses before or after spacing.

© Cengage Learning

Figure 2-5 Space-Bar technique

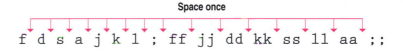

Space once

f d s a j k l ; ff jj dd kk ss ll aa ;;

Hard Return at Line Endings

To return the insertion point to the left margin and move it down to the next line, tap **Enter**. This is called a **hard return.** Use a hard return at the end of all drill lines. Use two hard returns to leave a blank line between drill lines.

To key a hard return, reach the little finger of the right hand to the Enter key, tap the key, and return the finger quickly to home-key position.

1. Study Figure 2-6.
2. Practice the Enter key reach several times.
3. Review proper position at the keyboard (6B).
4. Key the line in 6D above again.

© Cengage Learning

Figure 2-6 Enter-key reach

0 *Right little* finger

5 *Left index* finger

Learn 0

1 ; 0 ; 0|;; 00 ;; 00|;0; ;0;|00; 00;|0;0 0;0|0; 0;0

2 Reach from the ; to the 0. The license was 00H00.

3 Kia keyed 000 after the decimal; Tonya keyed 0000.

Learn 5

4 f 5 f 5|ff 55 ff 55|f5f f5f|55f 55f|5f5 5f5|5f 5f;

5 Ken had 55 points on the quiz; Jay also scored 55.

6 Of the 55 exhibits, only 5 won grand prize awards.

Combine 0 and 5

7 Debra told us the number was 505.550, not 550.505.

8 Lance hit .500 during July and .505 during August.

9 Orlando bought 500 pounds of grain on September 5.

3C

Practice: Keying Numbers

TIP Reach up without moving your hands away from your body.

Key each line twice.

1 Mario dialed 594.1880 instead of dialing 495.1880.

2 He drove 598 miles one day and 410 miles the next.

3 He bowled 98, 105, and 94 the last time he bowled.

4 Orlando said the odometer read 58,940 on March 15.

5 Maryann was born in 1980; Marsha was born in 1954.

3D

Timed Writings

Key each ¶ once. DS between ¶s. Key a 1' timed writing on each ¶; determine *gwam*. Record your best timing.

 all letters used

You must realize by now that learning to key requires work. However, you will soon be able to key at a higher speed than you can write just now.

You will also learn to do neater work on the computer than you can do by hand. Quality work at higher speeds is a good goal for you to have next.

MicroType 6

Use *MicroType* Numeric Keyboarding Lesson 3 for additional practice.

Home-Key, Space-Bar, and Enter-Key Practice

Fingers curved and upright

Down-and-in spacing motion

1. Place your hands in home-key position (left-hand fingers on **f d s a** and right-hand fingers on **j k l ;**).
2. Key each line once.
3. DS between 2-line groups. (Tap Enter twice to insert a DS between 2-line groups. Do not key line numbers.)

```
1 a aa s ss d dd f ff

2 a aa s ss d dd f ff
                        DS

3 j jj k kk l ll ; ;;

4 j jj k kk l ll ; ;;
                        DS

5 aj lf d; ks ja fl ;d aja

6 aj lf d; ks ja fl ;d aja
                          DS

7 djd kak s;s flf jal d;k;

8 djd kak s;s flf jal d;k;
```

6G

Enter-Key Practice

★TIP Reach out with the little finger; tap the Enter key quickly; return finger to home key.

Key each line once; DS between 2-line groups. Do not key the numbers.

```
1 jj ss ll

2 jj ss ll
          DS

3 aa kk dd ;; ff

4 aa kk dd ;; ff
              DS

5 ll ff jj dd kk ss ;;

6 ll ff jj dd kk ss ;;
                      DS

7 aa aa fd l; kj j; lk af ds

8 aa aa fd l; kj j; lk af ds
```

ws/sw

7 ws sw was saw laws rows cows vows swam sways swing

8 Swin swims at my swim club and shows no big flaws.

ed/de

9 ed de led ode need made used side vied slide guide

10 Ned said the guide used a video film for her talk.

ju/ft

11 ju ft jug oft jet aft jug lift just soft jury loft

12 Ted said the guide used a video film for her talk.

LESSON 3

New Keys: 0 and 5

OUTCOMES

- Learn reach technique for **0** and **5**.
- Improve skill at keying copy with numbers.

3A

Warmup

Key each line twice.

Alphabet   1   Jewel amazed Vic by escaping quickly from the box.

Spacing   2   It will be fun for us to try to sing the old song.

Easy   3   He paid the men for the work they did on the dock.

gwam 1' | 1 | 2 | 3 | 4 | 5 | 6 | 7 | 8 | 9 | 10 |

3B

New Keys: 0 and 5

Key each line on the next page twice. If time permits, rekey lines 7–9.

6H

Home-Key Mastery

★TIP Space once after semicolon (;) used as punctuation.

Correct finger alignment

1. Place your fingers curved and upright over the home keys with the right thumb just barely touching the Space Bar.
2. Key each line twice; DS between 2-line groups. Do not key the line numbers or the vertical lines separating word groups.

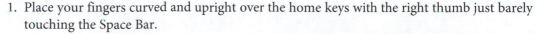

```
1 j j jk jk l l l; l; a a as as d d df df af kl dsj;
2 jj kjk kjk ll ;l; ;l; ja ja dk dk ls ls ;f ;f kjd;
3 sad sad|lad lad|all all|ask ask|jak jak|fall fall;
4 a sad lass; ask all dads; a lad ask; a salad; as a
5 as a dad; add a fall; ask all lads; as a fall fad;
```

6I

End-of-Lesson Routine

At the end of each lesson, complete the following steps.

1. Save the document if you have not already done so. Use the word *lesson* and the lesson number (*lesson 6*) for the filename unless directed to use another filename.
2. Exit the software.
3. Turn off equipment if directed to do so.
4. Store materials as instructor directs.
5. Clean up your work area and push in your chair before you leave.

6J

Enrichment

For additional practice:

MicroType 6

Alphabetic Keyboarding Lesson 1

Key each line twice; DS between 2-line groups.

```
1 ja js jd jf f; fl fk fj ka ks kd kf d; dl dk dj a;
2 la ls ld lf s; sl sk sj ;a ;s ;d ;f a; al ak aj fj
3 as as ask ask ad ad lad lad all all fall fall lass
4 as a fad; as a dad; ask a lad; as a lass; all lads
5 a sad dad; all lads fall; ask a lass; a jak salad;
6 add a jak; a fall ad; all fall ads; ask a sad lass
```

Learn 9

1 1 9 1 9|11 99 11 99|191 191|991 991|919 919|19 19;
2 My baseball number is 9; my football number is 99.
3 There were 999 racers; only 9 of the 999 finished.

Learn 4

4 f 4 f 4|ff 44 ff 44|f4f f4f|44f 44f|4f4 4f4|f4 f4;
5 He read pages 4 to 44. Janet has 44 extra points.
6 Tim added 4, 44, and 444. Jason scored 44 points.

Combine 9 and 4

7 Jay scored 44 of the 99 points; Joe had 49 points.
8 Is his average .449 or .494? Today it is at .449.
9 She keyed a 49 rather than a 94 in the number 494.

9 *Right ring* finger

4 *Left index* finger

2C

Key Script Copy

Key each line twice.

1 Script is copy that is written with pen or pencil.
2 Copy that is written poorly is often hard to read.
3 Read script a few words ahead of the keying point.
4 Doing so will help you produce copy free of error.
5 Leave proper spacing after punctuation marks, too.
6 With practice, you can key script at a rapid rate.

2D

Practice: Keying Technique

Key each line twice.

ol/lo

1 ol lo loaf cold sold hold lock loan fold long load
2 Lou told me that her local school loans old locks.

za/az

3 za az zap adz haze zany lazy jazz hazy maze pizzas
4 A zany jazz band played with pizzazz at the plaza.

ik/ki

5 ik ki kit ski kin kid kip bike kick like kiwi hike
6 The kid can hike or ride his bike to the ski lake.

(continued)

LESSON 7

Review Home Keys (fdsa jkl;)

OUTCOMES

- Learn home keys (**fdsa jkl;**).
- Learn the **Space Bar** and **Enter** keys.

7A

Practice Home Keys

1. Get ready to key:
   - Place your fingers curved and upright over the home keys with the right thumb just barely touching the Space Bar.
   - Your wrists should be low, but not touching the keyboard.
   - You should be sitting back in the chair with your body erect.
   - Your eyes should be on the copy.

2. Key each line twice; DS between 2-line groups. Do not key the numbers.

1 s s ss l l ll d d dd k k kk f f ff j j jj a; a; ;a

2 f f ff j j jj d d s sl fl lf al la ja aj sk ks jj;

3 sa as ld dl af fa ls sl fl lf al la ja aj sk ks jj

4 fj dk sl a; jf kd ls ;a ds kl df kj sd lk sa ;l jj

5 fa ds jk ;f jf kd ls ;a f; dl sk aj sj ak d; fl ad

7B

Improve Enter-Key Technique

Key each line twice; DS between 2-line groups.

1 alj; ksf; dak;

2 sff; ldd; ajj; lkk;

3 jaj; sls; kdk; fjf; sks;

4 ljd; fss; jdj; skj; asj; fdl;

5 afsd klj; fsda lj;k flaj s;dk fj;k

6 akdj ls;f daj; kfls jlja fsdl ;skd ajsa

© Cengage Learning

Keep fingers curved

1E

Timed Writing

MicroType 6

Use MicroType Numeric Keyboarding Lesson 1 for additional practice.

Key each ¶ once. DS between ¶s. Key a 1' timed writing on each ¶.

E all letters used

      •   2   •   4   •   6   •   8   •
Keep in home position all of the fingers not
10   •   12   •   14   •   16   •   18   •
being used to tap a key. Do not let them move out
20   •   22   •   24   •   26   •   28
of position for the next letters in your copy.
      •   2   •   4   •   6   •   8   •
Prize the control you have over the fingers.
10   •   12   •   14   •   16   •   18   •
See how quickly speed goes up when you learn that
20   •   22   •   24   •   26   •   28   •
you can make them do just what you expect of them.

LESSON 2

New Keys: 9 and 4

OUTCOMES

- Learn reach technique for **9** and **4**.
- Key from script copy.

2A

Warmup

Key each line twice.

Alphabet	1	By solving the tax quiz, Jud Mack won first prize.
Caps Lock	2	Jay used the CAPS LOCK key to key CAPITAL letters.
Easy	3	Six of the eight firms may make a bid for the bus.

gwam 1' | 1 | 2 | 3 | 4 | 5 | 6 | 7 | 8 | 9 | 10 |

2B

New Keys: 9 and 4

Key each line on the next page twice. If time permits, rekey lines 7–9.

7C

Key Words

Keep fingers upright

© Cengage Learning

Key each line twice; DS between 2-line groups.

1 a fall; a fall; a jak; a jak; asks dad; asks dad;;
2 all ads; all ads; a fad; a fad; as a lad; as a lad
3 a sad lad; a sad lad; a fall; a fall; ask a ask a;
4 a fad a fad; ask a lass; ask a lass; a dad; a dad;
5 all fall ads; all fall ads; a sad fall; a sad fall
6 a lad asks a lass; a lad asks a lass; a lad; a lad

7D

Home-Key Mastery

Key each line twice; DS between 2-line groups.

1 ff jj dd kk ss ll aa ;; fj dk sl a; jf kd ls ;a a;
2 aa ;; ss ll dd kk ff jj ja js jd jf fj fk fl f; fj
3 fjf dkd sls a;a jfj kdk lsl ;a;a a;sldkfj a;sldkfj
4 a a as as ask ask ad ad lad lad add add fall falls
5 a jak ad; a sad dad; a lad asks; a lad asks a lass
6 a sad fall; all fall ads; as a lass asks a sad lad

7E

End-of-Lesson Routine

For additional practice:

MicroType 6

Alphabetic Keyboarding
Lesson 2

At the end of each practice session, complete the following steps.

1. Save the document if you have not already done so. Use the word *lesson* and the lesson number (*lesson 7*) for the filename unless directed to use another filename.
2. Exit the software.
3. Turn off equipment if directed to do so.
4. Store materials as instructor directs.
5. Clean up your work area, and push in your chair before you leave.

8 **Right middle** *finger*

1 **Left little** *finger*

Learn 8

1 k 8 k 8|kk 88 kk 88|k8k k8k|88k 88k|8k8 8k8|k8 k8;

2 Add the figures 8 and 888. Only 8 of 88 finished.

3 Felipe lives at 88 Pine; Oscar lives at 88 Spruce.

Learn 1

4 a 1 a 1|aa 11 aa 11|a1a a1a|11a 11a|1a1 1a1|a1 a1;

5 Key the figures 11 and 111. Read pages 11 to 111.

6 Travis keyed 1 instead of 11; I keyed 111, not 11.

Combine 8 and 1

7 His time was 8 min. 1 sec.; mine was 8 min. 8 sec.

8 June 18 was the day Ricardo Santo biked 181 miles.

9 Jane keyed 818 and 181; Michael keyed 811 and 118.

1C

Key Proofread Copy

Proofreaders' Marks

∧ = insert

\# = add space

∿ = transpose

∂ = delete

⊃⊂ = close up

≡ = capitalize

lc = lowercase

Study the proofreaders' marks shown at the left and in the sentences. Key each sentence double-spaced, making all handwritten changes.

1 Rough draft is ~~work~~ *keyed copy* with hand written change *s*.

2 Special marks *are* used to show changes *to be* made.

3 *First* Read a sentence notting changes; then key it.

4 *Next* Check to see *that* if you made *all of* the changes ~~correctly~~.

5 Read rough draft *slightly* a bit ahead of *the* keying pint.

6 Doing *so* ~~this~~ will help *you to* make *all* the change s right.

7 You *soon* will key often from script and *rough* draft.

1D

Practice: Balanced-Hand Sentences

⭐ **TIP** Keep your fingers curved and upright.

Key each line twice.

1 Jane is to pay for the eight audit forms for them.

2 Rich is to go to the lake to fix the signs for us.

3 I may go to the city to do the work for the firms.

4 Profit is a problem for the big firms in the city.

5 The eight maps may aid them when they do the work.

LESSON 8 — New Keys: h and e

- Learn reach technique for **h** and **e**.
- Improve keying techniques.

8A

Home-Key Review

1. Arrange your work area as shown on p. 33 (6A).
2. Review the *Get Ready to Key* procedure on p. 38 (7A).
3. Key each line twice; DS between 2-line groups.

All keystrokes learned

```
1 ss jj ff ;; dd ll aa kk jj ff kk ss dd ll ;; aa kk
2 fk ja ld s; aj d; fl sk ka jf ls d; jd kf sl ;a dj
3 a sad lass; all ads; ask a lad; all fall; a flask;
4 a lad ask; a salad; a fall ad; ask a dad; all fall
5 as a fall fad; add a jak salad; as a sad lad falls
```

> **★ TIP** Space once after semicolon (;) used as punctuation.

8B

Plan for Learning New Keys

All keys except the home keys (**fdsa jkl;**) require the fingers to reach in order to tap them. Follow the *Standard Plan for Learning New Keys* shown below to learn the proper reach for each new key.

Standard Plan for Learning New Keys

1. Find the new key on the keyboard illustration shown on the page where the new key is introduced.
2. Look at your keyboard and find the new key.
3. Study the reach-technique picture near the practice lines for the new key.
4. Identify the finger to be used to tap the new key.
5. Curve your fingers; place them in home-key position (over asdf jkl;).
6. Watch your finger as you reach to the new key and back to home position a few times (keep it curved). The reach with the finger should be made without moving the hands or arms.
7. Key the set of drill lines to the right of the reach-technique illustration. Key each line twice SS—once slowly to learn the new reach and then again at a faster rate. DS between 2-line groups.

Appendix A Numeric Keys and Numeric Keypad

Lesson 1	New Keys: 8 and 1	Lesson 6	Numeric Keypad Keys 4/5/6/0
Lesson 2	New Keys: 9 and 4	Lesson 7	Numeric Keypad Keys 7/8/9
Lesson 3	New Keys: 0 and 5	Lesson 8	Numeric Keypad Keys 1/2/3
Lesson 4	New Keys: 7 and 3	Lesson 9	Subtraction & Multiplication
Lesson 5	New Keys: 6 and 2	Lesson 10	Division & Math Calculations

LESSON 1   New Keys: 8 and 1

OUTCOMES

- Learn reach technique for **8** and **1**.
- Improve skill on straight-copy sentences.
- Key rough-draft copy.

1A

Warmup

Key each line twice.

Alphabet 1 Levi Kintz packed my bag with six quarts of juice.

Spacing 2 is he|to me|and is|of us|to the|was it|it is|at my

Easy 3 A box with the forms is on the shelf by the bowls.

gwam 1' | 1 | 2 | 3 | 4 | 5 | 6 | 7 | 8 | 9 | 10 |

1B

New Keys: 8 and 1

★TIP Keep the fingers not being used to tap the number key anchored to the home keys.

Key each line on the next page twice. If time permits, rekey lines 7–9.

New Keys: h and e

1. Use the *Standard Plan for Learning New Keys* (p. 40) for each key to be learned. Study the plan now.
2. Relate each step of the plan to the illustrations and copy below.
3. Key each line twice; DS between 2-line groups. Do not key the line numbers, the vertical lines separating word groups, or the labels.

Learn h

1 j h jh jh|hj hj|ha ha|has has|dash dash|hall hall;
2 jh jh|had had|ash ash|has has|half half|lash lash;
3 ha ha; a half; a dash; has had; a flash; had half;

Learn e

4 d e de de|ed ed|elk elk|elf elf|see see|leak leak;
5 fake fake|deal deal|leaf leaf|fade fade|lake lake;
6 jade desk; see a lake; feel safe; see a safe deal;

Combine h and e

7 he he|she she|shelf shelf|shake shake|shade shade;
8 he has; half ashes; he fed; held a shelf; she has;
9 held a sale; he has a shed; he has a desk; she has

h *Right index* finger

© Cengage Learning

e *Left middle finger*

© Cengage Learning

New-Key Mastery

Key each line twice; DS between 2-line groups.

home row
1 add add|dad dad|jak jak|ask ask|lad lad|fall falls
2 all fall; as a jak; a sad lad falls; all salad ads

h/e
3 he he|had had|see see|she she|held held|shed shed;
4 half a shelf; a jade sale; she has a jak; he deals

all keys learned
5 jell jell|half half|sale sale|lake lake|held held;
6 a lake; she has half; he held a flask; a jade sale

all keys learned
7 she held a deed; a flash; a jade keel; has a shed;
8 a jak; half a flask; he has a desk; he held a sale

For additional practice:

MicroType 6

Alphabetic Keyboarding Lesson 3

Assess Database Skills

Open the *Route 153 Customer List* database table from *df 90d database*, and do the following:

- Using the *Subscription Data* form, key each subscriber's type of service—*Daily* or *Weekend Only*. The subscribers shown in the following table are *Weekend Only*; all others are *Daily* subscribers.
- Sort the table by *Last Name* in ascending order and then by *Type of Service* in descending order.
- Print a copy of the table.

Last Name	First Name	Courtesy Title	Address
Sherman	Stuart	Mr. and Mrs.	216 Lincoln Place
Furyk	Lindsey	Mrs.	228 Berkeley Place
Jackson	Duncan	Mr. and Mrs.	333 Flatbush Avenue
Monrow	Tyler	Mr. and Mrs.	318 Flatbush Avenue
Koszo	Miguel	Mr. and Mrs.	320 St. Johns
York	Kiesha	Ms.	1206 8th Avenue

90E

Assess Database Skills

1. Open the database file *df 90d database*, and key and verify the four new subscriptions shown below.

Mr. Justin Willoughby
220 Lincoln Place
Brooklyn, NY 11217
Daily Service

Ms. Tisha Farve
1217 8th Avenue
Brooklyn, NY 11215
Weekend Only Service

Mr. & Mrs. Jay Biltmore
321 Flatbush Avenue
Brooklyn, NY 11238
Daily Service

Mrs. Tiffany Talawanda
337 Sterling Place
Brooklyn, NY 11238
Weekend Only Service

2. Make the following changes:
   - Chelsea Hathaway's address should be **210** rather than 220.
   - Natalie Madison has moved; delete her record from the file.
3. Sort the table by *Last Name* in ascending order and then by *Type of Service* in ascending order.
4. Print a copy of the table.

© 2012 Jack Hollingsworth/Jupiterimages Corporation

LESSON 9 New Keys: i and r

- Learn reach technique for **i** and **r**.
- Improve keying speed.

9A
Get Ready to Key

Follow the steps in the *Standard Plan for Getting Ready to Key* on p. 38.

9B
Warmup

Correct finger technique

Key each line twice; DS between 2-line groups. Key the line at a slow, steady pace, tapping and releasing each key quickly. Key the line again at a faster pace; move from key to key quickly.

home keys 1 `ll aa ff jj ss kk dd ;; jd f; ls ak sj ;a df kl ak`

h/e 2 `he he|she she|held held|heed heed|shed shed|ahead;`

all keys learned 3 `she had a sale; a jade desk; she ask a as he fled;`

9C
Speed Building

Using the Space Bar

Key each line twice; DS between 2-line groups. At the end of each line, tap Enter key quickly and start the new line without a pause. Keep your eyes on the copy as you tap the Enter key.

1 `had a deal`

2 `she sells jade;`

3 `she fled; he has ash`

4 `she leads all fall sales;`

5 `she sells sleds; he sells jade`

6 `she ask dad; he has had a sad fall;`

7 `she added all fall sales; as she fell he`

8 `she has a shed; half a flask; she has a desk;`

1. Design an 8.5" × 11" flyer that looks similar to the one below by using shapes and text boxes.
2. **Save as:** *90c flyer*.

Wednesday, December 5
7:15 p.m.
River Valley Health and Fitness Club

CPR Instructions

Instructor:
Dr. Marilyn Guiterez
River Valley Hospital

A two-hour CPR (cardiopulmonary resuscitation) class for those interested in learning how to administer CPR to adults and infants.

Participants will gain the confidence needed to respond in an emergency situation with skills that can save a life.

New Keys: i and r

1. Use the *Standard Plan for Learning New Keys* (p. 40).
2. Key each line twice; DS between 2-line groups.

Learn i

1 k i|ki ki|ik; ik;|is; is;|lid lid|kid kid|aid aid;
2 ill; ill;|said said|like like|jail jail|file file;
3 he likes; file a lease; a slide; if he is; his kid

Learn r

4 f r|fr fr|far far|red red|are are|ark ark|jar jar;
5 dark dark|real real|rake rake|hear hear|rear rear;
6 a red jar; hear her; dark red; a real rake; read a

Combine i and r

7 ride ride|fire fire|hair hair|hire hire|liar liar;
8 air air|risk risk|fair fair|dire dire|rifle rifle;
9 fire risk; hire a; her side; like air; a fire; sir

i Right middle finger

r Left index finger

New-Key Mastery

Key each line twice; DS between 2-line groups. As you key, keep your fingers curved and upright, your eyes on the copy, and your wrists low, but not resting on the keyboard.

reach review

1 de ki jh fr ed ik rf ik ki rf jh ed ik fr jh de ki
2 are are|hair hair|hear hear|risk risk|shear shear;

h/e

3 she she|her her|seeks seeks|shed sheds|shelf shelf
4 her shelf; he had; he held a jar; he heard; he has

i/r

5 ir ir|air air|hair hair|hired hired|riddle riddle;
6 hire a kid; ride like; her hair; like her; a fire;

all keys learned

7 jar jar|half half|fire fire|liked liked|lake lake;
8 fire fire|jail jail|hire hire|sake sake|deal deal;

all keys learned

9 if she is; he did ask; he led her; he is her aide;
10 she has had a jak sale; she said he had a red fir;

For additional practice:

MicroType 6

Alphabetic Keyboarding Lesson 4

Assess Word Processing (Special Documents) and Database Skills

- Use word processing features to format and key special documents from templates for assessment purposes.
- Use database features to create a database for assessment purposes.

90B

Memo

1. Open *df 90b memo*, a template file, and use it and the information below to create a memo.
2. Proofread and correct errors.
3. Save as: *90b memo*.

TO: Longfellow Astronomers Club Members | **FROM:** Jesus Clavijo, Secretary | **DATE:** Current date | **SUBJECT:** CLUB MEETING AGENDA

The next meeting of the Longfellow Astronomers Club is scheduled for 7:30 p.m. on Friday, September 23, in Room 102 of the Longfellow Observatory.

As the enclosed agenda indicates, the primary purpose of the meeting is to plan next year's schedule of events. As usual, the events are likely to include a lecture series and one or two star parties. A project to involve high school students in astronomy needs to be planned and approved.

Please mark your calendar for this important meeting. If you are unable to attend, please call me at 555-0151.

xxx | Enclosure

LESSON 10   Review

OUTCOMES

- Increase keying speed.
- Improve **Space Bar** and **Enter** technique.

10A

Space-Bar Mastery

Key each line twice; DS between 2-line groups. Space quickly after keying a letter or a word; begin keying the next letter or word immediately.

1 a s d f; a s d f; j k l; j k l; as; ask; he; held;
2 ask her; ask her; fall sale; fall sale; if he asks
3 a red jar; a red jar; she said half; she said half
4 hear a lark; hear a lark; a fire sale; a fire sale
5 he fired her; he fired her; a dark red; a dark red
6 ask her kids; ask her kids; he has had; he has had

10B

Enter-Key Mastery

Key each line twice; DS between 2-line groups. At the end of the line, tap Enter quickly and begin the new line immediately.

1 she said;
2 a red file is;
3 ask her if she has;
4 she said her ad is here;
5 she asked if he had a red jar
6 here is a jar; he hired a sad lad;

10C

Increase Keying Speed

For additional practice:

MicroType 6

**Alphabetic Keyboarding
Lesson 5**

Key each line twice; DS between 2-line groups. Key the word the first time at an easy speed; repeat it at a faster speed.

1 had had|sad sad|her her|lake lake|dad dad|has has;
2 is is|lad lad|red red|jade jade|lake lake|far far;
3 sad; sad;|ask ask|desk desk|fall fall|hired hired;
4 sir sir|jar jar|like like|ash ash|far far|are are;
5 fair fair|fall fall|read read|risk risk|here here;

4. Insert your name, your instructor's name, your course title, and the current date in the report identification lines.
5. Insert a header containing your last name and page number.
6. Hyphenate the report, check spelling, proofread, and correct errors. Adjust page endings as needed.
7. **Save as:** *89d report*.

89E

Worksheet

1. Open *df 89e worksheet*.
2. Delete the row for Everett.
3. Insert the information for employees Kennyman and Means so the last names are in alphabetic order.

| Tom Kennyman | 112 | 36 | 10.55 | 0 | | 48.65 |
| Margaret Means | 119 | 40 | 10.55 | 2 | | 52.45 |

4. Cut and paste the rows as needed so employees are listed in alphabetic order by last name.
5. Calculate the Overtime Pay Rate for each employee at 1.5 times the Regular Pay Rate. Display the answer with two decimal places.
6. Add a **Gross Pay** column to the right of *Overtime Pay Rate* and calculate Gross Pay for each employee. Display answer with two decimal places.
7. Add a **Net Pay** column to the right of *Total Deductions* and calculate the Net Pay for each employee. Display answer with two decimal places.
8. Calculate column totals and averages in unshaded cells in rows 15 and 16. Display averages with two decimal places.
9. Format numbers in columns D, F, G, H, and I as Accounting. Adjust column widths as needed to fit the contents.
10. Add a title, **Jefferson Medical Association Payroll—Week 6**, in row 1 in 24-pt. bold font.
11. Center-align and bold the column headings.
12. Apply a cell style to and bold the text in cells I2:I17 and cells A16:H17.
13. Prepare the worksheet to print without gridlines and headings.
14. **Save as:** *89e worksheet*.

89F

Charts

1. Open *df 89f worksheet*.
2. Create a pie chart using a Chart Style of your choice. Use **Investment Portfolio** as the title.
3. **Save as:** *89f chart 1*. Do not close the file.
4. Convert **89f chart 1** to a column chart. Use a Chart Style of your choice. Use **Investment Portfolio** as the title. Delete the legend.
5. **Save as:** *89f chart 2*.

WP Applications

For each activity, read and learn the feature described; then complete the activity as directed.

Activity 1a

Insert

Insert

The **Insert** feature is active when you open a software program. Move the insertion point to where you want to insert text; key the new text.

1. Open *df aa2 activity 1a*.
2. Use the insert feature to insert the text highlighted in yellow.

   Tom said, "Did you hire John?"

   Mary has five red blocks.

   I will ask her for a jar of peaches.

   She hired a man to fix the desk last fall.

   She wore a dark red dress to the dance.

3. Save the file as **aa2 activity 1a** by deleting the *df* at the beginning of the filename that appears in the File Name box when you click on *File* and then *Save As*.

Activity 1b

Overtype

Overtype

Overtype allows you to replace (type over) current text with newly keyed text.

1. Open *df aa2 activity 1b*.
2. Use the overtype feature to change the text highlighted in yellow.

   She had half a jar of red jam.

   Ask Chen if he has a file for sale.

   Felipe's ad is here at the lake.

   Kellee has a new desk and file.

   David heard a lark in his tree.

3. **Save as:** *aa2 activity 1b*.

Activity 1c

AutoCorrect

AutoCorrect

The **AutoCorrect** feature detects and corrects *some* typing, spelling, and capitalization errors for you automatically.

Key the following lines; note how the errors are corrected automatically by the AutoCorrect feature.

   a redd file is heree;

   hirred a sadd lass;

[2] Patsy Fulton-Calkins and Karin M. Stulz, *Procedures & Theory for Administrative Professionals* (Mason, OH: South-Western Cengage Learning, 2004) p. 543.

3. Format and key the following as a separate reference page at the end.

References

Fulton-Calkins, Patsy and Karin M. Stulz. *Procedures & Theory for Administrative Professionals*. Mason, OH: South-Western Cengage Learning, 2004.

Jordan, Ann K. and Lynne T. Whaley. *Investigating Your Career*. 2nd ed. Mason, OH: South-Western Cengage Learning, 2011.

4. Number the pages at the top right, and hide the number on p. 1.
5. Hyphenate the report, check spelling, proofread, and correct all errors. Adjust page endings as necessary.
6. **Save as:** *89b report*.

89C

Cover Page

1. Using the Sideline built-in style, create a cover page for the report you keyed in 89B. Include the report title, your name, your school name, and the current date. Delete unused placeholders as well as the blank page following the cover page.
2. **Save as:** *89c cover page*.

89D

MLA Report with Textual Citations

1. Open *df 89d report*.
2. Format the text in MLA report format with textual citations and a separate Works Cited page.
3. Format and key the text below as a table after the ¶ that begins with "Table 1." Center headings; left-align the text in column 1; center the text in the other three columns.

Table 1: Metric Units of Length

Unit	Abbreviation	Equivalent in Meters	Common English Equivalent
Millimeter	mm	0.001 m	.03937 inch
Centimeter	cm	0.01 m	.3937 inch
Decimeter	dm	0.1 m	3.937 inches
Meter	m	1 m	39.37 inches
Dekameter	dam	10 m	32.808 feet
Hectometer	hm	100 m	328.08 feet
Kilometer	km	1000 m	.621 mile

Activity 1d

Underline

Home/Font/
Underline

★ TIP ▶ Ctrl + U
Underline

Underline

The **Underline** feature underlines text as it is keyed.

1. Open *df aa2 activity 1d*.
2. DS after the heading and key lines 1–5 DS. Do not key the line numbers.

1.   if <u>he</u> is;
2.   as if <u>she</u> is;
3.   <u>he</u> had a fir desk;
4.   <u>she</u> has a red jell jar;
5.   <u>he</u> has had a lead all fall;

3. **Save as:** *aa2 activity 1d*.

Activity 1e

Italic

Home/Font/
Italic

★ TIP ▶ Ctrl + I
Italic

Italic

The **Italic** feature prints letters that slope up toward the right.

1. Open *df aa2 activity 1e*.
2. DS after the heading and key lines 1–5 DS. Do not key the line numbers.

1.   had *had* sad *sad* her *her* lake *lake* dad *dad* has *has*;
2.   if *he* is; as *he* fled; risk a *lead*; has a red *sled*;
3.   a *jade* fish; ask if *she* slid; *she* has asked a kid;
4.   as if *he* did; *he* asked a lad; *his* aide has a sled;
5.   *he* has a sled; if *he* has a jar; see if *he* is here;

3. **Save as:** *aa2 activity 1e*.

Activity 1f

Bold

Home/Font/
Bold

★ TIP ▶ Ctrl + B
Bold

Bold

The **Bold** feature prints text darker than other copy as it is keyed.

1. Open *df aa2 activity 1f*.
2. DS after the heading and key lines 1–5 DS. Do not key the line numbers.

1.   a **red** jar;
2.   she said **half** a
3.   **she** asked if **he** had;
4.   a **red** desk; he fired **her**;
5.   a **kid** led; **he** is fair; ask **her**

3. **Save as:** *aa2 activity 1f*.

LESSON 89

Assess Word Processing (Reports) and Spreadsheet Skills

OUTCOMES

- Use word processing features to create, format, and key unbound and MLA-style reports with textual citations and footnotes.
- Use spreadsheet software features to key, revise, and format worksheets.

89B

Unbound Report with Footnotes

1. Format and key the text below as an unbound report, using styles appropriately for the title and side headings. Do not key the text in red.

Career Planning

Career planning is an important, ongoing process. It is important because the career you choose will affect your quality of life.

One important step in career planning is to define your goals.

> Finding your path to a satisfying career requires careful planning and thoughtful decisions. . . . Your journey to a successful career begins with setting goals. Although your goals may change over time, the things that you enjoy doing and the talents that you have do not change. Your career choice depends on you. [Insert footnote 1 here.]

Another useful step in career planning is to develop a personal profile of your skills, interests, and values.

Skills

An analysis of your skills is likely to reveal that you have many different kinds: (1) functional skills that determine how well you manage time, communicate, and motivate people; (2) adaptive skills that determine your efficiency, flexibility, reliability, and enthusiasm; and (3) technical skills such as keyboarding, computer, and language skills that are required for many jobs.

Values

Values are "principles that guide a person's life," [Insert footnote 2 here.] and you should identify them early so that you can pursue a career that will improve your chances to acquire them. Values include the importance you place on family, security, wealth, prestige, creativity, power, and independence.

Interests

Interests are best described as activities you like and enthusiastically pursue. By listing and analyzing your interests, you should be able to identify a desirable work environment. For example, your list is likely to reveal if you like to work with things or people, work alone or with others, lead or follow others, or be indoors or outdoors.

2. Insert the following footnotes where indicated in the text.

[1] Ann K. Jordan and Lynne T. Whaley, *Investigating Your Career*, 2nd ed. (Mason, OH: South-Western Cengage Learning, 2011) p. 7.

LESSON 11

New Keys: o and t

- Learn reach technique for **o** and **t**.

11A

Warmup

Key each line twice; DS between 2-line groups.

Fingers curved

Fingers upright

h/e 1 her head; has had a; see here; feed her; hire her;

i/r 2 hire a; fire her; his risk; fresh air; a red hair;

all keys learned 3 a lake; ask a lad; a risk; here she is; a red jar;

11B

New Keys: o and t

1. Use the *Standard Plan for Learning New Keys* (p. 40).
2. Key each line twice; DS between 2-line groups. If time permits, key lines 7–9 again.

Learn o

1 l o lo lo|olo olo|fold fold|sold sold|holds holds;

2 of of|do do|oak oak|soil soil|does does|roof roof;

3 load of soil; order food; old oil; solid oak door;

Learn t

4 f t ft ft|tf tf|the the|tea tea|eat eat|talk talk;

5 at at|fit fit|set set|hit hit|talk talk|test tests

6 flat feet; the treats; the first test; take a hike

Combine o and t

7 total total|tooth tooth|toast toast|otters otters;

8 the total look; other tooth; took a toll; too old;

9 those hooks; the oath; old tree fort; took a tool;

o *Right ring* finger

t *Left index* finger

Key two 3' timings on all ¶s combined; determine *gwam* and number of errors.

 A all letters used

	gwam	3'	5'

Character is often described as a person's combined moral **4 | 2 | 43**
and ethical strength. Most people think it is like integrity, **8 | 5 | 46**
which is thought to be a person's ability to adhere to a code or **12 | 7 | 48**
a set standard of values. If an individual's values are accepted **17 | 10 | 51**
by society, others are likely to view her or him as having a some- **21 | 13 | 53**
what high degree of integrity. **23 | 14 | 55**

You need to know that character is a trait that everyone **27 | 16 | 57**
possesses and that it is formed over time. A person's character **31 | 19 | 59**
reflects his or her definition of what is good or just. Most **35 | 21 | 62**
children and teenagers model their character after the words and **40 | 24 | 65**
deeds of parents, teachers, and other adults with whom they have **44 | 26 | 67**
regular contact. **45 | 27 | 68**

Existing character helps mold future character. It is impor- **49 | 29 | 70**
tant to realize that today's actions can have a lasting effect. **53 | 32 | 73**
For that reason, there is no better time than now to make all your **58 | 32 | 73**
words and deeds speak favorably. You want them to portray the **62 | 37 | 78**
things others require of people who are thought to possess a high **67 | 40 | 80**
degree of character. **68 | 41 | 81**

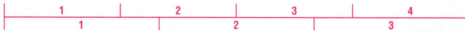

gwam	3'	1	2	3	4
	5'	1	2	3	

New-Key Mastery

⭐TIP

- curved, upright fingers
- down-and-in spacing
- wrists low, but not resting
- eyes on copy as you key

Key each line twice; DS between 2-line groups. Speed up the second keying of each word in lines 3, 5, and 7.

reach review

1 ki lo de ft jh fr ei or th olo ere hjh iki edr iro
2 here is; the fort; their old trail; first look at;

h/e

3 the the|hear hear|here here|heat heat|sheet sheet;
4 the sheets; hear her heart; their health; heat the

i/t

5 sit sit|fit fit|silt silt|kites kites|tried tried;
6 a little tire; he tried to tilt it; he tied a tie;

o/r

7 tort tort|tore tore|fort fort|road road|roof roof;
8 a road|a door|a rose|or a rod|a roar|for her offer

space bar

9 to do it he as are hit dot eat air the ask jar let
10 if he|do it|to see|had it|is the|for her|all of it

all keys learned

11 ask jet art oil old fit hit the sad did soil risk;
12 oil the; the jail; oak door; he said; their forts;

11D

Enrichment

Key each line twice; DS between 2-line groups. At the end of each line, tap the Enter key quickly and start the new line without a pause.

For additional practice:

MicroType 6

**Alphabetic Keyboarding
Lesson 6**

1 it is
2 the jet is
3 he had the rose
4 ask to hear the joke
5 she took the old shirt to
6 she told her to take the tests
7 at the fort; the lake road; did she
8 take the test; it is the last; he did it
9 the last jar; the old fort; he took the offer
10 take a jet; solid oak door; a red rose; ask her to

Slide 5: Section Header

Slide 6: Title and Content

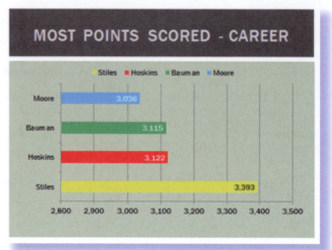

Slide 7: Title and Content

LESSON 12　　New Keys: n and g

• Learn reach technique for **n** and **g**.

12A

Warmup

Key each line twice; DS between 2-line groups.

e/r 1 rare doer fear feet tire hire read ride rest after

o/t 2 toad told took other hotel total tools tooth torte

i/h 3 hits idle hail hiked their fifth faith heist hairs

12B

New Keys: n and g

Key each line twice; DS between 2-line groups. If time permits, key lines 7–9 again.

Learn n

1 j n jn jn|njn njn|an an|on on|no no|in in|and and;

2 kind kind|none none|loan loan|find find|land land;

3 not till noon; not a need; not in; a national need

Learn g

4 f g fg fg|gfg gfg|go go|dog dog|gas gas|goes goes;

5 age age|logs logs|glad glad|eggs eggs|legal legal;

6 great grin; large frog; gold dog; eight large eggs

Combine n and g

7 gone gone|sing sing|king king|gnat gnat|ring rings

8 sing along; a grand song; green signs; long grass;

9 eight rings; a grand king; long gone; sing a song;

n *Right index* finger

g *Left index* finger

12C

Enter-Key Mastery

Key each line three times; DS between 3-line groups. At the end of a line, tap the Enter key quickly and start a new line immediately.

1 large gold jar;

2 take the last train;

3 did he take the last egg;

4 she has to sing the last song;

5 join her for a hike at the lake at;

Reach out and tap Enter

LESSON 88

Assess Presentation and Input Skills

OUTCOMES

- Use presentation software features to create slide shows for assessment purposes.
- Key straight-copy text for assessment purposes.

88B

Assess Presentation Skills

1. Create the slides displayed below using the slide layouts shown beneath each slide. Choose appropriate clip art if the art shown isn't available with your software.

Note: Text on some slides has been enlarged for readability.

2. **Save as:** *88b pp slides*.

Slide 1: Title Slide

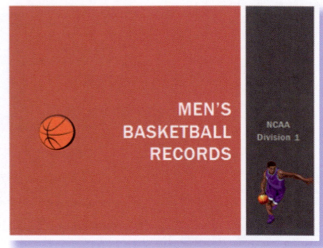

Slide 2: Section Header

Slide 3: Title and Content

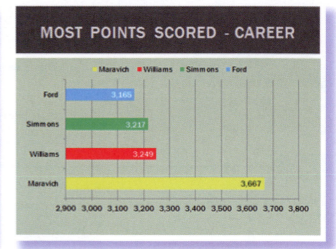

Slide 4: Title and Content

New-Key Mastery

TIP

- curved and upright fingers
- wrists low, but not resting
- down-and-in spacing
- eyes on copy as you key

Key each line twice; DS between 2-line groups.

reach review
1 rf ik hj tf ol ed nj gf; lo fr ft jn de ki jh fgf;
2 it it|oil oil|the the|ink ink|here here|song song;

n/g
3 sing gone night seeing doing going ringing longest
4 sing one song; going along; long night; good angle

space bar
5 if he no as to it is so do at in so of did elk jet
6 it ask and the are let oil oar ill son odd fan sat

all keys learned
7 desk soil lark joke that done find join gold lake;
8 tank logs hand jade free toil seek said like tear;

all keys learned
9 oil free; did join; has half; go get; near the end
10 tell jokes; right here; ask her; fine desk; is it;

12E

Enrichment

TIP

- space immediately after each word; down-and-in motion of thumb
- maintain pace to end of line; tap Enter quickly and start new line immediately

For additional practice:

MicroType 6

Alphabetic Keyboarding Lesson 7

Key each line twice; DS between 2-line groups.

Reach review

1 jh jh|jn jn|fg fg|fr fr|ft ft|de de|ki ki|lo lo|jh
2 no no|hot hot|oil oil|the the|gold gold|rest rest;
3 hold nest gone that nails there going alert radio;

Space Bar

4 is at if so no do as he of go it to an or is on in
5 of hen got ink and the ask jar let hit jet den far
6 no ink|on the go|hit it|ask her to|did not see the
7 he is to join her at the lake; she is not the one;

Enter key

8 he is there;
9 ask if it is far;
10 the sign for the lake;
11 she still has three of the;
12 did he join her at the lake the;

Short words and phrases

13 on on|do do|in in|it it|go go|or or|as as|are are;
14 see see|the the|and and|are are|for for|hire hire;
15 jet jet|kid kid|fit fit|ask ask|ton ton|risk risk;
16 he is go to the ski lodge; he lost the three jars;

1. Format and key the table below as shown, using AutoFit to Contents.
2. Center the table on the page.
3. **Save as:** *87d table 1*.

FBLA FUNDRAISING CAPTAINS			
First	**Last**	**Homeroom**	**Community Area**
Phillip	Dillon	106	1
Aparna	Iozzi	110	4
Juno	Taylor	208	6
Austin	Gruber	213	5
Seth	Garrity	218	3
Sandra	Mamajek	115	2

4. Apply a grid table style using Accent 2 and include only the Banded Row feature from the Table Styles group.
5. Sort the table by Homeroom number in ascending order.
6. Proofread and correct errors.
7. **Save as:** *87d table 2*.

1. Open *df 87e table*.
2. Adjust the column widths to fit the contents.
3. Insert two columns after the *Number Elected* column, and add the following information.

Democrats	Republicans
2	0
8	5
7	10

4. Add a row below the column headings, and insert the following in that row.

1925–1950	2	2	0	TX, WY

5. Increase row heights to 0.5".
6. Use Align Center for title, column headings, and columns 1–4 of the remaining rows. Use Align Center Left for the rows in column 5.
7. Use a bold 18-pt. font for the title, and bold the column headings.
8. Change orientation to landscape; center the table on the page.
9. Apply a 3-pt. red outside border to the table.
10. Apply a light red shading to rows 1, 3, and 5.
11. **Save as:** *87e table*.

LESSON 13   New Keys: Left Shift and Period (.)

OUTCOMES

- Learn reach technique for **left shift** and . (period).
- Improve **Space Bar** and **Enter** key technique.

13A

Warmup

Key each line twice; DS between 2-line groups.

reach review 1   ft jn fr jh de ki gf lo tf nj rf hj ed ik fg ol ng

space bar 2   so it if at or on is go do ask the and jar art lid

all keys learned 3   join the; like those; ask her to sing; define the;

13B

New Keys: Left Shift and . (period)

Key each line twice; DS between 2-line groups. Space once after the period (.) following abbreviations and initials. Space twice after a period at the end of a sentence except at the end of a line. There, return without spacing.

Left Shift *Left little finger*

. (period) *Right ring finger*

Learn left shift key

1 a J|a J|Ja Ja|Jan Jan|a K a K|Kate Kate|Hank Hank;

2 Idaho; Kansas; Ohio; Oregon; Indiana; Illinois; IL

3 Lane and I; Ida and Jane; Hal and Kate; John and I

Learn . (period)

4 l . l .|l. l.|a.l. a.l.|d.l. d.l.|j.l j.l|k.l. k.l

5 hr. hr.|ft. ft.|in. in.|rd. rd.|ea. ea.|ltd. ltd.;

6 fl. fl.|fed. fed.|alt. alt.|ins. ins.|asst. asst.;

Combine left shift and . (period)

7 I took Linda to Lake Harriet. Lt. Kerns is there.

8 I did it. Lana took it. Jett Hill left for Ohio.

9 Karl and Jake got Ida and Janet to go to the fair.

 TIP

1. Hold down left shift key with little finger on the left hand.
2. Tap the letter with the finger on the right hand.
3. Return finger(s) to home key(s).

Assess Word Processing (Letters and Tables) Skills

OUTCOME

- Use word processing features to prepare block format personal-business and business letters, envelopes, and tables for assessment purposes.

87B

Personal-Business Letter

1. Format and key the text below as a personal-business letter in block format with open punctuation. Use Times New Roman 12-pt. font and the Insert Date feature, but do not update automatically.
2. Prepare a large envelope with a return address.
3. Check spelling, proofread, and correct errors.
4. **Save as:** *87b letter*.

315 Princeton Drive | Mars, PA 16046-1463 | [Insert date] | Ms. Margaret McQuade | Butler County Symphony | 259 South Main Street | Butler, PA 16001-2693 | Dear Ms. McQuade

I want to thank you and the Rising Musician of Note Committee for sponsoring the "Rising Musician of Note" program and for selecting me to be recognized for my keen interest in music and ability.

I plan to attend the concert entitled "Fire" to be recognized. I will need tickets for myself and my mother, father, two brothers, and two of my grandparents. Enclosed is a check for $60 for reserved seating. Please send the tickets to me at the above address.

Again, thank you and the committee for the recognition you have given me and others from my school. My family and I look forward to meeting you at the concert.

Sincerely | Kyle Jon | Enclosure

87C

Business Letter

1. Format and key the text below as the opening lines of a business letter in block format with mixed punctuation. Use the Insert Date feature with automatic update.

[Insert date] | Mrs. Vera L. Bowden | 3491 Rose Street | Minneapolis, MN 55441-5781 | Dear Mrs. Bowden | SUBJECT: YOUR DONATION

2. Insert the text in file *df 87c body* as the body of the letter.
3. Format and key the text below as the closing lines of the letter.

Yours truly | Miss Amelia R. Carter | Beta Xi Sponsor | xx | Enclosure | c Thomas Turnball, Treasurer

4. Hyphenate the letter. Check spelling, proofread, and correct errors.
5. Prepare a large envelope without a return address.
6. **Save as:** *87c letter*.

13C

New-Key Mastery

Down-and-in spacing

Key each line twice; DS between 2-line groups. Keep your eyes on copy. Immediately tap Space Bar after the last letter in each word.

abbrev./initials
1 J. Hart and K. Jakes hired Lila J. Norton to sing.
2 Lt. Karen J. Lane took Lt. Jon O. Hall to the jet.

3rd row emphasis
3 I told her to take a look at the three large jets.
4 Iris had three of her oldest friends on the train.

key words
5 if for the and old oak jet for oil has egg jar oar
6 told lake jade gold here noon tear soil goes fade;

key phrases
7 and the|ask for|go to the|not so fast|if he|to see
8 if there is|to go to the|for the last|none of the;

all letters learned
9 Jodi and Kendra Jaeger are in the National finals.
10 Jason Lake did not take Jon Hoag for a train ride.

13D

Space-Bar and Enter-Key Mastery

Quick out-and-tap Enter

Key each line twice; DS between 2-line groups. Tap Enter quickly and start each new line immediately.

1 Linda had fish.
2 Jan is on the train.
3 Nat took her to the lake.
4 He is here to see his friends.
5 Kathleen sold the large egg to her.
6 Kate and Jason hired her to do the roof.

13E

Enrichment

For additional practice:

MicroType 6

Alphabetic Keyboarding Lesson 8

Key each line twice; DS between 2-line groups.

Spacing/shifting

1 Kellee and I did see Jed and Jonathan at the lake.
2 Jane and Hal are going to London to see Joe Hanks.
3 Lee left for the lake at noon; Kenneth left later.
4 Jo and Kate Hanson are going to take the test soon.

Keying easy sentences

5 Jessie is going to talk to the girls for the kids.
6 Harold Lett took his friends to the train station.
7 Lon and Jen are going to see friends at the lodge.
8 Natasha and Hansel are taking the train to London.

Key two 3' timings on all ¶s combined; determine *gwam* and number of errors.

 A all letters used

	gwam	3'	5'

There are many opportunities for jobs in the physical 　　4　2
fitness industry. The first step for many people is to be a 　8　5
fitness instructor in a fitness center or program. A genuine 　12　7
interest in the field as well as evidence of a personal com- 　16　9
mitment to good fitness are frequently the major things needed 　20　12
to land a job as a fitness instructor. 　22　13

Another opportunity in the fitness industry is to become 　26　16
a strength coach for an athletic team. This person works to 　30　18
make the team members fit and strong at the same time the 　34　21
athletic coach works to maximize their skills. A college 　38　23
degree in physical education or a related field is usually 　42　25
needed for this kind of job. 　44　26

Others in the fitness field often get a job in a big 　47　28
company or hospital as a fitness program director. These 　51　31
directors run programs that improve the fitness and overall 　55　33
health of the people who work in the hospital or company. 　59　36
Directors usually need a college degree and a lot of training 　63　38
in fitness skills, health promotion, and business. 　67　40

gwam	3'	1		2		3		4	
	5'		1		2		3		

LESSON 14 Review

OUTCOMES

- Increase keying speed.
- Improve **Space Bar, left shift,** and **Enter** technique.

14A

Keyboard Mastery

For additional practice:

MicroType 6

Alphabetic Keyboarding Lesson 9

Key each line twice; DS between 2-line groups. Keep your fingers curved and upright with your eyes on the copy. Don't rest your wrists on the keyboard.

o/t

1 too took foot told hot toes lot dot toil toga torn
2 Otto has lost the list he took to that food store.

n/g

3 gin song sing sign long ring gone green gnat angle
4 Link N. Nagle is going to sing nine songs at noon.

Left shift/.

5 Lake Ontario; Hans N. Linder; Lake Larson; J. Hill
6 Jake left for Indiana; Kathleen left for Illinois.

14B

Enter-Key Mastery

Key each line twice; DS between 2-line groups. At the end of the line, tap Enter quickly and begin the next line immediately.

1 I like the dog.
2 Jan has a red dress.
3 Hal said he left it here.
4 Kate has gone to the ski hill.
5 Lane said he left the dog in Idaho.
6 Kristi and Jennifer are hiking the hill.

14C

Increase Keying Speed

Key each line twice; DS between 2-line groups. Key the word the first time at an easy speed; repeat it at a faster speed.

1 add add|ask ask|hot hot|ring ring|eat eat|off off;
2 jar jar|ago ago|feet feet|hotel hotel|other other;
3 sand sand|join join|lake lake|half half|dear dear;
4 Janet said she left three letters on his old desk.

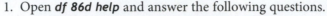

86D

Assess Using Help

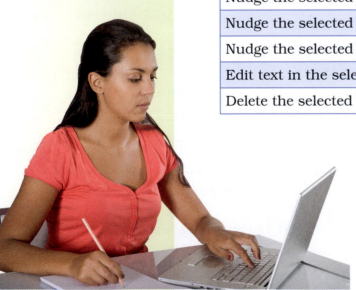

1. Open *df 86d help* and answer the following questions.
    1. What are two ways to access Help?
    2. How do you access the Table of Contents for the Help feature?
    3. You have heard that *Training Courses* and *Videos* are available through the Help feature. When you open the Help Table of Contents, they do not appear. What is the problem?
    4. You want to complete a step-by-step procedure using the Help feature. Every time you click in the document you are working on, the Help feature disappears. What do you do to get the Help feature to stay on top?
2. **Save as:** *86d help.*

86E

Assess Using Help

1. Open *df 86e help.*
2. Access Help and locate the article *Keyboard shortcuts for SmartArt graphics.* Scroll down to *Work with shapes in a SmartArt graphic.*
3. Position the Help menu to the right of the table included in *df 86e help.*
4. Activate the *Keep on Top* feature of Help so that you can complete the *Press* column of the table with the information from the article.
5. **Save as:** *86e help.*

Keyboard Shortcuts for SmartArt Graphics

To Do This	Press
Select the next element in a SmartArt graphic.	
Select the previous element in a SmartArt graphic.	
Select all shapes.	
Remove focus from the selected shape.	
Nudge the selected shape up.	
Nudge the selected shape down.	
Nudge the selected shape left.	
Nudge the selected shape right.	
Edit text in the selected shape.	
Delete the selected shape.	

Marco Mayer/Shutterstock.com

WP Applications (continued)

Activity 2

Select Text

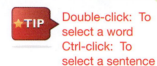

> **★TIP**
> Double-click: To select a word
> Ctrl-click: To select a sentence

Once you have keyed text, you can make changes to it. To do so, you must select it first. The Select Text feature allows you to select (highlight) text to apply formatting changes or perform other actions. Text can be selected using the mouse or the keyboard. As little as one letter of text or as much as the entire document (Select All) may be selected.

Once selected, the text can be bolded, italicized, underlined, deleted, copied, moved, printed, saved, etc.

1. Open **df aa2 activity 2**.
2. Use the Select Text feature to select and change the copy as shown below.

John F. Kennedy: *"And so, my fellow Americans: ask not what your country can do for you—ask what you can do for your country."*

Dwight D. Eisenhower: *"Love of liberty means the guarding of every resource that makes freedom possible—from the sanctity of our families and the wealth of our soil to the genius of our scientists."*

Franklin D. Roosevelt: *"I see a great nation, upon a great continent, blessed with a great wealth of natural resources."*

Abraham Lincoln: *"Both parties deprecated war, but one of them would make war rather than let the nation survive, and the other would accept war rather than let it perish, and the war came."*

3. **Save as:** *aa2 activity 2*.

Activity 3

Cut, Copy, and Paste

Home/Clipboard/Cut, Copy, or Paste

> **★TIP**
> Ctrl + x: Cut
> Ctrl + c: Copy
> Ctrl + v: Paste

After you have selected text, you can use the Cut, Copy, and Paste features. The **Cut** feature removes selected text from the current location; the **Paste** feature places it at another location. The **Copy** feature copies the selected text so it can be placed in another location (pasted), leaving the original text unchanged.

1. Open file **df aa2 activity 3**. Copy the text in this file, and paste it a TS (tap Enter 3 times) below the last line of text.
2. In the second set of steps, use Cut and Paste to arrange the steps in order.

Step 1. Select text to be cut (moved).

Step 2. Click **Cut** to remove text from the current location.

Step 3. Move the insertion point to the desired location.

Step 4. Click **Paste** to place the cut text at the new location.

3. **Save as:** *aa2 activity 3*.

1. Create a new Contacts file called **86c Contacts**.
2. Key the information from the three business cards shown below into the Contacts file.
3. Print a copy of the file in Business Card View with Card Style.
4. **Save as:** *86c contacts*.

**General
Dynamics**

383 Roosevelt Pl.
Atlantic City, NJ 08401
Phone: 609.339.7215
Fax: 609.339.0032

mjfitzge@gendyn.com

Martin J. Fitzgerald

Director of Human
Resources

**General
Dynamics**

383 Roosevelt Pl.
Atlantic City, NJ 08401
Phone: 609.339.2841
Fax: 609.339.0032

ralafaye@gendyn.com

Rosslyn A. Lafayette

VP - Marketing

**General
Dynamics**

383 Roosevelt Pl.
Atlantic City, NJ 08401
Phone: 609.339.5389
Fax: 609.339.0032

dplincol@gendyn.com

Duncan P. Lincoln

Director of IS

New Keys: u and c

- Learn reach technique for **u** and **c**.

15A

Warmup

Key each line twice; DS between 2-line groups.

reach review 1 hjh tft njn gfg iki .l. ede olo rfr it go no or hi

space bar 2 so ask let jet his got ink are and the kid off did

left shift 3 Jason and I looked for Janet and Kate at the lake.

15B

New Keys: u and c

Key each line twice; DS between 2-line groups. Reach the finger up to the 3rd-row keys and down to the 1st-row keys without moving hands or arms.

Learn u

1 j u|juj juj|uju uju|us us|due due|jug jug|sun sun;

2 suit suit|dusk dusk|four four|fund fund|huge huge;

3 just for fun; under the rug; unusual urt; found us

Learn c

4 d c|dcd dcd|act act|cash cash|card card|ache ache;

5 Jack Jack|sack sack|lock lock|calf calf|rock rock;

6 acted sick; tic toc goes the clock; catch the cat;

Combine u and c

7 duck duck|accuse accuse|cruel cruel|actual actual;

8 crucial account; cute cousin; chunk of ice; juice;

9 such success; rustic church; no luck; count trucks

10 June and Laura told us to take four cans of juice.

11 Jack asked us for a list of all the codes he used.

12 Louise has gone to cut the cake on the green cart.

u *Right index* finger

c *Left middle* finger

© Cengage Learning

UNIT 17   Assessment

Lesson 86	Assess E-mail, PIM, Help, and Input Skills	Lesson 89	Assess Word Processing (Reports) and Spreadsheet Skills
Lesson 87	Assess Word Processing (Letters and Tables) Skills	Lesson 90	Assess Word Processing (Special Documents) and Database Skills
Lesson 88	Assess Presentation and Input Skills		

LESSON 86   Assess E-mail, PIM, Help, and Input Skills

OUTCOMES

- Prepare e-mail messages, use PIM features, and use Help for assessment purposes.
- Key straight-copy text for assessment purposes.

86A-90A

Warmup

Key each line twice at the beginning of each lesson; first for control, then for speed.

alphabet	1	Weber excluded a quick jaunt to the big zoo from my travel plans.
figures	2	My agents will sell 43 tables, 59 beds, 187 chairs, and 206 rugs.
speed	3	Their neighbor may pay the downtown chapel for the ancient ivory.

| gwam | 1' | 1 | 2 | 3 | 4 | 5 | 6 | 7 | 8 | 9 | 10 | 11 | 12 | 13 | |

86B

Assess E-mail Skills

1. Format and key the e-mail message below; send to your instructor's e-mail address. Use **Macbeth Quote** for the subject line.
2. Proofread your copy; correct all errors.
3. **Save as:** *86b e-mail*.

I enjoyed our visit last week at the class reunion. How quickly time passes; it seems like only yesterday that we graduated. Of course, a class reunion is a quick reminder that it wasn't yesterday.

I was able to find the quote that we discussed with the group on Friday. Your memory definitely serves you better than mine; it was a quote from George Bernard Shaw. However, he was referring to Shakespeare's *Macbeth*. Here is the exact quote by Shaw: "Life is not a 'brief candle.' It is a splendid torch that I want to make burn as brightly as possible before handing it on to future generations."

I was glad to see that so many of our classmates are living lives as "splendid torches" rather than as "brief candles."

15C

New-Key Mastery

Key each line twice; DS between 2-line groups. Reach the finger up to the 3rd-row keys and down to the 1st-row keys without moving hands or arms.

3rd/1st rows
1 run car nut nice cute noon touch other clean truck
2 Lincoln coin; strike three; cut the cards; four or

left shift and .
3 Jack and Nicholas are going to Otter Lake in Ohio.
4 Lucille took a truck to Ohio. Janet sold her car.

key words
5 call fund kind race neck golf half just toil lunch
6 cause guide hotel feast alike joins; laugh; judge;

key phrases
7 if she can|he can do the|it is the|and then|all of
8 till the end|tie the knot|faster than|a little red

all keys learned
9 Jack or Lance Hughes said the four girls are here.
10 Hugh likes to run on the lakefront; Jack does not.

15D

Space-Bar and Left-Shift Mastery

Key the lines once; DS between 3-line groups.

space bar
1 Lucas asked the girls to get the dogs at the lake.
2 Lance said he can go to Oregon to get the old car.
3 Janice and her three dogs ran along the shoreline.

left shift
4 Jack and Joe Kern just left to go to Lake Ontario.
5 Jo thinks it takes less than an hour to get there.
6 Kanosh and Joliet are cities in Utah and Illinois.

15E

Enrichment

For additional practice:

MicroType 6

Alphabetic Keyboarding
Lesson 10

Key each line once; DS between 2-line groups. Try to reduce hand movement and the tendency of unused fingers to fly out or follow reaching finger.

u/c
1 cut luck such cuff lunch crush touch torch justice
2 Okichi Kinura had juice. Lucius caught the judge.

n/g
3 gone ring fang long eggnog length; sing sang song;
4 Jake thinks Jerald Leung can sing the eight songs.

all keys learned
5 Julian and Hector left a note for Leticia Herrera.
6 Juan and Luisa took Jorge and Leonor to the dance.

all keys learned
7 Jack Lefstad said to take the road through Oregon.
8 Janet and Linda caught eight fish in Lake Ontario.

10. In the next row, display the maximum for each column that contains dollars or percent.

11. In the next row, display the minimum for each column that contains dollars or percent.

12. Insert a row at the top and insert an appropriate title for this worksheet. Format the spreadsheet attractively.

13. Print the worksheet so it appears on one page.

Project 20

Employee	Present Salary
Parker, Natasha	$104,958
St. Claire, Helen	$37,650
Carter, Jamal	$78,728
DeCosta, Serena	$75,389
Lopez, Miguel	$79,539
Powell, Steven	$73,899
Thomas, Erika	$83,762

Project 21

1. HPJ is an equal opportunity employer. Ms. Parker would like you to do a query to determine if men and women have received equal opportunities in upper-level positions within the organization. Create a query with the following fields:

> Last Name
> First Name
> Branch
> Job Title
> Gender

You will need to set the "Criteria" for Job Title to "***Branch Manager***" to show only those at the branch manager level.

> Query Name: **M/F Branch Managers**

2. Create a query for Ms. Parker showing first and last name, job title, branch, and salary. She would like the query sorted by job title in ascending order before you print a copy of the query for her.

> Query Name: **Salary by Job Title**

LESSON 16   New Keys: w and Right Shift

OUTCOMES

- Learn reach technique for w and right shift.
- Learn correct spacing of punctuation.

16A

Warmup

Key each line twice; DS between 2-line groups.

reach review 1 jn de ju fg ki ft lo dc fr l. jtn ft. cde hjg uet.

u/c 2 cut cue duck luck cute success accuse juice secure

all keys learned 3 Jake and Lincoln sold us eight large ears of corn.

16B

New Keys: w and Right Shift

w *Left ring* finger

Right Shift *Right little* finger

Key each line twice; DS between 2-line groups.

Learn w

1 s w sw sw|we we|saw saw|who who|wet wet|show show;

2 will will|wash wash|work work|down down|gown gown;

3 white gown; when will we; wash what; walk with us;

Learn right shift key

4 ;A ;A;|A1; A1;|Dan; Dan;|Gina; Gina;|Frank; Frank;

5 Don saw Seth Green and Alfonso Garcia last August.

6 Trish Fuentes and Carlos Delgado left for Atlanta.

Combine w and right shift

7 Will Wenner went to show the Wilsons the two cars.

8 Wes and Wade want to know who will work this week.

9 Willard West will take Akiko Tanaka to Washington.

10 Rafael and Donna asked to go to the store with us.

11 Walt left us at Winter Green Lake with Will Segui.

12 Ted or Walt will get us tickets for the two shows.

 TIP

1. Hold down right shift key with little finger on the right hand.
2. Tap the letter with the finger on the left hand.
3. Return finger(s) to home key(s).

Slide 4

Business Etiquette:
You Cannot Not Communicate!

▸ If business etiquette is important to you, don't miss this seminar. Learn what's acceptable—and what's not—in formal business settings.

Project 19

HPJ From the Desk of
Helen St. Claire

I need to give Ms. Parker information about our Communication Specialists' present and proposed salaries. The proposed salary is based on an across-the-board raise for all specialists meeting expectations and a merit raise for those exceeding expectations. Find the worksheet named *df HPJ project19*, which has the present salaries and the performance appraisal scores. Use the directions at the right to complete the worksheet. Also, this is very sensitive data, so please keep it secure and confidential.

June 14   HSC

	A	B	C	D	E	F	G
1	Name	Present Salary	PR Points	Base Raise	Merit Rais	Proposed	% Increase
2	Ammari, Ann	46320	71				
3	Ashley, David	48240	58				
4	Black, Virginia	42562	47				
5	Casey, Shawn	47212	65				
6	Cey, Donald	38568	69				
7	Cody, William	52643	58				
8	Dent, Marsha	45508	49				

1. Insert a column after each name, and insert the name of the branch in which each employee works.
2. Delete Jan Polacheck from the list, as she just notified us that she will be leaving the company at the end of the month.
3. In the *Base Raise* column, write and key a formula that provides everyone with more than 45 performance review points (PRP) a 2% salary increase (round to nearest dollar). Key **0** for those employees not getting a base raise. Format all amount columns as "Accounting."
4. In the *Merit Raise* column, key **$1,500** for each employee with more than 66 PRP.
5. In the *Merit Raise* column, key **$750** for each employee with at least 45 PRP but not more than 66 PRP. Key **0** for those employees not getting a merit raise.
6. In the *Proposed Salary* column, compute the proposed salary for each employee.
7. In the *% Increase* column, compute the percent that each person receives as a raise (round percent to one decimal place).
8. In the row beneath the last employee, compute a sum for each column that contains dollar amounts. Label the row appropriately.
9. In the row below the totals, compute an average for each column that contains a value. Round the PRP average to the nearest whole point.

16C

New-Key Mastery

Key each line twice; DS between 2-line groups. Space quickly after keying each word.

w and right shift
1 Alaska; Wisconsin; Georgia; Florida; South Dakota.
2 Dr. Wick will work the two weekends for Dr. Woods.

n/g
3 eight or nine|sing the songs again|long length of;
4 Dr. Wong arranged the song for singers in Lansing.

key words
5 wet fun ask hot jar cot got use oil add run are of
6 card nice hold gnaw join knew face stew four feat;

key phrases
7 will see|it is the|as it is|did go|when will|if it
8 I will|where is the|when can|use it|and the|of the

all keys learned
9 Nikko Rodgers was the last one to see Jack Fuller.
10 Alfonso Garcia and I took Taisuke Johns to Newark.

16D

Punctuation Spacing

Key each line twice; DS between 2-line groups. Do not space after an internal period in an abbreviation; space once after each period following initials.

No space   Space once.

1 Use i.e. for that is; cs. for case; ck. for check.
2 Dr. West said to use wt. for weight; in. for inch.
3 Jason F. Russell used rd. for road in the address.
4 Dr. Tejada got her Ed.D. degree at Colorado State.

16E

Enrichment

Key each line twice; DS between 2-line groups.

u/c
1 cute luck duck dock cure junk clue just cuff ulcer
2 Luci could see the four cute ducks on the counter.

w and right shift
3 Wade and Will; Don W. Wilson and Frank W. Watkins.
4 Dr. Wise will set the wrist of Sgt. Walsh at noon.

left shift and
5 Julio N. Ortega|Julia T. Santiago|Carlos L. Sillas
6 Lt. Lou Jordan and Lt. Jan Lee left for St. Louis.

n/g
7 gain gown ring long range green grind groan angle;
8 Last night Angie Nagai was walking along the road.

o/t
9 foot other tough total tooth outlet outfit notice;
10 Todd took the two toddlers towards the other road.

i/r
11 ik rf or ore fir fir sir sir ire ire ice ice irons
12 Risa fired the fir log to heat rice for the girls.

For additional practice:

MicroType 6

Alphabetic Keyboarding Lesson 11

Project 17

HPJ From the Desk of
Helen St. Claire

Prepare (don't send) this message as an e-mail to the communication specialists in the Minneapolis branch from Erika Thomas. You will need to get the e-mail addresses from their web page. **New Communication Specialist** is the subject.

June 13   HSC

Communication Specialists,

Stewart Peters will be joining our branch as a Communication Specialist on Monday, July 15.

Stewart grew up in New York, where he completed an undergraduate degree in organizational communication at New York University. He recently completed his master's degree at the University of Minnesota.

Stewart's thesis dealt with interpersonal conflict in the corporate environment. Since we intend to develop a seminar in this area, he will be able to make an immediate contribution.

Please welcome Stewart to HPJ and our branch when he arrives on the 15th.

Erika

Project 18

HPJ From the Desk of
Helen St. Claire

I've started an electronic slide presentation for the annual meeting (*df HPJ project18*). Please insert slides 2–8. I've attached sketches of slides 2, 3, and 4. Slides 5–8 will be similar to slide 4, showing a description of each of the new seminars. Get the information for the slides from the Organizational Chart (Project 16) and from the New Seminar Descriptions table (Project 7) that you completed earlier.

June 13   HSC

Slide 2

Slide 3

New Seminars

▸ Business Etiquette: You Cannot Not Communicate!

▸ Gender Communication: "He Says, She Says."

▸ International Communication

▸ Listen Up!

▸ Technology in the Workplace

LESSON 17   New Keys: b and y

- Learn reach technique for **b** and y.
- Improve **Space Bar** and **Enter** key technique.
- Learn to determine *gwam*.

17A

Warmup

Key each line twice; DS between 2-line groups.

reach review 1 sw ju ft fr ki dc lo .l jh fg ce un jn o. de gu hw

c/n 2 cent neck dance count clean niece concert neglect;

all letters learned 3 Jack and Trish counted the students on the risers.

17B

Space-Bar Mastery

Key each line twice; DS between 2-line groups. Space with a down-and-in motion immediately after each word.

1 Ann has an old car she wants to sell at this sale.

2 Len is to work for us for a week at the lake dock.

3 Gwen is to sign for the auto we set aside for her.

4 Jan is in town for just one week to look for work.

5 Juan said he was in the auto when it hit the tree.

17C

Enter-Key Mastery

1. Key each line twice; at the end of each line, quickly tap the Enter key and immediately start new line.
2. On line 4, see how many words you can key in 30 seconds (30").

1 Dot is to go at two.

2 Joe said he will see us there.

3 Sarah cooked lunch for all of the girls.

4 Glenda took the left turn at the fork in the road.

gwam 30"	2	4	6	8	10	12	14	16	18	20

A **standard word** is five characters or any combination of five characters and spaces, as indicated by the number scale under line 4. The number of standard words keyed in 1' is called **gross words a minute** *(gwam)*.

To find 1-minute (1') *gwam*:

1. Note on the scale the number beneath the last word you keyed. That is your 1' *gwam* if you key the line partially or only once.
2. If you completed the line once and started over, add 10 to the figure determined in step 1. The result is your 1' *gwam*.

To find 30-second (30") *gwam*:

1. Find 1' *gwam* (total words keyed).
2. Multiply 1' *gwam* by 2. The resulting number is your 30" *gwam*.

Here is the company organization chart we have on file (df HPJ project16). Some of the information is missing or outdated. Each branch's website contains the most up-to-date information. Print a copy of the file; then verify the information against that on the website. Mark the changes on the printed copy; finally, make the changes to the master file. Be sure to change the date to today's date, June 12.

HPJ COMMUNICATION SPECIALISTS

Organizational Chart

January 2, 20--

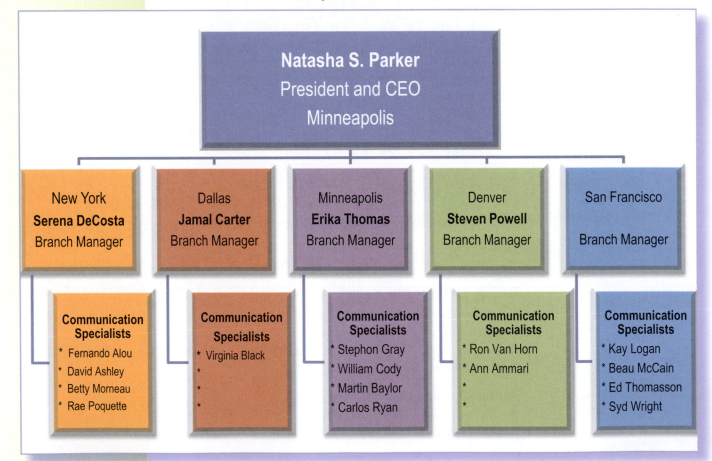

Natasha S. Parker
President and CEO
Minneapolis

New York	Dallas	Minneapolis	Denver	San Francisco
Serena DeCosta	**Jamal Carter**	**Erika Thomas**	**Steven Powell**	
Branch Manager	Branch Manager	Branch Manager	Branch Manager	Branch Manager

Communication Specialists
* Fernando Alou
* David Ashley
* Betty Morneau
* Rae Poquette

Communication Specialists
* Virginia Black
*
*
*

Communication Specialists
* Stephon Gray
* William Cody
* Martin Baylor
* Carlos Ryan

Communication Specialists
* Ron Van Horn
* Ann Ammari
*
*

Communication Specialists
* Kay Logan
* Beau McCain
* Ed Thomasson
* Syd Wright

New Keys: b and y

b *Left index* finger

y *Right index* finger

Key each line twice; DS between 2-line groups.

Learn b

1 f b | fb fb | fob fob | tub tub | bug bug | bat bat | bus bus;

2 bfb bfb | boat boat | boot boot | jobs jobs | habit habit;

3 blue bus; bit bat; brown table; a bug; big hubbub;

Learn y

4 j y | jy jy | yet yet | eye eye | dye dye | say say | day day;

5 yjy yjy | yell yell | stay stay | easy easy | style style;

6 Sunday or Friday; your youth; fly away; any jockey

Combine b and y

7 by by | baby baby | bury bury | lobby lobby | gabby gabby;

8 bay bridge | blue eyes | busy body | noisy boys | baby toy

9 Tabby and Barry had a baby boy with big blue eyes.

New-Key Mastery

Key each line twice; DS between 2-line groups. Reach the finger up to the 3rd-row keys and down to the 1st-row keys without moving hands or arms.

reach review
1 jnj ftf ded kik hjh dcd fgf juj jyj sws lol 1.1 hg
2 how got eat was rat you ice not bat fun done only;

3rd/1st rows
3 nice hit | not now | only twice | were busy | they can be;
4 Cody told both boys before they left for the show.

key words
5 and are the can did was ask far you foil boat note
6 joke dine call ball gold feet hold wash yard flute

key phrases
7 to the | and then | if you want | when will you | you were
8 here is the | this is the | you will be able to | is the

all letters learned
9 Julio and Becky forgot to show Dick their new dog.
10 Barry found two locks by his jacket in the garage.

gwam 1' | 1 | 2 | 3 | 4 | 5 | 6 | 7 | 8 | 9 | 10 |

For additional practice:

MicroType 6

Alphabetic Keyboarding Lesson 12

Internal barriers. Internal barriers are those that deal with the mental or psychological aspects of listening. The perception of the importance of the message, the emotional state, and the ~~running~~ *tun*ing in and out of the speaker by the listener are examples of internal barriers.

External Barriers. External barriers are barriers other than those that deal *with* the mental and psychological makeup of the listener that tend to keep the listener from devoting *full* attention to what is being said. Telephone interruptions, *uninvited* visitors, noise, and the physical environment are examples of external barriers.

Ways to Improve Listening

Barrier*s* to listening can be overcome. However, it does take a sincere ef*f*ort on the part of the ~~speaker~~ *listener*. Neher and Waite suggest the following ways to improve listening skills.[3]

- Be aware of the barriers that are especially troublesome for you. Listening difficulties are individualistic. Developing awareness is an important step in overcoming *such barriers.*

- Listen as though you will have to paraphrase what is being said. Listen for ideas rather than for facts.

- Expect to work *a*t listening. Work at overcoming distractions, such as the speaker's delivery or nonverbal mannerisms.

- Concentrate on summarizing the presentation as you listen. If possible, think of additional supporting material that would fit with the point that the speaker is making. Avoid trying to refute the speaker. Try not to be turned off by remarks *you* disagree with.

---

[1]H. Dan O'Hair, James S. O'Rourke IV, and Mary John O'Hair, *Business Communication: A Framework for Success* (Cincinnati: South-Western Publishing, 2001), p. 211.

[2]Ronald B. Adler and Jeanne Marquardt Elmhorst, *Communicating at Work* (New York: The McGraw-Hill Companies, 2008), p. 77.

[3]William W. Neher and David H. Waite, *The Business and Professional Communicator* (Needham Heights, MA: Allyn and Bacon, 1993), p. 28.

LESSON 18   Review

- Improve spacing and shifting technique.
- Increase keying control and speed.

18A
Keyboard Mastery

Key each line twice; DS between 2-line groups.

Space bar (Space immediately after each word.)

1 She will be able to see the show in a week or two.

2 Jack lost the ball; Gary found it behind the door.

3 Kay and Jo went to the beach to look for starfish.

Shift keys (Shift; tap key; release both quickly.)

4 Dick and Allene went with Elaine to New York City.

5 The New York Knicks host the Boston Celtics today.

6 Don and Jack used the new bats that Jason brought.

18B
Speed Check

Key three 20" timings on each line. Try to go faster on each timing.

1 He can go to town for a shelf.

2 Gary can fish off the dock with us.

3 Jo thanked the girls for doing the work.

4 Becky took the girls to the show on Thursday.

5 Lance and Jared will be there until noon or later.

6 Jose and I should be able to stay for one or two hours.

gwam 20"	3	6	9	12	15	18	21	24	27	30	33

18C
Increase Keying Speed

For additional practice:

MicroType 6

Alphabetic Keyboarding Lesson 13

Key each line twice; DS between 2-line groups. Key the word the first time at an easy speed; repeat it at a faster speed.

1 Juan hikes each day on the side roads near school.

2 Taki and I will take the algebra test on Thursday.

3 Fran told the four boys to take the bus to school.

4 Jordan took the dogs for a walk when he got there.

5 Sandra and I went to the store to buy new outfits.

6 Jennifer will buy the food for the January social.

Project 15

HPJ From the Desk of
Helen St. Claire

Format the text as an unbound report with footnotes (shown at bottom of attached copy). Format the paragraph headings using Heading 3 style. The report will be a handout for the "Listen Up!" seminar.

June 12   HSC

According to Raymond McNulty, Everyone who expects to succeed life should realize that success only will come if you give careful consideration to other people"[1] To acomplish this you must be an excellent listener. One of the most critical skills that an individual acquires is the ability to listen. studies indicate that a person spends 70 percent to 80 percent of their time communicating, of which 32.7% is spent listening. Adler and Elmhorst give the following breakdown for the average individual of time spent communicating.[2]

- Writing 18.8%

- Reading 22.6%

- Speaking 25.8%

- Listening 32.7%

Since most of the time spent communicating is spent listening, it is important to overcome any obstacles that obstruct our ability to listen and to learn new ways to improve our listening ability.

Barriers to Listening

Anything that interferes with our ability to listen is classified as a barrier to listening. Barriers that obstruct our ability to listen can be divided into two basic categories--external and internal barriers.

(Report continued on next page)

WP Applications (continued)

For each activity, read and learn the feature described; then complete the activity as directed.

Activity 4

Undo and Redo

Undo Redo

Use the **Undo** feature to reverse the last change you made in text. Undo restores text to its original location, even if you have moved the insertion point to another position. Use the **Redo** feature to reverse the last Undo action.

1. Create a new document and key the sentence below.

The final show featured the Brooklyn **Band** in concert at the Lincoln Center and the San Francisco **Band** at the Herbst Theatre in the Arts Center.

2. Change *Band* to *Orchestra* in both places.
3. Use the Undo feature to reverse both changes.
4. Use the Redo feature to reverse the last Undo action.
5. **Save as:** *aa2 activity 4*.

Activity 5

Zoom

View/Zoom/
Select Feature

★TIP The – and + on the right side of the Status Line can also be used to zoom out and zoom in.

Use the **Zoom** feature to increase or decrease the amount of the page appearing on the screen. As you decrease the amount of the page appearing on the screen, the print will be larger. Larger print is easier to read and edit. As you increase the amount of the page appearing on the screen, the print becomes smaller. Other options of the Zoom feature include viewing one page, two pages, or multiple pages on the screen.

1. Learn how to use the Zoom feature of your software.
2. Open the *df aa2 activity 5* file. Complete the steps given below. Keep the file open; you will use it in Activity 6.
   a. Step 1: View the document at 75% using the Zoom feature.
   b. Step 2: View the document as a whole page.
   c. Step 3: View the document at 200%.

Activity 6

Print Preview and Print

File/Print

Print

File/Print/Print

Quite often you will want to see the whole page on the screen to check the appearance (margins, spacing, graphics, tables, etc.) of the document prior to printing. You can display an entire page by using the **Print Preview** feature (see Figure 2-7). After previewing the document, you can return to it to make additional changes, or, if no additional changes are required, you can print the document.

1. Learn how to use the Print Preview feature of your software.
2. View the document as a whole page using Print Preview.
3. Print the document.
4. Close the file.

Figure 2-7 Print Preview

HPJ From the Desk of
Helen St. Claire

Prepare a final draft of the attached memo to Natasha from Erika Thomas. The subject is **Monthly Progress Report**. Be sure to include the attachment.

Use Calibri 12 pt. font to key the memo. Use Heading 1 style for the headings in the body of the memo.

June 9   HSC

Here is an update on recent progress of the Minneapolis Branch.

Seminar Bookings

We are fully booked through April and May. Additional communication specialists are desperately needed if we are going to expand into other states in our region. Most of our current bookings are in Minnesota, Iowa, and Wisconsin. We will be presenting in Illinois for the first time in May. I anticipate this will lead to additional bookings that we won't be able to accommodate. This is a problem that I enjoy having. Michigan, Indiana, and Ohio provide ample opportunities for expansion, when resources are made available.

New Seminar

A lot of progress has been made on the new seminar we are developing, "Technology in the Workplace" (see attachment for seminar objectives). Our branch will be ready to preview the seminar at our annual meeting. Not only will the seminar be a great addition to our seminar offerings, but also I believe HPJ can use it to communicate better internally. I will present my ideas when I preview the seminar. The seminar covers:

- Videoconferencing
- Teleconferencing
- Data conferencing
- GroupSystems
- Internet resources

Graphic Designer

A graphic artist has been hired to design all of the materials for the new seminar. He will design promotional items as well as content-related items. Currently he is working on the manual cover and divider pages. These items will be coordinated with the emblems used in the slide show portion of the presentation, along with name tags, promotional paraphernalia, and business cards.

This should give our seminar a more professional appearance. If it works as well as I think it is going to, we will have the designer work on materials for our existing seminars to add the "professional" look.

LESSON 19   New Keys: m and x

OUTCOMES

- Learn reach technique for **m** and **x**.
- Improve reaches to the 1st- and 3rd-row keys.

19A

Warmup

Key each line twice; DS between 2-line groups.

reach review 1 car hit bus get ice not win boy try wait knit yarn

b/y 2 body obey baby busy bury bully byway beauty subway

all letters learned 3 Jerry will take the four cans of beans to Douglas.

19B

New Keys: m and x

Key each line twice; DS between 2-line groups.

Learn m

1 j m | jm jm | jam jam | arm arm | aim aim | man man | ham hams

2 lamb some game firm come dome make warm mark must;

3 more magic; many firms; make money; many mean men;

Learn x

4 s x | sx sx | six six | axe axe | fix fix | box box | tax tax;

5 Lexi Lexi | oxen oxen | exit exit | taxi taxi | axle axle;

6 fix the axle; extra exit; exact tax; excited oxen;

Combine m and x

7 Max Max | mix mix | exam exam | axiom axiom | maxim maxim;

8 tax exams; exact amount; maximum axles; six exams;

9 Max Xiong took the extra exam on the sixth of May.

10 Mary will bike the next day on the mountain roads.

11 Martin and Max took the six boys to the next game.

12 Marty will go with me on the next six rides today.

m *Right index* finger
© Cengage Learning

x *Left ring* finger
© Cengage Learning

Project 12

HPJ Communication Specialists
Interview Schedule for **Jamal Carter**
June 29, 20--, Room 101

Time	Name of Interviewee
1:00 – 1:15	Joan Langston
1:20 – 1:35	Tim Wohlers
1:40 – 1:55	Mark Enqvist
2:00 – 2:15	Stewart Peters
2:20 – 2:35	Felipe Valdez
2:40 – 2: 55	Katarina Dent
3:00 – 3:15	Jennifer Kent
3:20 – 3:35	Sandra Baylor

Project 13

Seminar Objectives for:
Technology in the Workplace
Minneapolis Branch

1. Discuss the role of communication technology in today's business environment and how it has changed over the past ten years.
2. Inform participants of various technological communication tools presently available.
3. Highlight the advantages/disadvantages of these tools presently available.
4. Demonstrate:
   - Videoconferencing
   - Teleconferencing
   - Data conferencing
   - GroupSystems
   - Internet resources
5. Inform participants of various technological communication tools that are in development.
6. Discuss Internet resources available to participants.
7. Discuss how using high-speed communication in today's business environment can give a firm a competitive advantage in the global marketplace.

19C

New-Key Mastery

Key each line twice; DS between 2-line groups. As you key the lines, focus on making the reaches to the 1st- and 3rd-row keys without moving your hands or arms. The movement should be in the fingers.

Goal: finger-action keystrokes; quiet hands and arms

3rd/1st rows
1 no cut not toy but cow box men met bit cot net boy
2 torn core much oxen only time next yarn into north

space bar
3 as ox do if go oh no we of is he an to by in it at
4 jar ask you off got hit old box ice ink man was in

key words
5 mend game team card exam back hold join form enjoy
6 were time yarn oxen four dent mask when dark usual

key phrases
7 she can|go to the|if they will|make the|at the end
8 when will|we will be able|need a|take a look|I can

all keys learned
9 Fabio and Jacki said you would need the right mix.
10 Glen said that he would fix my bike for Jacob Cox.

19D

Spacing and Punctuation

Key each line twice; DS between 2-line groups. Do not space after an internal period in an abbreviation, such as Ed.D.

1 Dr. Smythe and Dr. Ramos left for St. Louis today.
2 Dr. Chen taught us the meaning of f.o.b. and LIFO.
3 Keith got his Ed.D. at NYU; I got my Ed.D. at USU.
4 Sgt. J. Roarke met with Lt. Col. Christina Castro.

19E

Enrichment

For additional practice:

MicroType 6

Alphabetic Keyboarding Lesson 14

Key each line twice; DS between 2-line groups. Keep the insertion point moving steadily across each line (no pauses).

m/x
1 Mary Fox and Maxine Cox took all six of the exams.

b/y
2 Burly Bryon Beyer barely beat Barb Byrnes in golf.

w/right shift
3 Carlos DeRosa defeated Wade Cey in the last match.

u/c
4 The clumsy ducks caused Lucy Lund to hit the curb.

./left shift
5 Keith and Mike went to St. Louis to see Mr. Owens.

n/g
6 Glen began crying as Ginny began singing the song.

o/t
7 Tom bought a total of two tons of tools yesterday.

i/r
8 Rick and Maria tried to fix the tire for the girl.

h/e
9 Helen Hale heard her tell them to see the hostess.

Project 10

HPJ From the Desk of
Helen St. Claire

Format the attached agenda for the Branch Manager Annual Meeting that Ms. Parker will be facilitating. Use the agenda template (*df HPJ project10 template*). You will need to modify the template to fit the agenda items. The meeting will start at 9 a.m. on June 26. All branch managers will be invited to attend the meeting.

June 8   HSC

Agenda

I.   Call to order
II. Greetings
III. Roll call
IV. Approval of minutes from last meeting
V.   Discussion items
     a) Seminars
        1. Enhancement
        2. Expansion
        3. Client base
     b) Leadership
     c) Company growth
        1. Regional expansion
        2. International expansion
     d) Employee incentives
        1. Branch managers
        2. Communication specialists
     e) Technology
VI. Miscellaneous
VII. Adjournment

Project 11

HPJ From the Desk of
Helen St. Claire

Ms. Parker would like the attached letter sent to the branch managers. Enclose a copy of the agenda and the hotel confirmation (when it's available) with the letter. Save each letter with the last name of the addressee, e.g., *HPJ project11 Carter.*

June 8   HSC

Attached is the agenda for the annual meeting. I didn't hear from any of you about additions to the agenda; so if you have items to discuss, we can include them under Miscellaneous.

Your accommodations have been made for the McIntyre Inn. Your confirmation is enclosed. A limousine will pick you up at the Inn at 8:30 a.m. on Monday. Activities have been planned for Monday and Wednesday evenings. Tuesday and Thursday mornings have been left open. You can arrange something on your own, or we can make group arrangements. We'll decide on Monday before adjourning for the day.

I'm looking forward to seeing you on the 26th.

LESSON 20 New Keys: p and v

New Keys: p and v

- Learn reach technique for **p** and **v**.
- Improve Shift and Enter key technique.

20A
Warmup

Key each line twice SS; DS between 2-line groups.

Fingers curved

Fingers upright

Hard return

one-hand words
1 rare gear seed hill milk lion bare moon base onion

balanced-hand words
2 town wish corn fork dish held coal owns rich their

all letters learned
3 Gabe Waxon may ask us to join him for lunch today.

20B
New Keys: p and v

Key each line twice; DS between 2-line groups. If time permits, key lines 7–9 again.

p *Right little* finger

v *Left index* finger

Learn p

1 ; p ;p ;p|put put|pin pin|pay pay|pop pop|sap sap;

2 pull pull park park open open soap soap hoop hoops

3 a purple puppet; pay plan; plain paper; poor poet;

Learn v

4 f v fv fv|van van|vain vain|very very|value value;

5 over over|vote vote|save save|move move|dove dove;

6 drive over; seven verbs; value driven; viable vote

Combine p and v

7 cave push gave pain oven pick jive keep very river

8 have revised; river view; five to seven; even vote

9 Eva and Paul have to pick papa up to vote at five.

Project 8

HPJ From the Desk of
Helen St. Claire

Ms. Parker would like you to create an HPJ Communication Specialists database with a table for *Employee Information* with the fields that are shown at the right. Key the information for all employees into the database.

I've attached a file (*df HPJ project8 notes*) with notes that should help you complete the project. The information for the database can be found in the data file (*df HPJ project8*), on the company website, and given at the right. I've also created a worksheet (*df HPJ project8 worksheet*) that you may want to use for gathering the data.

June 6   HSC

Project 9

HPJ From the Desk of
Helen St. Claire

Compose (don't send) an e-mail to the Webmaster (jensenra@cengage.com) asking her to update the address information for the New York branch on the company website. Ask her to correct Serena DeCosta's e-mail address on the website, also. It should be decostsl instead of decostas. You will need to make that correction in the contacts file you created for Project 1.

June 6   HSC

Employee Information

ID	1	E-mail Address	parkerns
Last Name	Parker	Work Phone Number	(612) 555-0418
First Name	Natasha	Extension	1200
Middle Initial	S.	Date of Birth	June 15, 1970
Branch	Headquarters	Employee ID	547-18
Job Title	President and CEO	Gender	Female
		Employment Start Date	9/1/1991

Employee ID Numbers

Employee	ID No.	Employee	ID No.
Ammari, Ann	382-49	Morina, Jarrod	302-18
Ashley, David	497-23	Morneau, Betty	279-43
Black, Virginia	127-88	Parker, Natasha	547-18
Carter, Jamal	385-61	Polacheck, Jan	675-66
Casey, Shawn	420-29	Poquette, Rae	150-32
Cey, Donald	303-61	Powell, Steven	576-39
Cody, William	569-17	Redford, Jason	295-36
DeCosta, Serena	202-57	Ryan, Carlos	129-54
Dent, Marsha	801-74	St. Claire, Helen	350-32
Gibbons, Tracy	245-71	Thomas, Erika	465-01
Gray, Stephon	908-17	Thomasson, Ed	394-29
Logan, Kay	570-45	Van Horn, Ron	616-89
Lopez, Miguel	129-06	Wright, Syd	545-11
McCain, Beau	609-40		

20C

New-Key Mastery

Key each line twice; DS between 2-line groups. As you key the lines, focus on making the reaches to the 1st- and 3-row keys without moving your hands or arms. The movement should be in the fingers.

reach review
1 fv fr ft fg fb jn jm jh jy ju l. lo sx sw dc de ;p
2 free kind junk swim loan link half golf very plain

3rd/1st rows
3 oven cove oxen went been nice more home rice phone
4 not item river their newer price voice point crime

key words
5 pair pays pens vigor vivid vogue panel proxy opens
6 jam kept right shake shelf shape soap visit visual

key phrases
7 pay them|their signs|vote for|when will|if they go
8 you will be|much of the|when did they|to see their

all letters learned
9 Crew had seven of the votes; Brooks had only five.
10 They just left the park and went to see Dr. Nixon.

20D

Shift and Enter-Key Mastery

1. Key each line once; at the end of each line, quickly tap the Enter key and immediately start the next line.
2. On lines 7 and 8, see how many words you can key in 30".

1 Mary was told to buy the coat.
2 Vern is to choose a high goal.

3 Jay and Livan did not like to golf.
4 Ramon Mota took the test on Monday.

5 Lexi told Scott to set his goals higher.
6 Eric and I keyed each line of the drill.

7 Roberto excels in most of the things he does.
8 Vivian can key much faster than Jack or Kate.

gwam 1' | 1 | 2 | 3 | 4 | 5 | 6 | 7 | 8 | 9 | 10 |

20E

Enrichment

For additional practice:

MicroType 6

Alphabetic Keyboarding
Lesson 16

Key each line twice; DS between 2-line groups.

m/p
1 plum bump push mark jump limp camp same post maple
2 Pete sampled the plums; Mark sampled the apricots.

b/x
3 box exact able except abide job expand debt extend
4 Dr. Nixon placed the six textbooks in the taxicab.

y/v
5 very verb eyes vent layer even days save yard vast
6 Darby Vance may take the gray van to Vivian today.

Project 5

HPJ From the Desk of
Helen St. Claire

Prepare (don't send) the attached message as an e-mail from Ms. Parker to the branch managers. Attach the job description that you created. Get e-mail addresses from your contacts file you created for Project 1.

June 7   HSC

SUBJECT: JOB DESCRIPTION FOR COMMUNICATION SPECIALISTS

I've attached a draft of the job description for the communication specialists that we will be hiring for each branch. I wanted to give each of you an opportunity to review it before we advertise for the positions in the newspaper.

If there are additional responsibilities that you would like to see included with the job description before we post it, please let me know by Friday. The advertisement will run in the <u>Star</u> on Sunday and appear on its Job Board website next week. I'm confident that we will have an even greater interest in the positions than we had when we hired a couple of communication specialists last January.

Project 6

HPJ From the Desk of
Helen St. Claire

The New York branch has moved into their new office located at 488 Broadway. The ZIP Code is 10012-3871. Update your contact file information for Serena DeCosta to reflect this change.

June 7   HSC

New Seminar Descriptions

Seminar Title	Seminar Description	Cost per Person
Business Etiquette: You Cannot Not Communicate!		$99
Gender Communications: "He Says, She Says"		$75
International Communication		$75
Listen Up!		$99
Technology in the Workplace		$125

Project 7

HPJ From the Desk of
Helen St. Claire

Create the attached *New Seminar Descriptions* table. You can copy and paste seminar descriptions from our website. Leave one blank line before and after each description.

June 7   HSC

LESSON 21

OUTCOMES

New Keys: q and Comma (,)

- Learn reach technique for **q** and , (comma).
- Improve reach technique to 1st- and 3rd-row keys.

21A

Warmup

Key each line twice; DS between 2-line groups.

all letters learned 1 dash give wind true flop comb yolk joke hunt gain;

p/v 2 prove vapor above apple voted super cover preview;

all letters learned 3 Mary forced Jack to help move six big water units.

21B

New Keys: q and , (comma)

Key each line twice; DS between 2-line groups.

q *Left little* finger

, (comma) *Right middle* finger

TIP Space once after , (comma) used as punctuation.

Learn q

1 a q aq|quit quit|aqua aqua|quick quick|quote quote

2 quest quest|quart quart|quite quite|liquid liquid;

3 quite quiet; quick squirrel; chi square; a quarter

Learn , (comma)

4 , k ,k ,k one, two, three, four, five, six, seven,

5 Akio, Baiko, Niou, and Joji are exchange students.

6 Juan, Rico, and Mike voted; however, Jane did not.

Combine q and , (comma)

7 Quota, square, quiche, and quite were on the exam.

8 Quin can spell Quebec, Nicaragua, Iraq, and Qatar.

9 Joaquin, Jacque, and Javier sailed for Martinique.

10 Quin, Jacqueline, and Paque quickly took the exam.

11 Rob quickly won my squad over quip by brainy quip.

12 Quit, quiet, and quaint were on the spelling exam.

Project 3

HPJ From the Desk of
Helen St. Claire

I've started the attached letter from Ms. Parker to the branch managers. It is saved as *df HPJ project3*. Please finish the letter. Refer to the Application Guide for formatting the heading for the second page of a letter. Save each letter with the last name of the addressee, e.g., *HPJ project3 Carter*.

June 5   HSC

Technology. The changed marketplace is demanding that we explore new ways of delivering our seminars. How can we better use technology to deliver our product? This may include putting selected seminars online, inter- and intra-company communication, etc.

Company growth. What steps can we take to increase company growth? Last year revenues grew by 15 percent; our expenses grew by 8 percent.

Employee incentives. Last year we implemented a branch manager profit-sharing plan. Some of you have indicated that we need to expand this profit-sharing plan to include our communication specialists.

Regional expansion. Some of the regions have been very successful. How do we capitalize on that success? Is it time to divide the successful regions?

International expansion. **HPJ** has put on several seminars overseas—at a very high cost. Is it time to start thinking about creating a branch of **HPJ** at a strategic overseas location?

I am proud of what we have been able to accomplish this year. The foundation is in place, and we are ready to grow. Each of you plays a critical role in the success of **HPJ**. Thank you for your dedication and commitment to making our company the "leader in providing corporate and individual communication training." Best wishes for continued success. I'm looking forward to discussing **HPJ's** future at this year's annual meeting. If you have additional items that you would like included on the agenda, please get them to me before June 15.

Project 4

HPJ From the Desk of
Helen St. Claire

Format the attached Job Description. I've included some notes. In order to get the title on two lines, you need to key the entire title on one line and then go back and tap Enter before HPJ.

June 6   HSC

2" TM—Use 12 pt. Calibri for body

Job Description
HPJ Communication Specialist

HPJ Communication Specialists work cooperatively with other branch members to develop and deliver communication seminars throughout the United States.

Position Requirements

a. College degree
b. Excellent oral and written communication skills
c. Excellent interpersonal skills
d. Technology skills
e. Knowledge of business concepts

Duties and Responsibilities

a. Research seminar topics
b. Develop seminars
c. Prepare electronic presentations for seminars
d. Prepare seminar manual
e. Present seminars

21C

New-Key Mastery

Key each line twice; DS between 2-line groups. As you key the lines, focus on keeping all movement in the fingers.

reach review
1 jh fg l. o. k, I, ft sw aq de ;p fr jn jb fv jn jm
2 We can leave now. Take Nancy, Michael, and Jorge.

3rd/1st rows
3 nice bond many when oxen come vent quit very prom;
4 drive a truck|know how to|not now|when will you be

key words
5 have jail wept quit desk from goes cave yarn boxer
6 brand extra cycle event equip know fight made show

key phrases
7 when will you|may be able to|if you can|he will be
8 ask about the|need to be|where will|as you can see

all letters learned
9 The quaint old maypole was fixed by Jackie Groves.
10 Very fixed the job growth plans quickly on Monday.

21D

Spacing with Punctuation

Key each twice; DS between 2-line groups. Space once after , (comma) or ; (semicolon) used as punctuation.

1 Jay asked the question; Tim answered the question.

2 Ann, Joe, and I saw the bus; Mark and Ted did not.

3 I had ibid., op. cit., and loc. cit. in the paper.

4 The Mets, Dodgers, Cardinals, and Padres competed.

21E

Enrichment

Key each line twice; DS between 2-line groups.

Adjacent keys

1 ew mn vb tr op iu ty bv xc fg jh df ;l as kj qw er

2 week oily free join dash very true wash tree rash;

3 union point extra river tracks water cover weapon;

Long direct reaches

4 ny many ce rice my myself mu mute gr grand hy hype

5 lunch hatch vouch newsy bossy yearn beyond crabby;

6 gabby bridge muggy venture machine beauty luncheon

Double letters

7 book feet eggs seek cell jeer keep mall adds occur

8 class little sheep effort needle assist happy seem

9 Tennessee Minnesota Illinois Mississippi Missouri;

For additional practice:

MicroType 6

**Alphabetic Keyboarding
Lesson 16**

LESSONS 81–85 HPJ Communication Specialists: An Integrated Project

OUTCOMES

- Apply *Word, Outlook, PowerPoint, Access,* and *Excel* application skills in an integrated project.
- Use your decision-making skills to process documents.
- Improve your ability to read and follow directions.

81A–85A

Warmup

Key each line twice daily.

alphabet	1	Seven complete textbooks were required for the new zoology major.
figures	2	Shipping charges ($35.98) were included on the invoice (#426087).
speed	3	A sick dog slept on the oak chair in the dismal hall of the dorm.

gwam 1' | 1 | 2 | 3 | 4 | 5 | 6 | 7 | 8 | 9 | 10 | 11 | 12 | 13 |

81–85B

Project 1

HPJ From the Desk of
Helen St. Claire

You will be corresponding with the branch managers frequently. Create an HPJ Branch Managers contact folder, and key contact information for each of the branch managers as shown at the right. You will need to get the information for the other three managers from the company website.

June 5   HSC

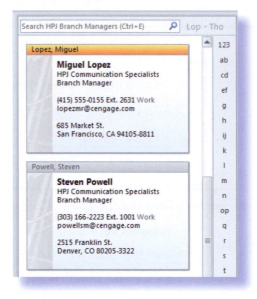

Search HPJ Branch Managers (Ctrl+E)   Lop - Tho

Lopez, Miguel

Miguel Lopez
HPJ Communication Specialists
Branch Manager

(415) 555-0155 Ext. 2631 Work
lopezmr@cengage.com

685 Market St.
San Francisco, CA 94105-8811

Powell, Steven

Steven Powell
HPJ Communication Specialists
Branch Manager

(303) 166-2223 Ext. 1001 Work
powellsm@cengage.com

2515 Franklin St.
Denver, CO 80205-3322

123 ab cd ef g h ij k l m n op q r s t

Project 2

HPJ From the Desk of
Helen St. Claire

Ms. Parker wants the attached letter sent to each branch manager. Find mailing addresses from your contacts. Save each letter with the last name of the addressee, e.g., *HPJ project2 Carter.*

June 5   HSC

Dear

Each of you has indicated a need for additional personnel. I've heard your requests. With this quarter's increase in seminar revenues, I am now in a position to respond to them. Five new communication specialist positions, one for each branch, have been added.

Since training for the positions takes place here at the home office, it is more cost effective to hire communication specialists from this area. I will take care of recruitment and preliminary screening. However, since each of you will work closely with the individual hired, I think you should make the final selection.

When you are here for the annual meeting, I'll schedule time for you to interview eight individuals. If you are not satisfied with any of the eight, we will arrange additional interviews. I should have a job description created within the next week. When it is completed, I'll send it to you for your review.

LESSON 22   Review

• Improve keying technique and speed.

22A

Keyboarding Skill Mastery

Key each line twice; DS between 2-line groups.

1 Vivian may make their formal gowns for the social.
2 It may be a problem if both men work for the city.
3 The antique box is in the big field by the chapel.
4 The man paid a visit to the firm to sign the form.
5 He works with the men at the dock to fix problems.
6 The rich man may work with Jan to fix the bicycle.

22B

Speed Check

Key three 20" timings on each line. Try to go faster on each timing.

1 You will need to buy the book.
2 Jana will have to pay the late fee.
3 Scott and James left for Utah yesterday.
4 Reed has not set a date for the next meeting.
5 I will not be able to finish the book before then.
6 Enrique took the final exam before he left for Georgia.

gwam 20" | 3 | 6 | 9 | 12 | 15 | 18 | 21 | 24 | 27 | 30 | 33 |

22C

Increase Keying Speed

For additional practice:

MicroType 6

Alphabetic Keyboarding Lesson 17

Key each line twice; DS between 2-line groups. If time permits, key a 30" timing on each line.

1 It is a civic duty to handle the problem for them.
2 Six of the city firms may handle the fuel problem.
3 Jay may make an authentic map for the title firms.
4 Hal and Orlando work at the store by the big lake.
5 I may make a shelf for the neighbor on the island.
6 Rick and I may go to town to make the eight signs.
7 He may blame the boy for the problem with the bus.
8 Jan Burns is the chair of the big sorority social.

gwam 30" | 2 | 4 | 6 | 8 | 10 | 12 | 14 | 16 | 18 | 20 |

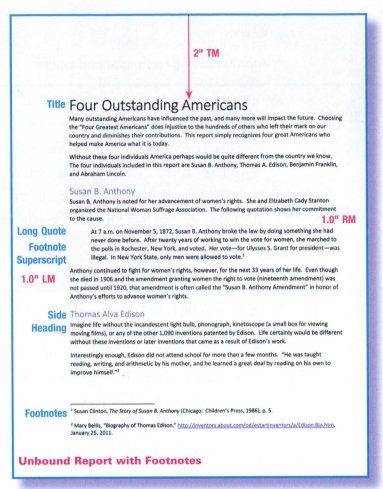

2" TM

Title Four Outstanding Americans

Many outstanding Americans have influenced the past, and many more will impact the future. Choosing the "Four Greatest Americans" does injustice to the hundreds of others who left their mark on our country and diminishes their contributions. This report simply recognizes four great Americans who helped make America what it is today.

Without these four individuals America perhaps would be quite different from the country we know. The four individuals included in this report are Susan B. Anthony, Thomas A. Edison, Benjamin Franklin, and Abraham Lincoln.

Susan B. Anthony

Susan B. Anthony is noted for her advancement of women's rights. She and Elizabeth Cady Stanton organized the National Woman Suffrage Association. The following quotation shows her commitment to the cause.

1.0" RM

Long Quote At 7 a.m. on November 5, 1872, Susan B. Anthony broke the law by doing something she had
Footnote never done before. After twenty years of working to win the vote for women, she marched to
Superscript the polls in Rochester, New York, and voted. Her vote—for Ulysses S. Grant for president—was
illegal. In New York State, only men were allowed to vote.[1]

1.0" LM Anthony continued to fight for women's rights, however, for the next 33 years of her life. Even though she died in 1906 and the amendment granting women the right to vote (nineteenth amendment) was not passed until 1920, that amendment is often called the "Susan B. Anthony Amendment" in honor of Anthony's efforts to advance women's rights.

Side Thomas Alva Edison
Heading Imagine life without the incandescent light bulb, phonograph, kinetoscope (a small box for viewing moving films), or any of the other 1,090 inventions patented by Edison. Life certainly would be different without these inventions or later inventions that came as a result of Edison's work.

Interestingly enough, Edison did not attend school for more than a few months. "He was taught reading, writing, and arithmetic by his mother, and he learned a great deal by reading on his own to improve himself."[2]

Footnotes [1] Susan Clinton, *The Story of Susan B. Anthony* (Chicago: Children's Press, 1986), p. 5.

[2] Mary Bellis, "Biography of Thomas Edison," http://inventors.about.com/od/estartinventors/a/Edison.Bio.htm, January 25, 2011.

Unbound Report with Footnotes

Figure 16-3 Format Guide: Report

When sending an e-mail to all five branch managers, use **Branch Managers** for the opening line and *Natasha* for the closing line of the e-mail message, as shown in the illustration below.

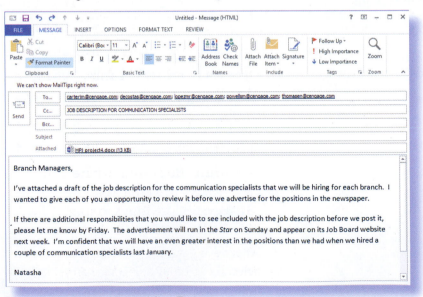

Figure 16-4 Format Guide: E-mail

Activity 7

Margins

Page Layout/Page Setup/
Margins

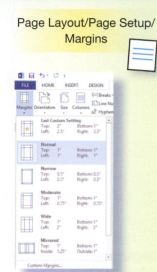

Figure 2-8 Setting margins

For each activity, read and learn the feature described; then complete the activity as directed.

Use the **Margins** feature to change the amount of blank space at the top, bottom, right, and left edges of the paper (see Figure 2-8). The default margin settings are not the same for all software.

1. Open the **df aa2 activity 7** file.
2. Change the margins to the Wide margin option.
3. Change the left and right margins to 2.5" and the top margin to 2" using the Custom Margins option.
4. **Save as:** *aa2 activity 7*.

Margins are the white space left between the edge of the paper and the print. When the right and left margins are increased, the length of the line of text will be decreased. When the top and bottom margins are increased, the number of lines of text that can be placed on a page will be decreased.

Of course, increasing or decreasing the size of the font also changes the amount of text that appears on a page. You will understand this concept better when you learn about fonts later in the book.

Activity 8

Line and Paragraph Spacing

Home/Paragraph/Line and
Paragraph Spacing

Line and Paragraph
Spacing

Use the **Line Spacing** feature to change the amount of white space left between lines of text. Single spacing, one-and-a-half spacing, and double spacing are common to most software.

There is a default setting of 10 points (Word 2010) or 8 points (Word 2013) after each paragraph. This allows a little more white space between lines of type than a default setting of 1. The default is treated as single spacing.

1. Open the **df aa2 activity 8** file.
2. Move the cursor to the end of the file following the word *spacing*.
3. Change the line spacing to 1 and *remove space after paragraph*.
4. Finish keying the first line and the next three lines shown below. (The line numbers will appear automatically; you will not need to key them.)

   1. Click the I-beam where you want the line spacing changed.
   2. Access the Line Spacing feature.
   3. Specify the line spacing.
   4. Begin or continue keying.

5. After keying the last line, copy and paste the four lines a triple space below the last line.
6. Select the last four lines and change the line spacing to 2.
7. **Save as:** *aa2 activity 8*.

Note: If a letter or memo is longer than one page, a header is placed on all pages except the first using the Header feature. The header consists of three lines blocked at the left margin. Line 1 contains the addressee's name, line 2 contains the word *Page* and the page number, and line 3 contains the date.

Ms. Charla Ramirez
Page 2
May 28, 20—

Figure 16-2 Format Guide: Letter

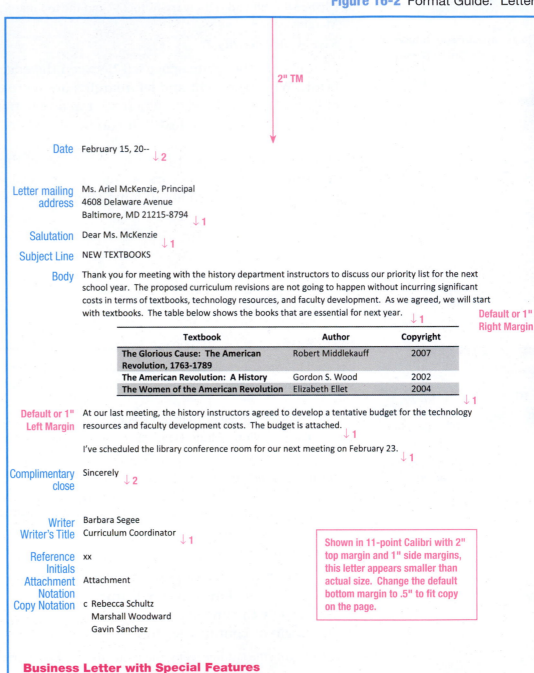

Date February 15, 20-- ↓ 2

Letter mailing address Ms. Ariel McKenzie, Principal
4608 Delaware Avenue
Baltimore, MD 21215-8794 ↓ 1

Salutation Dear Ms. McKenzie ↓ 1

Subject Line NEW TEXTBOOKS

Body Thank you for meeting with the history department instructors to discuss our priority list for the next school year. The proposed curriculum revisions are not going to happen without incurring significant costs in terms of textbooks, technology resources, and faculty development. As we agreed, we will start with textbooks. The table below shows the books that are essential for next year. ↓ 1

Default or 1" Right Margin

Textbook	Author	Copyright
The Glorious Cause: The American Revolution, 1763-1789	Robert Middlekauff	2007
The American Revolution: A History	Gordon S. Wood	2002
The Women of the American Revolution	Elizabeth Ellet	2004

↓ 1

Default or 1" Left Margin At our last meeting, the history instructors agreed to develop a tentative budget for the technology resources and faculty development costs. The budget is attached. ↓ 1

I've scheduled the library conference room for our next meeting on February 23. ↓ 1

Complimentary close Sincerely ↓ 2

Writer Barbara Segee
Writer's Title Curriculum Coordinator ↓ 1

Reference Initials xx

Attachment Notation Attachment

Copy Notation c Rebecca Schultz
  Marshall Woodward
  Gavin Sanchez

Shown in 11-point Calibri with 2" top margin and 1" side margins, this letter appears smaller than actual size. Change the default bottom margin to .5" to fit copy on the page.

Business Letter with Special Features

2" TM

LESSON 23

OUTCOMES

New Keys: z and Colon (:)

- Learn reach technique for **z** and : (colon).
- Improve keying speed on paragraph copy.

23A

Warmup

Key each line twice; then key a 1' timing on line 3; determine *gwam*.

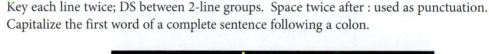

all letters learned	1	Jack quickly helped Mary Newton fix the big stove.
spacing	2	it is|if you can|by the end|when will he|to be the
easy	3	Helen may go to the city to buy the girls a shake.
gwam	1'	1 | 2 | 3 | 4 | 5 | 6 | 7 | 8 | 9 | 10 |

23B

New Keys: z and : (colon)

Key each line twice; DS between 2-line groups. Space twice after : used as punctuation. Capitalize the first word of a complete sentence following a colon.

z Left little finger

: Left Shift and tap : key

Learn z

1 a z a z|az az|zap zap|zip zip|raze raze|size size;

2 daze daze|maze maze|lazy lazy|hazy hazy|zest zest;

3 Utah Jazz; hazel eyes; loud buzz; zoology quizzes;

Learn : (colon)

4 ;: ;:|a:A b:B c:C d:D e:E f:F g:G h:H i:I j:J kK1L

5 M:m N:n O:o P:p Q:q R:r S:s T:t U:u V: w: X: y: Z:

6 Dear Mr. Baker: Dear Dr. Finn: Dear Mrs. Fedder:

Combine z and :

7 Liz invited the following: Hazel, Inez, and Zach.

8 Use these headings: Zip Code: Zone: Zoo: Jazz:

9 Buzz, spell these words: size, fizzle, and razor.

10 Dear Mr. Perez: Dear Ms. Ruiz: Dear Mrs. Mendez:

Document Formats

During your training program, you were instructed to use block format for all company letters and the unbound format for company reports. Additional general instructions will be attached to each document you are given to process. Use the date included on the instructions for all documents requiring a date.

As with a real job, you will be expected to work independently and learn on your own how to do some things that you haven't previously been taught using resources that are available to you. You will also be expected to use your decision-making skills to arrange documents attractively whenever specific instructions are not provided. Since HPJ has based its word processing manual on the *Century 21* textbook, you can refer to this text in making formatting decisions. In addition to your textbook, you can use the Help feature of your software to review a feature you may have forgotten or to learn new features you may need.

HPJ is extremely concerned about the image it presents to the public. You are expected to produce error-free documents, so check spelling, proofread, and correct your work carefully before presenting it for approval. Errors are unacceptable.

Use the following formatting guides to prepare memos, letters, reports, and e-mails. If you have additional questions about format, refer to your textbook.

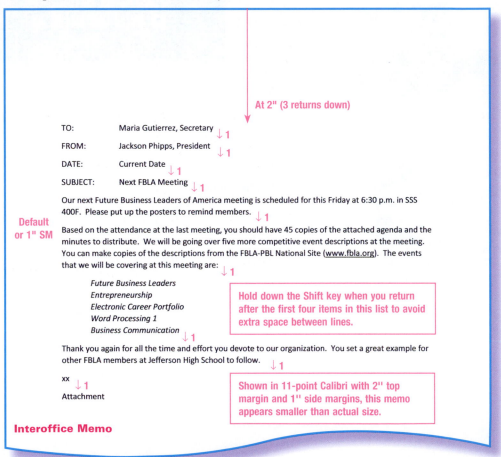

Figure 16-1 Format Guide: Memo

23C

New-Key Mastery

Key each line twice; DS between 2-line groups. Keep fingers curved and upright.

q/z
1 zoom hazy quit prize dozen freeze quizzed equalize
2 Zoe was quite amazed by the quaint city of La Paz.

p/x
3 pox expect example explore perplex explain complex
4 Tex picked six apples for a pie for Rex and Pedro.

v/m
5 move vase mean veal make vice mark very comb above
6 Mavis came to visit Mark, Vivian, Val, and Marvin.

easy
7 Their maid may pay for all the land by the chapel.
8 The auditor may do the work for the big city firm.

alphabet
9 Glenn saw a quick red fox jump over the lazy cubs.
10 Gavin quickly explained what Joby made for prizes.

23D

Block Paragraphs

1. Key each paragraph (¶) once SS; DS between ¶s; then key them again faster.
2. Key a 1' timing on each ¶; determine your *gwam*.

Paragraph 1

gwam 1'

A good team member is honest, does a fair share of   10
the work, and is eager to help another team member   20
if there is a need to do so. Quite often the best   30
team member must be a superb follower as well as a   40
good leader.   43

Paragraph 2

There are several other skills that a person ought   10
to acquire in order to become a good leader. Such   20
skills as the ability to think, listen, speak, and   30
write are essential for a good leader to possess.   40

gwam 1' | 1 | 2 | 3 | 4 | 5 | 6 | 7 | 8 | 9 | 10 |

Company Website

The company has a website (www.cengage.com/school/keyboarding/hpj) containing the following information:

- HPJ branch locations
- Address and phone number for each branch
- Contact information and bios for each branch manager
- Contact information and bios for each communication specialist
- New seminar descriptions

Dallas Branch
Jamal Carter, Manager

New York Branch
Serena DeCosta, Manager

Denver Branch
Steven Powell, Manager

San Francisco Branch
Miguel Lopez, Manager

Minneapolis Branch
Erika Thomas, Manager

Employee Bios
Link to Upcoming Seminars

You will need to access the website to gather information to complete some of the projects you are working on for Ms. St. Claire.

Data Files

Some of the projects you will be working on have already been started or require information from previously created documents. You will need to access the company data files to complete these projects.

File Naming

In order to quickly access information, HPJ has established a *file-naming* system that is used by company employees. It is very simple. All files you create should be named with *HPJ*, followed by the project number (*HPJ project1, HPJ project2*, etc.).

23E

Timed Writing

1. Key a 1' timing on each ¶.
2. Key two 2' timings on ¶s 1–2 combined; determine *gwam*.

LA all letters used

		gwam	2'
Laura Ingalls Wilder is a beloved writer of books for			5
children. Most of her books are based on her own experiences			12
as a youth. Her first book was about her life in Wisconsin.			18
From just reading such a book, children fantasize about what			24
it would have been like to live with the pioneers during this			30
time period of our nation.			33
Besides writing about her own life and the lives of her			38
family members, she also wrote about the life of her husband,			45
Almanzo, and his family. Her second book was about the early			51
years of his life growing up on a farm near the Canadian bor-			57
der in the state of New York. Through these exquisite books,			63
this period of time in our history is preserved forever.			69

gwam 2' | 1 | 2 | 3 | 4 | 5 | 6 |

23F

Enrichment

For additional practice:

MicroType 6

Alphabetic Keyboarding
Lesson 18

Key each line twice SS; DS between 2-line groups.

One-hand words (Think and key by letter response.)

1 bear aware data gave edge states race great street

2 ink pin you hook milk moon only join union million

Balanced-hand words (Think and key by word response.)

3 oak box land sign make busy kept foal handle gowns

4 chair disown mantle right world theme towns theory

One-hand sentences (Think and key by letter response.)

5 Jim gazed at a radar gadget we gave him in a case.

6 Dave saved a dazed polo pony as we sat on a knoll.

Balanced-hand sentences (Think and key by word response.)

7 Rick may make them turn by the lake by their sign.

8 Jane may go to the city to work for the six firms.

HPJ Communication Specialists: An Integrated Project

Work Assignment

© Ryan McVay/Photodisc/Getty Images

Ms. Natasha Parker
President & CEO

© Ryan McVay/Photodisc/Getty Images

Ms. Helen St. Claire
Administrative Assistant

HPJ Communication Specialists prepares, organizes, and delivers communication training seminars. Three partners—Stewart **H**errick, Natasha **P**arker, and Spencer **J**orstad—founded the company in 1991. In 1998, Ms. Parker bought out the other two partners. Today the company has five branches located in Dallas, Denver, Minneapolis, New York, and San Francisco. Company headquarters are located in Minneapolis, Minnesota.

You have been hired by HPJ to work part-time on some of the projects that have been assigned to Helen St. Claire. Ms. St. Claire is an administrative assistant for the president and CEO, Natasha S. Parker, as well as for Erika Thomas, the Minneapolis branch manager.

In this position you will be required to use:

- *Word* to prepare letters, memos, reports, agendas, etc.
- *Outlook* for e-mail communication and to manage contact information
- *Access* to create and maintain a database of employee information
- *Excel* to construct a worksheet to calculate salary increases
- *PowerPoint* to design slide presentations for meetings

Photo Courtesy of the Author.

HPJ Communication Specialists
3251 Wayzata Blvd.
Minneapolis, MN 55461-4533
Telephone (612) 555-0418

LESSON 24 New Keys: Caps Lock and Question Mark (?)

OUTCOMES

- Learn reach technique for **Caps Lock** and **?** (question mark).
- Improve keying speed on paragraph copy.

24A

Warmup

Key each line twice; then key a 1' timing on line 3; determine *gwam*.

alphabet	1	Zosha was quick to dive into my big pool for Jinx.
z/:	2	To: Ms. Lizza Guzzo From: Dr. Beatriz K. Vasquez
easy	3	The firms paid for both of the signs by city hall.

gwam 1' | 1 | 2 | 3 | 4 | 5 | 6 | 7 | 8 | 9 | 10 |

24B

New Keys: Caps Lock and ? (Question Mark)

Tap the Caps Lock to key a series of capital letters. To release the Caps Lock to key lowercase letters, tap it again.

Caps Lock *Left little* finger

? (question mark) *Left shift*; then *right little* finger

Key each line twice; DS between 2-line groups.

© Cengage Learning, 2013

Learn caps lock

1 The CARDINALS will play the PHILLIES on Wednesday.

2 Use SLC for SALT LAKE CITY and BTV for BURLINGTON.

3 THE GRAPES OF WRATH was written by JOHN STEINBECK.

Learn ? (question mark)

Space twice.

4 :? :? ;? ;? ?; ?; Who? ↓ What? ↓ When? ↓ Where? ↓ Why? ↓

5 When will they arrive? Will you go? Where is he?

6 What time is it? Who called? Where is the dance?

Combine caps lock and ?

7 Is CSCO the ticker symbol for CISCO? What is MMM?

8 MEMORIAL DAY is in MAY; LABOR DAY is in SEPTEMBER.

9 When do the CUBS play the TWINS? Is it on SUNDAY?

10 Did Julie fly to Kansas City, MISSOURI, or KANSAS?

11 Did Dr. Rodriguez pay her DPE, PBL, and NBEA dues?

12 Did you say go TWO blocks EAST or TWO blocks WEST?

1. Key a 1' timing on ¶ 1; determine *gwam*.

2. Add 2–4 *gwam* to the rate attained in step 1; determine quarter-minute checkpoints from the chart at the left.

3. Key two 1' guided timings on ¶ 1 to increase speed.

4. Practice ¶ 2 in the same way.

5. Key two 3' timings on ¶s 1 and 2 combined; determine *gwam* and the number of errors.

Quarter-Minute Checkpoints

gwam	1/4'	1/2'	3/4'	1'
24	6	12	18	24
28	7	14	21	28
32	8	16	24	32
36	9	18	27	36
40	10	20	30	40
44	11	22	33	44
48	12	24	36	48
52	13	26	39	52
56	14	28	42	56
60	15	30	45	60

A all letters used

	gwam	3'	5'

One of the great statesmen of our nation was Benjamin — 4 | 2

Franklin. Among other things, the man is quite well known for his — 8 | 5

work as an author, as a philosopher, as a scientist, and as a — 12 | 7

diplomat and representative of our country. Recognized as one of — 16 | 10

the excellent leaders of the Revolution, he is considered a founding — 21 | 13

father of the United States. His name can be seen on the — 25 | 15

Declaration of Independence as well as the United States — 29 | 17

Constitution. — 29 | 18

Some of the things that Franklin is given the credit for — 33 | 20

include the Franklin stove, the lightning rod, bifocals, and many, — 38 | 23

many witty quotes in his almanac. Franklin once said, "If you — 42 | 25

would not be forgotten as soon as you are dead, either write — 46 | 27

something worth reading or do things worth the writing." Because — 50 | 30

of his many personal accomplishments and the written documents — 54 | 33

that his signature appears on, Mr. Franklin will not likely be — 58 | 35

forgotten very soon! He is a role model that all Americans should — 63 | 38

try to model their life after. — 65 | 39

gwam 3' | 1 | 2 | 3 | 4 |
      5' | 1 | 2 | 3 |

24C

New-Key Mastery

To find 1' gwam:
Add 10 for each line you completed to the scale figure beneath the point at which you stopped in a partial line.

Key each line twice; DS between 2-line groups.

caps lock/?
1 UTAH is the BEEHIVE state. What is HAWAII called?
2 Who did Mark select to play CASSIE in CHORUS LINE?

z/v
3 Vince Perez and Zarko Vujacic wore velvet jackets.
4 Zurich, Zeist, Venice, and Pskov were on the quiz.

q/p
5 Paula, Pepe, and Peja took the quiz quite quickly.
6 Quincy Pappas and Enrique Quin were both preppies.

key words
7 very exam calf none disk quip wash give just zebra
8 lazy give busy stop fish down junk mark quit exact

key phrases
9 if you can|see the|when will you|it may be|when he
10 where will|and the|as a rule|who is the|to be able

Alphabet
11 A complex theory was rejected by Frank G. Vizquel.
12 Lock may join the squad if we have six big prizes.

gwam 1' | 1 | 2 | 3 | 4 | 5 | 6 | 7 | 8 | 9 | 10 |

24D

Block Paragraphs

Key each ¶ once. If time permits, key a 1' timing on each ¶.

Paragraph 1

gwam 1'

Dance can be a form of art or it can be thought of   10
as a form of recreation. Dance can be utilized to   20
express ideas and emotions as well as moods.   29

Paragraph 2

One form of dance that is quite common is known as   10
ballet. The earliest forms of ballet are believed   20
to have taken place in Western Europe.   30

Paragraph 3

To excel at ballet, you must take lessons when you   10
are very young. It is not uncommon to see a three   20
year old in a dance studio taking ballet lessons.   30

Paragraph 4

In addition to starting at a very young age, hours   10
and hours of practice are also required to develop   20
into a skilled performer of ballet.   30

gwam 1' | 1 | 2 | 3 | 4 | 5 | 6 | 7 | 8 | 9 | 10 |

For additional practice:

MicroType 6

Alphabetic Keyboarding
Lesson 19

80C

Speed-Forcing Drill

Key each line twice at top speed.

Emphasis: high-frequency balanced-hand words

```
       4|    8|   12|   16|   20|   24|   28|   32|   36|   40|   44|   48|   52|

Jay and I may make a bid for the antique pen.
Clem may make a big profit for the six firms.

Pamela may pay for the eight pens for the auditor.
Nancy bid for the antique chair and antique rifle.

If the pay is right, Sue may make their gowns for them.
When did the auditor sign the audit forms for the city?

Laurie kept the men busy with the work down by the big lake.
Diana may go with us to the city to pay them for their work.

Did the firm bid for the right to the land downtown by city hall?
Jay may suspend the men as a penalty for their work on the docks.
```

gwam 15" | 4| 8| 12| 16| 20| 24| 28| 32| 36| 40| 44| 48| 52|

80D

Technique: Number Keys/Tab

Set tabs at 2" and 4". Key the copy below.

Concentrate on figure location; quick tab spacing; eyes on copy.

102 Cottonwood Drive	534 Knox Street	221 Auckland Drive
934 McDonald Street	761 Lincoln Street	909 Atlantic Street
768 Indian Hills Drive	792 Pleasant Terrace	387 Landmark Avenue
530 Memorial Drive	837 Wilson Road	546 Wright Street
196 Bourque Street	657 Woodbridge Road	161 Tomiyasu Lane
578 Brookdale Avenue	809 Broadway Street	243 Fernandez Court

80E

Speed-Forcing Drill

Key each line once at top speed; then try to complete each sentence on the 15", 12", or 10" call. Force speed to higher levels as you move from sentence to sentence.

Emphasis: high-frequency balanced-hand words

Janel may go to the dock to visit the eight girls.	40|50|60
She is to go with them to the city to see the dog.	40|50|60
The sorority girls paid for the auto to go to the city.	44|55|66
She is to go to the city with us to sign the six forms.	44|55|66
Dick may go to the big island to fix the auto for the widow.	48|60|72
Hank and the big dog slept by the antique chair on the dock.	48|60|72
Rick is to make a turn to the right at the big sign for downtown.	52|65|78
Vivian may go with us to the city to do the work for the auditor.	52|65|78

LESSON 25   New Keys: Backspace, Quotation Mark ("), and Tab

OUTCOMES

- Learn reach technique for **Backspace key**, **quotation mark**, and **Tab key**.
- Improve and check keying speed.

25A

Warmup

Key each line twice; then key a 1' timing on line 3; determine *gwam*.

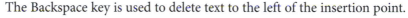

alphabet	1	Jacky can now give six big tips from the old quiz.
caps lock	2	Find the ZIP Codes for the cities in IOWA and OHIO.
easy	3	It may be a problem if both girls go to the docks.

gwam   1' | 1 | 2 | 3 | 4 | 5 | 6 | 7 | 8 | 9 | 10 |

25B

**New Key:
Backspace Key**

★TIP   When you hold down the Backspace key, letters to the left of the insertion point will be deleted continuously until the Backspace key is released.

Backspace Key *Right little* finger; keep right index finger anchored to *j* key.

© Cengage Learning

The Backspace key is used to delete text to the left of the insertion point.

1. Locate the Backspace key on your keyboard.
2. Reach up to the Backspace key with the right little finger (keep the index finger anchored to the *j* key); tap the BACKSPACE key once for each letter you want deleted; return the finger to the ; key.

This symbol means to delete.

Learn Backspace

1. Key the following.

   The delete

2. Use the Backspace key to make the changes shown below.

   The ~~delete~~ backspace

3. Continue keying the sentence as shown below.

   The backspace key can be

4. Use the Backspace key to make the change shown below.

   The backspace key ~~can be~~ is

5. Continue keying the sentence as shown below.

   The backspace key is used to fix

6. Use the Backspace key to make the change shown below.

   The backspace key is used to ~~fix~~ make

7. Continue keying the sentence shown below.

   The backspace key is used to make changes.

Key each line twice at top speed.

Emphasis: high-frequency balanced-hand words

4	8	12	16	20	24	28	32	36	40	44	48	52

```
Nancy and Helen may make the eight signs for them.
Bob and I paid the man for the shanty by the dock.
Helen paid the man to fix the signals down by the lake.
Rodney kept the box with the bugle for the man by the chair.
Nancy and Glen may hang the signs by the door of the shanty.
The man is to pay for the fieldwork both of the girls did for us.
The girl may make them the big signs when they pay for the forms.
```

gwam	15"	4	8	12	16	20	24	28	32	36	40	44	48	52

LESSON 80

Input Skill Development

OUTCOMES

- Build speed and accuracy.
- Enhance keying technique.

80A

Warmup

Key each line twice.

alphabet 1 Jackie Hudson won first prize by solving a tax quiz in less time.

figures 2 Dr. Juan Unit 19 on pages 605–635 includes Graphs 29, 37, and 48.

speed 3 He may wish to dismantle the antique chair for the busy neighbor.

gwam	1'	1	2	3	4	5	6	7	8	9	10	11	12	13

80B

Technique: One-Hand Words

Key each line twice.

One-hand words of 2–5 letters

1 be no up we at in ax my as on add bag car dad war tax sat saw see

2 dad oil egg lip cab joy fee pop art you age him sad mom seat look

3 save milk race pull star pink grade onion grass polio serve pupil

4 as my|at a rate|we are|no war|get set|at my best|you were|a great

5 as few|you set a date|my card|water tax|act on a|tax date|in case

6 my only date|water rate|my tax case|tax fact|my best date|my card

7 No, you are free only after I act on a rate on a state water tax.

8 Get him my extra database only after you set up exact test dates.

9 You set my area tax rate after a great state case on a water tax.

gwam	1'	1	2	3	4	5	6	7	8	9	10	11	12	13

25C

New Key: Quotation Mark

Quotation Mark: Press left shift and tap " (shift of ') with the *right little* finger.

Key each line twice; DS between 2-line groups.

Learn " (quotation mark)

1 ;; "; "; ";" ";" "I believe," she said, "you won."

2 "John Adams," he said, "was the second President."

3 "James Monroe," I said, "was the fifth President,"

4 Alison said "attitude" determines your "altitude."

NOTE: On your screen, quotation marks may look different from those shown in these lines.

25D

Speed Check: Sentences

1. Key a 30" timing on each line.
2. Key another 30" timing on each line. Try to increase your keying speed.

1 Karl did not make the ski team.

2 Jay shared his poem with all of us.

3 Doris played several video games online.

4 Their next game will be played in four weeks.

5 She will register today for next semester classes.

6 She quit the team so she would have more time to study.

| gwam 30" | 2 | 4 | 6 | 8 | 10 | 12 | 14 | 16 | 18 | 20 |

25E

Keyboard Mastery

★TIP

- fingers curved and upright
- forearms parallel to slant of keyboard
- body erect, sitting back in chair

1. Key each line twice; DS between 2-line groups.
2. Key a 1' timing on lines 4–6.

Shift key emphasis (Reach *up* and reach *down* without moving the hands.)

1 Jan and I are to see Ms. Han. May Lana come, too?

2 Bob Epps lives in Rome; Vic Copa is in Rome, also.

3 Oates and Co. has a branch office in Boise, Idaho.

Easy sentences (Think, say, and key the words at a steady pace.)

4 Eight of the girls may go to the social with them.

5 Corla is to work with us to fix the big dock sign.

6 Keith is to pay the six men for the work they did.

| gwam 1' | 1 | 2 | 3 | 4 | 5 | 6 | 7 | 8 | 9 | 10 |

79C

Technique: Number Keys/Tab

Key each line twice (key number, tap Tab, and key next number).

Concentrate on figure location; quick tab spacing; eyes on copy.

264	189	357	509	768	142	642	135	9,607
258	147	630	911	828	376	475	390	1,425
763	905	481	208	913	475	609	173	2,458

gwam 1' | 1 | 2 | 3 | 4 | 5 | 6 | 7 |

79D

Timed Writings

1. Key a 1' timing on ¶ 1; determine *gwam*.
2. Add 2–4 *gwam* to the rate attained in step 1; determine quarter-minute checkpoints from the chart at the left.
3. Key two 1' guided timings on ¶ 1 to increase speed.
4. Practice ¶ 2 in the same way.
5. Key two 3' timings on ¶s 1 and 2 combined; determine *gwam* and the number of errors.

Quarter-Minute Checkpoints

gwam	1/4'	1/2'	3/4'	1'
24	6	12	18	24
28	7	14	21	28
32	8	16	24	32
36	9	18	27	36
40	10	20	30	40
44	11	22	33	44
48	12	24	36	48
52	13	26	39	52
56	14	28	42	56
60	15	30	45	60

A all letters used

gwam 1' | 3'

When you talk about famous Americans, it doesn't take 4 | 2
long to come up with a long list. However, some individuals would 8 | 5
appear on nearly everyone's list. George Washington would be one 13 | 8
of those on most people's list. He is often referred to as the 17 | 10
Father of our Country because of the role he played in the Ameri- 21 | 13
can Revolution and being our first president. 24 | 15

Abraham Lincoln would also be included on most lists. He is 29 | 17
often referred to as Honest Abe. He always gave the extra ef- 33 | 20
fort. Because of this, he was successful. Whether the job was 37 | 22
splitting logs, being a lawyer, or being president, Lincoln gave 42 | 25
it his best. Dealing with the Civil War required a president who 46 | 28
gave his best. 47 | 28

Harriet Tubman is recognized as another prominent individ- 51 | 31
ual. She risked her own life for the freedom of others. After 55 | 33
becoming a free woman in the North, she returned to the South to 60 | 36
assist several hundred slaves escape. She also took part in the 64 | 38
Civil War, serving the country as a Union spy and scout. 68 | 41

gwam 1' | 1 | 2 | 3 | 4 | 5 | 6 | 7 | 8 | 9 | 10 | 11 | 12 | 13 |
3' | 1 | 2 | 3 | 4 |

New Key: Tab Key

Tab key *Left little* finger

The Tab key is used to indent the first line of ¶s. Word processing software has preset tabs called **default** tabs. Usually, the first default tab is set 0.5" to the right of the left margin and is used to indent ¶s.

1. Locate the Tab key on your keyboard (usually to the left of the letter *q*).
2. Reach up to the Tab key with the left little finger; tap the key firmly and release it quickly. The insertion point will move 0.5" to the right.
3. Key each ¶ once SS. As you key, tap the Tab key to indent the first line of each ¶. Use the Backspace key to correct errors as you key.
4. If time permits, key the ¶s again to master Tab key technique.

Tab ➔ The tab key is used to indent blocks of copy such as these. It should also be used for tables to arrange data quickly and neatly into columns.

Tab ➔ Learn how to use the tab key by touch; doing so will add to your keying skill. Tap the tab key firmly and release it very quickly. Begin the line without a pause.

Tab ➔ If you hold the tab key down, the insertion point will move very quickly from tab to tab across the line.

Speed Check: Paragraphs

For additional practice:

MicroType 6

Alphabetic Keyboarding Lesson 18

Key two 1' timings on each ¶; determine *gwam* on each timing.

 all letters used

```
            •     2   •    4    •    6    •    8    •
        Keep in home position all of the fingers not
  10    •    12   •    14   •    16   •    18   •
being used to tap a key.  Do not let them move out
  20    •    22   •    24   •    26   •    28
of position for the next letters in your copy.
            •     2   •    4    •    6    •    8    •
        Prize the control you have over the fingers.
  10    •    12   •    14   •    16   •    18   •
See how quickly speed goes up when you learn that
  20    •    22   •    24   •    26   •    28   •
you can make them do just what you expect of them.
```

UNIT 15 Enhance Input Skills

Lesson 79 Input Skill Development
Lesson 80 Input Skill Development

LESSON 79 Input Skill Development

OUTCOMES
- Build speed and accuracy.
- Enhance keying technique.

79A

Warmup

Key each line twice.

Alphabet 1 An exclusive photo of a tornado by Dr. Jackson was quite amazing.

Figures 2 As of July 10, Justin's inbox contained 3,975 e-mails, not 2,864.

Speed 3 Pam paid the six men to go to the city to do the work on the map.

gwam 1' | 1 | 2 | 3 | 4 | 5 | 6 | 7 | 8 | 9 | 10 | 11 | 12 | 13 |

79B

Technique: Balanced-Hand Words

Key each line twice.

Balanced-hand words

1 ivory risks panel signs their widow visit aisle blame chair eight

2 if me go he so us to am or by an of is to row she box air pay the

3 dig got due map jam own she box ant busy when city fish half rush

4 goal down dial firm keys pens rock odor sick soap tubs wish title

5 to do|to us|by the|if they|held a|the pen|their dog|is it|to make

6 a big fox|do the work|the gown is|when is it|he may go|a rich man

7 by the chair|he may make|did he spend|for the girls|for the firms

8 eight formal gowns|blame the girls|six city maps|burn the emblems

9 The maid may make the usual visit to the dock to work on the map.

10 Dick and Jay paid the busy man to go to the lake to fix the dock.

11 The girls may visit them when they go to the city to pay the man.

12 Glen may go with the city auditor to the dock to fix the problem.

gwam 1' | 1 | 2 | 3 | 4 | 5 | 6 | 7 | 8 | 9 | 10 | 11 | 12 | 13 |

WP Applications (continued)

Activity 9

Tabs

View/Show/Ruler

 Left tab

 Right tab

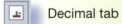 Decimal tab

Most software has left tabs already set at half-inch (0.5") intervals from the left margin. However, tabs can be set at intervals you determine. When you set a tab, the preset tabs are automatically cleared up to the point where you set the tab. Most software lets you set left tabs, right tabs, and decimal tabs. You will work with decimal tabs in Unit 7.

Left tabs align all text evenly at the left by placing the text you key to the right of the tab setting. Left tabs are commonly used to align words.

Right tabs align all text evenly at the right by placing the text you key to the left of the tab setting. Right tabs are commonly used to align whole numbers.

1. Open the *df aa2 activity 9* file.
2. DS after the heading and set a left tab at **2"** and at **4.5"**.
3. Key the four lines a DS below the heading using these tab settings. TS after keying the fourth line.

Left tab at 2"		Left tab at 4.5"	
(Tab) Sheryl Ho	(Tab)	Moorcroft	(Enter)
Hector Lopez		Gillette	
Pierre Pizarro		Upton	
Janice Robinson		Sundance	

4. Reset a left tab at **1"** and at **5"**; key the lines again.
5. **Save as:** *aa2 activity 9*.

21st Century Skills: Initiative and Self-Direction

Initiative and self-direction are important skills and attributes to attain as you develop as a student and as a person. These skills and attributes will help you succeed in any task you set out to do in the course of your personal and professional life, including learning keyboarding and computer applications. Taking initiative means making the decision to do something—a job, a project, a specific task—without needing to be prompted by someone else. It means you don't need to have a teacher, parent, or friend tell you that you must do something. You see what needs to be done, and you do it. Self-direction means you are able to guide yourself and motivate yourself through the various steps of a job, project, or task. You make good decisions about what needs to be done next, and if necessary, you push yourself to do it. As with any other skill, learning to keyboard properly requires a certain amount of initiative and self-direction.

Think Critically

1. What prompted you to want to learn keyboarding and computer applications?
2. Now that you have worked through the first lessons of this book, how do you think you can demonstrate initiative and self-direction as you learn these skills?
3. Describe some ways in which you have demonstrated initiative and self-direction at home, at school, or on a job.

© Konstantin Chagin /Shutterstock.com

Complete this activity to help prepare for the **Database Design & Applications** event in FBLA-PBL's Information Technology division. Participants in this event demonstrate their understanding of database usage in business and their skills in developing database objects.

In Unit 13, you created business documents for an ice cream and dessert shop named the Sweet Stop. The owner would now like you to develop a database for the business. She has given you the information shown here:

First Name	Last Name	Position	Address	City	State	ZIP	Phone	Hourly Rate
Jen	Maddox	Manager	448 Sawyer Court	Mason	OH	45040	513-555-6599	$12.00
Grant	Powers	Server	110 Concord Drive	Lebanon	OH	45036	513-555-3102	$ 8.00
Leah	Valdez	Server	45 Maple St.	Lebanon	OH	45036	513-555-7475	$ 8.00
Jackson	Volz	Server	310 East St.	Cincinnati	OH	45224	513-555-4720	$ 8.00
Ben	Nguyen	Server	7636 Bethel Road	Mason	OH	45040	513-555-3382	$ 8.00
Haley	Ashe	Server	309 Wright Ave.	Lebanon	OH	45036	513-555-0387	$ 8.00
Eric	Rose	Assistant Manager	2209 Miiller Road	Lebanon	OH	45036	513-555-6219	$10.00
Claire	Ghent	Assistant Manager	155 Pleasant View, Apt. 8	Monroe	OH	45050	513-555-2886	$10.00

1. Start a new database and name it **Sweet Stop**.
2. Create a table named *Employees*. Use the information above to set up the table's fields. Apply appropriate data types and field descriptions.
3. Create a form based on the *Employees* table and enter the records shown above.
4. Create a query that shows only those employees who live in Lebanon. Include the *First Name, Last Name,* and *Phone* fields in the query. Save it as **Lebanon Employees**.
5. Create a report based on the *Employees* table that includes only the *First Name, Last Name, Position,* and *Hourly Rate* fields. Name the report **Hourly Rate**.

For detailed information on this event, go to www.fbla-pbl.org.

Think Critically

1. What other tables might the Sweet Stop owner want in her business database?
2. How can a database help a business operate more efficiently?
3. How might you use a database to organize information related to school?

School and Community
Have you ever gone to a public park, hiked through a forest, or canoed down a river and been dismayed by the amount of litter you see? Despite the efforts of law enforcement agencies, trash collectors, and recyclers to halt littering and polluting, many people still drop their trash wherever they please. That's why more and more volunteers are needed for community cleanups. A community cleanup brings volunteers together to clean, repair, or improve public spaces, such as parks, riverbanks, and biking/hiking trails.

1. Identify a public space in your area that would benefit from a community cleanup.
2. Contact a community council member or civic leader to find out the requirements to prepare and carry out the cleanup.
3. Create a database table of family, friends, and other potential volunteers to contact to help with the cleanup.
4. Create another table that lists additional sites to target for cleanup.
5. Using the information you have gathered, organize and lead the cleanup.

LESSON 26

New Keys: Apostrophe (') and Hyphen (-)

OUTCOMES

- Learn reach technique for ' (apostrophe) and - (hyphen).
- Improve and check keying speed.

26A

Warmup

Key each line twice SS; then take a 1' timing on line 3; determine *gwam*.

alphabet	1	Glenn saw a quick red fox jump over the lazy cubs.
caps lock	2	STACY works for HPJ, Inc.; SAMANTHA, for JPH Corp.
easy	3	Kamela may work with the city auditor on the form.

gwam | 1' | 1 | 2 | 3 | 4 | 5 | 6 | 7 | 8 | 9 | 10 |

26B

New Keys: ' (Apostrophe) and – (Hyphen)

Key each line twice; DS between 2-line groups.

TIP On your screen, apostrophes may look different from those shown in these lines.

Learn ' (apostrophe)

1 ;' ;' ;' '; '; I've told you it's hers, haven't I.
2 I'm sure it's Ray's. I'll return it if he's home.
3 I've been told it isn't up to us; it's up to them.

Learn - (hyphen)

4 ;- ;- -;- -;- - on the up-and-up; play tug-of-war;
5 part-time job; attorney-at-law; my brother-in-law;
6 The sources are up-to-date. Joan works part-time.

Combine ' and -

7 ;' ;' ;- ;- ;-' ;-' -'; -'; up-to-date list; x-ray
8 Didn't he say it couldn't be done? I don't agree.
9 I told him the off-the-cuff comment wasn't needed.

10 That isn't a cause-and-effect relationship, is it?
11 The well-known guest is a hard-hitting outfielder.
12 Put an apostrophe in let's, it's, isn't, and don't.

Apostrophe *Right little* finger

Hyphen Reach *up* to hyphen with *right little* finger

© 2012 Creatas/Jupiterimages Corporation

Planning a Career in Government and Public Administration

The highest-ranking job in the U.S. government and one of the most powerful positions in the world—that of President of the United States—falls within this career cluster. This field is for those individuals who are interested in setting and implementing public policy, protecting citizen's rights, and helping to shape the future of their city, their state, and their country.

What's It Like?

Workers in this field are involved in planning and performing government functions at the local, state, and federal levels. This includes governance, national security, foreign service, planning, revenue and taxation, and regulations. For example:

- They oversee budgets, ensure that resources are used properly, nominate citizens to boards and commissions, encourage business investment, and promote economic development.
- They carry out and supervise the fundamental operations of the military in combat, administration, construction, engineering, health care, human services, and other areas.
- They develop laws and statutes.
- They review filed tax returns for accuracy and determine whether tax credits and deductions are allowed by law.

Jobs in this field often require long hours, including evenings and weekends. Individuals in public administration typically work in offices, while those in security and regulations often work in the field in different locations around the country and around the world.

Employment Outlook

Employment opportunities in the various pathways of this cluster range significantly. Little to no change is expected in the area of governance; those in the military and other national security areas can expect excellent job growth; those in planning, taxation, and regulations can expect job growth to be about as fast as average, or 7 to 13 percent.

Education requirements range widely, too. Some positions require on-the-job training in an administrative role or as a member of the armed forces; others may require a two-year college degree in public administration, health-care administration, human services management, or political science; and still others may require a four-year college degree or higher in political science, public administration, national security, or law.

What About You?

This career cluster is covered in box 7 of the Interest Survey Activity you completed in Unit 1 of this text. If this box had one of the three highest scores on your survey, you should further explore the cluster's pathways and related occupations.

1. Why do you think a career in this field could be a good choice?
2. What skills can you develop now that would be helpful to a career in this field?
3. Why are these jobs important to our country's prosperity and well-being?

26C

**Speed Check:
Sentences**

Key two 30" timings on each line. Your rate in *gwam* is shown word-for-word below the lines.

gwam 30"

	gwam 30"
When do you think you will go?	12
Tara just finished taking her exam.	14
Nancy told the man to fix the car brake.	16
Val could see that he was angry with the boy.	18
Karen may not be able to afford college next year.	20

gwam 30" | 2 | 4 | 6 | 8 | 10 | 12 | 14 | 16 | 18 | 20 |

If you finish a line before time is called and start over, your *gwam* is the figure at the end of the line PLUS the figure above or below the point at which you stopped.

26D

Speed Building

1. Key each line twice; DS between 2-line groups.
2. Key a 1' writing on each line; determine *gwam* on each timing.

1 Pamela may make a profit off the land by the lake.
2 Eight of the firms may handle the work for Rodney.
3 Vivian may make a map of the city for the six men.
4 Helen held a formal social for eight of the girls.
5 He may work with the men on the city turn signals.
6 The dog and the girl slept in a chair in the hall.

gwam 1' | 1 | 2 | 3 | 4 | 5 | 6 | 7 | 8 | 9 | 10 |

26E

**Speed Check:
Paragraphs**

For additional practice:

**Alphabetic Keyboarding
Lesson 21**

Key two 1' timings on each ¶; determine *gwam* on each timing.

EA all letters used

gwam 1'

Are you one of the people who often look from   10
the copy to the screen and down at your hands? If   20
you are, you can be sure that you will not build a   30
speed to prize. Make eyes on copy your next goal.   40

When you move the eyes from the copy to check   49
the screen, you may lose your place and waste time   59
trying to find it. Lost time can lower your speed   69
quickly and in a major way, so do not look away.   79

gwam 1' | 1 | 2 | 3 | 4 | 5 | 6 | 7 | 8 | 9 | 10 |

Academic and Career Connections

Complete the following exercises that introduce various topics that involve academic themes and careers.

@ VEER.COM/STILLFX

Grammar and Writing: Spelling and Modifiers

MicroType 6

- References/Communication Skills/Spelling
- References/Communication Skills/Modifiers
- CheckPro/Communication Skills 11
- CheckPro/Word Choice 11

1. Go to *MicroType 6* and use this feature path for review: References/Communication Skills/Spelling.
2. Click Rules and review the rules of spelling.
3. Then, under *Spelling*, click *Posttest*.
4. Follow the instructions to complete the posttest.
5. Repeat this process for *Modifiers*.

Optional Activities:

1. Go to this path: CheckPro/Communication Skills 11.
2. Complete the activities as directed.
3. Go to this path: CheckPro/Word Choice 11.
4. Key the Apply lines, and choose the correct word.

As desired, complete Word Choice 12–18.

Communications: Reading

Open the data file **df u14 communications**. Carefully read the brief and then close the file. Start a new document and key answers to the following questions, using complete sentences.

1. What was the final score of yesterday's soccer match?
2. Will last year's City League champion be playing in this year's championship match?
3. Will the top-ranked team in the city be playing in the championship match?
4. Has either of the teams in the match won a City League championship before?
5. Save the document as **u14 communications**.

Math Skills: Measures of Central Tendency

The measures of central tendency are mean, median, and mode. The **mean**, or average, is a value that is intermediate between other values; the **median** is the middle number in a data set when the data are arranged in numerical order; the **mode** is the value in the data set that occurs most often. Courtney has pulled this information from her company's database.

1. During the month of December, the company recorded these transactions:

   East: 814 transactions, $76/transaction   **West**: 637 transactions, $46/transaction

   North: 870 transactions, $53/transaction   **South**: 749 transactions, $67/transaction

   Find the mean number of transactions for the four stores during the month (rounded to the nearest whole number). What was the average amount of money spent per transaction?

2. The best-selling items are priced as follows. What is the median-priced item?

New game: $36	Used game: $16	New handheld device: $169
Used handheld device: $80	New game console: $299	Used game console: $199
Accessory starter kit: $34	Car adapter kit: $12	Carrying case: $19

WP Applications (continued)

Activity 10

Apply What You Have Learned

1. Create a new document and key lines 1–6, applying formatting as shown. Do not key the line numbers.

   1. **Kennedy** was a *Democrat*; **Lincoln** was a *Republican*.
   2. Is the correct choice <u>two</u>, <u>too</u>, or <u>to</u>?
   3. Is *Harry Potter and the Deathly Hallows* still on the bestseller list?
   4. There was an article on her in the *New York Times*.
   5. Are the names to be **bolded** or <u>underlined</u> or <u>**bolded and underlined**</u>?
   6. The <u>underscore</u> is being used less frequently than *italic*.

2. After keying the lines, make the following changes.
   line 1
   Change *Kennedy* to *Washington* and *Democrat* to *Federalist*.
   line 4
   Change *New York Times* to *Washington Post*.
   line 6
   Delete *frequently*. Insert or **bold** after *italic*.

3. **Save as:** *aa activity 10*.

Digital Citizenship and Ethics

More everyday activities such as finding directions, making purchases, and transferring data are happening over the Web, and social networking sites such as Facebook, Twitter, and FourSquare enable users to connect with friends and family by sharing photos, videos, music, status updates, and even their current locations.

© SuriyaPhoto/Shutterstock.com

In addition, online services enable you to store and retrieve data such as music, photos, and videos on the Web so the files are accessible anywhere, any time. This is sometimes known as **cloud computing**.

One downside to storing and transferring all this personal data online is the possibility of identity theft. Because people consider PCs, laptops, tablets, and cell phones to be personal devices, they may be unaware that nearly anything they send online can be accessed by others if it is not sent or posted in a secure manner.

Identity theft can occur when malicious users gain access to personal data such as credit card information, bank account data, Social Security numbers, personal photographs, phone numbers, or addresses.

Think Critically

1. What do you think might happen to a victim of identity theft?
2. Refer to Unit 1, Lesson 5C for a brief description of ways to avoid identity theft. Describe some things you can do to help yourself avoid identity theft.
3. Do you think identity theft will become more or less prevalent as more businesses and services store data online with cloud computing? State the reasons for your answer.

e. Kayla Maas has a new address and telephone number:
    1125 Westbrook Lane
    Minneapolis, MN 55436-2837
    612-348-8211
3. Save and close the database.

Sort Information for Eastwick School of Dance

1. Open the *Eastwick School of Dance* database.
2. Run sorts to answer the following questions.
3. Open *df 78G* and record your answers.
4. **Save as:** *78G Eastwick School of Dance.*

	Eastwick School of Dance	
No.	**Question**
1	How many of the students enrolled in Eastwick School of Dance are from Wisconsin?
2	How many of the students are from Minneapolis?
3	How many students are taking beginning jazz for their first class?
4	How many students are taking beginning jazz for their first or second class?
5	How many students have not paid their September fees?
6	How many students have not paid their October fees?
7	How many students are taking advanced ballet for their first or second class?

Compose Letter for Eastwick School of Dance

Several of the students have fallen behind in paying their dance fees. Compose and format a letter to the parents of the dancers reminding them that their September dance fees have not been paid.

www.cengage.com/school/
keyboarding/c21key

Activity 11

Apply What You Have Learned

1. Open *df aa2 activity 11*.
2. Use the Select Text feature to select and change the formatting of the copy using bold and italic as shown below.
3. Use the copy and paste feature to arrange the presidents in the order they served: Roosevelt 1901–1909, Wilson 1913–1921, Truman 1945–1953, Reagan 1981–1989.
4. **Save as:** *aa2 activity 11*.

Harry S. Truman: *"The American people stand firm in the faith which has inspired this Nation from the beginning. We believe that all men have a right to equal justice under law and equal opportunity to share in the common good. We believe that all men have the right to freedom of thought and expression."*

Theodore Roosevelt: *"Much has been given us, and much will rightfully be expected from us. We have duties to others and duties to ourselves; and we can shirk neither."*

Ronald Reagan: *"We are a nation that has a government--not the other way around. And this makes us special among the nations of the Earth. Our government has no power except that granted it by the people. It is time to check and reverse the growth of government, which shows signs of having grown beyond the consent of the governed."*

Woodrow Wilson: *"We have built up, moreover, a great system of government, which has stood through a long age as in many respects a model for those who seek to set liberty upon foundations that will endure against fortuitous change, against storm and accident."*

Activity 12

Apply What You Have Learned

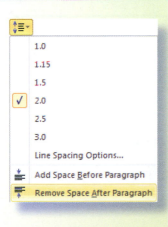

1. Open a new document.
2. Set the Line Spacing to 2.
3. Remove Spacing After Paragraph (see illustration at left).
4. Set left tabs at 2.5 and 5.
5. Key the following.

Please invite the following individuals to be our guests at the July 15 reception:

Mr. and Mrs. Jason Beckett	Dr. Michelle White	Ms. Faye Culver
Ms. Maria Ortiz	Ms. Maxine Aguilar	Ms. Alexandra Harper
Mr. Ashton Schumann	Dr. Theodore Benning	Mr. Mitchell Parizo
Mr. and Mrs. Paul Sorrento	Mr. and Ms. Jay Becker	Mrs. Stephen Chen
Mrs. Alison Greenfield	Mr. Felipe Nolan	Dr. Janette Ramirez

6. **Save as:** *aa activity 12*.

www.cengage.com/school/ keyboarding/c21key

78D

Update Table for Eastwick School of Dance

1. Open the *Eastwick Fees* table.
2. Input the following records in the table.
3. Save and close the database after you key the information.

Name	Dance Class 1	Dance Class 2	Monthly Fees	Sept. Fees	Oct. Fees	Nov. Fees	Dec. Fees
Tarin Chan	Inter. Ballet	Adv. Jazz	$62	$62	$62		
Marcia Moreno	Inter. Jazz		$29	$29			
Elizabeth Pingel	Beg. Tap		$25	$25	$25		
Sonja Phelps	Inter. Jazz	Adv. Tap	$62	$62	$62	$62	
Charlotte Ross	Beg. Ballet		$28	$28	$28		
Lynda Sackett	Inter. Ballet	Adv. Tap					

78E

Edit Records for Eastwick School of Dance

1. Open the *Eastwick Fees* table.
2. Make the following changes.
    a. Stacy Rice is enrolled in Inter. Jazz and Inter. Ballet (be sure to change fees).
    b. Byrns should be spelled **Burns**.
    c. Tasha Lang should be **Trisha Lang**.
    d. Diane Bunnell is enrolled in Adv. Ballet, not Inter. Make the necessary adjustments.
    e. Lynda Sackett decided not to take Adv. Tap. Make the necessary adjustments to reflect this change. The September Fees will stay at $63.00; however, change the Monthly Fee to $30.00 to reflect this change for future months.
3. Save and close the database.

78F

Edit Records for Eastwick School of Dance

1. Open the *Eastwick School of Dance-Address* table.
2. Make the following changes.
    a. Diane Bunnell has a new address and telephone number:
       380 Innsbruck Drive
       St. Paul, MN 55112-8271
       612-329-7621
    b. Jackqueline Finley's name should be spelled **Jacqueline**. Her phone number should be **715-386-6764**.
    c. Make sure you change the spelling of Brook Byrns (**Burns**) and Tasha Lang (**Trisha**).
    d. Change Judy Higgins's mother's name to **Ms. Erin Schultz**.

© VEER.COM/STILLFX

Academic and Career Connections

Complete the following exercises that introduce various topics that involve academic themes and careers.

Grammar and Writing: Terminal Punctuation

MicroType 6

- References/Communication Skills/Terminal Punctuation
- CheckPro/Communication Skills 2
- CheckPro/Word Choice 2

1. Go to *MicroType* 6 and use this feature path for review: References/Communication Skills/ Terminal Punctuation.
2. Click *Rules* and review the rules of using terminal punctuation.
3. Then, under *Terminal Punctuation*, click *Posttest*.
4. Follow the instructions to complete the posttest.

Optional Activities:
1. Go to this path: CheckPro/Communication Skills 2.
2. Complete the activities as directed.
3. Go to this path: CheckPro/Word Choice 2.
4. Key the Apply lines and choose the correct word.

Communications: Listening

1. Listen carefully to the sounds around you for three minutes.
2. As you listen, key a list of every different sound you hear.
3. If requested, give the document you have keyed to your instructor.

Math Skills

1. Julian and Maria have started a new business after school and on weekends selling artwork they and their classmates have made in an online store. They have decided to price each item as follows:

   a. Art photographs: $10 each
   b. Paintings and drawings: $15 each
   c. Sculptures: $20 each
   d. Jewelry: $15 each
   e. Clothing: $15 each

2. How much money will Julian and Maria collect in the first month of operations if they sell the following items: 7 photos, 3 paintings, 2 sculptures, 6 pieces of jewelry, and 3 T-shirts.
3. Julian and Maria have determined that they need to sell at least $175 per month to cover the operating costs of the business, including website design and hosting fees, marketing expenses (creating ads and posting them on other sites), and the cost of their time. What will their gross profit be for the first month? This is the amount they sold minus monthly operating expenses (and doesn't include paying any taxes).
4. How much money will Julian and Maria each make if they divide the gross profits among themselves and the three other classmates who contributed items to the business? (*Hint:* Divide the gross profit by five.)
5. What is the average selling price of each item in the first month? (*Hint:* Divide the total amount sold by the number of items sold.)

Add Fields and Input Data for Eastwick School of Dance

1. Open the *Eastwick Fees* table.
2. Add the fields shown below.

September Fees
October Fees
November Fees
December Fees

3. Update the records in the database table to include the new information shown below.
4. Print the revised table in landscape orientation.
5. Save and close the database.

Eastwick School of Dance

Name	Sept. Fees	Oct. Fees	Nov. Fees	Dec. Fees
Stewart	55	55	55	
Vaughn				
Martin	53	53		
Finley				
Garcia	57	57		
Edmonds	59	59		
Ramirez	58	58		
Rice				
Rizzo				
Higgins	27			
Giani	28	28		
Griffith	59	59		
Boyer	52	52		
Bunnell				
Byrns	57	57	57	
Koosman	66	66		
Lang				
Maas	25	25	25	
McDowell	28	28		

Planning a Career in Business Management and Administration

Every type of business needs people to help manage it and run it. Whether the business is a multibillion-dollar international corporation or a neighborhood shop run by a single owner, the same basic principles apply in developing the business—from creating a product or service, marketing and selling the product or service, to administering all the financial and staffing needs of the company.

The business management and administration services industry is one of the highest-paying career pathways, with a wide variety of opportunities for workers in both large and small business settings. Workers in entrepreneurial or small business settings often must apply many different kinds of skills in the course of running their businesses.

What's It Like?

When you see a new store opening in your community or hear about an international corporation providing a new product or service, the skills of workers in business management have made it happen. Entrepreneurs can take an idea for a new product and develop it into a business that will earn thousands or millions of dollars for themselves and for the people who work and invest in the company.

One example is the story of Bert and John Jacobs, two brothers who worked for five years selling their T-shirts at street fairs and college dorms. One day, the inspiration for the Life Is Good character hit, and they sold out all 48 shirts they printed for a local street fair. Sales took off from there, and Life Is Good is now a multimillion-dollar corporation.

Figure 2-9 Entrepreneur Bert Jacobs Selling Life Is Good T-shirts

© Eric Fowke / Alamy

Employment Outlook

Employment is expected to grow faster than average for most business management and administration careers, especially business information management and human resources management, with predicted growth of up to 17 percent.

Most workers in this field work in offices, and most jobs require at least a bachelor's degree from a four-year college or university. Entrepreneurial and jobs at small business can provide a more varied workday in a store, home, or small office setting.

What About You?

1. Why do you think a career in business management and administration could be a good choice? Can you picture yourself doing this type of job?
2. Why are these jobs important to our economy?

Fee Schedule

Beg. Ballet	$28
Beg. Tap	25
Beg. Jazz	27
Inter. Ballet	$30
Inter. Tap	29
Inter. Jazz	29
Adv. Ballet	$34
Adv. Tap	33
Adv. Jazz	32

Eastwirk
School of Dance

Name	Dance Class 1	Dance Class 2	Monthly Fees
Julie Stewart	Beg. Ballet	Beg. Jazz	$55
Julie Vaughn	Adv. Ballet		$34
Lauren Martin	Beg. Ballet	Beg. Tap	$53
Jacqueline Finley	Inter. Ballet		$30
Angela Garcia	Beg. Jazz	Inter. Ballet.	
Kirsten Edmonds	Beg. Tap	Adv. Ballet	
Camille Ramirez	Inter. Tap	Inter. Jazz	$58
Stacy Rice	Inter. Jazz		
Loren Rizzo	Beg. Ballet		$28
Judy Higgins	Beg. Jazz		
Jill Giani	Beg. Ballet		$28
Anne Griffith	Inter. Ballet	Inter. Jazz	$59
Jayne Boyer	Beg. Tap	Beg. Jazz	$52
Diane Bunnell	Inter. Ballet		
Brook Byrns	Beg. Jazz	Inter. Ballet	$57
Alison Koosman	Adv. Ballet	Adv. Jazz	$66
Tasha Lang	Beg. Ballet	Inter. Tap	$57
Kayla Maas	Beg. Tap		$25
Carolyn McDowell	Beg. Ballet		

Dmitriy Shironosov /Shutterstock.com

Complete this activity to help prepare for the **Keyboarding Production** event in BPA's Administrative Support division. Participants in this event use word processing software to produce different types of business documents. In your word processing program, compose a paragraph about each of the following common business documents. Discuss the purpose of the document and provide two examples of how it could be used in a workplace setting.

- **Business letter:** This is written to communicate with other businesses or individuals. The basic parts of a business letter include the return address, date, inside address, salutation, body, and signature line.
- **Memo:** This is typically used to communicate with other workers within a company. The basic parts of a memo are the organization name; the word *Memo*, the headings *To*, *From*, *Date*, and *Subject*; and the memo text.
- **Report:** This is typically two or more pages long and is based on research and information gathered on a specific topic. The basic parts include a title, the body of the report (with subheadings, if applicable), and a list of references.

You may use references to assist in preparing the paragraphs. When you are finished:

- Insert an appropriate title for the text you wrote. Apply bold formatting.
- Increase the line spacing after the title and between the paragraphs.
- Proofread the text for accuracy, content, grammar, spelling, and punctuation.
- Use paragraph formatting, tab indents, and text formatting as appropriate.
- Save and print the document as directed by your instructor.

For detailed information on this event, go to www.bpa.org.

Think Critically

1. How can strong writing skills contribute to your academic and career success?
2. What opportunities do you have in school to help you develop writing skills?
3. How do you think well-written and attractively formatted documents reflect on the individual who wrote them?

School and Community

Volunteering in your school and community is an important part of developing your leadership and professional skills. One way to express your interest in the arts is to volunteer at a local museum or theater. Volunteer work at an arts organization can include helping with administrative work such as keying documents, and preparing flyers or brochures. Student volunteers may help with sets or costumes or usher in a theater. Volunteers at museums may work in a gift shop or serve as exhibit guides.

1. Get started with volunteer work in the arts by researching volunteer opportunities in your community. What kinds of arts organizations can use your help?
2. Identify your two favorite types of artistic expression, and describe how you might apply these interests to volunteer work in your school or community.
3. Write a brief summary of the importance of art in your school and community. Describe how art has contributed to your own personal development and how you can use this experience to develop your resume or work portfolio.

77F

Create a Query for Franklin HS FBLA

Since Franklin High School has outgrown its facility, the city of San Francisco is considering the possibility of rezoning in order to shift the overflow of students to a high school with extra space. If this rezoning occurs, the students living in the 94111 ZIP Code would be moved to another school. The Membership Director for Franklin FBLA would like you to use the Query Wizard to create a query to determine the number of current FBLA members that could be lost if the rezoning were to occur.

1. Review the Query feature in the Application Guide (pp. 295-296); learn how to create a query.
2. Create a query using *94111 ZIP Code Members* for the filename. Include all the fields in the query.

77G

Create a Query for Executive Development Seminars

Mr. Blackburn would like to know how many individuals have registered for all four of the seminars when they are offered in Atlanta on July 15-19.

1. Create a query that will produce a table for him that includes the following information:

ID

Last Name

First Name

State

All Four Seminars

2. Use *Orlando Registrants for All Four* for the query name.

Hint: Use **750** as the criteria in the *All Four Seminars* field to filter out only those individuals who have registered for all four seminars.

LESSON 78

Database Application Assessment

OUTCOME

- Assess database application skills.

78B

Create a New Table for Eastwick School of Dance

Tupungato/Shutterstock.com

The owner of Eastwick School of Dance, Ashley Eastwick, would like you to create another table (*Eastwick Fees*) in the *Eastwick School of Dance* database to keep track of student fees. She would like you to use the field names shown below.

Last Name

First Name

Dance Class 1

Dance Class 2

Monthly Fees

1. Open the **df Eastwick School of Dance** database, and save it as **Eastwick School of Dance**.
2. Create and save a new table using the name **Eastwick Fees**.
3. Key the information from the records on the next page into the *Eastwick Fees* database table. If the monthly fee is not given, use the Fee Schedule information shown at the left to calculate the fee.
4. Save and close the database.

UNIT 3 Enhance Input Skills

Lesson 27	Input Skill Development
Lesson 28	Input Skill Development

LESSON 27 — Input Skill Development

MicroType with CheckPro
Note that CheckPro is an effective feedback and grading tool. If you have MicroType with CheckPro, you may start using it with this lesson.

OUTCOMES
- Build speed and accuracy.
- Enhance keying technique.

27A

Warmup

Key each line twice; DS between 2-line groups.

Alphabet 1 J. Fox made five quick plays to win the big prize.

? (Question mark) 2 Where is Helen? Did she call? Is she to go, too?

Easy 3 Pam owns the big dock, but they own the lake land.

gwam 1' | 1 | 2 | 3 | 4 | 5 | 6 | 7 | 8 | 9 | 10 |

27B

Speed Check: Sentences

Key each line three times at the speed level (see box below); DS between 3-line groups.

1 She has three more games left.

2 When will he make the payment?

3 Felipe left for school an hour ago.

4 Mary has four more puppies to sell.

5 The girls won the game by eleven points.

6 Taisho finished the report on Wednesday.

7 Their runner fell with less than a lap to go.

8 Inez will finish the project by the deadline.

9 You can register for classes starting next Friday.

10 Jessica was elected president by just three votes.

★TIP

- After keying the last letter of a word, quickly tap the Space Bar and immediately begin keying the next word.
- After keying the period or question mark at the end of each line, quickly tap Enter and immediately begin keying the next line.

Speed Level of Practice
When the purpose of practice is to reach a new speed, use the **speed level**. Take the brakes off your fingers and experiment with new stroking patterns and new speeds. Do this by:
- reading two or three letters ahead of your keying to foresee stroking patterns;
- getting the fingers ready for the combinations of letters to be keyed;
- keeping your eyes on the copy in the book;
- keying at the word level rather than letter by letter.

Sort information for Rockwell Technologies

1. Open **df 77d Rockwell Technologies** to use to record your answers for this activity.
2. Open the *Sales Reps – District 13* database table.
3. Run sorts to answer the following questions.
4. **Save as: 77d Rockwell Technologies.**

RT	ROCKWELL TECHNOLOGIES
No.	**Question**
1	How many Arizona sales reps are in District 13?
2	How many sales reps sold over $60,000 in July?
3	How many sales reps sold over $60,000 in August?
4	How many sales reps' last names start with **H**?
5	Do any of the sales reps have the same first name?
6	Do any of the sales reps have the same last name?
7	Which sales reps had less than $30,000 in sales in July?
8	Which sales reps had less than $30,000 in sales in August?

Create a Filter for Executive Development Seminars

Mr. Blackburn, the Executive Director for Executive Development Seminars, would like a table showing only the Georgia and South Carolina registrants attending the seminar to be held in Orlando on July 15–19.

1. Review the Filter feature in the Application Guide (p. 300); learn to use the Filter feature.
2. Open the *Orlando Seminar* table, and use the filter feature to provide a table showing the requested information.
3. Print a copy of the Georgia and South Carolina Registrants.

27C

Technique: Response Patterns

TIP

Word response: Key easy (balanced-hand) words as words.

Letter response: Key letters of one-hand words steadily and evenly, letter by letter.

1. Key each line twice; DS between 2-line groups.
2. Key 1' timings on lines 10–12; determine *gwam* on each timing.

Balanced-hand words

1 us so an by is or it do of go he if to me of ox am

2 an box air wig the and sir map pen men row fix jam

3 girl kept quay town auto busy firm dock held mango

One-hand words

4 be my up we on at no as oh as ax in at my up be we

5 no cat act red tax was you pin oil hip ear fat few

6 milk fast oily hymn base card safe draw pink gates

Balanced-hand phrases

7 to go|it is due|to the end|if it is|to do so|he is

8 pay the|for us|may do the|did he|make a|paid for a

9 he may|when did they|so do they|make a turn|to the

Balanced-hand sentences

10 I am to pay the six men if they do the work right.

11 Title to all of the lake land is held by the city.

12 The small ornament on their door is an ivory duck.

gwam 1' | 1 | 2 | 3 | 4 | 5 | 6 | 7 | 8 | 9 | 10 |

27D

Timed Writings

1. Key a 1' timing on each ¶; determine *gwam* on each timing.
2. Key two 2' timings on ¶s 1–2 combined; determine *gwam*.

LA   all letters used   gwam   2'

His mother signed her name with an X. His   5
father had no schooling. Could a President come   10
from such a humble background? President Lincoln   14
did. Lincoln was not just a President, he is often   20
recognized as one of the best to ever hold the office.   25

Honest Abe, as he was often called, always gave   30
the extra effort needed to be a success. Whether the   35
job was splitting logs, being a lawyer, or being   40
President, he always gave it his best. Dealing with   45
the Civil War required a man who gave his best.   50

gwam 2' | 1 | 2 | 3 | 4 | 5 |

LESSON 77 Sorts, Filters, and Queries

OUTCOMES

- Learn to create single and multiple data sorts.
- Learn to create filers.
- Learn to create queries.

77B

Sort Information for Franklin HS FBLA

Home/Sort & Filter/Select Type of Sort or Filter

1. Review the Sort feature in the Application Guide (p. 298); learn how to create sorts.
2. Open the *FHS FBLA Members* table file.
3. Perform the following sorts.

Single Sorts – *Ascending* Order
1. Last Name
2. ZIP Code

Single Sorts – *Descending* Order
1. Last Name
2. ZIP Code

4. Print the single sort by Last Name in Descending order.
5. Save and close the database.

77C

Sort Information for Software Professionals

TIP Sorts and queries can be used to arrange information to provide quick answers to questions.

1. Open *df 77c Software Professionals* to use to record your answers for this activity.
2. Open the *Software Professionals Inventory* database table.
3. Run sorts to answer the following questions.
4. **Save as:** *77c Software Professionals*.

Software Professionals	
No.	Question
1	What were the top three software packages in terms of number of copies sold?
2	What were the two software packages with the lowest beginning inventory?
3	How many software packages were designed mainly for education?
4	How many software packages sell for more than $250?
5	How many software packages sell for less than $100?

Technique: Response Patterns

1. As you key the lines, focus on making the reaches to the 1st- and 3rd-row keys without moving your hands or arms. The movement should be in the fingers.
2. Key each line twice; DS between 2-line groups.

za/az
1 zap lazy lizard pizza hazard bazaar frazzle dazzle
2 Zack and Hazel zapped the lazy lizard in the maze.

ol/lo
3 old load olive look fold lost bold loan allow told
4 Olympia told the lonely man to load the long logs.

ws/sw
5 swing cows sweet glows swept mows sword knows swap
6 He swung the sword over the sweaty cows and swine.

ju/ft
7 often jury draft judge left just hefty juice after
8 Jud, the fifth juror on my left, just wants juice.

ed/de
9 deal need debit edit deed edge deli used dent desk
10 Jed needed to edit the deed made by the defendant.

ik/ki
11 kick like kind bike kiln hike kids strike king ski
12 I like the kind of kids who like to hike and bike.

27F

Timed Writings

1. Key a 1' timing on each ¶; determine *gwam*.
2. Key two 2' timings on ¶s 1–2 combined; determine *gwam*.

E all letters used   gwam 2'

```
        •         2         •         4         •         6         •         8         •
      To risk your own life for the good of others          5
        10        •        12         •       14         •        16        •        18         •
has always been seen as an admirable thing to do.          10
  20        •        22         •       24         •        26         •       28         •
Harriet Tubman was a slave in the South.  She became       16
30        •        32         •       34         •        36         •       38         •
a free woman when she was able to run away to the          21
40        •        42         •       44         •        46         •       48         •       50
North.  This freedom just did not mean much to her         26
          •        52         •       54         •        56         •
while so many others were still slaves.                    30
        •         2         •         4         •         6         •         8         •
      She quickly put her own life at risk by going        35
        10        •        12         •       14         •        16        •        18         •
back to the South.  She did this to help others get        41
  20        •        22         •       24         •        26         •       28         •       30
free.  She was able to help several hundred.  This is      46
          •        32         •       34         •        36         •       38         •       40
a large number.  During the Civil War she continued        51
  •        42         •        44         •       46         •        48         •       50         •
to exhibit the traits of an amazing hero.  She served      57
  52        •        54         •       56         •       58
the Union as a spy and as a scout.                         60
```

gwam 2' | 1 | 2 | 3 | 4 | 5 |

For additional practice:

MicroType 6
Alphabetic Keyboarding

RT	SALES REPRESENTATIVES			
Last Name	Territory	ZIP	July Sales	August Sales
Carter	Wyoming	82001-1837	45,351	37,951
Hull	Colorado	30233-0070	53,739	49,762
McRae	Utah	84404-2835	33,371	38,978
Hernandez	Utah	84057-1572	39,371	40,790
Camby	Idaho	83702-8312	42,173	65,386
Henneman	Montana	59102-6735	17,219	29,737
Reed	Wyoming	82607-9956	53,791	59,349
Logan	Montana	59404-3883	49,712	21,790
Cirillo	Idaho	83202-7523	29,731	37,956
LeClair	Colorado	81503-2270	63,212	40,321
Donovan	Colorado	80123-0091	37,198	45,865
Young	Utah	84118-0111	44,876	56,791
Tapani	South Dakota	57702-9932	59,145	39,645
Rivera	Colorado	81005-8376	55,400	37,751
Walker	Idaho	83402-3326	43,900	44,750
Wetteland	Montana	59803-8388	33,650	40,765
Chi	Arizona	85224-1157	39,750	48,621
Finley	Arizona	85711-5656	19,765	35,765
Reese	Arizona	85268-0012	67,890	45,780
Bell	Colorado	80401-7529	39,200	43,286
Doolittle	South Dakota	57106-7621	64,890	37,102
Butler	Arizona	85302-1300	35,975	46,873
Hulett	Arizona	85023-2766	56,730	46,720

LESSON 28   Input Skill Development

OUTCOMES
- Build speed and accuracy.
- Enhance keying technique.

28A

Warmup

Key each line twice; DS between 2-line groups.

Alphabet   1 Levi Lentz packed my bag with six quarts of juice.

Caps Lock 2 KANSAS is KS; TEXAS is TX; IDAHO is ID; IOWA is IA.

Easy   3 Jan may name a tutor to work with the eight girls.

gwam 1' | 1 | 2 | 3 | 4 | 5 | 6 | 7 | 8 | 9 | 10 |

28B

Technique: Response Patterns

Key each line twice; DS between 2-line groups.

letter response
1 pink safe tree face hill look only fact date start
2 red dress|extra milk|union awards|pink car|you are
3 Jim Carter started a car in my garage in Honolulu.

word response
4 with work dock half coal hair both busy city civic
5 when they|fix their|pay the|did she|cut down|to it
6 Diana and Jan may go to the island to do the work.

combination response
7 big cat air act did fat due joy got pin rug was us
8 pink bowl|city street|their jump|extra chair|is at
9 Ed Burns was with Steve when we started the feast.

letter   10 Jim saw a fat cat in a cab as we sat in my garage.
combination 11 Jay was the man you saw up at the lake in the bus.
word   12 I may go to the lake with the men to fix the door.

28C

Speed Check: Sentences

Key two 30" timings on each line. Try to increase your keying speed the second time you key the line. Determine *gwam* for the faster timing of each line.

1 Ben will be ready before noon.
2 Sam will bring his dog to the lake.
3 Jack did not fill the two cars with gas.
4 Jon will take the next test when he is ready.
5 Susan is to bring two or three copies of the play.
6 This may be the last time you will have to take a test.

gwam 30" | 2 | 4 | 6 | 8 | 10 | 12 | 14 | 16 | 18 | 20 | 22 |

	Record 1	Record 2	Record 3
Software:	Basic Spreadsheets	Computer Geography	Computerized Reading
Purchases:	1200	400	500
Sales:	1578	850	674

	Record 4	Record 5	Record 6
Software:	Creative Bus. Letters	Data Controller	English Enhancement
Purchases:	250	0	1000
Sales:	400	240	1200

	Record 7	Record 8	Record 9
Software:	Financial Advisors	Graphics Designer	Keyboard Composition
Purchases:	1000	500	1000
Sales:	1987	437	1753

	Record 10	Record 11	Record 12
Software:	Language Arts Skills	Quick Key WP	Spelling Mastery
Purchases:	500	1000	0
Sales:	759	1378	300

	Record 13	Record 14	Record 15
Software:	Tax Assistant	Telephone Directory	Art Gallery
Purchases:	0	1000	500
Sales:	980	1873	673

	Record 16	Record 17	Record 18
Software:	Your Time Manager	Office Layout	Math Tutor
Purchases:	1000	300	0
Sales:	1379	475	39

76G

Add New Fields to a Table and Update Records for Rockwell Technologies

1. Open the *Sales Reps – District 13* table.
2. Add new fields for **Territory**, **ZIP**, **July Sales**, and **August Sales**.
3. Update the records in the database table to include the new information provided on the next page.
4. Add another new field with a field name of **Courtesy Title**. Use **Ms.** for all female reps except McRae, Donovan, and Finley. They prefer to use **Mrs.** for their courtesy title. Use **Mr.** for all male reps.
5. Print the revised table in landscape orientation.
6. Save and close the database.

Quarter-Minute Checkpoints				
gwam	1/4'	1/2'	3/4'	Time
16	4	8	12	16
20	5	10	15	20
24	6	12	18	24
28	7	14	21	28
32	8	16	24	32
36	9	18	27	36
40	10	20	30	40

Guided (Paced) Timing Procedure

Establish a goal rate

1. Key a 1' timing on ¶ 1 of a set of ¶s that contain superior figures for guided timings, as in 28D below.

2. Using the *gwam* as a base, add 4 *gwam* to set your goal rate.

3. From column 1 of the table at the left, choose the speed nearest your goal rate. In the quarter-minute columns beside that speed, note the points in the copy you must reach to attain your goal rate.

4. Determine the checkpoint for each quarter minute from the word count above the lines in ¶ 1. (*Example:* Checkpoints for 24 *gwam* are 6, 12, 18, and 24.)

Practice procedure

1. Key two 1' timings on ¶ 1 at your goal rate guided by the quarter-minute calls (1/4, 1/2, 3/4, time). Try to reach each checkpoint before the guide is called.

2. Key two 1' timings on ¶ 2 of a set of ¶s in the same way.

3. If time permits, key a 2' writing on the set of ¶s combined, without the guides.

28D

Timed Writings

1. Key a 1' timing on each ¶; determine *gwam*.

2. Using your better *gwam* as a base rate, set a goal rate and key two 1' guided timings on each ¶ as directed above.

3. Key two 2' unguided timings on ¶s 1–2 combined; determine *gwam*.

 all letters used   gwam 2'

```
             •      2      •      4      •      6      •      8      •
       Is it possible for a mouse to make an individual        5
10        •      12     •      14     •      16     •      18     •      20
quite wealthy?  Yes, of course it is.  If you do not           11
             •      22     •      24     •      26     •      28     •      30
believe it, consider Walt Disney.  This individual            16
        •      32     •      34     •      36     •      38     •      40     •
came from a very humble beginning.  But in the end,           21
  42        •      44     •      46     •      48     •      50     •
he was a very wealthy person.  He was a person whose          26
52        •      54     •      56     •      58     •      60     •
work brought great enjoyment to the lives of many            31
  62        •
people.                                                       31
             •      2      •      4      •      6      •      8      •
       A mouse, duck, and dog are just a few of the           36
10        •      12     •      14     •      16     •      18     •
exquisite personalities he brought to life.  After           41
  20        •      22     •      24     •      26     •      28     •
all these years, his work is still a part of our             46
  30        •      32     •      34     •      36     •      38     •
lives.  People travel miles to step into the amazing         51
40        •      42     •      44     •      46     •      48     •      50
world of Disney.  It would be impossible to picture          56
        •      52     •      54     •
this world without his work.                                 59
```

gwam 2' | 1 | 2 | 3 | 4 | 5 |

28E

Technique: Response Patterns

Key each line twice; DS between 2-line groups.

Double letters
1 took yell meet carrot need cross spoon little loop
2 Dianna has lived in Massachusetts and Mississippi.

Shift keys
3 New Jersey, South Dakota, New Mexico, North Dakota
4 The Padres play the Cubs on Tuesday and Wednesday.

76C

Edit Records for Software Professionals

Editing existing database records is similar to editing wp documents. Simply move the insertion point to the location where the change is to be made and use the Insert, Delete, or Backspace keys to make changes.

1. Open the *Software Professionals Inventory* database table.
2. Make the following changes.
   a. Change the price of Computer Geography to **$279**.
   b. Change the name of Creative Business Letters to **Creative Letters**.
   c. Change the price of Basic Spreadsheets to **$159**.
   d. The beginning inventory of Data Controller should have been **300**.
   e. Change the name of Language Arts Skills to **Language Skills**.
3. Save and close the database.

76D

Edit Records for Rockwell Technologies

1. Open the *Sales Reps – District 13* table.
2. Make the following changes.
   a. Carrie Chi's first name should be spelled **Karrie**.
   b. Jay Reese has moved; his new address is:
      1811 Olympic Way, N.
      Scottsdale, AZ
   c. Marsha Logan should have been entered as **Marshall** Logan.
   d. Mary Carter would like her name recorded as **Mary Carter-Bond.**
3. Save and close the database.

76E

Edit Records for Franklin FBLA

1. Open the *FHS FBLA Members* table to correct data entry errors.
2. Make the following changes to the table.
   a. Ms. Radclif's first name should be spelled **Julia**, not Julie.
   b. Ms. Sanchez moved to **748 Market Street**; the ZIP Code didn't change.
   c. Ms. Hawthorne's address should be **874** Montgomery Street.
   d. Mr. Lockwood's first name is **Greg**, not Gregg.
   e. Mr. Foster's address should be **874** Franklin Street.
3. Save and close the database.

76F

Add New Fields to Table for Software Professionals and Update Records

Over time a database may need to be modified in order to meet the information needs of the user. Some of the original information may no longer be needed, or additional information may be needed. Database tables may be modified by adding and deleting fields in order to accommodate the changing needs of the user.

1. Learn how to add new fields to a table.
2. Add two new fields to the *Software Professionals Inventory* database table, one for **Purchases** and one for **Sales.**
3. Update the records in the *Software Professionals Inventory* database table to include the new information provided on the next page.
4. Print a copy of the revised table in landscape orientation.
5. Save and close the database.

Rough Draft: Edited Copy

∧	= insert
#	= add space
∼	= transpose
ℓ	= delete
⊂⊃	= close up
≡	= capitalize

1. Study the proofreaders' marks shown at the right.
2. Key each sentence twice; DS between 2-line groups. Make all editing (handwritten) changes.

1 A first ~rough~ draft is a preliminary orr tentative one. ~revision~

2 It is where the ~creator~ ~writer~ gets his/~her~ thoughts on paper.

3 After the ~rough~ draft is created, it will be ~looked over~ ~edited~.

4 ~Reviewing~ ~Editing~ is the step where a ~person~ ~writer~ refines ~the~ copy.

5 Proof readers' marks are used to edit the ~original~ ~rough draft~ copy ~original~.

6 The ed~i~ting changes will be then be made to the ~copy~.

7 After the change~s~ have been made read the copy ag~ai~n.

8 ≡more changes ~still may~ need to be made to the copy.

9 Ed~i~ting ~and~ proof reading does take ~a lot~ time and effort.

10 ~an~ error free ~message~ ~copy~ is worth the trouble, how ever.

Timed Writings

Quarter-Minute Checkpoints

gwam	1/4'	1/2'	3/4'	1'
20	5	10	15	20
24	6	12	18	24
28	7	14	21	28
32	8	16	24	32
36	9	18	27	36
40	10	20	30	40
44	11	22	33	44
48	12	24	36	48
52	13	26	39	52
56	14	28	42	56

For additional practice:

MicroType 6

Alphabetic Keyboarding

www.cengage.com/school/
keyboarding/c21key

1. Key one 1' unguided and two 1' guided timings on each ¶.
2. Key two 2' unguided timings on ¶s 1–2 combined; determine gwam.

LA all letters used

	gwam	2'

Respect the kid who brings your newspaper. He or she 5
may be one of our next great leaders. One of the first jobs 12
Benjamin Franklin had was that of delivering papers. Later 18
in life he became recognized for the work he did in other 23
areas. 24

He was a printer. He was an author. He was a 29
philosopher. He is also known for his work as a scientist. 35
In addition, he is quite well known for the work he did as a 41
diplomat. He took part in the American Revolution. You 47
combine all this, and you have one of the greatest statesmen 53
of our country. 54

gwam 2' | 1 | 2 | 3 | 4 | 5 |

LESSON 76

Editing Records, Adding Fields, and Deleting Records

OUTCOMES

- Learn efficient ways to navigate within tables and forms.
- Edit records in tables and forms.
- Add new fields to a table.

76B

Navigate Within Tables and Forms

There are several ways to move the insertion point to a new location in a database table and a database form. Some methods take more keystrokes than others.

INSERTION POINT MOVES—TABLE

To move:	Keys
One field left	←
One field right	→
One line up	↑
One line down	↓
Leftmost field	Home
Rightmost field	End
Down one window	PgDn
Up one window	PgUp
To first record	Ctrl + Home
To last record	Ctrl + End

INSERTION POINT MOVES—FORM

To move:	Keys
Next field	↓
Previous field	↑
Top of form	Home
Bottom of form	End
First record	Ctrl + Home
Last record	Ctrl + End
Next record*	PgDn
Previous record*	PgUp
*If the record has more than one screen, use Ctrl + PgUp (PgDn).	

1. Open the *FHS FBLA Members* database membership table that you worked with in Lesson 75, and practice navigating within it.

2. Open the *FHS FBLA Members* database membership form file, and practice navigating within it.
   - Find Mitchell Wickman's record.
   - Go to Record 23.
   - Find all the records with a ZIP Code of 94111 (key **94111** in the Search box at the bottom of the screen, and tap Enter until it remains on the same record).

3. Close the database.

Lesson 29   Help Basics
Lesson 30   Special Features

LESSON 29   Help Basics

OUTCOMES
- Gain an overview of software Help features
- Learn to use software Help features

29A

Overview

Word Help

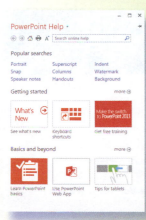

PowerPoint Help

Figure 4-1 Similar Help screens

Application software offers built-in Help features that you can access directly in the software as you work. **Help** is the equivalent of a user's manual on how to use your software. Listed below are some of the main functions that most software Help features allow you to do.

- Search for topics
- Browse a table of contents of Help topics organized by categories (Office 2010 users only)
- Point to screen items for a concise explanation of their use
- Access technical resources, free downloads, and other options at the software manufacturer's website

The Help features work the same way for each software application in the Office suite. For example, the Microsoft Help feature works the same in *Word* or *Excel* as it does in *PowerPoint* or *Access* (see Figure 4-1).

The software's Help features can be accessed by tapping F1 or by clicking on the question mark located in the upper-right corner of the screen (see Figure 4-2).

Figure 4-2 Access Help feature

Help button

The Maximize button at the upper-right corner of the Help screen fills the entire computer screen with the Help feature. Once the Maximize button is activated, it becomes the Restore Down button, which is used to restore the Help screen to its original size (see Figure 4-3).

The Minimize button removes the Help feature from the screen but keeps it open. Once the minimize button is clicked, you can restore the Help feature by clicking the question mark that appears beneath the status bar along with the other programs that are open.

The Help feature can be closed by clicking the **Close** button located at the upper right of the Help feature.

Minimize   Maximize/Restore Down   Close

Figure 4-3 Minimize, Maximize, and Close buttons

	SALES REPRESENTATIVES			
Last Name	**First Name**	**Address**	**City**	**State**
Walker	Trent	872 Texas Avenue	Idaho Falls	ID
Wetteland	Cynthia	380 Clearview Drive	Missoula	MT
Chi	Carrie	310 Sagebrush Court	Chandler	AZ
Finley	Ann	388 Oxford Drive	Tucson	AZ
Reese	Jay	330 Shiloh Way	Scottsdale	AZ
Bell	Scott	7211 Larkspur Drive	Golden	CO
Doolittle	Lisa	872 Kingswood Way	Sioux Falls	SD
Butler	Warren	398 Navajo Drive	Glendale	AZ
Hulett	Sandra	450 La Paz Court	Phoenix	AZ

75D

Update Database for Franklin FBLA

1. Open the *Franklin HS FBLA* database.
2. Add the three new memberships shown below to the membership table.
3. Save and close the database.

Franklin High School FBLA

Last Name: *Van Buren*
First Name: *Dianna*
City: *San Francisco*
Street Address: *773 Broadway Street*
State: *CA*   ZIP: *94133*

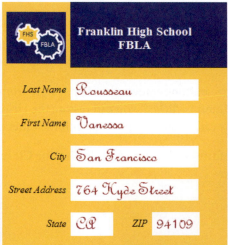

Franklin High School FBLA

Last Name: *Rousseau*
First Name: *Vanessa*
City: *San Francisco*
Street Address: *764 Hyde Street*
State: *CA*   ZIP: *94109*

Franklin High School FBLA

Last Name: Underwood
First Name: Katelin
City: San Francisco
Street Address: 834 Van Ness Avenue
State: CA   ZIP: 94109

Access Help

NOTE
The size of the Help box can be adjusted by clicking and dragging the edges of the dialog box. The Help box can also be moved to a different location on the screen (click the title bar at the top of the dialog box and drag to a new location) to allow you to see other parts of the screen.

1. Access Microsoft Office Word Help (see Figure 4-4).
2. Click the Maximize button.
3. Click the Minimize button.
4. Click the **?** beneath the status line to reactivate the Help feature.
5. Click the Close button.

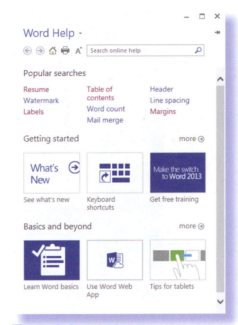

Figure 4-4 Help menu

Digital Citizenship and Ethics

The widespread use of the Internet for shopping and conducting financial transactions has led to scams in which online thieves trick users into supplying credit card and bank account numbers as well as other personal information.

One such scam is known as **phishing**. In this scam, you get an official-looking e-mail that appears to be from your bank or other financial institution. The e-mail tells you there is a problem with your account and asks you to confirm your account number, Social Security number, or some other personal information. But the message is a fake.

You should never respond to e-mails asking for personal information. If your bank needs to contact you about something, an employee will call or send a letter. The bank will not ask for personal information via an e-mail. You should always be suspicious if you get an e-mail or a phone message asking you to verify an account. Also, keep your antivirus and antispyware software up to date.

As a class, discuss the following.

1. What are ways you can verify that an e-mail message comes from a legitimate source?
2. If you suspect that you received a phishing e-mail from a party posing as your bank, what course of action would you take?

TEAMWORK

Adding Records to Update a Database

OUTCOMES

- Update an existing database.
- Add new records to a table.

75B

Update Database for Software Professionals

Database software lets you add records to update a table at any time. Lynda Smoltz provided the information below to be added to the *Software Professionals* database.

1. Open the *Software Professionals Inventory* table.
2. Add the following records to the table.
3. Save and close the database.

	Record 13	Record 14	Record 15
Stock No.:	B952	B658	B839
Software:	Tax Assistant	Telephone Directory	Art Gallery
Price:	$129	$119	$249
Beg. Invt.:	5000	5000	1000

	Record 16	Record 17	Record 18
Stock No.:	B794	B833	E910
Software:	Your Time Manager	Office Layout	Math Tutor
Price:	$69	$129	$59
Beg. Invt.:	2500	500	2000

75C

Update Database for Rockwell Technologies

Mr. Vermillion would like the information about the additional sales reps listed below added to the *Sales Reps – District 13* table.

1. Open the *Sales Reps – District 13* table.
2. Add the records shown below to the table.
3. Save and close the database.

1. Access Microsoft Office Word Help.
2. Study the Help Buttons shown in Figure 4-5 and on Microsoft Office Word Help.

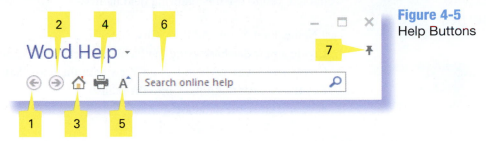

Figure 4-5
Help Buttons

1. Back
2. Forward
3. Home
4. Print

5. Change Font Size
6. Search online help
7. Keep on Top (Not on Top)

3. Click *Learn Word basics* in the lower left corner. Use the scroll bar to scroll down to see what is included with *Learn Word basics*.
4. Increase the font size; decrease the font size (see Figure 4-6).

Large Font Size

Small Font Size

Word Help ·

Basic tasks in Word 2013

Touch Guide

Microsoft Word 2013 is a word-processing program designed to help you create professional-quality documents. Word helps you organize and write your documents more efficiently.

Your first step in creating a document in Word 2013 is to choose whether to start from a blank document or to let a template do much of the work for you. From then on, the basic steps in creating and sharing documents are the same. Powerful editing and reviewing tools help you work with others to make your document perfect.

TIP   For a training course to help you

Word Help ·

Basic tasks in Word 2013

Touch Guide

Microsoft Word 2013 is a word-processing program designed to help you create professional-quality documents. Word helps you organize and write your documents more efficiently.

Your first step in creating a document in Word 2013 is to choose whether to start from a blank document or to let a template do much of the work for you. From then on, the basic steps in creating and sharing documents are the same. Powerful editing and reviewing tools help you work with others to make your document perfect.

TIP   For a training course to help you create your first document, see Create your first Word 2013 document. To learn about the features that are new to Word 2013, see What's new in Word 2013.

Choose a template

It's often easier to create a new document using a template instead of starting with a blank page. Word templates are ready to use with themes and styles. All you

Figure 4-6 Font sizes in Help

5. Use the Back button to return to the Work Help screen.
6. Use the Forward button to return to *Basic tasks in Word 2013* and scroll down to *Open a document*.
7. Click the Maximize button; click the Restore Down button.
8. Use the Home button to return to the Home screen.
9. Click the Keep Help on Top button. Click outside of the Help dialog box. Click the Keep Help on Top button again to change it to Don't Keep Help on Top pin. Click outside the Help dialog box. Notice what happens to the dialog box each time.
10. Reactivate the Help feature by clicking on the ? beneath the status line.
11. Close the Help feature.

Create a Database for Rockwell Technologies

Goran Bogicevic/Shutterstock.com

Paul M. Vermillion, District 13 sales manager for *Rockwell Technologies,* would like you to create a database containing the names and addresses of all sales representatives in his district. He would like you to use the following field names:

Last Name, First Name, Address, City, State

1. Create a new database using the filename **Rockwell Technologies**.
2. Create and save a table in Design View with the name **Sales Reps – District 13**.
3. Key the records that follow into the table.
4. Save and close the database.

SALES REPRESENTATIVES				
Last Name	**First Name**	**Address**	**City**	**State**
Carter	Mary	310 Old Trail Road	Cheyenne	WY
Hull	Dale	2710 Blue Jay Lane	Denver	CO
McRae	Jessica	475 Canyon Road	Ogden	UT
Hernandez	Erika	375 Highland Drive	Orem	UT
Camby	Sue	378 Ranchero Road	Boise	ID
Henneman	Jason	762 Nugget Drive	Billings	MT
Reed	Jessica	817 Herrington Drive	Casper	WY
Logan	Marsha	905 Chickadee Court	Great Falls	ID
Cirillo	Mathew	1208 Whitaker Road	Pocatello	ID
LeClair	Justin	830 Whitehead Drive	Grand Junction	CO
Donovan	Kellee	765 Coal Mine Avenue	Littleton	CO
Young	Marsha	7563 Ferncrest Circle	Salt Lake City	UT
Tapani	Devlin	543 Lookout Mountain	Rapid City	SD
Rivera	Jose	756 Royal Crest Drive	Pueblo	CO

Help Table of Contents for Office 2010 Users

1. Read the information below.
2. Access the Table of Contents by clicking the book icon Help button. When you click the icon, the book opens and the Table of Contents appears. The Table of Contents can be closed by clicking the open book icon.
3. Click a category in the Table of Contents that interests you. Read the topic information (for ease of reading, use the Maximize button and increase font size to Largest). Go to related topics, if any.
4. Read two other categories that interest you. Print any information you think will be helpful in the future.

Like the table of contents in a book, the Table of Contents feature in Help lets you look for information that is organized by categories. In the Table of Contents shown below in the left-hand pane, a book icon indicates a category. Click on the book to open it and reveal the topics available on the category. Some categories have subcategories (see Figure 4-7). The topics available for the subcategories can also be viewed by clicking on the book to open. Click on the desired topic, and information on the topic will be displayed in the right-hand pane.

Figure 4-7 Help Table of Contents

21st Century Skills: Access and Evaluate Information

The Internet and World Wide Web have given computer users quick and easy access to information on virtually any topic. As you learned in this unit, that includes helpful information on your computer's operations and the software you use. But how do you know that the information is accurate, timely, and written by a reliable and knowledge-able source? Following are some tips:

- Verify any information by checking another source.
- Identify the author or organization that publishes or sponsors the site and identify the date the content was created or last updated.
- On the home page, look for a statement or purpose for the site.
- Examine the language of the site. Does it provide facts, opinions, or both? A reliable site should present information in a balanced and objective manner and should be free of spelling and grammatical errors.

Think Critically

Open a new word processing document and compose answers to these questions.

1. Why is it important to evaluate information you read on the Web?
2. Do you think the Internet is as reliable a source of information for computer help as the documentation that comes with your computer or software?
3. Describe ways in which you evaluate information you obtain in various formats, including the Internet, television, print publications, and in person.
4. **Save as:** *u04 21century*.

**Add Records
to Software
Professionals
Database**

1. Key the records below into the *Software Professionals Inventory* table.
2. Save and close the table.

	Record 1	Record 2	Record 3
Stock No.:	B929	E246	E786
Software:	Basic Spreadsheets	Computer Geography	Computerized Reading
Price:	$139	$259	$189
Beg. Invt.:	2000	2500	1000

	Record 4	Record 5	Record 6
Stock No.:	E561	B821	E320
Software:	Creative Bus. Letters	Data Controller	English Enhancement
Price:	$125	$309	$219
Beg. Invt.:	500	500	800

	Record 7	Record 8	Record 9
Stock No.:	B689	B586	E758
Software:	Financial Advisors	Graphic Designer	Keyboard Composition
Price:	$99	$165	$155
Beg. Invt.:	2500	400	3000

	Record 10	Record 11	Record 12
Stock No.:	B615	B731	E641
Software:	Language Arts Skills	Quick Key WP	Spelling Mastery
Price:	$139	$75	$139
Beg. Invt.:	1500	2500	2000

LESSON 30   Special Features

- Learn to use the pop-up description feature
- Access additional software support on the Internet

30A

ScreenTips

1. Read the information below.
2. Learn how to use the pop-up description feature of your software.
3. Take a pop-up description tour of your screen. Use the feature to learn what unfamiliar screen items do.

A valuable Help feature for new users is the pop-up description box. This feature may be called ScreenTips, Quick Tips, or something similar. It allows you to use the mouse to point to commands or other objects on the screen. After a brief period of time, a pop-up box appears, giving a concise description of the feature.

Figure 4-8 shows what happens when you point at the **Format Painter** command found in the **Clipboard** group of the Home tab. For this particular command, the pop-up box tells you:

- The name of the command (for some commands, the shortcuts to activate the command are also given)
- What it is used for
- How to use it

Sometimes the box will offer more information about the command (see Figure 4-9) by telling you to *Press F1 for more help* (**Office 2010**) or having you click on *Tell me more* at the bottom of the pop-up box (**Office 2013**). When you are finished reading the information, move the pointer away from the command to close the description box.

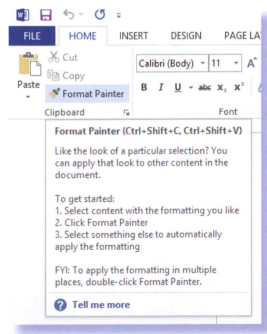

Figure 4-8 Pop-up Box information

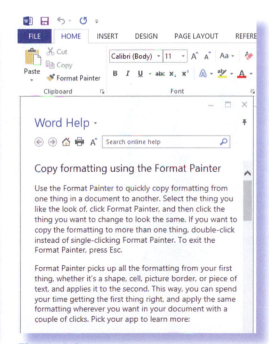

Figure 4-9 Help description box

LESSON 74

OUTCOMES

- Create a new database and table.
- Add records to a new database.

Creating a Database and Table

74B

Create a Database for Software Professionals

Create/Tables/Table Design

Vladitto/Shutterstock.com

Information has always been critical to the successful operation of a business. In today's business environment, more and more information is being stored and accessed through the use of databases. As noted earlier, a database is a computerized filing system that is used to organize and maintain a collection of data. The data is stored in tables. A database may contain one table or any number of tables. A few examples of different types of databases include customers' names and addresses, personnel records, sales records, payroll records, telephone numbers, and investment records.

One of the databases you worked with in Lesson 73 was a membership file that contained information about each member; the other database contained seminar registration information. In the remainder of this unit, you will be creating and working with several different databases.

The first database you will create is for *Software Professionals*. Lynda Smoltz, the manager, would like you to create a database for the software products they sell. She would like the database table to include the following field information:

Stock Number

Software

Price

Beginning Inventory

1. Review the information on defining and sequencing fields of a database table in the Application Guide on pp. 293-294
2. Learn how to create a new database.
3. Create a new database using the filename *Software Professionals*.
4. Learn how to create a table in Design View.
5. Create a table using Design View; save it using the name *Software Professionals Inventory*.

30B

Use ScreenTips

1. Use the pop-up description to learn about each of the features shown below.
2. Key a sentence or two explaining the purpose of each feature.

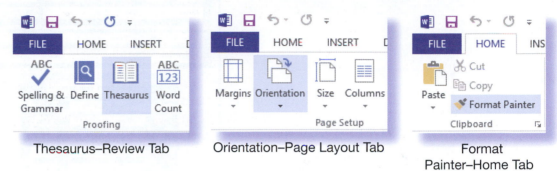

Thesaurus–Review Tab

Orientation–Page Layout Tab

Format Painter–Home Tab

30C

Office Online

1. Read the information below.
2. Access http://office.microsoft.com/en-us/ (shown in Figure 4-10) or the manufacturer's website of the software you are using.
3. Spend some time browsing what is available online from the software manufacturer. Microsoft provides:

- **MY OFFICE** to sign in for working in the cloud.
- **PRODUCTS** to view information about the latest products from the manufacturer.
- **SUPPORT** to access training videos for each of the Office applications.
- **IMAGES** to download free images.
- **TEMPLATES** to download business and personal templates available through the manufacturer.
- **STORE** to access applications which are available to download for purchase or for free.

Figure 4-10 Office Online

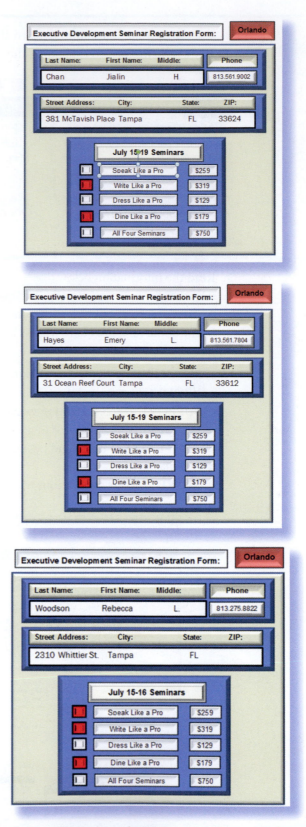

Ms. Woodson didn't include a ZIP Code on her registration form. Use http://zip4.usps.com to get a ZIP Code for Ms. Woodson.

1. Access http://office.microsoft.com/en-us/; see Figure 4-11.
2. Click on **Support** at the top of the screen; then click on *Free Training*.

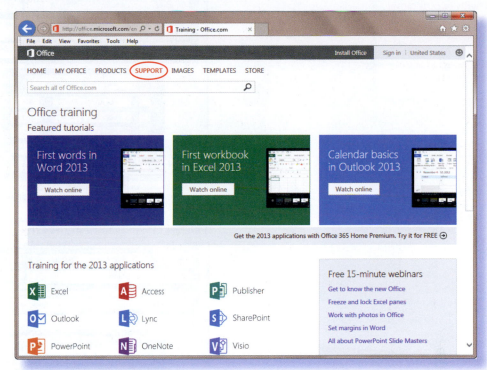

Figure 4-11 Support menu

3. Find training for Word 2013. Note that there are training applications for Office 2013, Office 2010, and Office 2007.
4. Click on *Download*; a screen will appear at the bottom. Click on *Open*.

5. Follow the instructions provided to view the training for Word.

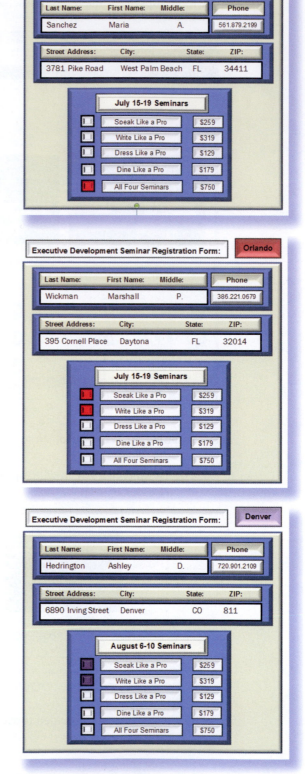

TIP The data type for the seminar fields was set to *currency* with two decimal places. When you key **750**, the format will automatically be changed to **$750.00** when you tap the Tab or Enter key.

Something is wrong with Ms. Hedrington's ZIP Code on her registration form. Use http://zip4.usps.com to get a ZIP Code for Ms. Hedrington.

Connected to Office.com for Office 2010 Users

1. Access Microsoft Office Word Help.
2. Access the Table of Contents.
3. Change from working *Offline* to *Connected to Office.com* by clicking *Offline* and then clicking *Show content from Office.com* (see Figure 4-12).
4. Click Creating documents to see help and videos available online about creating documents. Preview some of the videos by clicking on the video icon (see Figure 4-13).

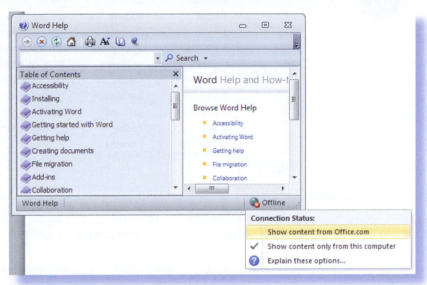

Figure 4-12 Connect to Office.com

Figure 4-13 Training Courses and Videos

www.cengage.com/school/keyboarding/c21key

Print a Database Table

Open the *Franklin HS FBLA* database, and print a copy of the *FHS FBLA Members* table in landscape orientation. It should look similar to Figure 14-22.

ID	First Name	Last Name	Address	City	State	ZIP
1	Jason	McWilliams	138 Van Ness Avenue	San Francisco	CA	94102
2	Maria	Sanchez	298 Hyde Street	San Francisco	CA	94102
3	Julie	Radclif	208 Broadway Street	San Francisco	CA	94111
4	Tyler	Saxon	586 California Street	San Francisco	CA	94104
5	Estella	Covington	670 Stockton Street	San Francisco	CA	94108
6	Sherri	Williams	780 Castle Street	San Francisco	CA	94133
7	Threse	Farina	430 Davis Street	San Francisco	CA	94111
8	Lauren	Alexander	783 Calhoun Terrace	San Francisco	CA	94133
9	Grant	Stewart	608 Winter Place	San Francisco	CA	94133
10	Lacy	Taylor	510 Market Street	San Francisco	CA	94104
11	Mitchell	Wickman	651 Battery Street	San Francisco	CA	94111

FHS FBLA Members (Lesson 72C & 72D)

Figure 14-22 Table

73F

Add Records to a Database

The FBLA database that you worked with included fields for name and address. The next database that you will work with consists of additional fields of information as well as two tables.

The **Executive Development Seminar** company uses a database to track registration information for their seminars. A separate database table is created for each seminar that includes the *name*, *address*, and *telephone* information of each registrant and the seminars they want to attend.

Notice that all the registration forms shown below and on the next page are for the seminar to be held July 15–19 in Orlando except for one, which will be held August 6–10 in Denver. Open the *df Executive Development Seminar* database, and save it as **Executive Development Seminar**. Open the *Orlando Seminar* form file, and key the information from the five registration forms shown below. You will need to key the Denver registrant in the table file since a form for the Denver registrants has not yet been created.

For consistency, key the telephone numbers in the same format as the current records in the file: *(516) 879-2199* rather than *561.879.2199*, as shown on the registration forms. For the seminars, key the dollar amount paid for the seminar. Leave the fields blank for any seminar that the registrant hasn't selected. For example, on the first registration form you would key $750 in the *All Four Seminars* field, leaving the other fields blank.

Academic and Career Connections

Complete the following exercises that introduce various topics that involve academic themes and careers.

Grammar and Writing: Commas

MicroType 6

- References/Communication Skills/Terminal Punctuation
- CheckPro/Communication Skills 3
- CheckPro/Word Choice 3

1. Go to MicroType 6 and use this feature path for review: References/Communication Skills/ Commas.
2. Click *Rules* and review the rules of using commas.
3. Then, under *Commas*, click *Posttest*.
4. Follow the instructions to complete the posttest.

Optional Activities:

1. Go to this path: CheckPro/Communication Skills 3.
2. Complete the activities as directed.
3. Go to this path: CheckPro/Word Choice 3.
4. Key the Apply lines and choose the correct word.

Communications: Reading

1. Open *df u04 communications*.
2. Read the document carefully, and then close the file.
3. In a new document, key your answers to the following questions.
   a. Pearl Buck was the first American woman to win what award?
   b. What award did Pearl Buck win in 1932 for her novel *The Good Earth*?
   c. What country is the setting for *The Good Earth*?
   d. Which award discussed in the document is an international award given to writers from many different countries and cultures?
   e. Which award discussed in the document recognizes American authors?
   f. What is the main topic of the first paragraph in the document?
4. **Save as: *u04 communications*.**

Math Skills

1. Ben uses his word processing software's built-in Help system to access the software manufacturer's website. He sees that there are a number of software updates that he can download for free. He selects a security update and sees that the application is 7.25 MB. He begins the download process. At one point, a message box opens that says the download is 40% complete. How much of the application has been downloaded?
2. If 1 megabyte (MB) equals 1,048,576 bytes, how many bytes is the security update? (*Hint*: When multiplying by a decimal, count the total number of decimal places in both factors and then insert a decimal point in the answer so that it has the same total number of decimal places as the factors.)
3. Ben wants to find out how much hard disk space he has left on his computer. The size of his hard disk is 148 GB and 3/4 of the space is being used. How many gigabytes are free?
4. Ben reviews a folder on his hard disk. The folder contains a total of 256 files. Of the total, roughly 1/3 are word processing documents; 1/4 are presentation files; 1/6 are picture files; 1/8 are spreadsheet files; and the remaining 1/8 are various other formats. How many of each type of file are in the folder? (Round to the nearest whole number.)

1. Open the *FHS FBLA Members* form file in the *Franklin HS FBLA* database.
2. Input the information contained on the following membership applications into the database form.
3. After keying the last record, close the file.

Franklin High School
FBLA

Last Name   Matsuzaka

First Name   Vanessa

City   San Francisco

Street Address   773 Broadway Street

State CA   ZIP 94133

Franklin High School
FBLA

Last Name   Pierzynski

First Name   Kim

City   San Francisco

Street Address   574 California Street

State CA   ZIP 94108

Franklin High School
FBLA

Last Name   Cordova

First Name   Roberto

City   San Francisco

Street Address   38 Stockton Street

State CA   ZIP 94108

Planning a Career in Information Technology

Almost every type of business uses some form of information technology in its day-to-day activities. For example, a multinational corporation might maintain a wireless network connecting thousands of employees around the world; or an entrepreneur might launch a new website to market his services; or a doctor's office might supply medical personnel with handheld computers to access patient information at the touch of a button. Information technology, or IT, refers to the design, development, support, and management of hardware, software, multimedia, and systems integration services.

Individuals who work in the IT industry help build links between people and technology, whether that's developing an application for your smart phone or providing Internet access to a classroom of students. Workers in this industry might focus on network systems, information support and services, Web and digital communications, and programming and software development.

What's It Like?

Those who work in the IT field are charged with setting up, managing, and maintaining an organization's computer systems. For example:

© Benis Arapovic/Shutterstock.com

- They coordinate the installation of new hardware, such as individual workstations, printers and other peripherals, and companywide networks.
- They develop programs to meet the specific needs of the organization, such as an application that helps the business monitor its inventory needs.
- They develop Internet and intranet sites that enable both those within the organization (employees) and external customers to access information.
- They are increasingly involved with the upkeep, maintenance, and security of systems and networks.

IT professionals typically work in offices. They are employed by large and small businesses, nonprofit organizations, and public institutions such as schools and government offices. Jobs in this field can often be high pressure and require long hours, especially in those organizations where timely access to information and data is critical.

Employment Outlook

Faster than average employment growth is forecasted for the IT industry, and job prospects are strong. According to the Bureau of Labor Statistics, employment is expected to grow 17 percent over the 2008–2018 decade, which is faster than the average for all occupations. Most employers require that IT workers have a bachelor's degree in a computer-related field, although many prefer a graduate degree, such as an MBA.

What About You?

The Information Technology career cluster is covered in box 11 of the Interest Survey Activity you completed in Unit 1 of this text. If this box had one of the three highest scores on your survey, you should further explore the cluster's pathways and related occupations.

1. Why do you think a career in information technology could be a good choice?
2. Can you picture yourself doing this type of job?
3. Why are these jobs important to our economy?

Add Records to a Table

© iStockphoto.com/Steve Shepard

1. Open the *df Franklin HS FBLA* database, and save it as *Franklin HS FBLA*. Open the *FHS FBLA Members* table.
2. Franklin High School FBLA has had five new students join. Include them in the FBLA database. They are all from San Francisco. Key the membership information shown below directly into the database table.
3. Close the database file after keying the last record.

New Members
September 16–September 30, 20xx

First Name	Last Name	Address	ZIP
Michael	Gutierrez	635 California Street	94108
Karla	Fitzgerald	368 Mission Street	94105
Justin	Saevig	573 Annie Street	94105
Shannon	Covington	670 Stockton Street	94108
Cody	Foster	873 Franklin Street	94102

© iStockphoto.com/Juanmonino

21st Century Skills: Use and Manage Information

Educational institutions use databases to organize information on students, teachers and staff, and class offerings. Governments use databases to manage information on personnel, taxes, and public programs and facilities. Businesses use databases to store information about customers, sales, inventories, and more.

But how is all this information obtained? Most of it is provided voluntarily. For example, individuals provide information when they enroll at a school or college, apply for a driver's license, fill out a job application, or answer a survey.

Think Critically

1. Most organizations obtain and use database information for legitimate business reasons. Provide examples of how a business might use customer purchasing information to increase sales.
2. What dangers or risks are involved with supplying information about yourself that will be stored in an electronic database?
3. If you created a database of friends, family, and other contacts, what type of information would you store on each person? Is there any information you think would be inappropriate to share with others?

© Edw/Shutterstock.com

Complete this activity to help prepare for the **Computer Literacy Open** event in BPA's Administrative Support division. Participants in this event are tested on their understanding of computer terminology related to operating systems, hardware, and software.

You have learned that a computer has five basic functions. In a new word processing document, write a descriptive paragraph about each of these functions:

- **Input:** Data you enter by keyboard, photos you scan, music you download, and video you record. Describe the ways you input data and the hardware and peripheral devices you use.
- **Processing:** Software that tells the computer what to do and in some way manipulates the data you input. Describe the different operating systems in use today and the types of software applications you use to complete common tasks.
- **Output:** Display of the processed data. Describe the ways you output data and the hardware and peripheral devices you use.
- **Distribution:** Enables the computer to share information with other computers, typically across a network. Describe the ways you distribute data to or share data with others.
- **Storage:** Enables you to keep data for use at a later time. Describe the two basic types of computer storage and the hardware and media you use to store data.

You may use electronic and hard copy references to assist in preparing the paragraphs. When you are done writing, be sure to proofread and revise the document as necessary. Apply formatting and text enhancements (bold, italics, and underline) as appropriate. Save and print the document as directed by your instructor.

For detailed information on this event, go to www.bpa.org.

Think Critically

1. How can a strong understanding of the computer's basic functions help you in your career?
2. Why do you think basic computer skills are important to an employer?
3. What activities can you participate in now that will strengthen your computer skills and knowledge?

School and Community

Recycling has become a way of life for many people, but most associate recycling with aluminum cans, plastic bottles, and paper. With the substantial increase in the use of electronic products over the last 20 years, though, many communities and organizations have launched programs to properly dispose of and recycle a variety of electronic devices and equipment. These include computers, printers, cell phones, televisions, gaming systems, and digital cameras.

In addition, many schools are involved in fund-raising programs in which they collect electronics from students, parents, and other community members, and then get paid upon delivery of them to a recycler.

1. Research the electronics recycling programs or events sponsored by your community. What are the guidelines? How often are they held?
2. Is your community or school in need of an electronics recycling program? If yes, what can you do to contribute to the start of one?
3. Write a brief summary of the importance of recycling electronics and the benefits to the community and the environment.

Currently the database has two tables: one for the Denver registration information and one for the Orlando registration information. Double-click the Denver table to open it to view the information included in the table. How many registrants are currently listed in the database? (44) Open the Orlando table. How many registrants are currently listed? (38)

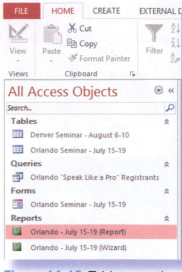

Under the Queries object is a table that shows only the individuals who have registered to attend the *Speak Like a Pro* seminar in Orlando. Open the query by double-clicking on *Orlando "Speak Like a Pro" Registrations*. How many individuals are currently registered? (15)

The Forms object allows the viewer to see each registrant's data individually. Double-click *Orlando Seminar – July 15-19* under the Forms object. The arrows at the bottom of the screen are used to move from record to record. Each arrow is explained below.

Figure 14-19 Tables, queries, forms, reports

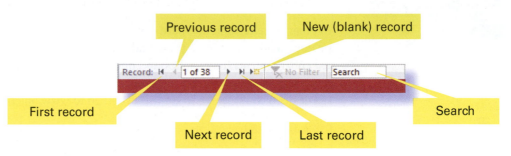

Figure 14-20 Moving from record to record

To find a specific piece of information, click Search and key the information you are looking for. Notice what happens when you click Search and then key *Valencia*. You are automatically taken to Hanna Valencia's registration information.

Figure 14-21 Search for a record

The last object shown on the left is the Reports object. Open both reports and note the difference between the one created using *Report* and the one created using the *Report Wizard*. The Wizard report groups the registrants by state and then sorts each state in ascending order by ZIP Code. When registrants have the same ZIP Code, only the first entry shows the ZIP and state.

UNIT 5

E-mail and Personal Information Management

Lesson 31 Format E-mail Messages
Lesson 32 Create and Format E-mail Messages

Lesson 33 Create and Format E-mail Messages
Lesson 34 Calendaring, Contacts, Tasks, and Notes

Application Guide

What Is Personal Information Management Software?

We live in a fast-paced world. Our schedules are filled with school, work, family, and extra-curricular activities. We are constantly communicating with others. The latest technological advances allow us to exchange more information faster than ever before. We are inundated with information. We schedule appointments and exchange addresses, telephone numbers, cell phone numbers, e-mail addresses, etc.

It is critical to be organized if we are to survive in this fast-paced world. Today's personal information manager software (PIMS) provides the solution for individuals to manage this abundance of information and to be personally and professionally organized. As shown in Figure 5-1, most PIMS has:

- an *E-mail* feature to send, receive, and manage e-mails
- a *Calendar* feature to keep track of schedules
- a *Contacts* feature to maintain information needed to contact others
- a *Tasks* feature to record items that need to be done
- a *Notes* feature to provide reminders

© StockLite/Shutterstock.com

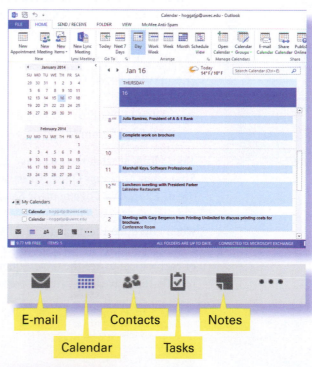

Figure 5-1 Components of PIMS

LESSON 73   Adding Records to an Existing Database

OUTCOMES

- Add records to an existing database.
- Print a database table.

73A–78A

Warmup

Key each line twice daily.

alphabet	1	Next week Zelda Jacks will become a night supervisor for quality.
figures	2	Scores of 94, 83, 72, 65, and 100 gave Rhonda an average of 82.8.
speed	3	Kay paid the maid for the work she did on the shanty by the lake.

| **gwam** | 1' | 1 | 2 | 3 | 4 | 5 | 6 | 7 | 8 | 9 | 10 | 11 | 12 | 13 |

73B

Database Overview

1. Read the Application Guide information on databases on pp. 291–300.
2. Read the information that follows about adding records to an existing database.
3. Learn how to add records to an existing database.

The executive director of Executive Development Seminars decided to use a database to keep track of individuals who have registered for seminars. Currently the director has the database set up for seminars in Orlando on July 15–19 and Denver on August 6–10 to include the following information about each member:

- Last Name
- First Name
- Middle Initial
- Street Address

- City
- State
- ZIP
- Phone

The director also included a field for each of the four seminars that individuals could register for. The field *All Four Seminars* is for those individuals who registered for all four seminars and are eligible for a discounted price.

- Speak Like a Pro
- Write Like a Pro
- Dress Like a Pro
- Dine Like a Pro
- All Four Seminars

Take a look at what the executive director created. First open *Microsoft Office Access*, and then open the ***df Executive Development Seminar*** database file. There are currently four objects that appear when you open the database: tables, queries, forms, and reports. Left-click the down arrow to the right of each object to see the tables, queries, forms, and reports that have already been created.

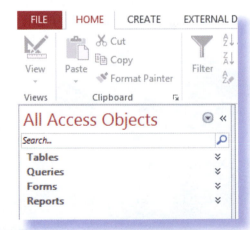

Figure 14-18 Access objects

E-mail

Mail/New/New E-mail

E-mail (electronic mail) is used in most business organizations. Because of the ease of creating and the speed of sending, e-mail messages have partially replaced the memo and the letter. Generally, delivery of an e-mail message takes place within seconds, whether the receiver is in the same building or in a location anywhere in the world. An e-mail message is illustrated in Figure 5-2.

E-mail heading. The format used for the e-mail heading may vary slightly, depending on the program used for creating e-mail. The heading generally includes who the e-mail is being sent to (**To**), what the e-mail is about (**Subject**), and who copies of the e-mail are being sent to (**Cc**). The name of the person sending the e-mail and the date the e-mail is sent are automatically included by the software. If you don't want the person receiving the e-mail to know that you are sending a copy of the e-mail to another person, the **Bcc** feature can be used.

E-mail body. The paragraphs of an e-mail message all begin at the left margin and are SS with a DS between paragraphs.

Message/Include/ Attach File

E-mail attachments. Attachments can be included with your e-mail by using the Attachment feature of the software. Common types of attachments include word processing, database, and spreadsheet files.

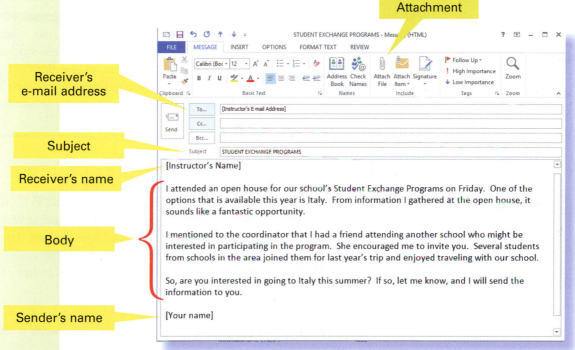

Figure 5-2 E-mail message

What Is a Filter?

Home/Sort & Filter/Filter

Filter

The **Filter** feature is used to display specific records in a table instead of all the records. In the example, the filter was used to show only the registrants from Georgia. This is done by clicking the field name (*State*) and then clicking on the filter icon in the Ribbon (shown at the left). This brings up the Filter box. Next, click *Select All* to remove the check marks. Then click on the items that you want to remain after the filter, in this case GA. See Figure 14-16. Finally, click OK. Figure 14-17 shows the filtered results.

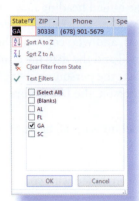

Figure 14-17 Filter results

Figure 14-16 Filter dialog box

Preview

In Unit 14, you will have the opportunity to work with databases from several companies and organizations. The first organization, **Franklin High School FBLA**, has a database of student membership information. The next database contains registration information for **Executive Development Seminars**. The **Software Professionals** keep an inventory of their software in a database, while **Rockwell Technologies** uses a database to keep track of their sales representatives. Finally, **Eastwick School of Dance** uses a database for student information and billing.

Digital Citizenship and Ethics

You've probably used the Internet to gather information for a school project, or maybe you visit websites as part of your classroom learning, or perhaps you've accessed an online tutorial to learn about effective study habits or how to write better essays. **E-learning**, or online education, has become a popular and accessible way for learners at all levels to take classes and further their academic pursuits. Many colleges and universities now offer online degree programs, and businesses often use online and computer-based training for employees.

E-learning offers many advantages, including:

- Flexible scheduling, which enables learners to complete coursework when it's convenient for them.
- Self-paced learning, which allows participants to learn at their own pace as long as coursework is turned in by the due date.
- No transportation costs or hassles, as you typically work from your home computer.

As a class, discuss the following.

1. How have you used e-learning at home or in school within the last six months?
2. What are some drawbacks of taking online courses?

TEAMWORK

E-mail tags. Tags (reminders) can be placed on your e-mail messages to mark them as unread, to categorize them, or to mark them for follow-up. This provides reminders for you to deal with specific e-mails at a later date or to easily find and access e-mails that have been categorized. The Tags group is located on the Home tab (see Figure 5-3).

The Unread/Read icon is used to mark a message that you have read as unread or to mark a message that you haven't read as read. The Categorize tag is used to mark messages as high importance or low importance or as another category that you create. If you wanted to mark all the messages that you receive from a particular person or a particular firm, you can rename a color tag with the name of the person or the name of the company. The Follow Up tag is used to mark messages that you plan on taking care of at a later time.

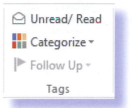

Figure 5-3 E-mail tags

Search People (Find a Contact). Use the Search People (Find a Contact) feature to quickly access e-mail address information about any person included in your contacts by clicking the Search People (Find a Contact) box and keying the name. This feature is located on the Home tab with the Find group (see Figure 5-4).

Figure 5-4 Search People (Find a Contact)

E-mail Inbox—Search and Arrange By. The e-mail inbox receives all incoming e-mail messages. Two features that are used to find e-mail messages are Search and Arrange By (see Figure 5-5).

The Search feature finds specific messages based on a word, phrase, or other text. Once the Search feature finds the desired messages, they can be arranged (organized) in a variety of ways using the Arrange By feature. The more common arrangements are by Date, From, To, Size, Categories, and Follow-up Flags. The example shown in Figure 5-6 searched for all the messages that included the word "Gary" and then arranged them by date.

Figure 5-5 Search and Arrange By

When a multiple sort is created, the first sort is called the **primary sort** and the second is called the **secondary sort**.

Figure 14-15 shows a multiple sort using the advanced filter/sort on the *Orlando* table of the *Executive Development Seminars* file. The file was first sorted by state in ascending order. This sort grouped all the registrants from each state together. The second sort was by city in ascending order. This sort put all the cities in each state in alphabetical order.

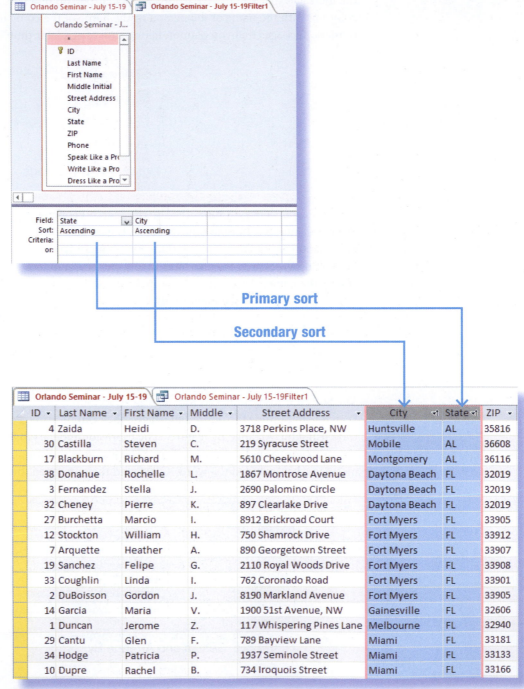

Figure 14-15 Multiple sort

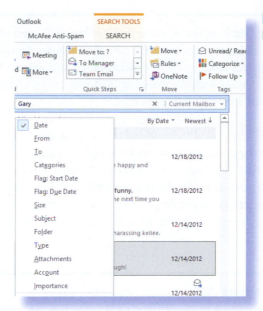

Figure 5-6 Search and Arrange By results

Calendar

Calendar/Home/New/
New Appointment

The Calendar feature is used to record and display appointments electronically. The calendar can be displayed and printed in a variety of ways (daily, weekly, or monthly), depending on how it will be used. The daily display is illustrated in Figure 5-7.

Appointments can be scheduled by using the Appointment dialog box (Ctrl + N) or by selecting the day and then clicking in the location where you want to key the information. Recurring appointments (those that occur repeatedly) can also be scheduled. For example, if you had a music lesson every Monday at 4 p.m, you could use the Recurrence feature to automatically place the music lesson on the calendar each Monday at 4 p.m.

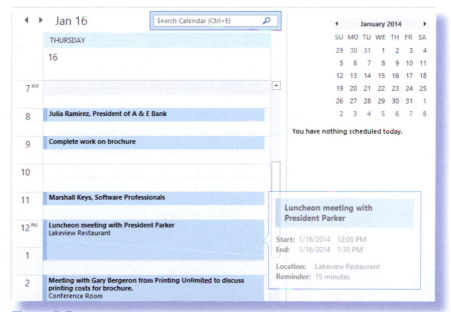

Figure 5-7 Daily Calendar with Appointments

A modified table or form is one that has been changed after it was created. Rather than creating a new database table or form each time information needs to be changed, database software allows changes to be made to existing tables and forms. Some of the most common changes that can be made include changing field properties, changing field names, adding new fields, and deleting fields no longer needed.

New fields often need to be added to accommodate additional information. Once the field is added, the new information can be keyed for each record. Once in a while the information in an existing field becomes outdated or is simply no longer needed. When this happens, the field can be deleted and all the information in that field is deleted. Before deleting a field, careful consideration should be given to make sure that the information will not be needed in the future. It is simple to delete the information, but time consuming to rekey information once deleted.

What Is a Sort?

Home/Sort & Filter/
Ascending

A↓Z Ascending

Z↓A Descending

The **Sort** feature can be used to sequence (order) records and forms. This feature allows sorts in ascending or descending order of words (alphabetically) or numbers (numerically). Ascending order is from A to Z and 0 to 9; descending order is from Z to A and 9 to 0.

A sort can be done on one field or on multiple fields. Figure 14-13 shows a sort by state in ascending order. All of the registrants from Alabama are grouped together followed by all the registrations from Florida. Note that the records within a group remain in ID order. The first three records are for Alabama registrants, IDs 4, 17, and 30.

ID	Last Name	First Name	Middle	Street Address	City	State	ZIP
4	Zaida	Heidi	D.	3718 Perkins Place, NW	Huntsville	AL	35816
17	Blackburn	Richard	M.	5610 Cheekwood Lane	Montgomery	AL	36116
30	Castilla	Steven	C.	219 Syracuse Street	Mobile	AL	36608
1	Duncan	Jerome	Z.	117 Whispering Pines Lane	Melbourne	FL	32940
2	DuBoisson	Gordon	J.	8190 Markland Avenue	Fort Myers	FL	33905
3	Fernandez	Stella	J.	2690 Palomino Circle	Daytona Beach	FL	32019
5	Holdern	Rita	W.	605 Mendavia Aveune	Miami	FL	33146
7	Arquette	Heather	A.	890 Georgetown Street	Fort Myers	FL	33907

Figure 14-13 Sort by state

Figure 14-14 shows the outcome of a sort by city in ascending order. Note that the records are no longer grouped alphabetically by state, but are grouped alphabetically by city. If the desired outcome is to have the records grouped alphabetically by state and then have the cities in the state ordered alphabetically by city, a multiple data sort would have to be created.

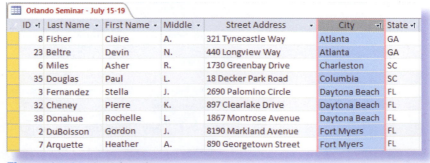

ID	Last Name	First Name	Middle	Street Address	City	State
8	Fisher	Claire	A.	321 Tynecastle Way	Atlanta	GA
23	Beltre	Devin	N.	440 Longview Way	Atlanta	GA
6	Miles	Asher	R.	1730 Greenbay Drive	Charleston	SC
35	Douglas	Paul	L.	18 Decker Park Road	Columbia	SC
3	Fernandez	Stella	J.	2690 Palomino Circle	Daytona Beach	FL
32	Cheney	Pierre	K.	897 Clearlake Drive	Daytona Beach	FL
38	Donahue	Rochelle	L.	1867 Montrose Avenue	Daytona Beach	FL
2	DuBoisson	Gordon	J.	8190 Markland Avenue	Fort Myers	FL
7	Arquette	Heather	A.	890 Georgetown Street	Fort Myers	FL

Figure 14-14 Sort by city

The Contacts feature is used to store information about your associates. Generally, the person's name, business address, phone number, and e-mail address are recorded. The notes portion can be used to record additional information about the person. Use the quick keys (Ctrl + N) to access the New Contact dialog box (see Figure 5-8).

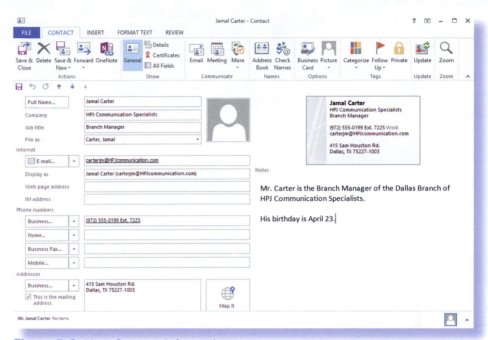

Figure 5-8 New Contact information

Information recorded in Contacts can be viewed electronically in several different views:

- Address Card
- Business Card
- Card
- List
- People
- Phone

The Business Card View is illustrated in Figure 5-9.

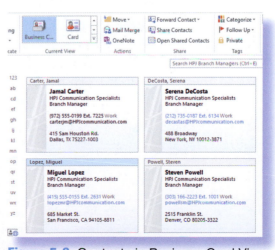

Figure 5-9 Contacts in Business Card View

Database reports are created from database tables and queries. **Reports** are used for organizing, summarizing, and printing information. The easiest way to generate a report is by simply clicking *Report* in the Reports group. This will give you a report of all the fields in the table. See Figure 14-11. Note that not all the fields are shown in the illustration.

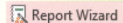
	Orlando Seminar - July 15-19		Orlando Seminar - July 15-19			

Orlando Seminar - July 15-19   Wednesday, December 5, 2012
                                                   10:14:21 AM

ID	Last Name	First Name	Middle Initia	Street Address	City	State
1	Duncan	Jerome	Z.	117 Whispering Pines Lane	Melbourne	FL
2	DuBoisson	Gordon	J.	8190 Markland Avenue	Fort Myers	FL
3	Fernandez	Stella	J.	2690 Palomino Circle	Daytona Beach	FL
4	Zaida	Heidi	D.	3718 Perkins Place, NW	Huntsville	AL
5	Holdern	Rita	W.	605 Mendavia Aveune	Miami	FL
6	Miles	Asher	R.	1730 Greenbay Drive	Charleston	SC
7	Arquette	Heather	A.	890 Georgetown Street	Fort Myers	FL
8	Fisher	Claire	A.	321 Tynecastle Way	Atlanta	GA
9	DuBois	Clarice	G.	3217 Ortega Drive	Tallahassee	FL
10	Dupre	Rachel	B.	734 Iroquois Street	Miami	FL
11	Montana	Marcus	M.	1839 Graham Drive	Miami	FL

Figure 14-11 Database report

Use the Report Wizard to customize the design of the report. Using the Report Wizard, specific fields can be selected to be included in the report, desired groupings can be specified, fields can be sorted in ascending or descending order, and layouts can be selected. Note in Figure 14-12 that the middle name has been left out. The records have been grouped by state in ascending order by ZIP Code.

	Orlando - July 15-19				

Orlando Seminar - July 15-19

State	ZIP	Last Name	First Name	Street Address	City
AL					
	35816	Zaida	Heidi	3718 Perkins Place, N	Huntsville
	36116	Blackburn	Richard	5610 Cheekwood Lan	Montgomery
	36608	Castilla	Steven	219 Syracuse Street	Mobile
FL					
	32019	Donahue	Rochelle	1867 Montrose Avenı	Daytona Beach
	32019	Fernandez	Stella	2690 Palomino Circle	Daytona Beach
	32019	Cheney	Pierre	897 Clearlake Drive	Daytona Beach
	32304	Farnsworth	Stephanie	2142 Scottsdale Road	Tallahassee
	32312	DuBois	Clarice	3217 Ortega Drive	Tallahassee
	32606	Garcia	Maria	1900 51st Avenue, N\	Gainesville
	32806	Teixeira	Barbara	2316 Kennedy Avenu	Orlando
	32807	Blankfein	Mary	260 Hibiscus Road	Orlando

Figure 14-12 Database report

Use the alphabet list on the right of the contacts to quickly access the person you are looking for by clicking the first letter of their last name. Note that the *L* was clicked, which then automatically highlighted the first name in the contacts that starts with an *L*.

Contact information can also be printed. The information can be printed in a variety of styles, including card style, small booklet style, medium booklet style, memo style, and phone directory style. Card style is illustrated in Figure 5-10.

Figure 5-10 Contacts printed in card style

As contact information changes, the cards can be edited by double-clicking on the business card.

Tasks

Tasks/Home/New/
New Task

The Tasks feature allows you to record tasks that you are responsible for completing. When a task is recorded, it is less likely to be forgotten. Completion dates and reminders can be set for each task. Once the task has been completed, it can be checked off, as shown in Figure 5-11. Use the quick keys (Ctrl + N) to access the Tasks dialog box. Use the *Change View (Current View)* feature to display different views of the tasks which have been entered.

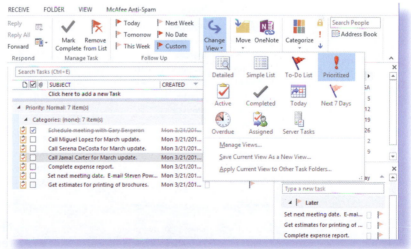

Figure 5-11 Tasks (ToDo/Did List)

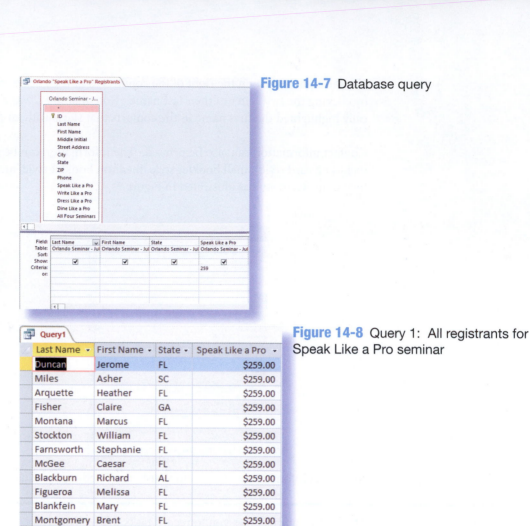

Figure 14-7 Database query

Figure 14-8 Query 1: All registrants for Speak Like a Pro seminar

Last Name	First Name	State	Speak Like a Pro
Duncan	Jerome	FL	$259.00
Miles	Asher	SC	$259.00
Arquette	Heather	FL	$259.00
Fisher	Claire	GA	$259.00
Montana	Marcus	FL	$259.00
Stockton	William	FL	$259.00
Farnsworth	Stephanie	FL	$259.00
McGee	Caesar	FL	$259.00
Blackburn	Richard	AL	$259.00
Figueroa	Melissa	FL	$259.00
Blankfein	Mary	FL	$259.00
Montgomery	Brent	FL	$259.00
Burchetta	Marcio	FL	$259.00
Hodge	Patricia	FL	$259.00
Donahue	Rochelle	FL	$259.00

Figure 14-9 Query 2: Florida residents registered for Speak Like a Pro seminar

Last Name	First Name	State	Speak Like a Pro
Duncan	Jerome	FL	$259.00
Arquette	Heather	FL	$259.00
Montana	Marcus	FL	$259.00
Stockton	William	FL	$259.00
Farnsworth	Stephanie	FL	$259.00
McGee	Caesar	FL	$259.00
Figueroa	Melissa	FL	$259.00
Blankfein	Mary	FL	$259.00
Montgomery	Brent	FL	$259.00
Burchetta	Marcio	FL	$259.00
Hodge	Patricia	FL	$259.00
Donahue	Rochelle	FL	$259.00

Figure 14-10 Query 3: Out-of-state registrants for Speak Like a Pro seminar

Last Name	First Name	State	Speak Like a Pro
Miles	Asher	SC	$259.00
Fisher	Claire	GA	$259.00
Blackburn	Richard	AL	$259.00

Notes

Notes/Home/New/
New Note

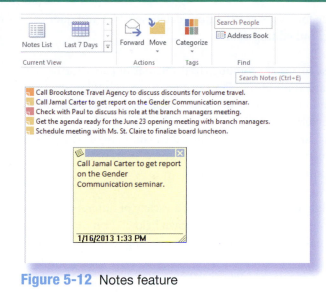

Figure 5-12 Notes feature

The Notes feature allows you to write yourself a reminder. The tags feature may be used to categorize the notes. Figure 5-12 shows five notes. The three gold notes were not categorized. The pink note was categorized as high priority; the orange note was tagged as low priority. The second note was opened for reading. Once the note is no longer needed, it can be deleted. The Notes feature can be used for anything that a paper note could be used for. To create a new note, tap Ctrl + N. Notes can be deleted by clicking on the note and tapping Delete.

21st Century Skills: Communicate Clearly

As you learned in this unit, e-mail has become one of the most common ways for computer users to communicate, both personally and for business purposes. Although e-mail is considered less formal than other business communications, it is still important to articulate your thoughts and ideas effectively in an e-mail message. You should:

- Write in complete, active sentences.
- Proofread and check your spelling.
- Avoid "bells and whistles," such as writing in all caps or inserting emoticons, that detract from your message.

Most importantly, you should always know your audience and understand that your message could be shared either intentionally or by mistake with someone else.

Think Critically

Open a new word processing document, and compose answers to the questions below.

1. What perception might you form of a person who sends an e-mail that has spelling and grammatical errors?
2. Under what circumstances in a business setting might e-mail *not* be the best form of communication?
3. Give an example of how you could use e-mail at work to instruct others on a topic.
4. **Save as:** *u05 21century*.

What Is a Database Form?

Create/Forms/Form

Database forms are created from database tables and queries. Forms are used for keying, viewing, and editing data.

Database forms are computerized versions of paper forms such as a job application or a credit card application. On a printed form, you fill in the blanks with the information that is requested, such as your name and address. In a database form, the blanks in which information is entered are called **fields**. In the example above, *Last Name, First Name, Address, City, State,* etc. are field names. When the blanks are filled in, the form becomes a **record**. The form illustrated in Figure 14-6 is Record 38 from the Orlando Seminar table of the Executive Development Seminars database.

Depending on the software used, a variety of different form formats are available. The form may show only one record (as shown below), or it may show multiple records in the database. Forms may be created manually or by using the software wizard.

Figure 14-6 Database form

What Is a Database Query?

Create/Queries/ Query Design

Queries are questions. The Query feature of a database software program allows you to ask for specific information to be retrieved from tables that have been created. For example, the query shown below is based on the Executive Development Seminars database. The query pulls information from the *Orlando Seminar – July 15-19* table to answer the question, "Who registered for the *Speak Like a Pro* seminar in Orlando?" The table resulting from the query is shown on the next page.

Perhaps you want to see the breakdown between those registrants who come from Florida versus those who come from out of state. Query 2 shows the individuals from Florida who are registered for that seminar; Query 3 shows the out-of-state individuals who are registered for the seminar. By using the Query feature, answers to questions can be made based on the information contained in database tables.

LESSON 31

Format E-mail Messages

OUTCOME

- Learn to format e-mail messages.

Warmup

alphabet   1   Jordan placed first by solving the complex quiz in one week.

spacing   2   When you get to the game, save two seats for Ron and Felipe.

speed   3   Jan paid the big man for the field work he did for the firm.

gwam   1' | 1 | 2 | 3 | 4 | 5 | 6 | 7 | 8 | 9 | 10 | 11 | 12 |

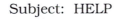

31B E-mail Messages

★TIP   E-mail can be saved using the same process used to save a *Word* document.

E-mail Message 1

1. Study the model e-mail illustration on p. 105.
2. Format and key the model illustration.
3. Proofread your copy; correct all errors.
4. **Save as:** *31b email1*.

E-mail Messages 2 and 3

1. Format and key the e-mail messages shown below and on the next page; send to your instructor's e-mail address.
2. Proofread your copy; correct all errors.
3. **Save as:** *31b email2* and *31b email3*.

E-mail Message 2

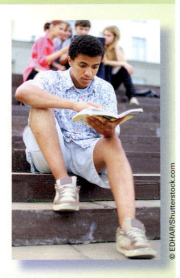

Subject: HELP

Hopefully, my sister told you that I would be e-mailing you. I'm writing a report on Mark Twain for my English class. Last weekend when Katherine was home, we were talking about this assignment. She mentioned that you were an English major and seemed to think that you had completed a course that focused on Mark Twain. She suggested that I contact you to see if you would be able to suggest some sources that I might use for this assignment.

As part of the report project, we have to read two of his books. I've already started reading *Life on the Mississippi*. Could you offer a suggestion as to what other book I should read for this assignment?

Katherine said that you are planning on coming home with her during spring break. I'll look forward to meeting you.

The **data type** determines the kinds of values that can be displayed in the field. The most common data types are **AutoNumber** (automatic sequential or random numbering of records), **Text** (text or a combination of text and numbers), **Number** (used in mathematical calculations), **Currency** (used in mathematical calculations), and **Date & Time** (date and time values).

When defining and sequencing fields in Design View, the fields in the table are defined before entering data. The *Description* field is used to describe the content of each field. At the bottom of the Design View screen, property values for each field can be set. The property values available change depending on the data type selected. Figure 14-5 shows the properties that can be set when you select *Currency* for the data type.

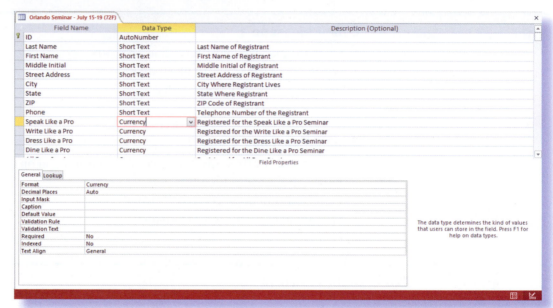

Figure 14-5 Design View

When feasible, fields should be arranged in the same order as the data in the **source document** (paper form from which data is keyed). Doing so reduces the time needed to enter the field contents and to maintain the records. The illustration above shows the field names (and sequence of the fields), data type, and description of the fields for the database table illustrated in 14-3. The **primary key** shown before the first field name is used to identify each record in the table with a number. In this case, a unique ID number would automatically be assigned each member's record.

E-mail Message 3

Subject: WEB PAGE CREATION

As we develop our Web page, we may want to review some of those developed by other symphonies. I have already looked at several on the Web. San Francisco's was one that I felt we could model ours after.

Theirs is clear, concise, and easy to navigate. In addition to the normal sections, they have a section called "More about the San Francisco Symphony." Here they include such things as:

1. A brief history
2. The mission statement
3. Community programs
4. News items about the Symphony

To view their Web page, go to www.sfsymphony.org. I'll look forward to working with you at our next committee meeting.

LESSON 32 — Create and Format E-mail Messages

OUTCOMES

- Learn to create e-mail messages.
- Learn tips for creating e-mail messages.

32B — Create E-mail Message

You have narrowed down to three the number of schools that you are considering attending when you graduate. A friend of yours started school this fall at one of your final three choices. Send an e-mail to your friend to gather additional information about the school he/she is attending to help you decide on which of the three schools to attend. Before starting the e-mail, think about all the things that are important to you in selecting a school to attend.

After completing your e-mail, print a copy of it, exchange it with one of your classmates, and complete 32C.

32C — Evaluate E-mail Message

1. Read the e-mail your classmate created for 32B.
2. Read the following Tips for Creating Effective E-mail Messages.
3. Evaluate your classmate's e-mail based on the tips below, using the E-mail Evaluation Form (*df 32c eval form*).

Tips for Creating Effective E-mail Messages

1. **Subject lines are important; use them.** A subject line entices the receiver to open and read the message immediately. Messages that aren't opened immediately often get overlooked. At a later date a subject line allows the receiver to quickly find and access e-mails. Consider the subject line to be the wrapping on a package. The package with the best wrapping attracts more attention than the other packages.

The table illustrated in Figure 14-3 has six of the fields showing—*Last Name*, *First Name*, *Middle Initial*, *Street Address*, *City*, and *State* (plus the ID number). Fourteen of the 38 records in the database are visible in the illustration.

Record 12, the registration record for William Stockton, is highlighted in the illustration and shows the information contained in each of the six fields. The database table is the foundation from which forms, queries, and reports are created.

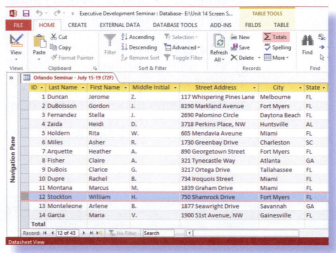

Figure 14-3 Database table

What Is Defining and Sequencing Fields of Database Tables?

Fields can be defined and sequenced in either **Datasheet View** (Figure 14-4) or **Design View** (Figure 14-5). In the Datasheet View, a field can be defined and sequenced by clicking on *Click to Add*, selecting a data type, and keying the field *name*.

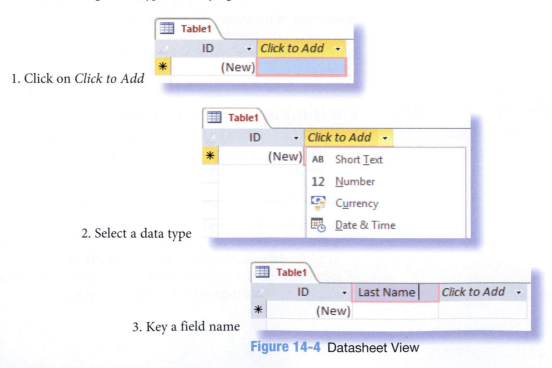

1. Click on *Click to Add*

2. Select a data type

3. Key a field name

Figure 14-4 Datasheet View

2. **The length of the message should be considered; keep them short.** The number of e-mails a person receives has steadily increased over the years. Keep your message short. By keeping your message short, you won't waste the time of the person you are sending it to, and the receiver is more likely to understand the main points you are making. Longer messages tend to be disorganized.

3. **Your e-mails reflect you; make a good impression.** An e-mail may be the first impression that the receiver has of you and your organization. The same care given to memos and letters should be given to e-mails. Make a good impression by having a well-organized message.

4. **Proofread your e-mail message before sending; errors are unacceptable.** Most e-mail messages require editing during writing and after they have been created. Proofread for correct spelling, punctuation, grammar, sentence structure, and capitalization. If you don't, you are either telling the receiver they are not important or that you lack the ability to create an error-free message.

5. **Respond to e-mails quickly; if you don't, you are still sending a message.** If you are not in a position to respond to an e-mail immediately, let the sender know when they can expect to receive an answer. Doing so builds goodwill.

6. **Be careful of sending negative messages; you can't retract them.** Often people say things in anger that they later regret. It is a good idea to write down your ideas to release your anger but wait until the next day to send the e-mail. A very high percentage of those messages are either never sent or revised considerably before being sent.

7. **Consider bullet points to emphasize specifics; they are easier to follow.** Important information can be lost in a long sentence using commas to separate points. A bullet list of points makes it easy to see exactly what you are requesting. If you have multiple questions, a bullet list may result in getting all questions answered.

8. **Consider whether e-mail is the best form of communication; oftentimes it is not.** Don't get in the habit of communicating everything with e-mail. There are times when face-to-face communication or a phone call will get you the desired result. Remember, it is much easier to say no in an e-mail than it is when the person is talking to you in person.

9. **Double-check dates and times; otherwise, you may have a surprise party.** Date errors are common; for example, keying Tuesday, January 20, when January 20 is really on Wednesday. This results in confusion or the possibility of a person showing up on the wrong date. Always double-check dates.

10. **Make it clear what you want; make it as easy as possible for the receiver to provide what you want.** After creating an e-mail, read it as though you were receiving it. Ask the question, "What does this person want?" If you are not sure, the reader definitely won't be. Another question you should ask is whether you have made it easy for the person to do what you want. The easier it is, the more likely the person will accommodate you.

© auremar/Shutterstock.com

What Are the Components of a Database?

A database may include **tables** for entering and storing information, **forms** for entering and displaying information, **reports** for summarizing and presenting information, and **queries** for drawing information from one or more tables. Figure 14-1 shows the components that can be created in a database. These components are accessed by clicking the Create tab in *Access*.

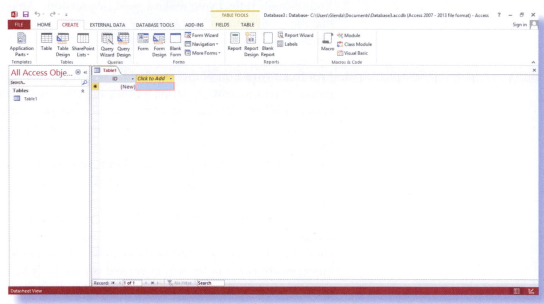

Figure 14-1 *Access* window with Create tab on the Ribbon

What Is a Database Table?

Database tables are created by the user in software programs such as *Access* for inputting, organizing, and storing information. The tables are set up to contain columns and rows of information. In a database table, the columns are called **fields** and the rows are called **records**. The cursor in Figure 14-2 is in Field 3 of Record 3.

Create/Tables/Table

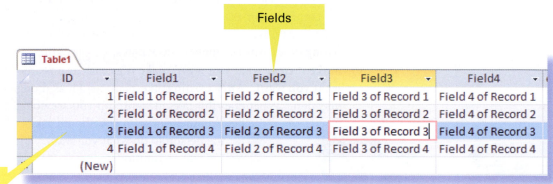

Figure 14-2 Fields and records

LESSON 33

Create and Format E-mail Messages

OUTCOMES
- Learn tips for managing e-mail messages.
- Create an e-mail message.

33B

Manage E-mail

Read the tips for managing e-mail given below.

Tips for Managing E-mail

✓ Set up separate accounts for personal and business e-mail messages.

✓ Set aside specific times each day to respond to e-mails. Don't let incoming e-mails take your attention away from important tasks that you are working on.

✓ Respond to an e-mail when you read it unless doing so will take too much time. Not responding clutters your mind as well as your inbox. Reading an e-mail a second time that could have been quickly dealt with in the first reading is a waste of time.

✓ Delete e-mails after responding to them unless a record is needed. Large e-mails with attachments take up a lot of disk space.

✓ Use shortcuts:
- Ctrl + D (Delete current e-mail.)
- Ctrl + R (Reply to current e-mail.)
- Ctrl + F (Forward current e-mail.)

✓ Use the Junk E-mail feature to block spam as well as to block individuals you don't want to receive e-mail messages from.

✓ Delete older messages that are no longer of value to you.

✓ Use the phone rather than e-mail for topics that require a great deal of discussion.

✓ Create separate folders for persons you correspond with frequently.

✓ Try to leave the office each day with an empty inbox.

33C

Create E-mail

Your instructor is having trouble managing his/her e-mail. Send an e-mail message to your instructor offering suggestions for managing e-mail. You can use the tips shown above as a basis for your e-mail, or you can come up with your own tips. Keep the message brief. Offer only three to five tips in the message.

LESSON 34

Calendaring, Contacts, Tasks, and Notes

OUTCOME
- Learn to use the Calendaring, Contacts, Tasks, and Notes features.

34B

Calendar

1. Open *df 34b answers* to use for your answers to the questions below.
2. Open *Outlook*. Learn how to use the Calendar feature.
3. Open *df 34b calendar* and answer the following questions.
4. **Save as:** *34b answers*.

Lesson 73	Adding Records to an Existing Database	**Lesson 76**	Editing Records, Adding Fields, and Deleting Records
Lesson 74	Creating a Database and Table	**Lesson 77**	Sorts, Filters, and Queries
Lesson 75	Adding Records to Update a Database	**Lesson 78**	Database Application Assessment

DB Applications

What Is Database Software?

Learning how to use *Access* is challenging, yet fun. Once you master how to define and sequence fields for recording information, you will be able to sort, filter, and run queries to access (gather) information for making sound decisions. In this unit, you will learn to:

- Work with a database
- Create a database
- Add records
- Edit records, add fields, and delete records
- Perform sorts, filters, and queries

© iStockphoto.com/EdStock

A **database** is an organized collection of facts and figures (information). The phone book, which includes names, addresses, and phone numbers, is an example of a database in printed form.

It is also quite common in today's environment to have databases stored in electronic form. Names and addresses, inventories, sales records, and client information are just a few examples of information that is stored in a database. Having information in a database makes it easy to compile and arrange data to answer questions and make well-informed decisions.

1. What is the title of the presentation Ms. Parker will be giving on Monday, June 16, 2014?

2. Who will Ms. Parker be meeting with at 10:00 a.m. on Tuesday, June 24, 2014?

3. Mr. Blackburn would like to schedule a meeting with Ms. Parker on Friday, June 20, 2014. Will that be possible?

4. What is the Flight No. of Ms. Parker's plane to New York on June 19, 2014?

5. How many people will Ms. Parker be interviewing on June 25, 2014? What is the position they are interviewing for?

34C

Contacts

Contacts/Home/New/
New Contact

Home/Current View/
Business Card

1. Open *Outlook*. Learn how to use the Contacts feature.
2. Create a new contacts file called **34c contacts**.
3. Key the information from the six business cards into the contacts file.
4. Print a copy of the file in Business Card View with card style.
5. **Save as: 34c contacts**.

Jackson W. Farrell
Agent

2701 Stanford Avenue
Dallas, TX 75225
jwfarrell@yahoo.com

Phone: 469-405-3288
Fax: 469-405-3290

www.AguilarRealty.com

Aguilar Realty

Old Home Studio

Maria Santos
Proprietor

381 Hilltop Drive
Longmont, CO 80501

Phone: 970-923-1655
Fax: 970-923-1600
Email: msantos@microsoft.com

The Winning Edge

Kheng Guan Toh/Shutterstock.com

Complete this activity to help prepare for the **Desktop Publishing** event in FBLA-PBL's Information Technology division. Participants in this event demonstrate skills in the areas of desktop publishing, creativity, and decision making.

A new ice cream and dessert parlor has just opened in your neighborhood. The owner asks you to develop and design her business documents. Following is information about the business:

Name: Sweet Stop
Address: 4032 Broadway, Lebanon, OH 45036
Phone: (513) 555-8787
Hours: Monday–Saturday 11 a.m.–8 p.m.; Sunday noon–6 p.m.
Menu: hand-dipped ice cream, sundaes, shakes, and floats; homemade pies, cookies, cupcakes, and other desserts; beverages, including various coffees, teas, and hand-squeezed lemonades

1. In a new word processing document, use clip art or ready-made shapes to create a logo for the business that incorporates its name and the tagline, "Your sweet tooth's dream come true!" Save the document as directed by your instructor.
2. Using the information above, create a menu for the business. If necessary, research the costs of similar menu items, and use your decision-making skills to set the price for each. Be sure to use the logo you already created. Save the document as directed by your instructor.
3. Use a template to create a business card. Save and print the document as directed.
4. Use a template to create a flyer. It should include the logo, address, phone, and hours of operation, and highlight items from the menu. Save and print the flyer as directed.

For detailed information on this event, go to www.fbla-pbl.org.

Think Critically

1. You have learned about a number of special business documents you can create using wp software. What special documents might you create for school activities? For social or family activities?
2. How does the design of a document or publication affect its message?

School and Community Community animal shelters rely heavily—and sometimes solely—on volunteers to help run the facility, fund services, and provide care for the animals. According to the Humane Society of the United States, there are more than 3,500 animal shelters in operation, and between six and nine million cats and dogs enter these shelters every year. You can make a difference in your community by volunteering at an animal shelter.

1. Using the Internet or the yellow pages, develop a list of animal shelters in your area. The list should include the name, address, and contact information.
2. Contact each shelter and find out the opportunities for volunteers in your age group. Add this information to the list.
3. Create a flyer that includes your list and any other pertinent information or graphics that you think will motivate others to volunteer. Print the flyer and make copies to post in your school.

Global Technologies

Jason Fennimore
Director of Human Resources
731 Chadwick Circle
Kissimmee, FL 34746

Phone (407) 382-1832
Fax (407) 382-1838
jpfennimore@microsoft.com

Printing Unlimited

Gary L. Bergeron
Design Associate

316 Huntington Avenue
Minneapolis, MN 55416

Phone (612) 901-7815
Fax (612) 901-7823

bergerongl@yahoo.com

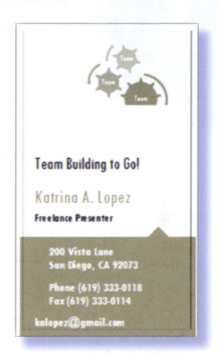

Team Building to Go!

Katrina A. Lopez

Freelance Presenter

200 Vista Lane
San Diego, CA 92073

Phone (619) 333-0118
Fax (619) 333-0114

kalopez@gmail.com

EZ Printing

Kaitlin A. Dixon

Marketing Rep

489 Melrose St. W
Chicago, IL 60657
Phone: 708.515.0689
Fax: 708.515.0688

dixonka@g-mail.com

Monkey Business Images/Shutterstock.com

Planning a Career in Agriculture, Food, and Natural Resources

From the food on our table to the clothes in our closet to the fuel that runs our car, we all are dependent in many ways on agriculture, food, and natural resources. Employees in this field work on farms, in dairies, and on rangelands, but they also work in manufacturing facilities and labs to develop and produce the raw materials used for clothing, shelter, energy, and medicine. In addition, they help maintain our parks and beaches; they care for animals and livestock; and they monitor air, soil, and water quality.

What's It Like?

Employees in this field are involved in the production, processing, marketing, distribution, financing, and development of agricultural commodities and resources including food, fiber, wood products, natural resources, horticulture, and other plant and animal products and resources. For example:

- They own or manage farms, ranches, nurseries, greenhouses, and timber tracts.
- They provide veterinary services for herds or individual animals.
- They identify, remove, and properly dispose of hazardous materials from buildings, facilities, and the environment.
- They patrol hunting and fishing areas and enforce fishing, hunting, and boating laws.
- They study plants and their interaction with other organisms and the environment.
- They design agricultural machinery, equipment, and structures, and develop ways to conserve soil and water and to improve the processing of agricultural products.

Jobs in this field often require work outdoors in all kinds of weather. Employees in some careers work long hours, with their schedules dictated by weather and environmental conditions. Others work standard 40-hour workweeks in offices and labs.

Employment Outlook

Employment opportunities in the various pathways of this cluster differ significantly. Jobs in farming are expected to decline; those in environmental and natural resource services can expect favorable employment opportunities; and those in plant and animal systems can expect much faster than average job growth. Education requirements range widely, too. A high school diploma and on-the-job training are sufficient for some jobs, while others require an associate's or bachelor's degree, or higher.

What About You?

This career cluster is covered in box 1 of the Interest Survey Activity you completed in Unit 1 of this text. If this box had one of the three highest scores on your survey, you should further explore the cluster's pathways and related occupations.

1. Why do you think a career in this field could be a good choice?
2. What skills can you develop now that would be helpful to a career in this field?
3. Why are these jobs important to our economy?

34D

Calendar

Calendar/Home/New/
New Appointment

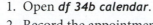

1. Open *df 34b calendar*.
2. Record the appointments shown below.
3. **Save as:** *34d calendar*.

1. Board Meeting on June 18, 2014, from 8 to 11:30 a.m. in the Lincoln Conference Room.
2. Board Luncheon on June 18, 2014, from 12:00 to 1:30 at Bartorolli's.
3. Jamison Russell, Vice President of Riley Manufacturing, on June 17, 2014, from 1:30 to 2:30.
4. Vivian Bloomfield, Manager of Garnett Enterprises, on June 19, 2014, from 8:30 to 9:30.
5. Chamber of Commerce meeting on June 24, 2014, from 5:30 p.m. to 7:30 p.m.

34E

Tasks

Task/Home/New/
New Task

1. Open *Outlook*. Learn how to use the Tasks feature.
2. Record the tasks shown below using the Tasks feature.
3. **Save as:** *34e tasks*.

1. Schedule an appointment with Jack Mason to discuss photo shoot.
2. Schedule a meeting with Marketing to discuss new products (Due Date: June 20).
3. Prepare May expense report (Due date: June 15).
4. Schedule meeting with Erin Hollingsworth to discuss layout of annual report (Due Date: June 10).
5. Create job description and advertisement for new marketing position (Due Date: June 8).

34F

Notes

Notes/Home/New/
New Note

1. Open *Outlook*. Learn how to use the Notes feature.
2. Record the notes shown below using the Notes feature.
3. **Save as:** *34f notes*.

1. Get the agenda ready for the June 23 opening meeting with branch managers. Tag as "*High Importance.*"
2. Call Brookstone Travel Agency to discuss discounts for volume travel.
3. Check with Paul to discuss his role at the branch managers meeting.
4. Schedule meeting with Ms. St. Claire to finalize board luncheon. Tag as "*High Importance.*"
5. Call Jamal Carter to get report on the Gender Communication seminar.

© VEER.COM/STILLFX

Academic and Career Connections

Complete the following exercises that introduce various topics that involve academic themes and careers.

Grammar and Writing: Pronoun Agreement and Pronoun Case

MicroType 6

- References/Communication Skills/Pronoun Agreement
- References/Communication Skills/Pronoun Case
- CheckPro/Communication Skills 10
- CheckPro/Word Choice 10

1. Go to *MicroType 6* and use this feature path for review: References/Communication Skills/ Pronoun Agreement.
2. Click *Rules* and review the rules of using pronoun.
3. Then, under *Pronoun Agreement*, click *Posttest*.
4. Follow the instructions to complete the posttest.
5. Repeat this process for *Pronoun Case*.

Optional Activities:

1. Go to this path: CheckPro/Communication Skills 10.
2. Complete the activities as directed.
3. Go to this path: CheckPro/Word Choice 10.
4. Key the Apply lines, and choose the correct word.

Communications: Listening

1. You have answered a telephone call from Maria MacDonald, who serves as an officer in the alumni association of which your mother is president. She asks you to take a message.
2. Open the data file *df u13 communications*, and listen to the message, taking notes as needed.
3. Close the file.
4. Start a new word processing document. Using your notes, key a message in sentence form for your mother.
5. Save the document as *u13 communications*.

Math Skills: Mental Math

Brian is a wildlife biologist. His main responsibilities are researching and monitoring plant and animal habitats within a 1,600-acre wildlife preserve. On a daily basis, Brian walks or drives around the area, making observations and recording data. He uses mental math (no calculator and no figuring with pencil and paper) to make estimations.

1. In a 10-acre area, Brian spots two honeybee hives. If three-fourths of the total preserve consists of the same type of plant and animal life as in the 10-acre area, how many hives would Brian estimate to be in the preserve?
2. Brian and his staff have been analyzing the predator/prey relationship between bobcats and rabbits in the preserve. One year ago, they counted six rabbits per acre. How many rabbits total were in the preserve? They then decided to double the number of bobcats in the preserve. After six months, they counted four rabbits per acre. By what percentage had the rabbit population been reduced? Round to the nearest whole number.
3. There is an average of 10 ash trees per acre in the preserve. If 50 percent of the trees in the preserve have been treated for emerald ash borer, how many trees are still at risk of being infected by the beetle? If these trees go untreated and are dying at four per week, how many untreated trees will still be alive after two years? Save as *u13 math*.

1. Look in the Contacts you created in 34C; open *Word* file **df 34g answers**.
2. Answer the following questions in the **df 34g answers** file.
3. **Save as: 34g answers**.

1. What company does Jackson Farrell work for?
2. What is Kaitlin Dixon's e-mail address?
3. What is the Fax No. where Maria Santos works?
4. What is Gary Bergeron's title?
5. What is Ms. Lopez's first name?

www.cengage.com/school/
keyboarding/c21key

Digital Citizenship and Ethics
Bullying comes in many forms, from teasing and name-calling to pushing and hitting to excluding others from a group. But, as you learned in Unit 1, technology has provided new ways for people to bully each other. Cyberbullying—or using online communications technology to harass or upset someone—has become increasingly common as more and more people gain access to cell phones and the Internet.

Now, cell phones and e-mail can be used to send hateful calls or messages or to share humiliating images. Threatening messages can be sent via chat rooms, message boards, and social networking sites. Name-calling and abusive remarks are thrown at players on gaming sites. What can you do about cyberbullying? As a class, discuss the following.

Think Critically
1. What are three things you can do so that you do not become a victim of cyberbullying?
2. If you've been the victim of cyberbullying, what course of action should you take?

www.cengage.com/school/
keyboarding/c21key

1. Open a new document. Key the application letter below as a personal-business letter in block format with mixed punctuation.
2. **Save as:** *72e letter*.

543 Lake View Boulevard | San Diego, CA 92130-2253 | May 15, 2014 | Mr. Hector Perez | Employment Coordinator | San Diego City Park | 1219 Park Road | San Diego, CA 92130-0120 | Dear Mr. Perez

Ms. Marcella Trent, San Diego City Park Coordinator, told me that there are several junior counselor positions available during the upcoming summer months.

I had the pleasure of meeting and working for Ms. Trent when I served as a volunteer at the San Diego City Park day camp last summer. Given what I learned about City Park while volunteering, I'm confident that I am qualified to be a junior counselor and would like to be considered for the position.

Currently, I am completing my sophomore year at North Beach High School. My work experience and school and volunteer activities have given me the opportunity to work with people of all ages, including those in the age group I would be counseling. I have enclosed my resume for you to see why I am qualified.

I would appreciate an opportunity to interview with you for this position. You can call me at (858) 555-0194 or e-mail me at maria.gomez@upstart.net to arrange an interview.

Sincerely | Maria Gomez | Enclosure

© 2012 PhotoAlto/Alix Minde/
Jupiterimages Corporation

TEAMWORK

21st Century Skills: Creativity and Innovation

Being a creative thinker and communicating ideas with others are important skills, whether you are in the classroom, on the job, or in a social situation. When you are willing to suggest and share ideas, you demonstrate your originality and inventiveness. When you are open and responsive to the ideas and perspectives of others, you show consideration and cooperation.

In teams of three to four, develop a class newsletter. The newsletter should be one to two pages. With your instructor's permission, you may use a newsletter template from Office.com. The newsletter should include a minimum of three articles and at least two graphics. Article ideas include recent projects, field trips, guest speakers, upcoming tests or assignments, study tips, teacher profiles, or student achievements. Divide duties as necessary. Save and print the newsletter as directed by your instructor.

Think Critically

1. Creativity can mean a lot of different things. How do you define *creativity*?
2. What idea creation techniques do you think work best for groups? What about for you individually?
3. What positive things can you learn from an idea that "flops"?

© VEER.COM/STILLFX

Academic and Career Connections

Complete the following exercises that introduce various topics that involve academic themes and careers.

MicroType 6

- References/Communication Skills/Number Expression
- CheckPro/Communication Skills 4
- CheckPro/Word Choice 4

1. Go to *MicroType* 6 and use this feature path for review: References/Communication Skills/Number Expression.
2. Click *Rules* and review the rules of using numbers.
3. Then, under *Number Expression*, click *Posttest*.
4. Follow the instructions to complete the posttest.

Optional Activities:

1. Go to this path: CheckPro/Communication Skills 4.
2. Complete the activities as directed.
3. Go to this path: CheckPro/Word Choice 4.
4. Key the Apply lines and choose the correct word.

Communications: Speaking

You have been selected to participate in an exchange program with students from different schools. Each time you visit one of their schools, you must stand up in front of the group and introduce yourself. In a new word processing document, prepare your introduction:

1. Write your name, grade, the name of your school, and the city in which it is located.
2. List the courses, activities, and organizations in which you are involved at school.
3. List your interests, hobbies, and anything else you feel is unique about you.
4. Discuss your goals for after you graduate.
5. Save the document as ***u05 communications***, and with your instructor's permission, print a copy.
6. Practice your introduction. Add transitions as necessary.
7. Then, either in front of a mirror or with your friends or family, continue to practice your introduction. Pay attention to your tone of voice, facial expressions, posture, and body language. Your goal is to introduce yourself without having to refer to your printed document.
8. As directed by your instructor, present your self-introduction to the class.

Math Skills

1. When Jennifer arrived at work on Monday morning, she had received 136 e-mail messages over the weekend. She skimmed through the list and deleted 42 that she knew were junk. What percentage of the e-mails did she delete? (Round to the nearest whole number.)
2. Of the remaining e-mails, Jennifer determined that she should reply to half of them before the end of the day. How many replies would she have to send?
3. Jennifer organizes the e-mails that she wants to keep into three different folders: Customers, Suppliers, and Coworkers. She has 35 messages in her Customers folder; 17 in her Suppliers folder; and 42 in her Coworkers folder. What percentage of the total does each represent? (Round to the nearest whole number.)
4. After lunch, Jennifer reviews her list of tasks to complete before the end of the day. She has only checked off 6 of the 18 tasks listed. What percentage must she still complete? (Round to the nearest whole number.)

1. Open a new document. Using the information below, key an electronic résumé for Maria Gomez. Use the default font, font size, line spacing, and spacing after ¶. Remove the space after ¶ as needed in the heading lines.
2. **Save as:** *72d resume*.

Maria Gomez
543 Lake View Boulevard
San Diego, CA 92130-2253
(858) 555-0194
maria.gomez@upstart.net

OBJECTIVE

To work as a junior counselor at day camp for the San Diego City Park

RELATED EXPERIENCE

Worked as a City Park volunteer in the summer of 2013 to clean up the park and coordinate special games for children's outings

Served as captain of the ninth-grade North Beach High School cross-country track team

Presently serve as babysitter for two children ages 4 and 6

EDUCATIONAL EXPERIENCE

North Beach High School, San Diego, CA, 2013-Present

Red Cross Babysitting, Safety, and CPR courses, San Diego, CA, 2012

WORK EXPERIENCE

Grocery bagger, Marta's Mini Mart, San Diego, CA 92135, 2013-Present

Paper courier, *San Diego Neighborhood News*, San Diego, CA 92130, 2010–2012

Mother's helper and babysitter, 2010-Present

ACHIEVEMENTS

North Beach High School Honor Student

Honorable Mention at the 2014 Science Explorers Club Invention Fair

REFERENCES

Marcella Trent, Park Coordinator, San Diego City Park, San Diego, CA 92130, (858) 555-0176, marcella.trent@sdcitypark.org

Janelle Travis, Store Manager, Marta's Mini Mart, San Diego, CA 92135, (858) 555-0101, janelle.travis@martas_minimart.com

Planning a Career in Marketing

Virtually every business in operation has to use marketing in some shape or form. Marketing is the process by which a company determines what products or services it can sell to others, and the strategy to use in sales, communications, and business development. The marketing function is closely tied to the organization's goals and objectives.

Marketing is a career area that provides a multitude of diverse and exciting job opportunities. For example, marketing professionals might conduct focus group interviews to determine consumers' wants and needs. Or they might travel the world to introduce a new product. Or they might organize a community event that is sponsored in part by their company.

What's It Like?

Individuals who work in marketing are responsible for planning, managing, and performing the marketing activities that meet the organization's objectives. For example:

© Golden Pixels LLC/Alamy

- They formulate business's policies and manage its operations.
- They conduct sales and ensure the timely delivery of products and services to the customer.
- They develop merchandising strategies aimed at promoting and sustaining sales of the company's products or services.
- They plan, coordinate, and implement advertising, promotion, and public relations activities.
- They collect and analyze data to develop comprehensive profiles of customers and their wants and needs.

Marketing professionals work in a variety of settings in all types of industries, including entertainment, technology, health care, and manufacturing. Businesses can be any size, ranging from a small start-up to a multinational corporation with thousands of employees. Positions are available at all levels, from CEOs and vice presidents to creative directors and account managers to sales clerks and public relations associates.

Employment Outlook

Employment in marketing careers is projected to grow between 7 and 13 percent over the 2008–2018 decade, with sales and marketing managers expected to experience the most growth. Most employers require marketing personnel to have a bachelor's or master's degree in business administration with an emphasis on marketing.

What About You?

The Marketing career cluster is covered in box 14 of the Interest Survey Activity you completed in Unit 1 of this text. If this box had one of the three highest scores on your survey, you should further explore the cluster's pathways and related occupations.

1. Why do you think a career in marketing could be a good choice?
2. What skills can you develop now that would be helpful to a career in marketing?
3. Why are these jobs important to a business?

LESSON 72 — Special Documents Application and Assessment

OUTCOMES

- Prepare documents using shapes, clip art or pictures, and text boxes.
- Prepare employment documents.

72B

Diagram

1. Open *df 72b diagram* and use it along with the Shapes and Text Box features to create a diagram similar to the one shown below. You decide the size, position, and format of the components of the diagram.
2. **Save as:** *72b diagram*.

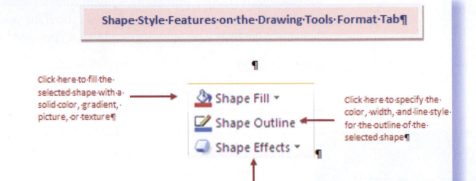

72C

Flyer

1. Open a new document. Using the information and directions below, design an 8.5" × 11" flyer. Include at least one text box and clip art or a picture. You decide all other formatting features.
2. **Save as:** *72c flyer*.

Laptop Computer for Sale

[Insert appropriate clip art or picture]

Contact: Juan Menendez

Phone: 419.555.0136

Model: Vostel 2100

Operating System: Optimum LX

Price: $435

Warranty: Transferable

The Winning Edge

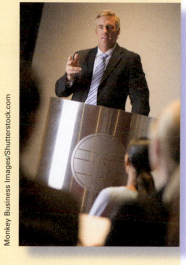

Monkey Business Images/Shutterstock.com

Complete this activity to help prepare for the **Business Communication** event in FBLA-PBL's Business Management and Administration division. Participants in this event demonstrate their business communication skills in writing, speaking, and listening.

1. In a new word processing document, use the information you learned in this unit to write a one-page report on how to write an effective e-mail message. Use the following guidelines.

   • **Introduction:** Define e-mail and discuss how it is used to communicate in business and professional settings.
   • **Body:** List and explain tips on writing an effective e-mail. Concepts to cover include subject line, recipients, organization, spelling and grammar, format, tone, and length.
   • **Conclusion:** Discuss the importance of preparing well-written e-mail messages and how their quality reflect on both the writer and the organization for which he or she works.

   You may use references to assist in preparing the paragraphs. When you are finished, be sure to proofread and revise the document as necessary. Apply formatting and text enhancements as appropriate. Save the document as directed by your instructor.

2. With your instructor's permission, send the document as an e-mail attachment to a classmate. Write a brief message explaining the document and asking your classmate to edit it.

3. Make revisions as necessary. Submit the document as directed by your instructor.

For detailed information on this event, go to www.fbla-pbl.org.

Think Critically

1. Why is writing considered an essential skill in just about any career you choose?
2. The writing process involves planning, composing, editing, proofreading, and revising. Why is each stage important to effective written communications?
3. What activities can you participate in now that will strengthen your writing skills?

School and Community

School and Community Many nonprofit and community-based organizations connect with members and volunteers through their websites, mass e-mails, and blogs. A blog is a type of website maintained by an individual or group on which regular entries of commentary as well as a listing of events and programs are posted. The commentary often deals with issues that are important to the organization. A feature of many blogs is the ability for readers to respond to content on the site with their own comments and thoughts.

1. Think of an organization in your community for which you would like to volunteer or perhaps for which you already volunteer.
2. Explore the ways in which the organization connects online with its members.
3. Assume you are going to write a blog for the organization. Investigate the procedures and requirements for starting a blog. (*Note*: You can use *Microsoft Word* to create a blog, but you must register your blog server in *Word* first. Or, you can create a free blog at various sites online.) What topics would you discuss in your blog and why? What benefits would your blog provide to the organization?

d. Select *Greeting line* from the task pane to insert a salutation. Make appropriate selections as shown in Figure 13-21. Click OK and tap Enter once.

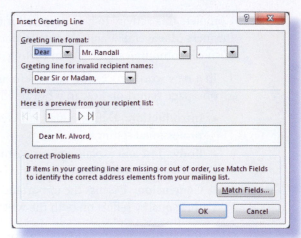

Figure 13-21 Insert Greeting Line dialog box

e. Key the following letter body and closing lines:

What a pleasant surprise it was to find your $100 donation to your alma mater's FBLA Chapter in my mail today. I think it is great that you think highly enough of FBLA and your high school to help fund our activities.

Your contribution will be used to pay the travel and lodging expenses for one of our members who will be competing at the upcoming state conference.

If you are ever in our area and would like to visit the school or speak to the FBLA members about your education, activities, or career; let me know. I would be happy to see what we can arrange.

Sincerely

Ms. Gretchen Tullis
FBLA Sponsor
xx

6. In Step 5 of 6, preview your letters and make any necessary revisions. Remove the space after the first two lines of the letter address, if needed.
7. In Step 6 of 6, print the first two letters and save the letters as *71d merged*.

UNIT 6 Enhance Input Skills

| Lesson 35 | Input Skill Development |
| Lesson 36 | Input Skill Development |

LESSON 35 Input Skill Development

OUTCOMES
- Build speed and accuracy.
- Enhance keying technique.

35A
Warmup

Key each line twice.

alphabet 1 Linda may have Jack rekey pages two and six of the big quiz.

spacing 2 if you | by the end of | it will be | you can see | when you | to your

easy 3 Jane is to go to the lake towns to do the map work for them.

| gwam | 1' | 1 | 2 | 3 | 4 | 5 | 6 | 7 | 8 | 9 | 10 | 11 | 12 |

35B
Technique: Letter Keys

1. Focus on limiting keystroking movement to the fingers.
2. Key each line twice.

A 1 Katrina Karrigan ate the meal of apples, bananas, and pears.

B 2 Bobby bought a beach ball and big balloons for the big bash.

C 3 Cody can serve cake and coffee to the cold campers at lunch.

D 4 David did all he could to dazzle the crowd with wild dances.

E 5 Elaine left her new sled in an old shed near the gray house.

F 6 Frank found a file folder his father had left in the office.

G 7 Gloria got the giggles when the juggler gave Glen his glove.

H 8 Hugh helped his big brother haul in the fishing net for her.

I 9 Inez sings in a trio that is part of a big choir at college.

J 10 Jason just joined the jury to judge the major jazz festival.

K 11 Nikki McKay kept the black kayaks at the dock for Kay Kintz.

L 12 Lola left her doll collection for a village gallery to sell.

M 13 Mona asked her mom to make more malted milk for the mission.

| gwam | 1' | 1 | 2 | 3 | 4 | 5 | 6 | 7 | 8 | 9 | 10 | 11 | 12 |

71C

Edit Data Source

A data source table contains unique information for each individual or item. Each individual or item is called a record, and each record contains fields. Fields are the information about each individual, such as title, first name, last name, street address, city, state, postal code, etc.; or about each item, such as item number, cost, selling price, size, etc. The column headings in the data source table are the names of the fields.

You can edit records in a data source. For example, you can add records to, delete records from, revise records in, or sort records in an existing data source file.

1. Open *df 71b data*.
2. Edit the data source by adding records for the three individuals below:

Mr.	Daniel	Raible	13811 Seagonville Road	Dallas	TX	75253-1380
Mrs.	Luz	Ruiz	13105 Timothy Lane	Mesquite	TX	75180-1310
Dr.	Jash	Sharik	2021 E. Park Boulevard	Plano	TX	75074-2021

3. Change Mrs. Alma Nolfi's address to **1919 Senter Road, Irving, TX 75060-1919**.
4. Save the file as *71c data*.

71D

Mail Merge: Create a Main Document

Mailings/Start Mail Merge/
Step by Step Mail Merge
Wizard

The main document file contains the generic text and format of the document that remains constant in each letter, plus the merge fields. The merge fields are inserted into the main document file where the variable information from the data source is to appear when the letter is written in the Wizard's Step 4 of 6.

1. Open a new *Word* document and access the Mail Merge Wizard.
2. In Step 1 of 1, choose *Letters*.
3. In Step 2 of 3, choose *Use the current document*.
4. In Step 3 of 6, choose *Use an existing list* and browse for *71c data*.
5. In Step 4 of 6, write your letter following the steps below:
   a. Format as a block letter with open punctuation.
   b. Key the current date. Tap Enter twice.
   c. Select *Address block* from the task pane to insert the fields for a person's title, name, and address. Make appropriate selections in the Insert Address Block dialog box, as shown in Figure 13-20. Click OK and tap Enter once.

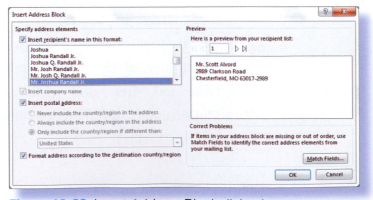

Figure 13-20 Insert Address Block dialog box

35C

Technique: Keying, Spacing, Shifting

1. Key each line twice.
2. Key a 1' writing on line 7 and then on line 8; determine *gwam* on each.

Spacing

1 Jay is in the city to buy an oak chair he wants for his den.

2 Jen may go to town by bus to sign a work form for a new job.

Shifting

3 Rico and Ty are in Madrid to spend a week with Jan and Juan.

4 Are you going in May or in June?   Rafael is leaving in July.

Balanced-hand sentences

5 Rick paid for both the visual aid and the sign for the firm.

6 Elvis kept all the work forms on the shelf by the big chair.

gwam 1' | 1 | 2 | 3 | 4 | 5 | 6 | 7 | 8 | 9 | 10 | 11 | 12 |

35D

Timed Writings

1. Key one 1' unguided and two 1' guided timings on each ¶; determine *gwam*.
2. Key two 2' unguided timings on ¶s 1–2 combined; determine *gwam*.
3. Record your best 2' timing.

A all letters used   gwam 2'

Quarter-Minute Checkpoints				
gwam	1/4'	1/2'	3/4'	1'
20	5	10	15	20
24	6	12	18	24
28	7	14	21	28
32	8	16	24	32
36	9	18	27	36
40	10	20	30	40
44	11	22	33	44
48	12	24	36	48
52	13	26	39	52
56	14	28	42	56

Who was Shakespeare? Few would question that he was the   6
greatest individual, or one of the greatest individuals, ever   12
to write a play.   His works have endured the test of time.   18
Productions of his plays continue to take place on the stages   24
of theaters all over the world.   Shakespeare was an expert   30
at creating comedies and tragedies, both of which often leave   36
the audience in tears.   38

Few of those who put pen to paper have been as successful   44
at creating prized images for their readers as Shakespeare.   50
Every character he created has a life of its own. It is   56
entirely possible that more middle school and high school   62
students know about the tragedy that Romeo and Juliet experi-   68
enced than know about the one that took place at Pearl Harbor.   74

gwam 2' | 1 | 2 | 3 | 4 | 5 | 6 |

OUTCOMES

- Use mail merge to create personalized letters.
- Edit a data source file.
- Create a main document file.

71B

Mail Merge Using Existing Files

Mailings/Start Mail Merge/
Step by Step Mail Merge
Wizard

The **Merge** feature is often used to merge a letter file (**main document**) with a name and address file (**data source**) to create a personalized letter (**merged file**) to each person in the data source file. Mail Merge can also be used to create labels for envelopes, name badges, etc.

Data sources can be word processing, spreadsheet, database, or e-mail files. In this lesson, you will use existing data sources created in *Word* and the Mail Merge Wizard to lead you through six steps to set up and perform a mail merge (See the Wizard's Step 1 of 6 task pane in Figure 13-19). Mail merges can also be performed by using the commands on the Mailings tab instead of the Wizard.

1. Open *Word* and then open *df 71b main*, which is the main document.

   Note that the main document contains merge fields in the letter address and salutation. These fields were inserted from the Wizard's task pane when the main document was created.

2. Use the path at the left to access the Mail Merge Wizard.

3. Complete Steps 1–3 in the Wizard. In the Step 1 of 6 task pane, select the type of document (choose *Letters*). In Step 2 of 6, select the starting document (choose *Use the current document*), and in Step 3 of 6, choose the recipients (choose *Use an existing list* and then browse for *df 71b data*).

   Note that the data file has three records; therefore, the mail merge will create three personalized letters.

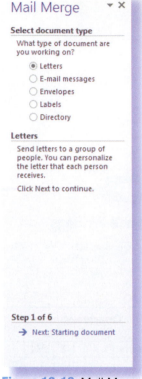

Figure 13-19 Mail Merge Wizard Step 1

4. Click OK to move to the Wizard's Step 4 of 6. In Step 4 of 6, the letter is written and the merge fields are inserted. Since the letter is already written and contains the desired merge fields, Step 4 is completed; so proceed to Step 5 of 6.

5. In Step 5 of 6, preview the three letters in the merged file by using the forward or backward chevrons in the task pane.

   Note that the merged fields in each letter have been replaced with the appropriate information from the data source file. Read the body of the letter to reinforce what you have learned about the mail merge feature.

6. In Step 6 of 6, select the Print option in the task pane and choose to print the Current record.

7. Save the three merged letters in one file named *71b merged* (see Tip at the left).

★TIP To save a copy of all the letters, click Edit Individual Letters in the task pane in Step 6 of 6 of the Mail Merge Wizard. Choose All in the Merge New Document dialog box. Click OK and then save the letters as *71b merged*. The letters may be saved before or after one or more of the letters are printed.

**Speed Check:
Sentences**

Key three 30" timings on each line. Try to go faster on each timing.

1 The firm kept half of us busy.

2 The girls work for the island firm.

3 Diane may blame the girls for the fight.

4 Pay the man for the work he did on the autos.

5 The social for the maid is to be held in the city.

6 Jake may sign the form if they do an audit of the firm.

| 30" | 2 | 4 | 6 | 8 | 10 | 12 | 14 | 16 | 18 | 20 | 22 |

35F

Timed Writings

1. Key one 1' unguided and two 1' guided timings on each ¶.
2. Key two 2' unguided timings on ¶s 1–2 combined; determine *gwam*.

A *all letters used* **gwam** 2'

	Quarter-Minute Checkpoints			
gwam	1/4'	1/2'	3/4'	Time
16	4	8	12	16
20	5	10	15	20
24	6	12	18	24
28	7	14	21	28
32	8	16	24	32
36	9	18	27	36
40	10	20	30	40

Whether you are an intense lover of music or simply 5
enjoy hearing good music, you are more than likely aware of 11
the work completed by Beethoven, the German composer. He is 17
generally recognized as one of the greatest composers to ever 24
live. Much of his early work was influenced by those who 29
wrote music in Austria, Haydn and Mozart. 33

It can be argued whether Beethoven was a classical or 39
romantic composer. This depends upon which period of time in 45
his life the music was written. His exquisite music has ele- 51
ments of both. It has been said that his early works brought 57
to a conclusion the classical age. It has also been stated 63
that Beethoven's later work started the romantic age of music. 69

| gwam 2' | 1 | 2 | 3 | 4 | 5 | 6 |

For additional practice:

MicroType 6

**Alphabetic Keyboarding
Lesson 1**

Interview Follow-Up Letter

Figure 13-18 Interview follow-up letter

1. Read the information below to learn about sending an interview follow-up letter.

Interview Follow-Up Letter. The **follow-up letter** is a thank-you to each person that had a significant role in your interview for the time given and courtesies extended to you (Figure 13-18). This personal-business letter lets each interviewer know that you are still interested in the job, it reminds him/her of your application and qualifications, and gives you an opportunity to create a favorable impression. This letter should be mailed within 24 hours after the interview to increase the likelihood that it will be received before an applicant is selected for the job.

2. Open a new document. Key the interview follow-up letter below as a personal-business letter in block format with mixed punctuation.

3. **Save as:** *70d letter*.

8503 Kirby Drive | Houston, TX 77054-8220 | May 25, 2014 | Ms. Jenna St. John | Personnel Director | Regency Insurance Company | 219 West Greene Road | Houston, TX 77067-4219 | Dear Ms. St. John

Thank you for discussing the customer service opening at Regency Insurance Company. I have a much better understanding of the position after meeting with you and Mr. Meade.

Mr. Meade was extremely helpful in explaining the specific job responsibilities. My previous jobs and my information technology classes required me to complete many of the tasks that he mentioned. With minimal training, I believe I could be an asset to your company.

Even though I realize it will be a real challenge to replace a person like Mr. Meade, it is a challenge that I will welcome. If there is further information that would be helpful as you consider my application, please let me know.

Sincerely | Douglas H. Ruckert

LESSON 36

Input Skill Development

OUTCOMES
- Build speed and accuracy.
- Enhance keying technique.

36A

Warmup

Key each line twice.

alphabet 1 Zelda might fix the job growth plans very quickly on Monday.

spacing 2 did go|to the|you can go|has been able|if you can|to see the

easy 3 The six men with the problems may wish to visit the tax man.

gwam 1' | 1 | 2 | 3 | 4 | 5 | 6 | 7 | 8 | 9 | 10 | 11 | 12 |

36B

Technique: Letter Keys

1. Focus on limiting keystroking movement to the fingers.
2. Key each line twice.

N 1 Nadine knew her aunt made lemonade and sun tea this morning.

O 2 Owen took the book from the shelf to copy his favorite poem.

P 3 Pamela added a pinch of pepper and paprika to a pot of soup.

Q 4 Quent posed quick quiz questions to his quiet croquet squad.

R 5 Risa used a rubber raft to rescue four girls from the river.

S 6 Silas said his sister has won six medals in just four meets.

T 7 Trisha told a tall tale about three little kittens in a tub.

U 8 Ursula asked the usual questions about four issues you face.

V 9 Vinny voted for five very vital issues of value to everyone.

W 10 Wilt wants to walk in the walkathon next week and show well.

X 11 Xania next expects them to fix the extra fax machine by six.

Y 12 Yuri said your yellow yacht was the envy of every yachtsman.

Z 13 Zoella and a zany friend ate a sizzling pizza in the piazza.

gwam 1' | 1 | 2 | 3 | 4 | 5 | 6 | 7 | 8 | 9 | 10 | 11 | 12 |

36C

Skill Building

Key each line twice.

Space Bar

1 and the big tub six she jam man oak row own fur did end keys

2 girl duck coal hand firm burn sick also city name when shelf

3 angle chair civic goals dials title cycle spend signs profit

Double Letters

4 book knee call pass wood eggs deed good look beet doll hoops

5 press little cottage college green depress bookseller letter

6 Illinois Mississippi Tennessee Missouri Massachusetts Hawaii

Figure 13-17 Employment form

Application for Employment
Regency Insurance Company

An Equal Opportunity Employer

PERSONAL INFORMATION

NAME (LAST FIRST)	SOCIAL SECURITY NO.	CURRENT DATE	PHONE NUMBER
Ruckert, Douglas H.	368-56-2890	5/22/2014	(713) 555-0121

ADDRESS (NUMBER, STREET, CITY, STATE, ZIP CODE)	U.S. CITIZEN	DATE YOU CAN START
8503 Kirby Dr., Houston, TX 77054-8220	☒ YES ☐ NO	6/10/2014

ARE YOU EMPLOYED NOW?	IF YES, MAY WE INQUIRE OF YOUR PRESENT EMPLOYER?	IF YES, GIVE NAME AND NUMBER OF PERSON TO CALL
☒ YES ☐ NO	☒ YES ☐ NO	James Veloski, Manager (713) 555-0149

POSITION DESIRED	SALARY DESIRED	STATE HOW YOU LEARNED OF POSITION
Customer Service	Open	From Ms. Anne D. Salgado Eisenhower Information Technology Instructor

HAVE YOU EVER BEEN CONVICTED OF A FELONY?
☐ YES ☒ NO   IF YES, EXPLAIN.

EDUCATION

	NAME AND LOCATION OF SCHOOL	YEARS ATTENDED	DID YOU GRADUATE?	SUBJECTS STUDIED
COLLEGE				
HIGH SCHOOL	Eisenhower Technical High School Houston, TX	2010 to 2014	Will graduate 06/2014	Information Technology
GRADE SCHOOL				
OTHER				

SUBJECTS OF SPECIAL STUDY/RESEARCH WORK OR SPECIAL TRAINING/SKILLS DIRECTLY RELATED TO POSITION DESIRED

Windows and Office Suite, including Word, Excel, Access, PowerPoint, and Publisher

Office Procedures course with telephone training and interpersonal skills role playing

FORMER EMPLOYERS (LIST LAST POSITION FIRST)

FROM - TO (MTH & YEAR)	NAME AND ADDRESS	SALARY	POSITION	REASON FOR LEAVING
9/2012 to present	Hinton's Family Restaurant, 2204 S. Wayside Avenue, Houston, TX 77023-8841	Minimum wage plus tips	Server	Want full-time position in my field
6/2010 to 9/2014	Tuma's Landscape and Garden Center 10155 East Freeway, Houston, TX 77029-4419	Minimum wage	Sales	Employed at Hinton's

REFERENCES (LIST THREE PERSONS NOT RELATED TO YOU, WHOM YOU HAVE KNOWN AT LEAST ONE YEAR)

NAME	BUSINESS ADDRESS	PHONE NUMBER	TITLE	YEARS KNOWN
Ms. Anne D. Salgado	Eisenhower Technical High School, 100 W. Cavalcade, Houston, TX 77009-2451	(713) 555-0134	Information Technology Instructor	Four
Mr. James R. Veloski	Hinton's Family Restaurant, 2204 S. Wayside Avenue, Houston, TX 77023-8841	(713) 555-0149	Manager	Two
Mrs. Helen T. Landis	Tuma's Landscape and Garden Center, 10155 East Freeway, Houston, TX 77029-4419	(713) 555-0182	Owner	Three

I UNDERSTAND THAT I SHALL NOT BECOME AN EMPLOYEE UNTIL I HAVE SIGNED AN EMPLOYMENT AGREEMENT WITH THE FINAL APPROVAL OF THE EMPLOYER AND THAT SUCH EMPLOYMENT WILL BE SUBJECT TO VERIFICATION OF PREVIOUS EMPLOYMENT DATA PROVIDED IN THIS APPLICATION, ANY RELATED DOCUMENTS, OR DATA SHEET. I KNOW THAT A REPORT MAY BE MADE THAT WILL INCLUDE INFORMATION CONCERNING ANY FACTOR THE EMPLOYER MIGHT FIND

RELEVANT TO THE POSITION FOR WHICH I AM APPLYING, AND THAT I CAN MAKE A WRITTEN REQUEST FOR ADDITIONAL INFORMATION AS TO THE NATURE AND SCOPE OF THE REPORT IF ONE IS MADE.

Douglas H. Ruckert
SIGNATURE OF APPLICANT

Speed Check: Sentences

Key three 30" timings on each line. Try to increase your keying speed each time you key the line. Determine *gwam* for the faster timing of each line.

1 Dr. Cox is running late today.
2 Ichiro baked Sandy a birthday cake.
3 Kellee will meet us here after the game.
4 Gordon will be leaving for college on Friday.
5 Juan and Jay finished the project late last night.
6 This is the first time that I have been to Los Angeles.

| gwam | 30" | 2 | 4 | 6 | 8 | 10 | 12 | 14 | 16 | 18 | 20 | 22 |

36E

Timed Writings

1. Key a 1' timing on each ¶; determine *gwam*.
2. Key two 2' timings on ¶s 1–2 combined; determine *gwam*.

 all letters used

| | gwam | 2' |

Who lived a more colorful and interesting 4
existence than this President? He was a rancher in 9
the west. He participated as a member of the Rough 14
Riders. He was a historian. He went on an African 20
safari. He was quite involved in the development of 25
the Panama Canal. He was the youngest person ever to 30
become President of the United States; however, he was 35
not the youngest person that was ever elected to the 41
office of President. And these are just a few of his 46
accomplishments. 48

Theodore Roosevelt was an active and involved 52
man. He lived life to the fullest and tried to make 57
the world a better place for others. Today, we still 63
benefit from some of his many deeds. Some of the 68
national forests in the West came about as a result of 73
legislation enacted during the time he was President. 78
He worked with college leaders to organize the 83
National Collegiate Athletic Association. 87

| gwam | 2' | 1 | 2 | 3 | 4 | 5 | 6 |

2. Check the contents of the application letter below against the guidelines in step 1 above. Note the kinds of information in each ¶.

3. Open a new document. Key the application letter below as a personal-business letter in block format with mixed punctuation.

4. **Save as:** *70b letter*.

8503 Kirby Drive | Houston, TX 77054-8220 | May 10, 2014 | Ms. Jenna St. John | Personnel Director | Regency Insurance Company | 219 West Greene Road | Houston, TX 77067-4219 | Dear Ms. St. John:

Ms. Anne D. Salgado, my business technology instructor, informed me of the customer service position with your company that will be available June 15. She speaks very highly of your organization. After learning more about the position, I am confident that I am qualified and would like to be considered for the position.

As indicated on the enclosed resume, I am currently completing my senior year at Eisenhower Technical High School. All of my elective courses have been computer and business-related courses. I have completed the advanced computer application class where we integrated word processing, spreadsheet, database, presentation, and Web page documents by using the latest suite software. I have also taken an office technology course that included practice in using the telephone and applying interpersonal skills.

My work experience and school activities have given me the opportunity to work with people to achieve group goals. Participating in FBLA has given me an appreciation of the business world.

An opportunity to interview with you for this position will be greatly appreciated. You can call me at (713) 555-0121 or e-mail me at dougr@ suresend.com to arrange an interview.

Sincerely, | Douglas H. Ruckert | Enclosure

70C

Application Form

1. Read the information below to learn about completing an application form for a position you are seeking.

Application Form. Many companies require an applicant to complete an application form even though a résumé and application letter have been received. Applicants often fill in forms at the company, using a pen to write on a printed form or keying information into an online form (Figure 13-16). Sometimes applicants may take an application form home, complete it, and return it by mail or in person. In this case, the information should be printed in blue or black ink on the form. You should strive to provide information that is accurate, complete, legible, and neat. To lessen the chance of error on a printed application, make a copy of the blank form to complete as a rough draft.

2. Open *df 70c form*. Print one copy of the form.

3. Using the information from the model copy on the next page, complete the form. Print neatly.

4. Submit the completed form to your instructor.

36F

Rough Draft: Edited Copy

∧	=	insert
#	=	add space
∼	=	transpose
ℓ	=	delete
◡	=	close up
≡	=	capitalize
/ℓc	=	lowercase

1. Review the proofreaders' marks shown at the left.
2. Key each sentence twice. Make all editing (handwritten) changes.

1. The manager, ~~Mr. Chen~~ *Ms. Ramirez*, left for New#york on Friday.

2. The ~~Texas~~ Rangers won the ~~Central~~ *Western* Divis∼oin of *the* American league.

3. Roger ~~got~~ *was* fitted for ∼knew eye glas∼sses *on Friday*.

4. Jamal∼l will study for#the ≡spanish exam this week◡end.

5. Did you know ~~their~~ *there* are three more exams in ≡History∼.?

36G

Timed Writings

1. Key one 1' unguided and two 1' guided timings on each ¶.
2. Key two 2' unguided timings on ¶s 1–2 combined; determine *gwam*.

Quarter-Minute Checkpoints

gwam	1/4'	1/2'	3/4'	1'
20	5	10	15	20
24	6	12	18	24
28	7	14	21	28
32	8	16	24	32
36	9	18	27	36
40	10	20	30	40
44	11	22	33	44
48	12	24	36	48
52	13	26	39	52
56	14	28	42	56

For additional practice:

MicroType 6

Alphabetic Keyboarding Lesson 2

A   all letters used   gwam   2'

Austria is a rather small country, about three times the size of Vermont, located between Germany and Italy. The best known of the cities in this country is Vienna. Over the years this city has been known for its contributions to the culture in the region, particularly in the area of performing arts. Another place that has played an important part in the exquisite culture of the area is the city of Salzburg.

Salzburg is recognized as a great city for the performing arts, particularly music. Just as important, however, is that the city is the birthplace of Wolfgang Amadeus Mozart, one of the greatest composers of all time. Perhaps no other composer had an earlier start at his professional endeavors than did Mozart. It is thought that he began playing at the age of four and began composing at the age of five.

gwam 2' | 1 | 2 | 3 | 4 | 5 | 6 |

Enrichment

Europe is a popular tourist destination. Millions of tourists visit such countries in Europe as Austria, France, Germany, Italy, and Spain each year.

If you could visit a country in Europe next year, which one would you select? Learn more about the country you selected by searching the Internet. Compose a paragraph or two explaining why you chose the country you did and what you would like to see in that country.

1. Read the information below to learn about preparing reference lists.

Reference List. When your résumé indicates that references will be furnished upon request, you should prepare a **reference list** to take with you to employment interviews. If you prefer, references may be listed on the résumé, at the end of the page.

Your reference list should contain the name, address, telephone number, and e-mail address (if the person uses e-mail) of three to six people (not relatives) who know you well. Teachers, clergy, and current or previous employers usually make good references. Ask each person in advance for permission to list her or his name as a reference, and describe the job for which you are applying. Be sure all names are spelled correctly and that addresses and telephone numbers are accurate. Include each person's organization and job title.

To format a separate reference list, use a 2" top margin and default side margins and line spacing. Include a centered title, such as **REFERENCE LIST FOR** (*insert your name*) in bold, 14-pt. font. List the references beneath the centered title.

2. Open *df 69d references*.
3. Insert the following title and reference above the two references in the file.

REFERENCE LIST FOR DOUGLAS H. RUCKERT

Ms. Anne D. Salgado, Information Technology Instructor, Eisenhower Technical High School, 100 W. Cavalcade, Houston, TX 77009-2451, (713) 555-0134, salgado@eths.tx.us.gov.

4. Verify that the format is correct and all errors are corrected.
5. **Save as:** *69d references*.

LESSON 70 — Employment Letters and Forms

OUTCOMES
- Format application letters.
- Complete application forms.
- Format thank-you letters.

1. Read the information below to learn about preparing application letters for a position you are seeking.

Application Letter. An **application letter** should always accompany a résumé. This personal-business letter should be limited to one page. See an example in Figure 13-16. The application letter should include three topics—generally in three to five ¶s. The first topic (¶) should specify the position for which you are applying and may state how you learned of the opening and something positive about the company. The second topic (one to three ¶s) should include evidence that you qualify for the position. This is the place to interpret information presented in your résumé and to show how your qualifications relate to the job for which you are applying. The last ¶ should request an interview and give precise information for contacting you to arrange it.

Figure 13-16 Application letter

Lesson 37   Personal-Business Letters—Block Format and Open Punctuation
Lesson 38   Personal-Business Letters—Mixed Punctuation
Lesson 39   Additional Letter Parts
Lesson 40   Business Letters
Lesson 41   Letters with Envelopes
Lesson 42   Letters—Application and Assessment

Application Guide

Letters

A letter written by an individual to deal with business of a personal nature is called a **personal-business letter**. A personal-business letter is typically printed on personal stationery that does not have a preprinted return address. A **business letter** is typically printed on letterhead stationery (stationery that has a preprinted return address). You compose letters using word processing software such as *Microsoft Word* (see Figure 7-1).

Block Letter Format

Block letter format (see p. 138) is commonly used to arrange the parts of a letter. All parts of a letter arranged in block format begin at the left margin. The ¶s are not indented. Use a 2" top margin (tap Enter three times), default side margins, and 1.08 line spacing unless otherwise specified below.

Basic Letter Parts

The basic parts of a letter are described below in order of placement on the paper. Differences between the parts of a personal-business letter and a business letter are identified.

Return address. The return address on a personal-business letter (start at or near the 2" line) consists of a line for the street address and one for the city, state, and ZIP Code. Tap Shift + Enter once after each line of the return address.

© iStockphoto.com/Lise Gagne

The return address on a business letter need not be keyed since the street, city, state, and ZIP Code are preprinted on letterhead stationery. In addition, the company name, phone numbers, and/or website are usually part of the letterhead.

Date. When keying a personal-business letter, key the month, day, and year on the line below the city, state, and ZIP Code and then tap Enter twice to begin the letter address.

When keying a business letter, begin the date at or near the 2" line or 0.5" below the last line of the letterhead, whichever is lower. Tap Enter twice to begin the letter mailing address.

Figure 13-15 Print résumé

Formatted as a 2" x 5" table. Default font and line spacing were used. All borders were removed.

Douglas H. Ruckert

8503 Kirby Drive
Houston TX 77054-8220
(713) 555-0121
dougr@suresend.com

Objective:	To use my computer, Internet, communication, and interpersonal skills in a challenging customer service position.
Education:	Will graduate from Eisenhower Technical High School in June 2014 with a high school diploma and business technology emphasis. Grade point average is 3.75. **Relevant Skills and Courses:** ❑ Proficient with most recent versions of Windows and Office, including Word, Excel, Access, PowerPoint, and FrontPage. ❑ Excelled in the following courses: Keyboarding, Computer Applications, Business Communications, and Information Technology. **Major Accomplishments:** ❑ Future Business Leaders of America: Member for four years, vice president for one year. Won second place in Public Speaking at the District Competition; competed (same event) at state level. ❑ Varsity soccer: Lettered three years and served as captain during senior year. ❑ Recognition: Named one of Eisenhower's Top Ten Community Service Providers at end of junior year.
Work Experience:	Hinton's Family Restaurant, Server (2012-present): Served customers in culturally diverse area, oriented new part-time employees, and resolved routine customer service issues. Tuma's Landscape and Garden Center, Sales (2010-2011): Assisted customers with plant selection and responsible for stocking and arranging display areas.
References:	Will be furnished upon request.

Letter address. Key the first line of the letter (delivery) address below the date. A personal title (Miss, Mr., Mrs., Ms.) or a professional title (Dr., Lt., Senator) is keyed before the receiver's name. Tap Shift + Enter to move from line to line within the mailing address. Tap Enter once after keying the last line of the mailing address to begin the salutation.

Salutation. Key the **salutation** (greeting). Include a courtesy title with the person's name, e.g., Dear Ms. Jones. Tap Enter after keying the salutation.

Body. Key the letter body (message) using the default line spacing, and tap Enter once after each paragraph (¶) and after the last line of the last ¶ in the body to begin the complimentary close.

Complimentary close. Key the **complimentary close** (farewell), and then tap Enter twice to key the name of the writer. Capitalize only the first word in the complimentary close.

Name of the writer. Key the name of the writer. The name may be preceded by a personal title (Miss, Mrs., Ms.) to indicate how a female prefers to be addressed in a response. If a male has a name that does not clearly indicate his gender (Kim, Leslie, Pat), the title Mr. may precede his name.

In many letters, a position title (Manager, President, Salesperson, etc.) is used with the name of the writer. The position title may be keyed on the same line as the name of the writer (separated with a comma) or on the next line. If placed on the next line, tap Shift + Enter once and then key the position title. Tap Enter once to begin the next letter part, if any.

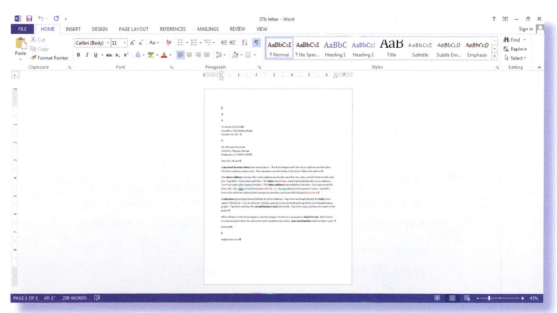

Figure 7-1 Letter shown on *Word* screen

Figure 13-14 Electronic résumé

Formatted with default margins, line spacing, and font.

Douglas H. Ruckert
8503 Kirby Drive
Houston TX 77054-8220
(713) 555-0121
dougr@suresend.com

SUMMARY

Strong communication and telephone skills; excellent keyboarding, computer, and Internet skills; and good organizational and interpersonal skills.

EDUCATION

Will graduate from Eisenhower Technical High School in June 2014 with a high school diploma and information technology emphasis. Grade point average is 3.75.

RELEVANT SKILLS AND COURSES

Proficient with most recent versions of Windows and Office, including Word, Excel, Access, PowerPoint, and Publisher.

Excelled in the following courses: Computer Applications, Business Communications, and Information Technology.

MAJOR ACCOMPLISHMENTS

Future Business Leaders of America: Member for four years, vice president for one year. Won second place in Public Speaking at District Competition; competed (same event) at state level.

Varsity soccer: Lettered three years and served as captain during senior year.

Recognition: Named one of Eisenhower's Top Ten Community Service Providers at end of junior year.

WORK EXPERIENCE

Hinton's Family Restaurant, Server (2012-present): Served customers in culturally diverse area, oriented new part-time employees, and resolved routine customer service issues.

Tuma's Landscape and Garden Center, Sales (2010-2012): Assisted customers with plant selection and responsible for stocking and arranging display areas.

COMMUNITY SERVICE

First Methodist Church Vacation Bible School teacher assistant (2012-2013).

Race for the Cure publicity committee (2013).

ETHS Senior Citizens Breakfast server (2011-2014).

United Youth Camp student helper (2013).

REFERENCES

Will be furnished upon request.

Open and Mixed Punctuation

When **mixed punctuation** is used, place a colon after the salutation and a comma after the complimentary close. When **open punctuation** is used, do not key any punctuation after the salutation and complimentary close.

Additional Letter Parts

The following letter parts are frequently included in letters following the writer's name and/or position title. If more than one of these parts is included in a letter, key them in the order listed below. To properly place each part, tap Enter once at the end of the line that precedes the part you are including.

Reference Initials. If someone other than the originator of the letter keys it, his/her initials are keyed in lowercase letters at the left margin below the writer's name and/or title.

Attachment/Enclosure notation. If another document is attached to a letter, the word *Attachment* is keyed at the left margin. If the additional document is not attached, the word *Enclosure* is used. If more than one document is attached or enclosed, make the notation plural.

Copy Notation. A copy notation indicates that a copy of the letter is being sent to someone other than the addressee. Key **c** and then tab to 0.5" to begin the name(s) of the person(s) to receive a copy. If there is more than one name, list names vertically as shown below (tap Shift + Enter between the names).

c   Hector Ramirez
         Ursula O'Donohue

TIP You may need to Undo Automatic Capitalization to key the first letter in the reference initials or the copy notation in lowercase if AutoCorrect options are not changed.

WP Applications

Activity 1

Font Group

For each feature, read and learn the feature described; then complete the activity as directed.

OUTCOMES
- Change Font attributes
- Insert a Text Wrapping Break (Remove Space After Paragraph)
- Use Spelling & Grammar, Synonyms, Hyphenation, Thesaurus, Envelope, Insert Date & Time, Decimal Tabs, and Bullets and Numbering

Home/Font

The Font group contains many features that can be used to change the appearance of text in a document. For example, the font, font size, and font color can be changed. Text can be highlighted, underlined, or have an effect applied to it. Numbers can be formatted in superscript or subscript formats. These features as well as others are contained in the Font group on the Home tab illustrated below in Figure 7-2.

1. Within the Font group, hover your mouse pointer over each of the 15 features to identify each feature and read the short description of it.

Figure 7-2
The Font group

Résumé do's and don'ts. Follow these guidelines when creating your résumé.

- Do use a simple format. Default top, bottom, and side margins and line spacing are acceptable but may vary slightly depending on the amount of information presented.
- Do key your name at the top of the page on a line by itself. Key your address below your name, and list e-mail address and telephone number on separate lines.
- Do arrange the résumé parts attractively on the page. The arrangement may vary with personal preference and the purpose of the résumé.
- Do use a basic font, such as 12-pt. Times New Roman or 11-pt. Calibri.
- Do use white, ivory, or light-colored (gray or tan) paper, standard size (8.5" × 11") for a print résumé.
- Don't use text effects (such as Outline, Shadow, Reflection, and Glow), borders, horizontal lines, or shading on electronic or printed résumés that are likely to be scanned.
- Don't insert your photograph in a résumé.

2. Study the electronic résumé model in Figure 13-14 on p. 276.
3. Key the electronic résumé from the model.
4. **Save as:** *69b resume*.

69C

Printed Résumé

1. Study the printed résumé model in Figure 13-15 on p. 277.
2. Using the Table feature, insert a 2" × 5" table. Set the width of column 1 at 1.5" and column 2 at 5". Merge the cells in row 1, and key the name and contact information as shown in the résumé model on p. 277.
3. Key the remaining text in the four rows, formatting it as shown in the model résumé on p. 277.
4. Remove all table borders, and make any desired adjustments to the white space between ¶s.
5. **Save as:** *69c resume*.

© 2011 Digital Vision/Jupiter Images Corporation

2. Read each sentence below; then key each sentence, applying the font commands as directed in the sentence.

Bold, italicize, and underline this text in a red, 11-pt., Arial font.

Apply a subscript number and superscript as shown: $H_2O.$[1]

Highlight this text in yellow and apply a text effect of your choice.

KEY AS SHOWN; USE CHANGE CASE TO MAKE IT SENTENCE CASE.

Use Strikethrough on this text and then grow it to 16-pt. Calibri.

3. Make a copy of the first sentence and paste it after the last sentence. Use the Clear Formatting feature to erase the font features applied to the text.
4. **Save as:** *aa7 activity 1*.

Activity 2

Hyphenation

Page Layout/Page Setup/
Hyphenation

The **Hyphenation** feature automatically divides (hyphenates) words that would normally wrap to the next line. This evens the right margin, making the text more attractive.

1. Open a new document, and change the right and left margins to 2.5".
2. Key the text below in Courier New 12 pt. with hyphenation off.
3. Use the Hyphenation feature (Automatic option) to hyphenate the document.

    Use the Hyphenation feature to give text a professional appearance. When the Hyphenation feature is activated, the software divides long words between syllables at the end of lines. Using hyphenation makes the right margin less ragged. This feature is particularly helpful when keying in narrow columns.

4. **Save as:** *aa7 activity 2*.

Activity 3

Spelling & Grammar

Review/Proofing/Spelling
& Grammar

Use the **Spelling & Grammar Check** to check for misspellings and grammar errors. The Spelling Check feature compares each word in the document to words in its dictionary (or dictionaries). If a word in a document is not identical to one in its dictionary, the word is flagged by a wavy red underline. Usually the Spelling Check lists words it *thinks* are likely corrections (replacements). The Grammar Check feature flags potential grammar errors with a wavy green underline. The Grammar Check also lists words it thinks will correct the grammar error. *Note:* The Grammar Check may or may not catch incorrect word usage (*too* for *to* or *two*). If it does, a blue wavy underline appears. Even when using these features, it is important to proofread your documents.

1. Key the ¶ below *exactly* as it is shown. Note how some errors are automatically corrected.
2. Use the Spelling & Grammar Check to identify errors. Correct all errors by editing or selecting a replacement.
3. Proofread after the Spelling & Grammar Check, and correct any errors Spelling & Grammar did not detect.

    Dr. Smith met with the students on Friday to reviiw for for there test. He told the students that their would be three sections to the test. The first secction would be multiplee choice, the second sction would be true/fals, and the last section would be shoot answer. He also said, "If you have spelling errors on you paper, you will have pionts deducted.

4. **Save as:** *aa7 activity 3*.

LESSON 69

OUTCOME

69B

Electronic Résumé

Figure 13-12 Electronic résumé

Figure 13-13 Print résumé

Employment Résumés

- Correctly format print and electronic résumés.
- Correctly format reference lists.

1. Read the information below and on the next page to learn about preparing employment documents in general and résumés in particular.

Employment Document Guidelines

Résumé. In most cases, a résumé should be limited to one page. The information presented usually covers six major areas: *personal information* (your name, home address, e-mail address, and telephone number[s]); *objective* (clear definition of position desired); *education* (courses and/or program taken, skills acquired, grade-point average [and grades earned in courses directly related to job competence], and graduation date); *school and/or community activities or accomplishments* (organizations, leadership positions, and honors and awards); *work experience* (position name, name and location of employer, and brief description of responsibilities); and a notation that *references* (names of people familiar with your character, personality, and work habits) will be provided upon request. In general, the most important information is presented first, which means that most people who have recently graduated from high school will list educational background before work experience. The reference section is usually last on the page.

Print versus electronic résumés. **Print résumés** are those printed on paper and mailed to prospective employers. **Electronic résumés** are those attached to e-mail or posted to a company web page or Internet job search site. (See Figures 13-12 and 13-13 and the model electronic and print résumés on pp. 276 and 277.)

Résumé scanning. Many companies scan both print and electronic résumés into database files and then search each file for specific information. They may search for education level, work experience, or keywords that are closely related to the position being filled. When you believe an employer is not likely to scan your résumé, your print résumé may contain format features, such as indentations and columns; and text enhancements, such as bold, bullets, several font designs and sizes, and underlines. These types of features and enhancements can cause errors or disappear entirely or partially when a résumé is scanned, attached to e-mail, or posted to a web page. Therefore they should be omitted from an electronic résumé—and from a print résumé that may be scanned. To increase the likelihood that their résumé will be selected in a database search, many people replace the Objective section with a Summary section (see the electronic résumé on p. 276). The summary contains keywords describing education, positions held, skills, and/or accomplishments that relate to the position being sought.

Activity 4

Thesaurus

Review/Proofing/
Thesaurus

A **thesaurus** in your word processing software can be quickly accessed to help you find synonyms that will convey an appropriate meaning of the message you are writing. To find synonyms for a specific word, select that word and then use the path at the left to access the thesaurus. Or right-click the selected word and click Synonyms to display a list of synonyms from which you can select the word you want.

1. Open *df aa7 activity 4*. Find appropriate synonyms for the four words in blue font, and insert them into the text.
2. **Save as:** *aa7 activity 4*.

Activity 5

Insert Date & Time

Insert/Text/Date & Time

The **Insert Date & Time** feature is used to enter the date into a document automatically. Choose the appropriate format of the date to be inserted from the list of available formats as shown in Figure 7-3. If desired, you can choose to have the date updated automatically each time the document is opened or printed. The date on your computer must be current to insert the correct date in a document.

Some software provides an Automatic Completion (AutoComplete) feature, which also inserts the date automatically. When you start keying a month, AutoComplete recognizes the word and shows it in a tip box above the insertion point. By tapping the Enter key, you enter the remainder of the month automatically, without keying the remaining letters. When you tap the Space Bar after the month has been inserted, the tip box shows the complete date. Tapping the Enter key enters the complete date.

1. Key the information below using 1.0 line spacing, Insert Date & Time as directed, and AutoComplete when applicable.
2. **Save as:** *aa7 activity 5*.

1. Insert date by using <Insert Date & Time; do not select Update automatically>.
2. Insert date by using <Insert Date & Time; select Update automatically>.
3. Today is <Use Insert Date & Time; do not Update automatically>.
4. Your balance as of Insert date <Use Insert Date & Time; select Update automatically> is $42.83.
5. I received your check today, <Use Insert Date & Time; select Update automatically>.
6. You will need to make sure to record today's date, <Use Insert Date & Time; do not Update automatically>, is included on the form.

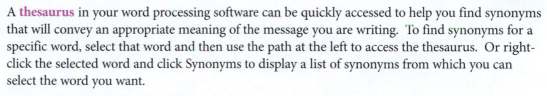

Figure 7-3 Date and Time formats

1. Open a new document. Design a flyer to present the information below on 8.5" × 11" paper. Use clip art or a picture in your flyer. You decide the use of color, shapes, clip art, pictures, tables, and/or text boxes and all other formatting features.

2. **Save as:** *68c flyer*.

> ## Dr. Ida Meinert
> ## Nutritionist, Blair Hospital
> ## will speak on the topic
> ## Recognizing Eating Disorders
> ## Wednesday, October 3
> ## Periods 1, 2, 5, 6, and 7
> ## Classroom 222

To attend, complete the form below and have the teacher of the class you will miss sign the form. By Monday, October 1, give the form to Mrs. Porterfield.

Permission to Attend Dr. Meinert Presentation	
Student's Name	
Course & Period Missed	
Teacher's Signature	

1. Open a new document. Using the suggestions for content that are given below, design a flyer your instructor can use to inform others of the value of the course in which you are using this textbook.

2. Use clip art or a picture in your flyer. You decide all formatting features.

3. **Save as:** *68d flyer*.

Suggested content:

- Include the title of the course.
- Identify some of the course activities you enjoy.
- Describe important things that you have learned.
- Specify reasons why others should take this course.
- Identify the software that you use.
- Explain how this course helps you in other classes or at work.

The default settings leave 8 pts. of white space between lines each time Enter is tapped. The space can be removed by using the **Remove Space After Paragraph** feature. This feature can be accessed by following the path at the left. Alternatively, the space can be removed by using the **Text Wrapping Break** feature. To use this feature, tap and hold down the Shift key and tap the Enter key. In this unit, you will be instructed to use the **Shift + Enter** method when the space after a ¶ is to be removed.

1. Key the text in the left column below, tapping Enter at the end of each line.
2. Tap Enter twice and key the text in the right column, holding down the Shift key and tapping Enter as instructed.
3. Compare the difference.
4. Select the first two lines of the text keyed from the left column, and use the Remove Space After Paragraph feature to remove the space after these two lines.
5. Compare the spacing of this text to the text where Shift + Enter was used to remove the space after the ¶s—the spacing should be the same.
6. **Save as:** *aa7 activity 6*.

Mr. Ricardo Seanez (Tap Enter)	Mr. Ricardo Seanez (Hold Shift; tap Enter)
1538 Village Square (Tap Enter)	1538 Village Square (Hold Shift; tap Enter)
Altoona, WI 54720 (Tap Enter)	Altoona, WI 54720 (Tap Enter)
Dear Ricardo (Tap Enter)	Dear Ricardo (Tap Enter)
I will be arriving in Altoona on July 15 for the next meeting.	I will be arriving in Altoona on July 15 for the next meeting.

Use the Envelopes feature to create envelopes for your letters. This feature allows you to select the size of the envelope, key the return address and the delivery address, and print the envelope (see Figure 7-4). The delivery address can be keyed, inserted automatically from the letter file, or inserted from your Address Book. Electronic postage software can be used with this feature.

1. Open a new document, and use the Envelopes feature to format a small envelope (No. 6 3/4) using this information:

Figure 7-4
The Envelopes and Labels dialog box

Return address:
Ms. Carson Sanchez
270 Rancho Bauer Drive
Houston, TX 77079-3703

Mailing address:
Ms. Susan Keane
872 Mayflower Drive
Terre Haute, IN 47803-1199

Flyers with Graphics

- Insert and modify shapes, text boxes, clip art, and/or pictures to enhance the content of flyers and make them attractive and easy to read.

68B

Flyer

1. Open a new document. Prepare a flyer to be printed on 8.5" × 11" paper, using shapes and/or text boxes and the information below. Use clip art or a picture in your flyer. You decide the size, color, and format of the shapes and the placement of all information.
2. **Save as:** *68b flyer*.

5K Run or Walk

Join RTHS Alumni

on

Saturday, August 14, 20--

at 9 a.m.

in East Park

$12 ENTRANCE FEE INCLUDES T-SHIRT, PRIZES, AND REFRESHMENTS

CALL (422) 555-0192 TO REGISTER

PRIZES WILL BE AWARDED TO
TOP THREE MEN AND WOMEN
FINISHERS IN THREE AGE
GROUPS

See our website at http://www.rths.org/5k

2. **Save as:** *aa7 activity 7a*.
3. Open a new document and use the Envelopes feature to format a large envelope (No. 10) using this information for the mailing address. A return address need not be keyed as it is assumed the business envelope has a preprinted return address on it.

Mr. Jacob Saunders
396 Hickory Hill Lane
Kalamazoo, MI 49009-0012

4. **Save as:** *aa7 activity 7b*.

Activity 8

Bullets and Numbering

Home/Paragraph/Bullets
Home/Paragraph/
Numbering

Bullets (special characters) are used to enhance the appearance of text. Bullets are often used to add visual interest or emphasis. Examples of bullets are illustrated in Figure 7-5.

Numbering is used to show the proper order of a series of steps. Use numbers instead of bullets whenever the order of items is important. Examples of number format are illustrated in Figure 7-6.

Figure 7-5 Bullet Library

Figure 7-6 Numbering Library

1. Key Activity A below using the ✓ Bullet style; tap Enter twice after keying the last bulleted item to end the bulleted list.
2. Key Activity B using the Numbering feature. Tap Enter twice after the last numbered item.
3. **Save as:** *aa7 activity 8*.

Activity A
Please be sure to bring the following:

- ✓ Paper
- ✓ Pencil
- ✓ Data files
- ✓ Keyboarding book

Activity B
The final 2010 standings in the American League East were:

1. Rays
2. Yankees
3. Red Sox
4. Blue Jays
5. Orioles

LESSON 67 Documents with Shapes and Text Boxes

OUTCOME

- Insert and modify shapes and text boxes to enhance the content of documents and make them attractive and easy to read.

67B

Letterhead

1. Open a new document. Using the information below, create a header that serves as letterhead on the company stationery. Use Verdana 36-pt. font within a text box to display the company name and colors similar to those shown below. You decide all other format features.
2. **Save as:** *67b letterhead*.

Paragon Group

Specialists in Actuarial Recruiting

22 East Ohio Street
Chicago, IL 60613

Phone: 312.555.0100
Fax: 312.555.0130
Email: actuarialrecruits@group-paragon.com
www.group-paragon.com

67C

Business Card

1. In a new document, draw a text box 2" high and 3.5" wide.
2. Within that text box, design a business card using black and shades of gray and the information below. You may choose different clip art for the logo. You decide all other formatting features.
3. **Save as:** *67c card*.

Tri-County Science Supplies

Deanne A. Gardner
6010 N. Scottsdale Road
Scottsdale, AZ 85253-6000
480.555.0110
480.555.0111
gardner@az-tcss.com

67D

Diagram

1. Open *df 67d diagram* and use it along with the Shapes and Text Box features to create an instructional diagram similar to the one shown below. You decide the size, position, and format of the components of the diagram.
2. **Save as:** *67d diagram*.

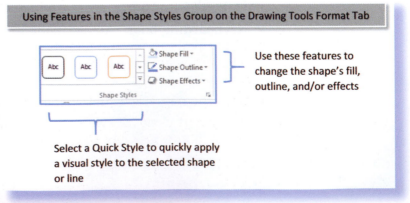

Using Features in the Shape Styles Group on the Drawing Tools Format Tab

Use these features to change the shape's fill, outline, and/or effects

Select a Quick Style to quickly apply a visual style to the selected shape or line

Activity 9

Decimal Tab

Decimal tab button

Decimal tabs are set in the same way as Left, Right, and Center tabs that you learned earlier. Decimal tabs align all text at the decimal point or any other character that you specify. If you key numbers in a column at the decimal tab, the decimal points will line up, regardless of the number of places before or after the decimal point. The decimal tab icon in the tab selector box on the Horizontal Ruler is illustrated at the right.

1. Open a new document. Set a left tab at 1", a right tab at 2.75", a decimal tab at 3.75", and another decimal tab at 5".
2. Key the four lines below, using the Tab key to move from one column to another. Tap Shift + Enter at the ends of the lines to remove the space between the ¶s.

James Hill	6,750	88.395	0.25
Mark Johns	863	1.38	13.6
Sue Chen	30	115.31	297.312
Seth Ramirez	1,397	24.6583	32.0167
Kay Kent	56,873	367.4142	1.58245

3. **Save as:** *aa7 activity 9*.

Activity 10

Show/Hide ¶

Home/Paragraph/
Show/Hide

Word processing documents contain invisible formatting marks that can be displayed. Commonly used marks (read the text in Figure 7-7) are

¶ to show the end of a ¶,

→ to show a tab,

. to show a space between words.

Being able to see the formatting marks is helpful when editing a document or solving formatting problems. The formatting marks do not print.

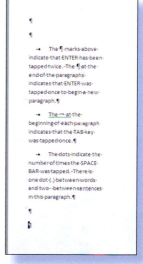

Figure 7-7 Formatting marks

1. Key the following text with Show/Hide ¶ activated. Tap Enter twice after the last bulleted item.

You can incorporate fitness into your daily routine by doing these three activities:
- Walk up stairs for one minute each day instead of taking the elevator. Within a year you should be a pound lighter without changing any other habits.
- Walk the dog, don't just watch the dog walk. In a nutshell—get moving!
- Perform at least 30 minutes of moderate activity each day. If necessary, do the 30 minutes in 10-minute intervals.

2. Review the keyed text, and note the formatting marks that are displayed.
3. **Save as:** *aa7 activity 10*.

II. **Roll call**

Jim Holman, Secretary, conducted a roll call. Thirteen members were present.

III. **Approval of minutes from last meeting**

Jim Holman, Secretary, read the minutes from the last meeting. The minutes were approved as read.

IV. **Open issues**

    a. Samantha Earl, Fundraising Chair, reported that her committee recommends that our chapter sell Better Candles to raise money to support our members who will compete at the state level. Better Candles will give us 50 percent of the sales. The committee's recommendation was accepted.

    b. Madeline Barry reported that our chapter sponsor, Ms. Dearborn, has gained permission to have our members compete in all team and individual events this year.

V. **New business**

    a. Madeline Barry suggested that our chapter use the Membership Brochure Template that the national office provides to recruit new members. Since we are a new club, many may not know the membership benefits of FBLA. The members approved the recommendation and appointed Maria Velman and Jack Imhoff to prepare a brochure at the next meeting.

VI. **Adjournment**

    Madeline Barry, President, adjourned the meeting at 3:15 p.m.

Minutes submitted by: Jim Holman, Secretary

© iStockphoto.com/Bob Ingelhart

TEAMWORK

Digital Citizenship and Ethics

From homework help to music downloads to online shopping, the Internet has become a valuable resource that provides many benefits when it is used responsibly. But searching on the Internet can lead you to websites containing inappropriate content, such as antisocial or reckless behavior, violence, pornography, and gambling.

Many search engines provide options for controlling access to inappropriate websites, but you can also limit your exposure to offensive content by understanding what constitutes illegal or misleading content. In general, anything that is illegal in the real world is also illegal in the online world. In addition, do not take everything you read on the Internet at face value, because anyone can set up a website and use it to publish just about anything they please, including extremist views and false information.

If you are upset by content you view on a website, you should tell an adult immediately. You can also contact your Internet service provider or a community hotline. If you feel you are in immediate danger because of your Internet activities, you should contact the local police.

As a class, discuss the following.

1. What search engines do you use regularly? What features do they offer to control access to inappropriate websites? What would you do if you came across an offensive website?

2. What does Internet safety mean to you?

Activity 11

Apply What You Have Learned

1. Open **df aa7 activity 11**.
2. Find and insert an appropriate synonym for "unit" in the first ¶.
3. Check the text for spelling and grammar, and make necessary corrections.
4. Bold the names of the Clubs.
5. Grow the title to 20 pts., and (for Word 2010) apply the Gradient Fill – Orange, Accent 6, Inner Shadow text effect to it. For Word 2013, use Gradient Fill – Purple, Accent 4, Outline – Accent 4.
6. Hyphenate the text.
7. Tap Enter three times after the last line, and key the following four lines, removing the space after the first three lines (¶s).

    Ms. Henrietta Killingsworth
    Roosevelt High School
    824 South Jackson Boulevard
    Chesterton, IN 46304-0860 <Tap Enter twice>

8. Insert a decimal tab at 3", and key the following numbers at the point. Remove the space between the ¶s.

    123.456

    12.3456

    1.23456

    0.12345 <Tap Enter twice>

9. Key the following bulleted list using a bullet of your choice. After keying the list, use the Insert Date & Time feature to key today's date using the xx/xx/xxxx format. Select the Update automatically option.

    Things to do:
    - Monday
    - Tuesday
    - Wednesday
    - Thursday
    - Friday <Tap Enter twice>

10. **Save as:** *aa7 activity11*.

on April 12. Their expenses for travel and meals will be reimbursed.

c. Three suggestions for a give-back gift were discussed. The possibilities include planting a tree near the student parking lot, donating one or more biology reference books to the school library, and purchasing a banner that can be used to welcome students back to school each fall. The Give-Back Committee, chaired by Annie Sexton, will study all three options and report back at the April meeting.

VI. <u>Adjournment</u>

Marcie Holmquist adjourned the meeting at 3:35 p.m.

Minutes submitted by: Jerry Finley, Secretary

66C

Template—Invitation

1. Open the template file *df invitation*. Prepare an invitation using the information below. Use the template settings for font, font size, line spacing, etc.
2. Adjust the position of the text box so the right and bottom margins are about equal.
3. Proofread and correct errors.
4. **Save as: *66c invite*.**

Date: September 15, 20—

Time: 7:30 p.m.

Location: 527 Longview Drive

RSVP: 724-555-0136

Your hosts: Don and Kathie

66D

Template—Certificate

1. Open the template file *df certificate 2*. Prepare a certificate for **Holly Wilson** for excellence in **Computer Applications and Keyboarding**. Insert **Thomas Jefferson High School** for the school name.
2. Increase the font size to 20 pt. for the text you inserted.
3. **Save as: *66d cert 1*** and keep the file open.
4. Replace Holly's name with **James Lyle**.
5. **Save as: *66d cert 2*.**

66E

Template—Meeting Minutes

1. Open the template file *df minutes*. Using the information below and the template file, prepare a set of meeting minutes. Use the template settings for font, font size, line spacing, etc. Add to and delete from the template content as needed.
2. Use bold and underline as shown in the copy below.
3. Proofread and correct errors.
4. **Save as: *66e minutes*.**

Aitken High School FBLA

Meeting Minutes

October 12, 20—

I. <u>Call to order</u>

Madeline Barry, President, called to order the regular meeting of the Aitken High School FBLA at 2:25 p.m. on October 12, 20— in Room 303.

(continued on next page)

Personal-Business Letters—Block Format and Open Punctuation

OUTCOMES

- Learn to format personal-business letters in block format with open punctuation.
- Use wp features for font, hyphenation, spelling and grammar check, and removing space after ¶s.

37–42A

Warmup

Key each line twice at the beginning of each lesson; first for control, then for speed.

alphabet 1 Jay asked four zany questions before each good example was given.

figures 2 My mutual fund fell 4.87 points to 65.92 on Friday, May 30, 1998.

speed 3 The men may pay for a big emblem of the chapel with their profit.

gwam	1'	1	2	3	4	5	6	7	8	9	10	11	12	13

37B

Personal-Business Letter from Model Copy

1. Study the application guides on pp. 128–130 and the model personal-business letter in Figure 7-8. Note the placement of letter parts and vertical spacing between them.
2. Format/key the model on p. 138. Proofread and correct errors. Hyphenate the document.
3. **Save as:** *37b letter*.

37C

Personal-Business Letter from Arranged Copy

1. Format/key the letter below in block format with open punctuation. Refer to the model on p. 138 as needed. Proofread and correct errors. Hyphenate the document.
2. **Save as:** *37c letter*.

853 North Highland Avenue
Atlanta, GA 30306-0403
October 15, 20—

Ms. Amy Mazanetz
4505 Ashford Road
Atlanta, GA 30346-0346

Dear Ms. Mazanetz

Thank you for speaking to our Community Service Club. Your points on the importance of giving back to our community were very well received by the club members. They will help motivate us to do more service work during this school year.

We enjoyed learning about the projects you described, and our members plan to adopt at least two of the projects this year. Your comments about what it takes to plan and carry out service projects will be very helpful to us.

Again, thank you for sharing your expertise with our club and agreeing to work with us in the future.

Sincerely

Alex Neu, Secretary

If you use Shift + Enter to remove space after the ¶s and tap Enter correctly between before and after the letter parts, the format codes shown below should display when the Show/Hide ¶ feature is used. The ↵ is the code to indicate that Shift + Enter has been used.

¶

Ms.·Amy·Mazanetz↵
4505·Ashford·Road↵
Atlanta,·GA·30346-0346¶

Dear·Ms.·Mazanetz¶

OUTCOME

- Use templates to efficiently prepare meeting minutes, certificates, and invitations.

66B

Template—Meeting Minutes

1. Open the template file **df minutes**. Using the information below and the template file, prepare a set of meeting minutes. Use the template settings for font, font size, line spacing, etc. Add to and delete from the template content as needed.

2. Use bold and underline as shown in the copy below, and number the pages at the upper right; hide the page number on p. 1.

3. Proofread and correct errors.

4. **Save as: 66b minutes**.

WOODWARD HIGH SCHOOL BIOLOGY CLUB

Meeting Minutes

March 2, 20—

I. <u>Call to order</u>

President Marcie Holmquist called to order the regular meeting of the Biology Club at 2:45 p.m. on March 2, 20— in Room 214.

II. <u>Roll call</u>

Jerry Finley, Secretary, conducted a roll call. The following persons were present: All officers, 23 members, and the faculty sponsor.

III. <u>Approval of minutes from last meeting</u>

Jerry Finley, Secretary, read the minutes from the last meeting. The minutes were approved as read.

IV. <u>Open issues</u>

    a. There will be five teams of four members each for the candy sale that begins on May 1. Team captains are Bruce Holstein, Anita Jones, Roberto Nuez, Ty Billops, and Gracie Walton. Each captain will select three members for his/her team.

    b. Bill Eaton will lead a team of 15 volunteers to pick up litter on Route 163 on May 15. The Rotary Club will provide supervision, safety vests, gloves, road signs, and collection bags. The volunteers are to meet at the Carriage Inn parking lot at 8:45 a.m. and will work until about 11:30 a.m.

    c. The officers recommended that the Club not provide financial support for an international student this coming year since the Club needs to provide financial assistance to members who attend the Fall Regional Leadership Conference. The officers' recommendation was approved.

V. <u>New business</u>

    a. President Holmquist appointed the Nominating Committee (Sissy Erwin, Roberta Shaw, and Jim Vance), and they are to present a slate of officers at the April meeting.

    b. The membership approved officers to attend the Spring Regional Leadership Conference at Great Valley Resort and Conference Center

(continued on next page)

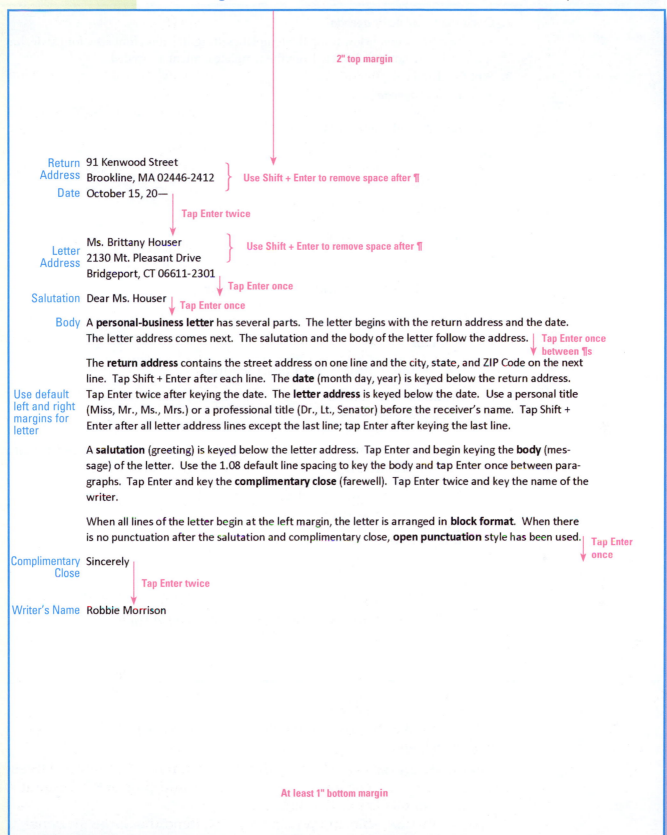

2" top margin

Return Address
91 Kenwood Street
Brookline, MA 02446-2412 } Use Shift + Enter to remove space after ¶

Date
October 15, 20—

Tap Enter twice

Letter Address
Ms. Brittany Houser
2130 Mt. Pleasant Drive } Use Shift + Enter to remove space after ¶
Bridgeport, CT 06611-2301

Tap Enter once

Salutation
Dear Ms. Houser

Tap Enter once

Body
A **personal-business letter** has several parts. The letter begins with the return address and the date. The letter address comes next. The salutation and the body of the letter follow the address.

Tap Enter once between ¶s

Use default left and right margins for letter

The **return address** contains the street address on one line and the city, state, and ZIP Code on the next line. Tap Shift + Enter after each line. The **date** (month day, year) is keyed below the return address. Tap Enter twice after keying the date. The **letter address** is keyed below the date. Use a personal title (Miss, Mr., Ms., Mrs.) or a professional title (Dr., Lt., Senator) before the receiver's name. Tap Shift + Enter after all letter address lines except the last line; tap Enter after keying the last line.

A **salutation** (greeting) is keyed below the letter address. Tap Enter and begin keying the **body** (message) of the letter. Use the 1.08 default line spacing to key the body and tap Enter once between paragraphs. Tap Enter and key the **complimentary close** (farewell). Tap Enter twice and key the name of the writer.

When all lines of the letter begin at the left margin, the letter is arranged in **block format**. When there is no punctuation after the salutation and complimentary close, **open punctuation** style has been used.

Tap Enter once

Complimentary Close
Sincerely

Tap Enter twice

Writer's Name
Robbie Morrison

At least 1" bottom margin

1. Open the template *df agenda*.
2. Key the information below using the template settings for font, font size, font style, line spacing, etc. Add to and delete from the template content as needed.
3. Proofread and correct errors.
4. **Save as:** *65d agenda*.

Woodward High School Biology Club

Meeting Agenda

March 2, 20—

2:45 p.m. in Room 214

Type of Meeting: Regular meeting

Meeting Facilitator: Marcie Holmquist, President

Invitees: All members and faculty sponsor

I.   Call to order

II.   Roll call

III. Approval of minutes from last meeting

IV.   Unfinished business

    a) Finalize team assignments for candy sale that begins May 1

    b) Plan approved community service project to care for one mile of State Route 163

    c) Discuss recommendation that the Club help support an international student

V.   New business

    a) Appoint nominating committee

    b) Discuss plans for regional leadership conference on April 12

    c) Discuss annual give-back gift to Woodward High

VI.   Adjournment

1. Open *65d agenda* and add this item as letter d under V. New business:

Discuss the request that club members tutor science students at the middle school

2. **Save as:** *65e agenda*.

1. Format/key the letter below in block format with open punctuation. *Note:* Line endings for opening and closing lines are indicated by color verticals.
2. Proofread and correct errors. Hyphenate the document.
3. **Save as:** *37d letter*.

4810 Smokey Road | Newman, GA 30263 | October 25, 20— | Ms. Denise Joyce | 3209 Snyder Avenue | Modesto, CA 95356-0140 | Dear Ms. Joyce

My English teacher, Mr. Merriman, has been discussing with me the importance of considering my audience when I write.

He emphasizes that the language I use when I am e-mailing or text messaging with my friends is not the language I should use when I am writing to adults. He tells me that the language my friends and I use when writing each other is quite informal and chatty, even though we may be writing about a topic that is important to us.

He has convinced me that I need to learn more about writing to adult audiences, and I've decided to write my report on this topic. I want to learn how to change the style and tone of my writing so that adults will have a favorable first impression when I write them.

Since you are a professional writer, Mr. Merriman suggested I write you and request the names of a few resources I can use to learn more about audience consideration. Thanks. I look forward to hearing from you.

Sincerely | Catherine Kessler

Digital Citizenship and Ethics

A **cyber predator** is someone who uses the Internet to hunt for victims whom they take advantage of in many ways—sexually, emotionally, psychologically, or financially. Cyber predators know how to manipulate kids. They create trust and friendship where none should exist.

Cyber predators are the dark side of social networking and other forms of online communication. They frequently log on to chat groups or game sites and pose as other kids. They try to gradually gain your trust and encourage you to talk about your problems. Even if you don't chat with strangers, personal information you post on sites such as Facebook can make you a target.

As a class, discuss the following.

1. Give examples of how to identify a cyber predator.
2. How can you avoid being the victim of a cyber predator?
3. What should you do if you receive a message that is suggestive, obscene, aggressive, or threatening?

TEAMWORK

© AresT/Shutterstock.com

4. Key the following for the body and closing lines of the memo:

I've enclosed copies of the announcement for this year's Science Information Evening for the parents of the middle school students. The middle school science teachers will distribute the announcement in their classes, and the district newsletter will also announce the date, time, and location.

As in the past, we will use this event to explain the high school science curriculum to interested students and parents so they will have a better idea of the courses, options, and activities our department has to offer.

xxx

Enclosure

5. Proofread and correct all errors.
6. **Save as:** *65b memo*.

65C

Template—Memo

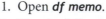

1. Open *df memo*.
2. Use the following information to prepare a memo. Use your school name in the top text box, and include reference initials and enclosure notation.
3. Proofread and correct errors.
4. **Save as:** *65c memo*.

TO: All Intermediate and Senior High School Science Teachers

FROM: Mudi Mutubu, Department Head

DATE: April 15, 20—

SUBJECT: LABORATORY RENOVATIONS

I've met several times with our school district architects and the science facility consultants they employed to plan the renovations needed for our biology, chemistry, and physics laboratories at the intermediate and senior high schools.

The architect is prepared to have us review and discuss the enclosed preliminary drawings that show the proposed changes to the facilities, including the preparatory rooms and laboratory furniture. I've scheduled a meeting for Wednesday, April 22, at 2:30 p.m. in the conference room near the Principal's Office.

Please arrange your schedules so you can attend this important meeting. The meeting should not last more than one hour, and we will then have ten days to make recommendations so the architect can prepare the second set of drawings.

OUTCOMES

- Learn to format personal-business letters with mixed punctuation.
- Use wp features for Thesaurus and Insert Date and previously applied features.

38B

Personal-Business Letter with Mixed Punctuation from Arranged Copy

1. Review mixed punctuation on p. 130.
2. Format/key the letter below using block format and mixed punctuation. Use the Insert Date & Time function to insert the date—do not select Update automatically. Change the font to 12-pt. Times New Roman.
3. Hyphenate the document. Proofread and correct errors.
4. **Save as:** *38b letter.*

207 Brainard Road
Hartford, CT 06114-2207
<Insert date>

Mr. Justin A. Alaron
Brighton Life Insurance Co.
I-84 & Route 322
Milldale, CT 06467-9371

Dear Mr. Alaron:

Your job in actuarial science is of great interest to me. I am a student at Milldale School and participate in the Shadow Experience Program (SEP) that is part of the curriculum. I learned about actuarial science while researching jobs related to mathematics. Math is my favorite subject, and I have done very well in all of my math classes. Math appears to be one of my strengths.

SEP encourages students to shadow a person who is working in a career field they are exploring. I would like to shadow you for one or two days so that I can learn more about what an actuary does and the skills and knowledge that are required. I would also like to learn about how you became an actuary and the process you completed to get your license.

I can arrange to be with you at your office for one or two days during the coming month. Please send your written response to me so that I can present it to Ms. Michelle Kish, the SEP coordinator. Thank you.

Sincerely,

Valerie E. Lopez

LESSON 65   Templates—Memos and Agendas

OUTCOME

- Use templates to efficiently prepare memos and agendas that are attractive and easy to read.

65–72A

Warmup

Key each line twice at the beginning of each lesson; first for content and then for speed.

alphabet 1 Frank questioned Tim over the jazz saxophone at my new nightclub.

fig/sym 2 The #5346 item will cost Ford & Sons $921.87 (less 10% for cash).

speed 3 If Jen signs the form, I may pay to dismantle the ancient chapel.

gwam 1' | 1 | 2 | 3 | 4 | 5 | 6 | 7 | 8 | 9 | 10 | 11 | 12 | 13 |

65B

Template—Memo

1. Read the information about memos in the special document section of the application guide on p. 259, and preview the template below that will be used to prepare memos in this unit.

This template requires you to insert a name for the organization in the text box at the top right and appropriate text in the TO, FROM, and SUBJECT heading lines. The current date will be inserted automatically, but it can be changed if needed. The placeholder text in the memo body will be replaced with the body of the memo you are creating. Reference initials and attachment, enclosure, and copy notations are added as needed after the body, using the default line spacing of the template.

Business/School Name

Memo

TO: [Click **here** and type name]

FROM: [Click **here** and type name]

DATE: January 13, 2014

SUBJECT: [Click **here** and type subject]

- -

To use this template, select the text you want to replace and key the replacement text. If you want to keep the changes you make as a new template for future use, choose Save As from the File menu. In the Save As Type box, choose Word Template. Next time you want to use it, choose New from the File menu, and then double-click your template in the document gallery or find it in the My Templates folder.

---

2. Open the template *df memo*.
3. Key the name of your school in the top text box. Key **Science Teachers** in the TO heading and **Mary Todd, Science Department Head** in the FROM heading. Use the current date and key **SCIENCE INFORMATION EVENING** (in all caps) in the SUBJECT heading.

Personal-Business Letter with Mixed Punctuation from Unarranged Copy

1. Format/key the letter below using block format and mixed punctuation. Use the Insert Date & Time function or AutoCorrect to insert the date—do not select Update automatically.
2. Change the font to 12-pt. Arial. Hyphenate the document. Proofread and correct errors.
3. **Save as:** *38c letter*.

6920 Dalzell Place | Pittsburgh, PA 15217-6000 | <Insert Date> | Mr. Phillip Hendon | 119 Cornwalis Drive | McKeesport, PA 15135-1000 | Dear Mr. Hendon:

I want to thank you for helping me with funds to attend Camp Kennedy Space Camp from August 11 through August 15.

My learning experience began with the flight from Pittsburgh to Orlando. It was my very first airplane ride. I was very nervous before taking off, but once we started to climb into the sky, I was thoroughly enjoying the view of Pittsburgh and the wonderful feeling that comes from the thrust of the engines taking us up through the soft clouds. The landing in Orlando was equally as exciting.

The five days at camp were just great. I learned so much! I experienced the thrill of spaceflight through an actual motion-based simulator. We got to work in teams to investigate space travel and to design space exploration vehicles and habitats. I really enjoyed meeting and talking with an astronaut who is training for an upcoming flight. She was so informative and knew exactly what to say to us. Furthermore, I got to enjoy the company of other youngsters who are as interested in space as I am.

Again, thanks for supporting me in achieving this important goal. Your generosity is greatly appreciated, and it has impacted my education in a very meaningful way.

Sincerely, | Josh Satterfield

Insert/Illustrations/Online Pictures

You can use Online Pictures to search Office.com and other sources for pictures and clip art to insert into your document (Figure 13-10). If you have saved your own pictures or clip art, you can use Pictures to find and insert them into your document. When the inserted picture or clip art is selected, options in the Size and Arrange groups on the Format tab of the Picture Tools ribbon can be used to size, crop, and position the picture in relation to the paper and text (Figure 13-11). Other options in the Adjust and Picture Styles groups on the Format tab can also be used to format your picture as desired.

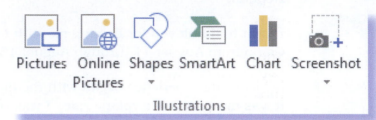

Figure 13-10 Insert illustrations

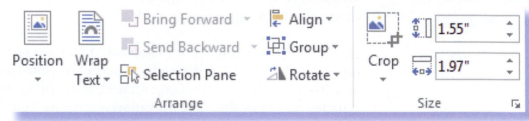

Figure 13-11 Format pictures

1. Open *df aa13 activity 4*.
2. From Online Pictures, search for a picture or clip art that represents a construction worker or one of the building trades named in ¶ 2.
3. Insert the picture into the middle of ¶ 2, wrapping text around it. Resize it so it does not extend above the first line of the ¶ or below the last line of the ¶.
4. Select a picture of a building from Online Pictures, and insert the picture into the middle of ¶ 3 so it is behind the text. Do not have it extend above the first line of the ¶ or below the last line of the ¶.
5. **Save as:** *aa13 activity 4*.

1. Open *df certificate 1*.
2. Insert your first and last name as the member and **Keystone Club** as the name of the organization. Use the current date.
3. **Save as:** *aa13 activity 5*.

1. Format/key the letter below using block format and open punctuation. Use the Insert Date & Time function to insert the date—select Update automatically.
2. Find and insert an appropriate synonym for "illness" and/or "recommended."
3. Proofread and correct errors.
4. **Save as:** *38d letter*.

14820 Conway Road | Chesterfield, MO 63025-1003 | <Insert Date> | Ms. Kelly Mueller | Fundraising Projects, Inc. | 15037 Clayton Road | Chesterfield, MO 63107-8734 | Dear Ms. Mueller

The Science Club at Jefferson High School is going to raise funds to help pay the medical bills of one of our members who is suffering from a life-threatening illness.

Our tentative plan is to fundraise during October, November, and December at each of the home varsity football, soccer, and basketball games. There are 20 such events scheduled during that time period. Our principal has given us permission to staff a table at each event.

We are interested in selling shirts, hats, sweats, etc. that have our school name and mascot, but we need to speak with you about this plan before proceeding further. We need to know the cost of the items, a recommended selling price, and payment arrangements. Our next meeting is scheduled for September 20 in Room 210 in the high school at 2:15 p.m. Can you meet with us for about an hour to tell us how your company can help us in this project?

You can e-mail your response to Seerhoff@stargate.net. I need to know your availability by September 15. Thank you.

Sincerely | Karen Seerhoff | President

LESSON 39   Additional Letter Parts

- Learn to format business letters with additional letter parts.
- Use wp features for Bullets and Numbering and previously applied features.

1. Review the application guides on pp. 128–130, paying particular attention to return address, date, and name of writer sections to learn differences between personal-business letters and business letters. Study the information on mixed punctuation and additional letter parts and preview the model business letter in Figure 7-9. Note the placement of letter parts, and spacing between them.
2. Format/key the model in Figure 7-9. Proofread and correct errors. Hyphenate the document.
3. **Save as:** *39b letter*.

2. Change the shape outline to a 3-pt. solid red line, and then resize the text box to fit the text on two lines, using center alignment.

3. Near the horizontal and vertical center of the page, draw a text box that is about 1" high × 3" wide. Shade the text box with a dark color and remove the shape outline. Using center alignment and bold, white 12-pt. Arial font, key the following copy in the text box. Resize the text box to fit the text on one line.

This is centered text in a shaded text box that has no shape outline.

4. Near the bottom right corner of the page, insert a text box, using either the Banded Quote or Braces Quote built-in design.

5. Key your first and last name, your school name, and the current date inside the box on three lines. Change the font color of the text and braces or bar to a dark burgundy. If needed, position the text box near the bottom right corner.

6. **Save as:** *aa13 activity 2*.

Activity 3

Shapes—Review

Insert/Illustrations/Shapes

This shape has text inserted.

As you learned in Unit 9, *Office* provides a variety of ready-made shapes (see Figure 13-9 for shapes in the following galleries: Recently Used Shapes; Lines; Basic Shapes, Block Arrows, Flowchart, Callouts, and Stars and Banners that you can add to a document). A freeform (a shape in the Lines gallery) can be used to create a customized shape by using your mouse as a pen.

Once a drawing shape is inserted into a document, features on the Drawing Tools Format ribbon can be used to insert a shape or text within a shape; change the shape size and form; apply styles, shadow, and 3-D effects; and specify the position and size of the shape. The illustration at the left shows a Cloud callout that has been inserted, sized, shaped, and shaded. Text has been added, and the outside border and text have been colored blue.

Shapes can be deleted by selecting the shape and then tapping Delete. Perfect squares or circles can be drawn by selecting the Oval or Rectangle button on the Shapes gallery and then holding down the Shift key as you drag to create the shape.

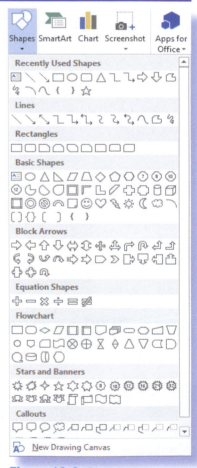

Figure 13-9 Shapes

1. Open a new document. Select a star shape. Draw a 2.5" star near the horizontal center at the top of the page. Insert your name using a 14-pt. bold font for the text. Resize and format the star as needed to attractively display your name on one or two lines.

2. Near the center of the page, draw a shape of your choice. Key your school name in the shape, center aligned. Format this shape using an Outer shadow and the Denim texture.

3. **Save as:** *aa13 activity 3*.

Figure 7-9 Business letter in block format with mixed punctuation

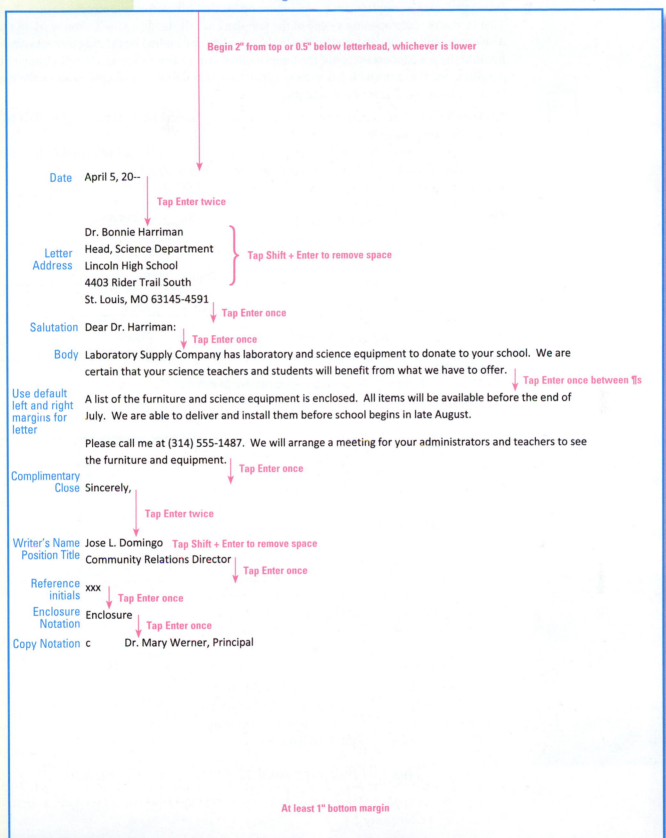

Begin 2" from top or 0.5" below letterhead, whichever is lower

Date — April 5, 20--

Tap Enter twice

Letter Address —
Dr. Bonnie Harriman
Head, Science Department
Lincoln High School
4403 Rider Trail South
St. Louis, MO 63145-4591

Tap Shift + Enter to remove space

Tap Enter once

Salutation — Dear Dr. Harriman:

Tap Enter once

Body — Laboratory Supply Company has laboratory and science equipment to donate to your school. We are certain that your science teachers and students will benefit from what we have to offer.

Tap Enter once between ¶s

Use default left and right margins for letter

A list of the furniture and science equipment is enclosed. All items will be available before the end of July. We are able to deliver and install them before school begins in late August.

Please call me at (314) 555-1487. We will arrange a meeting for your administrators and teachers to see the furniture and equipment.

Tap Enter once

Complimentary Close — Sincerely,

Tap Enter twice

Writer's Name Position Title —
Jose L. Domingo   Tap Shift + Enter to remove space
Community Relations Director

Tap Enter once

Reference initials — xxx

Tap Enter once

Enclosure Notation — Enclosure

Tap Enter once

Copy Notation — c   Dr. Mary Werner, Principal

At least 1" bottom margin

When you open a template, a new document opens that is based on the template you selected. That is, you're really opening a copy of the template, not the template itself. You work in that new document, using what was built into the template and adding or deleting as necessary. Because the new document is not the template itself, your changes are saved to the copy of the template, and the template is left in its original state. Therefore, one template can be the basis for an unlimited number of documents.

1. Open the Fax template, *df fax*, from your data files (or the Equity Fax template that is installed on your computer).
2. Replace the text in the template with that shown in italic in the fax transmittal sheet below to create a new fax transmittal sheet that is based on the template.
3. **Save as:** *aa13 activity 1*.

To:	Ms. Helen Fresco	From:	[Your Name]
Fax:	803-555-0195	Pages:	Five
Phone:	803-555-0198	Date:	[Pick the date]
Re:	Oliver Plaza Project	CC:	None

| Urgent | X | For Review | Please Comment | | Please Reply | Please Recycle |

Comments:
I'll call you on Thursday to set up an appointment to discuss the project.

Activity 2

Text Boxes—Review

Insert/Text/Text Box

This is a shaded text box without a border that illustrates reverse type (white letters on green background) using Calibri 12-pt. font. The text is center-aligned.

As you learned in Unit 9, text boxes are frequently used for labels or callouts in a document. You can use a built-in text box that has pre-designed information and formats, or you can draw a blank text box to hold your information and format it as desired (see Figure 13-8).

Once a text box is inserted in your document, you can edit it by using available features on the Text Box Tools Format ribbon that appears when a text box is selected. You can use the features within the groups on this ribbon to change the text or text box style, change shadow or 3-D effects, and specify the position and size of your text box as you did with WordArt.

1. Open a new document. Draw a text box that is approximately 1" high × 2" wide near the horizontal center on line 1. Key the following information in the text box, using a 12-pt. Arial italic font.

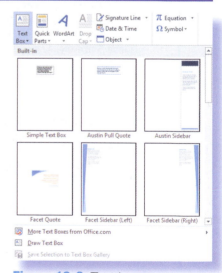

Figure 13-8 Text boxes

This text box uses Arial 12-pt. italic font for the letters.

Business Letter from Arranged Copy

1. Format/key the letter below in block format with mixed punctuation. Refer to the model on p. 143 as needed. Proofread and correct errors. Hyphenate the document.
2. **Save as:** *39c letter*.

August 15, 20—

Ms. Amy McKenery
2128 Magill Drive
Odessa, TX 79764-0700

Dear Ms. McKenery:

Thank you for expressing an interest in establishing a scholarship to be awarded to a student who will be graduated at the end of this school year. As we discussed briefly on the telephone, the deadlines we need to meet are listed below:

1. Prepare the scholarship application by September 30.
2. Post scholarships on the school district website by October 10.
3. Receive scholarship dollars by November 1.
4. Receive scholarship applications by March 1.
5. Select and notify recipients by May 1.

Please complete the enclosed form and return it to me by September 1 so I can have a draft of the application prepared for you to review. If you have any questions, please call me at (943) 555-4612.

Again, thanks for giving back to your community to assist a worthy student.

Sincerely,

Alex Neu, Principal

xxx

Enclosure

For each feature, read and learn about the feature described; then complete the activity as directed.

OUTCOMES

- Use templates to format and key documents.
- Use shapes, text boxes, clip art, and pictures to enhance the content of documents and make them more attractive and easier to read.

File/New

Many business and personal documents are keyed using a template. In this unit, you will use templates to create a variety of documents including agendas, certificates, faxes, invitations, meeting minutes, and memos.

A template is a master copy of a set of predefined styles for a particular type of document. The template may contain text and formatting for margins, line spacing, colors, borders, styles, themes, etc. The use of a template saves you time since you use it as a starting point rather than creating every document from scratch. For example, if you have weekly meetings and have to create a similar agenda for each meeting, starting out with a template that is formatted and has a lot of the repetitive information already in place will save time, since you will need to change only the details that differ from week to week. See the example memo template in Figure 13-6.

Normally, you select templates from the sample templates that are installed on your computer (see Figure 13-7), from Office.com Templates, or from templates you have created. In this unit, you will mostly use *Word* templates that have been created and saved to your data files.

Figure 13-6 Memo template

★TIP You can save any *Word* file as a template by selecting Word Template (.dotx) under Save As Type in the Save As dialog box.

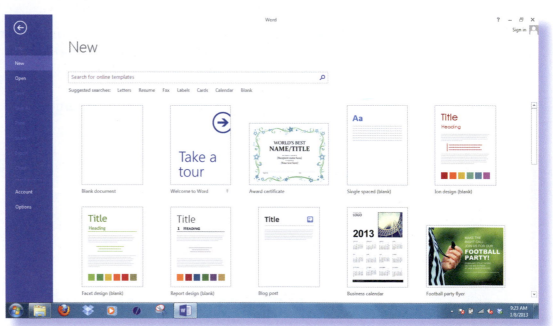

Figure 13-7 Sample templates

1. Format/key the letter below in block format with open punctuation. Change the font to 10-pt. Calibri.
2. Proofread and correct errors. Hyphenate the document.
3. **Save as:** *39d letter*.

November 1, 20— | Mr. Max R. Rice | Foster Plaza Seven | 23 Oak Street | Schiller Park, IL 60176-6932 | Dear Mr. Rice

If the dental plan you chose last year has not delivered everything you thought it would, we have some good news for you. Dental Benefits Plus is now available to all Barclay, Inc. employees during this open enrollment period.

Dental Benefits Plus is part of the All-American family of health care products. Members of Dental Benefits Plus enjoy many advantages, including:

- Convenience: a nationwide network of over 50,000 dentists
- Affordability: low copays for high-quality services
- Support: a qualified support staff you can contact 24 hours a day, 7 days a week
- Availability: offered in 50 states and the District of Columbia
- Honesty: no hidden costs or surprise fees

These advantages as well as others are described in greater detail in the enclosed booklet. You can enroll any time before December 31. Mr. James Rothie, the customer service representative in your area is available to assist you with any questions you may have. You can contact him at (866) 555-1258.

Thank you for considering Dental Benefits Plus.

Sincerely | Janet Kingston | Regional Enrollment Manager | xxx | Enclosure | c James Rothie

Figure 13-2 Agenda

Agenda

An **agenda** (Figure 13-2) is a list of topics to be discussed or actions to be taken, usually at a meeting. Agendas generally include the name of the group holding the meeting; the date, time, and location of the meeting; the purpose of the meeting; and information about who is conducting the meeting and who is expected to attend.

Meeting Minutes

Meeting minutes (Figure 13-3) are written records of what was discussed and decided at a meeting. Meeting minutes usually include the date, time, and location of the meeting; a list of the attendees; action taken on the minutes from the previous meeting; and information about the next meeting.

Certificates and Invitations

These documents are generally prepared on special stationery and include information pertinent to the document being prepared. For example, a certificate usually has the name of the recipient and organization/person issuing the certificate, a reason for the certificate, the signature of the person(s) authorized to present the certificate, and the date it was awarded. See an example in Figure 13-4.

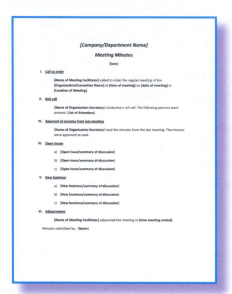

Figure 13-4 Certificate

Figure 13-3 Meeting minutes

Figure 13-5 Print résumé

Employment Documents

Employment documents provide applicants an opportunity to present their best qualities to prospective employers. These qualities are represented by the content of the documents as well as by their accuracy, format, and neatness. The care with which you prepare your documents suggests to employers how carefully you would work if hired. Therefore, give special attention to preparing your employment documents. In addition to a data sheet, or **résumé** (pronounced REZ oo MAY) as shown in Figure 13-5, common types of employment documents are an application letter, application form, reference list, and interview follow-up letter.

- Format business letters.
- Use wp features for Decimal Tabs and previously applied features.

40B

Business Letter in Block Format with Open Punctuation

1. Format/key the letter below in block format with open punctuation using 14-pt. Times New Roman font.
2. Proofread and correct errors. Hyphenate the document. Revise as needed to avoid splitting the e-mail address on two lines.
3. **Save as:** *40b letter*.

July 22, 20— | Financial Aid Office | Bethany College | P.O. Box 417 | Bethany, WV 26032-0417 | Ladies and Gentlemen

Cindy Stroka, who is entering Bethany College in the upcoming fall semester, was awarded the Donna Forde Keller Book Scholarship. The scholarship is valued at $500.

The scholarship is restricted to the purchase of textbooks; therefore, the $500 should be placed in a book fund for her use. Enclosed is a $500 check made payable to Bethany College for the scholarship.

This scholarship is administered by the Haverford High Alumni Association. If you need additional information, contact me at 412-555-1678 or harris.jim@fastmail.net. Thank you.

Sincerely | Jim Harris | HHAA Scholarship Chair | xxx | Enclosure | c Cindy Stroka

40C

Business Letter in Block Format with Mixed Punctuation

1. Format/key the letter below in block format with mixed punctuation. To key the listing, set a left tab at 1.5" for the company names (column 1), a decimal tab at 3.5" for the number of shares (column 2), and a decimal tab at 4.5" for the market value (column 3). Remove space between the items in the listing.
2. Proofread and correct errors. Hyphenate the document if needed.
3. **Save as:** *40c letter*.

November 15, 20— | Dr. Joseph Mullen | 9940 Maplested Lane | Richmond, VA 23235-9001 | Dear Dr. Mullen:

I am pleased to acknowledge your generous gift to Harris School of Business. This gift will be used to fund computer software that will be purchased to support projects in the Investment Portfolio course, which requires students to plan investment portfolios for clients that have different investment goals.

Listed below are the stock name, the number of shares you donated, and the market value per share on November 10, which is the transfer date for all shares. Since our institution is a non-profit institution, this information may help you prepare your federal taxes.

(continued on next page)

Lesson 65 Templates—Memos and Agendas
Lesson 66 Templates—Meeting Minutes, Certificates, and Invitations
Lesson 67 Documents with Shapes and Text Boxes
Lesson 68 Flyers with Graphics

Lesson 69 Employment Résumés
Lesson 70 Employment Letters and Forms
Lesson 71 Mail Merge
Lesson 72 Special Documents Application and Assessment

Application Guides

Special and Employment Documents

Special Documents

Special documents include a variety of documents other than letters, tables, and reports that are created using word processing software. In this unit, you will create memos, meeting minutes, agendas, certificates, and invitations (each is described below and shown at the left). Each special document can be formatted from "scratch" as you did with letters, tables, and reports; however, templates are frequently used for these documents to save formatting and keying time. A **template** is a master file with a set of predefined styles for a particular type of document. The template may contain text and formatting for margins, line spacing, colors, borders, styles, themes, etc.

Interoffice Memos

Memos (interoffice memorandums) are written messages used by employees within an organization to communicate with one another. See an example in Figure 13-1. Memos typically include heading lines—a **TO** line to identify the person(s) receiving the memo, a **FROM** line to identify the person(s) sending the memo, a **DATE** line to identify when the memo was prepared, and a **SUBJECT** line to describe what the memo is about. Following the heading lines is the body of the memo, which is similar to the body of a letter. Following the body, reference initials, attachment/enclosure notations, and copy notations may be included in the same manner as they are included in a letter.

Figure 13-1 Memo

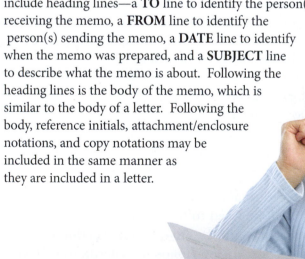

Otna Ydur/Shutterstock.com

Dominion Resources, Inc.	65.345	$43.11
Exelon Corporation	75.2	$42.11
Nike, Inc.	50.4824	$83.82
Citigroup, Inc.	112.402	$4.80

Thank you for supporting the Harris School of Business. I look forward to having you visit our campus within the next few months so you can see what our students are able to do with the software your gift helped us purchase.

Sincerely, | Katherine Heller, Dean | Harris School of Business | xxx

---

40D

Business Letter from Revised Copy

1. Format/key the letter below in block format with open punctuation.
2. Proofread and correct errors. Hyphenate the document, but do not divide the e-mail address. If needed, revise the final ¶ to improve line endings and appearance.
3. **Save as:** *40d letter*.

May 12, 20— | Ms. Danielle Murtha | 4263 Oak Drive | Monongahela, PA 15063-2582 | Dear Ms. Murtha

I am pleased to ~~tell~~ *inform* you that you have been granted a $2,000 loan from the Rivercrest District Student Aid Fund for the upcoming school year. You and your parents will need to schedule a time ~~from~~ *between* 6:30 p.m. and 8:30 p.m on July 9 or 10 to sign the note in the Rivercrest High School Guidance Office. You will receive your check at that time.

The interest rate for this loan is ~~6~~ *4*.5%. If you have one or more ~~loams~~ *loans* at different interest rates, a *consolidated* rate will be ~~figured~~ *computed* at the time payments are to begin and used for determining one payment amount to cover all ~~the~~ loans ~~you have with RDSAF~~ *RDSAF*.

¶ All RDSAF loans are to be repaid in five or fewer years with payments beginning shortly after graduation or withdrawal from college.

It is your responsibility to notify the RDSAF *treasurer* of any change in address and to complete a ~~Progress to Degree~~ form that will be sent to you each summer. The information on this form is needed to keep RDSAF records up to date.

~~If you have any questions or need~~ *To schedule your time or get* additional information, contact me at 412-555- 2133 or **harry.newton2@fastmail.net**.

Sincerely | Harry Newton | RDSAF Treasurer

© Yuri Arcurs/Shutterstock.com

Complete this activity to help prepare for the **Spreadsheet Applications** event in FBLA-PBL's Finance division. Participants in this event demonstrate the skills necessary to develop spreadsheets in business.

You are the sales manager for a magazine publisher. You record each agent's sales on a daily basis and then prepare a summary spreadsheet at the end of each quarter. Key the data as shown in a new worksheet. Then follow the steps below.

1. Use a formula in the Total row and Total column to sum the sales data by month and then by agent.

Sales Agent	April	May	June	Total	Commission
E. Juarez	$10,200	$12,549	$15,830		
M. Landon	$8,040	$9,927	$9,253		
R.Vaughn	$11,025	$10,449	$14,438		
S. Roos	$12,128	$14,497	$14,086		
B. Allison	$16,488	$14,323	$15,185		
Total					

2. Calculate the commission on each agent's total sales. The commission rate for Juarez, Roos, and Allison is 15 percent; the rate for Landon and Vaughn is 12 percent.

3. Create an embedded pie chart that shows what percent of the whole each agent's total sales represent. Add an appropriate title to the chart, and format it as desired.

4. Create an embedded column chart that illustrates each agent's sales by month. Add an appropriate title to the chart, and format it as desired.

5. Apply cell styles and other formats as necessary.

6. Save and print the worksheet as directed by your instructor. Save as *u12 winning edge*.

For detailed information on this event, go to www.fbla-pbl.org.

Think Critically

1. Spreadsheet programs such as *Microsoft Excel* are used extensively in business. How could you use such a program at home? At school?

2. Why are visual aids, such as charts, helpful in communicating ideas and information?

School and Community
Do you have a younger sibling who likes to tag along with you and your friends? Maybe you know a young neighborhood kid who's always checking in to see what you're up to. While this might be annoying at times, you should realize that young kids look up to teenagers and often view them as role models. There are many ways you can mentor young children. For example, you can volunteer for an after-school tutoring program or with your local library's reading program. You might volunteer at a daycare center or with a community program for children.

1. Research the need for youth mentors in your school district or community. You might contact elementary schools, preschools, daycare centers, and the library.

2. Create a spreadsheet that lists the following information: name of the organization, address, volunteer opportunities for youth mentors, and a contact name and number. Print the spreadsheet and make copies to post in your school.

OUTCOMES
- Format letters with envelopes.
- Use wp features for envelopes and previously applied features.

41B

Personal-Business Letter with Envelope

1. Format/key the letter below in block format with mixed punctuation. Use 12-pt. Arial font.
2. Proofread and correct errors.
3. Prepare a No. 10 envelope with a return and letter address.
4. **Save as:** *41b letter*.

325 Eighth Street | Elizabeth, PA 15037 | April 10, 20— | Mr. Steve Rippel | Rippel Capital Group, Inc. | 4032 Tuxey Avenue | Pittsburgh, PA 15220 | Dear Mr. Rippel:

Enclosed are the Rollover/Transfer Out Forms I received from RAIF. Please review them and let me know what else you need prior to our next meeting. Also enclosed are our most recent printouts of the three accounts we have with RAIF.

Carole and I would like to meet with you in the early afternoon on April 23, 26, 28, 29, or 30. We could also meet at the same time in early May except on May 5 or 7. We will be leaving on an extended vacation around May 20 and would like to have everything finalized before we leave.

Let me know which date works best for you. You can call me at (412) 555-1658 or e-mail me at simpson.james41@freemail.net. Thanks.

Sincerely, | James Simpson | Enclosures

© Blend Images/Ariel Skelley/Jupiterimages Corporation

21st Century Skills: Entrepreneurial Literacy

Business letters are a common form of communication for entrepreneurs, both to get their businesses up and running and then to keep them operating smoothly. For example, an entrepreneur might write a letter to potential investors asking them to help finance the business. Or she might write a letter to a supplier suggesting a volume pricing deal.

As you learned in this unit, writing a business letter is different from writing a letter, e-mail, or text message to a friend. It requires a certain degree of formality in tone and structure, as well as the ability to communicate ideas clearly.

Think Critically

Think of a business you would like to start. Using the information you learned in this unit, write a business letter to a potential investor. Use the following guidelines:

- **Paragraph 1:** Introduce the business, including its name, and describe the product or service you will sell.
- **Paragraph 2:** Discuss the market for the product or service, or who will buy it.
- **Paragraph 3:** Explain the skills and experience you have that qualify you to start and run such a business.

Save the document as *u07 21century*.

© 2011 Comstock Images/Getty Images/Jupiterimagescorporation

Planning a Career in Finance

The field of finance is focused on numbers and money, and, therefore, you probably immediately think of careers in banking. But the industry provides job opportunities at many different types of financial and even nonfinancial institutions. These include insurance companies, financial planners, accountant's offices, and investment banks as well as nonfinancial organizations that employ workers to handle these functions. This field is also directly tied to the stock market.

What's It Like?

Individuals who work in this field are involved in services for financial and investment planning, banking, insurance, and business financial management. For example:

- They advise companies about taxes or offer advice in areas such as compensation, employee health-care benefits, and investing.
- They advise everyday people ("retail investors") on appropriate investments based on their needs and financial ability.
- They guide clients through the process of applying for loans.
- They process routine transactions that customers conduct at banks, such as cashing checks and making deposits, loan payments, and withdrawals.
- They investigate and manage claims, negotiate settlements, and authorize payments to insurance policyholders who make a claim.

Employees in most of these fields work a standard five-day, 40-hour week in a typical office environment. Those in investment banking and stock market jobs often work longer hours under more stressful and demanding conditions.

Employment Outlook

Employment in the banking and insurance field is expected to grow more slowly than average, while employment in securities and investments will grow between 7 and 13 percent. Accountants and auditors should see much faster than average growth, or a 20 percent increase in employment. Employers typically require a bachelor's degree in a business or finance-related field. Many prefer a master's degree in business administration (MBA). Some jobs, such as bank tellers and loan officers, require a high school diploma, although previous banking, lending, or sales experience is highly valued.

What About You?

The Finance career cluster is covered in box 6 of the Interest Survey Activity you completed in Unit 1 of this text. If this box had one of the three highest scores on your survey, you should further explore the cluster's pathways and related occupations.

1. Why do you think a career in this field could be a good choice?
2. What skills can you develop now that would be helpful to a career in this field?
3. Why do you think the increase or decrease in employment in these fields is tied closely to the state of the country's economy?

1. Format/key the letter below in block format with open punctuation.
2. Proofread and correct errors. If needed, shrink the font so the letter appears on one page.
3. Prepare a No. 10 envelope with a letter address.
4. **Save as:** *41c letter*.

July 1, 20— | Mr. Denny Bezeck | 11024 Ditch Road | Carmel, IN 46032 | Dear Mr. Bezeck

A year ago, the Washington High Alumni Association began raising scholarship money for graduating seniors of Washington High School. To date, our efforts have been successful in that we have raised nearly $25,000 that was awarded to 15 members of last year's graduating class. Over 20% of the members in the class submitted applications. We believe this level of participation serves as evidence that there is need for the scholarship program.

Since your education at Washington High formed the foundation upon which you built a successful career, we are requesting that you consider participating in this worthwhile WHAA program. It is our hope that you will provide financial support to one or more deserving graduates in the upcoming year so they can get a better start on their way to a successful career. You can participate by pledging to award a scholarship of $1,000 or more.

Enclosed are four items:

- A participation form you can complete and return.
- Directions/explanations for the participation form.
- An article from the *Washington News* announcing last year's recipients.
- An addressed return envelope for your convenience.

WHAA would like you to commit to award your scholarship by August 1. The scholarship money may be paid any time before September so your scholarship can be announced early in the school year. If you have any questions or need additional information before deciding, please contact me at (317) 555-9401 or e.frantz60@jupiter.com.

Thank you for considering this worthwhile project.

Sincerely | Emilie Frantz | WHAA Scholarship Chair | xxx | Enclosures

© VEER.COM/STILLFX

Academic and Career Connections

Complete the following exercises that introduce various topics that involve academic themes and careers.

Grammar and Writing: Subject-Verb Agreement

MicroType 6

- **References/Communication Skills/Subject-Verb Agreement**
- **CheckPro/Communication Skills 9**
- **CheckPro/Word Choice 9**

1. Go to *MicroType 6* and use this feature path for review: References/Communication Skills/Subject-Verb Agreement.
2. Click *Rules* and review the rules of using subjects and verbs.
3. Then, under Subject-Verb Agreement, click *Posttest*.
4. Follow the instructions to complete the *posttest*.

Optional Activities:

1. Go to this path: CheckPro/Communication Skills 9.
2. Complete the activities as directed.
3. Go to this path: CheckPro/Word Choice 9.
4. Key the Apply lines, and choose the correct word.

Communications: Composition

1. Read the ¶ below.

Narcissus, a mythical young man, saw his image reflected in a pool of water; fell in love with his image; and starved to death admiring himself. Unlike Narcissus, our self-esteem or self-image should come not from mirror reflections but by thinking about who we are—inside. Further, our self-image is affected by the opinions of people who matter to us and whether they see us as strong or weak, good or bad, positive or negative. No one is perfect, of course; but we can all improve. It's time to start.

2. Start a new word processing document, and compose a ¶ about your self-image. The ¶ should include the following information:

   - The level of your self-esteem: high, low, or in-between; and factors that make it what it is.
   - Plans you have to raise your self-esteem.

3. Proofread, revise, and correct the document.
4. **Save as:** *u12 communications*.

Math Skills: Simple Interest

Interest is the fee paid to a lender for the use of borrowed money. Interest is always expressed as a percent. The *principal* is the amount of money borrowed. Simple interest (I) is calculated by multiplying the principal (P) by the annual interest rate (R) by the length of time in years (T). The formula is written as: $I = P \times R \times T$. Save the spreadsheet as *u12 math*.

1. Emily wants to buy a car when she goes to college in two years. She expects to pay about $20,000 for a reliable car. She figures her part-time job will allow her to save $250 a month toward a down payment. After two years, how much will she have saved?
2. Emily figures if she takes her first year of savings and buys a one-year certificate of deposit (CD) at her neighborhood bank, she can earn even more money toward her goal. If the CD pays a 4 percent annual interest rate, how much more money will she earn on one year of savings? How much money will she now have after two years?

Personal-Business Letter: Compose

© 2011 Comstock/Jupiterimages Corporation

1. Study the tips for writing effective personal-business and business letters below:

   - **Be concise**—do not include any words that are unnecessary or redundant. For example, use "My opinion is . . ." rather than "My personal opinion is . . ."
   - **Be complete**—be sure to tell your reader everything he or she needs to know. Avoid abbreviating words that are not usually abbreviated.
   - **Be correct**—make sure your facts such as times, dates, places, prices, etc. are correct.
     - **Be courteous**—maintain a polite tone throughout the letter. Also, use a personal title before the person's name in the letter address. Unless you know the person has a professional title (Dr., Senator, Lt., etc.), it is best to use "Mr." for males. If you do not know how a female prefers to be addressed, it is best to use "Ms."
     - **Do not use a comma after the salutation**—if mixed punctuation is used, use a colon after the salutation and a comma after the complimentary close.
     - **Proofread**—uncorrected typing or grammar errors are not acceptable. Use the spell check and grammar feature, but you still must proofread for undetected errors, format, and content after the feature has been used.
     - **Sign your letter**—your signature makes it official.

2. Open a new document.

3. Compose a block format personal-business letter to your teacher from you. Use your return address, insert the current date so that it does not update automatically, and address the letter to your teacher at your school's address. In the first ¶, identify a place you would like to visit for a class field trip. Give the name and the location or address. In the second ¶, describe the place and explain why you think this would be a good place for your class to visit. In the third ¶, thank your teacher for sponsoring a field trip and considering the desires of the students.

4. Proofread the letter carefully for content and check for synonyms that will improve your message. Check spelling and grammar. Correct any errors.

5. Prepare a No. 10 envelope with a return and letter address.

6. Save the letter as *41d letter*.

Optional: Print your letter, sign it, and exchange papers with a classmate. Proofread and mark any errors you find in your classmate's letter. Make corrections to your letter if necessary.

6. Insert these rows in alphabetic order:

   MACY | 80 | 75 | 83 | 93 | 95 |

   WEHNER | 67 | 72 | 85 | 92 | 88 |

7. Delete the Como, Rogers, and Stoehr rows.
8. Center-align all numbers in cell range B3:H23.
9. Shade every other row from Briggs to Zigerell, using the same color.
10. Copy row 2 to the row after MINIMUM; delete contents in cell A26, G26, and H26.
11. Change Gordon's score for Test 2 to **88** and for Test 5 to **78**.
12. Bold all cells in the TOTAL, MINIMUM, and AVERAGE columns and rows.
13. Apply appropriate cell styles to rows 1, 2, 24, 25, and 26.
14. **Save as:** *64c worksheet2*.

21st Century Skills: Productivity and Accountability
Spreadsheets are a powerful tool for calculating, managing, and analyzing numerical data. Businesses use spreadsheets to record market research, measure performance, and create financial documents. Another use of spreadsheets is creating charts and graphs to help illustrate numerical information and identify trends.

© iStockphoto.com/Doug Berry

Assume you are the production manager for a manufacturing company. You want to analyze the productivity of workers on first shift, second shift, and third shift. To do this, you have collected the following information on the number of units produced per shift.

	Shift 1	Shift 2	Shift 3
Monday	145	120	109
Tuesday	147	119	112
Wednesday	144	123	112
Thursday	147	125	111
Friday	140	124	110

1. Open a new worksheet, and key the data shown above.
2. Create a column chart to illustrate the number of units produced per shift. Save the spreadsheet as *u12 21century*.
3. Evaluate the chart. What might account for the lower outputs for shifts 2 and 3?

www.cengage.com/school/
keyboarding/c21key

Letters—Application and Assessment

- Apply/assess block format and punctuation styles for personal-business and business letters.
- Apply/assess envelopes.
- Apply/assess wp features.

42B

Business Letter with Envelope

1. Format/key the letter below in block format with mixed punctuation. Insert the current date, but do not update automatically.
2. Proofread and correct errors. Hyphenate the document if needed.
3. Prepare a No. 10 envelope with a letter address.
4. **Save as:** *42b letter*.

<Current date> | Ms. Juanita Ramirez | 3 Denford Drive | Newtown Square, PA 19073 | Dear Ms. Sanchez:

I'm pleased to report that the Challenge scholarship program in which you participate has been well received. Thirteen scholarships, totaling $16,000, were awarded to 13 outstanding seniors and alumni of Newtown Square High School.

Nine retired educators from the Newtown Square School District and community leaders served on three committees to review more than 70 applications and select the recipients. All reviewers were very impressed with the number of the applicants and their outstanding accomplishments. There were 11 applications for your scholarship.

Enclosed is a thank-you note from Joshua Greene, the senior who received your scholarship. I've also enclosed his application and resume so you can see what an outstanding young man you have helped with your financial support.

Your father will present your scholarship to Joshua at the Senior Awards Event on June 10 at 6:30 p.m. in the high school auditorium.

Again, I want to thank you for supporting this worthwhile program. I look forward to working with you in the future and will be in touch with you during the summer about next year's scholarship.

Sincerely, | Sara Jane Gilchrist | Challenge Scholarship Chair | xxx | Enclosures

Worksheet Application and Assessment

- Apply what you have learned to prepare worksheets and charts.

64B

Charts

Chart 1: Pie Chart

1. Open *df 64b worksheet1* and create a pie chart, using **Budget** as the title. Select a chart layout and chart style to show the data.
2. **Save as:** *64b worksheet1*.

Chart 2: Column Chart

1. Open *df 64b worksheet2* and create a column chart. Choose an appropriate chart layout to show **Participants** as the title and the number of participants in each column.
2. Choose an appropriate chart style and layout; delete the legend.
3. **Save as:** *64b worksheet2*.

64C

WorkSheets

Worksheet 1

1. Key the worksheet, keying column A as labels.

Ages	1950	1960	1970	1980	1990	2000	2010	2020
1-18	47.3	64.5	69.8	63.7	64.2	72.4	74.4	80.3
0-5	19.1	24.3	20.9	19.6	22.5	23.2	25.6	27.5
6-11	15.3	21.8	24.6	20.8	21.6	25.0	24.4	26.9
12-8	12.9	18.4	24.3	23.3	20.1	24.2	24.4	26.0

2. Use center alignment; Number format with one decimal place in cell range B2:I5; adjust column width to fit contents.
3. Insert a row at the top; in cell A1, key **MILLIONS OF U.S. CHILDREN UNDER AGE 18** using Heading 4 style.
4. In cell A7, key **Source: http://www.childstats.gov/** in italic.
5. **Save as:** *64c worksheet1*.

Worksheet 2

1. Open *df 64c worksheet2*.
2. In column G, calculate a total of all the test scores for each student.
3. In column H, calculate an average score (one decimal place) for each student.
4. In row 25, calculate an average class score (one decimal place) for each test.
5. In row 26, display the lowest score for each test.

42C

Business Letter with Envelope

1. Format/key the letter below in block format with open punctuation. Use 12-pt. Calibri font. Insert the current date, but do not update automatically.
2. Proofread and correct errors. Hyphenate the document if needed.
3. Prepare a No. 10 envelope with a letter address.
4. **Save as:** *42c letter*.

<Current date> | Mr. Pablo J. Lobos | 733 Marquette Avenue | Minneapolis, MN 55402-2736 | Dear Mr. Lobos

Congratulations! You are now the sole owner of the automobile you financed through Star Bank three years ago.

Thank you for choosing us to serve your needs and for being prompt in making your monthly payments. The original Certificate of Title and your Loan Contract marked "Paid in Full" are enclosed. We recommend that you file the papers in a safe place with your other important records.

You have a preferred credit rating with us; therefore, please let us know when we may serve you again.

Sincerely yours | Ms. Ilya Lindgren | Loan Manager | xxx | Enclosures | c Ms. Carla Perez, Records Manager

42D

Personal-Business Letter with Envelope

1. Format/key the letter below in block format with open punctuation. Use 12-pt. Times New Roman font.
2. Proofread and correct errors. Hyphenate the document if needed.
3. Prepare a No. 10 envelope with a return and letter address.
4. **Save as:** *42d letter*.

8503 Kirby Drive | Houston, TX 77054-8220 | May 5, 20— | Ms. Jenna St. John | Education Director | Regency Company | 219 West Greene Road | Houston, TX 77067-4219 | Dear Ms. St. John

Ms. Anne D. Salgado, my teacher, told me about your company's Information Technology course you offer to selected students each summer. She speaks very highly of your company and the computer course. She believes I would benefit greatly by enrolling in this summer's course. After reading about the course objectives and content on your company's website, I agree that the course would benefit me greatly.

I am in the ninth grade at Taft School. I have completed two computer software application courses. I am proficient with word processing, spreadsheet, database, and presentation software packages. I also have

(continued on next page)

1. Open **63b worksheet1** and change the column chart to an embedded line chart.
2. **Save as: 63c worksheet1.**
3. Open **63b worksheet2** and change the bar chart to an embedded area chart.
4. **Save as: 63c worksheet2.**
5. Open **63b worksheet3** and change the pie chart to an embedded doughnut chart.
6. **Save as: 63c worksheet3.**

63D

Change Chart Layout and Styles

Chart Tools/Design/Chart Layouts or Chart Styles

Once a chart has been created, you can change the chart layout to display or not display such chart parts as:

Titles—Headings that identify chart contents and the X-axis and/or Y-axis. To key your chart titles, click the default title names, and key the names you want.

Data labels—Numbers or words that identify values displayed in the chart.

Gridlines—Lines through a chart that identify intervals on the axes.

Legend—A key (usually with different colors or patterns) used to identify the chart's data categories.

Figure 12-21 Column Chart with Axis Titles and Chart Style

Chart Styles include several options that enable you to change the overall visual appearance of your chart, including the color of the bars, lines, pie slices, etc. See Figure 12-21 for an example of a chart style.

1. Open **63b worksheet1**.
2. Select a chart style that is similar to the style shown in Figure 12-21.
3. Key **Salesperson** as the X-axis title and **Sales and Returns** as the Y-axis title.
4. **Save as: 63d worksheet.**

63E

Charts

Chart 1: Bar

1. Open **df 63e worksheet1** and use the data to create a bar chart.
2. Choose an appropriate chart layout to show **Patient Report** as the title and **Month** and **Number of Patients** for the axis titles.
3. Select an appropriate chart style.
4. **Save as: 63e worksheet1.**

Chart 2: Column

1. Open df **63e worksheet2** and use the data to create a column chart, using **Prom Attendance** as the title and **Students** and **Number Attending** for the axis titles.
2. Select an appropriate chart style.
3. **Save as: 63e worksheet2.**

taken a programming course. It introduced me to Visual Basic and HTML. I developed and maintain a website for my baseball team. A copy of my transcript through the last grading period is enclosed.

I would like to visit you to learn more about the summer course and application process. I would also like you to learn about my educational and career goals. Please telephone me at (713) 555-0121 or e-mail me at dougs@suresend.com to suggest a meeting date. I can meet with you any day after 3:30 p.m. Thank you.

Sincerely | Douglas H. Spanos | Enclosure

42E

Business Letter with Envelope

1. Format/key the letter below in block format with mixed punctuation.
2. Find synonyms for the words in red font. If you believe a synonym will improve the message, use it in the letter.
3. Proofread and correct errors. Hyphenate the document if needed.
4. Prepare a No. 10 envelope with a letter address.
5. **Save as:** *42e letter*.

March 23, 20— | Mr. Glenn Rostello | 3480 Martin Drive | North Olmsted, OH 44070-3000 | Dear Mr. Rostello:

Thank you for your inquiry about the best perennial plants to use along walkways. I have researched this topic and found several low-growing plants that work well in our area.

- Yarrow
- Wormwood
- Geranium
- Evening Primrose
- Stonecrop
- Globeflower

Each of the above plants is available at our Ohio Street garden center. Anyone who buys plants before the end of April will receive a 10 percent discount. If more than 15 plants are purchased, we will deliver and plant them for a small fee. Plants that we plant have a one-year warranty.

Please say hello to me when you visit our store.

Sincerely, | Harry Piper | Owner

www.cengage.com/school/keyboarding/c21key

LESSON 63   Worksheets with Charts

- Create embedded column, bar, and pie charts using worksheet information.

63B

Charts

Insert/Charts

Spreadsheet software provides options to create a variety of charts including **column**, **bar**, **line**, and **pie** charts (see charts in Figures 12-15, 12-16, and 12-17). Usually, charts can be created as (1) an **embedded chart** that appears as an object in the worksheet along with the chart data or (2) a **chart sheet** where the chart appears on a separate worksheet.

In this activity, you will create simple embedded column, bar, and pie charts using the default chart layout.

Figure 12-15 Column chart

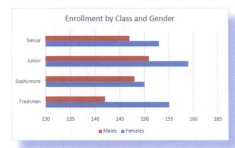

Figure 12-16 Bar chart

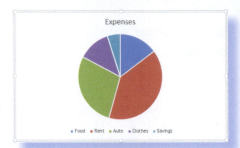

Figure 12-17 Pie chart

1. Open *df 63b worksheet1* and create an embedded column chart. Key **Sales and Returns** as the chart title.
2. **Save as:** *63b worksheet1*.
3. Open *df 63b worksheet2* and create an embedded bar chart. Key **Enrollment by Class and Gender** as the chart title.
4. **Save as:** *63b worksheet2*.
5. Open *df 63b worksheet3* and create an embedded pie chart. Key **Expenses** as the chart title.
6. **Save as:** *63b worksheet3*.

63C

Change Chart Type

Chart Tools/Design/Type/
Change Chart Type

There are several types of charts that you can select. In addition to bar, column, and pie charts, there are line, area, scatter, and doughnut charts (see examples in Figures 12-18, 12-19, and 12-20). The chart you initially select to display your data can be changed to other chart types to help you decide which type best presents your data.

Figure 12-18 Line chart

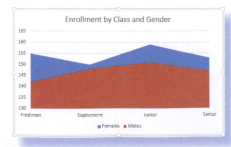

Figure 12-19 Area chart

Figure 12-20 Doughnut chart

Academic and Career Connections

Complete the following exercises that introduce various topics that involve academic themes and careers.

Grammar and Writing: Quotation Marks and Italics

MicroType 6

- References/Communication Skills/Quotation Marks and Italics
- CheckPro/Communication Skills 5
- CheckPro/Word Choice 5

1. Go to *MicroType* 6 and use this feature path for review: References/Communication Skills/ Quotation Marks and Italics.
2. Click Rules and review the rules of using quotation marks and italic.
3. Then, under Quotation Marks and Italics, click Posttest.
4. Follow the instructions to complete the posttest.

Optional Activities:

1. Go to this path: CheckPro/Communication Skills 5.
2. Complete the activities as directed.
3. Go to this path: CheckPro/Word Choice 5.
4. Key the Apply lines, and choose the correct word.

Communications: Composition

1. Open a new word processing document and key the ¶ below, correcting word-choice errors.
2. Key a second ¶ in which you identify the kinds of behavior that help earn your respect and those that cause you to lose respect for someone else. Describe the consequences of disrespectful behavior.

That all individuals want others to respect them is not surprising. What is surprising is that sum people think their due respect even when there own behavior has been unacceptable or even illegal. Key to the issue is that we respect others because of certain behavior, rather then in spite of it. Its vital, than, to no that what people do and say determines the level of respect there given buy others. Respect has to be earned; its not our unquestioned right to demand it. You should choose behaviors that will led others to respect you.

3. Proofread, check spelling and grammar, and revise your ¶s as necessary.
4. Save the document as **u07 communications**.

Math Skills

Thomas is in the process of starting up his own business for making personalized stationary and note cards. He has sent a letter to a potential investor in which he provided the details below. In a new word processing document, key the ¶, filling in the blanks with the correct percentages (rounded to the nearest whole number). Save the document as **u07 math**.

I estimate that I will spend $8,000 on the start-up and operation of my business for the first year. I have raised $4,600 so far. This represents _____% of the total $8,000. In the first year of operation, I am projecting that my sales revenue will be $10,000. Of that, I expect $7,000, or _____%, to be generated by online sales. My variable and fixed costs will total about $4,400, which is _____% of my sales revenue.

2. Key a formula in column F (cells F1:F9) to calculate the individual batting averages (Hits/At Bats) to three decimal places.

3. In row 10 (cells B10:E10), use the SUM function to calculate the team totals.

4. In row 11 (cells B11:F11), use the MIN function to calculate the team lows.

5. In row 12 (cells B10:F10), use the MAX function to calculate the team highs.

6. Use cell styles as desired.

7. Adjust column widths to fit cell contents.

8. In cell A13, key **BASEBALL TEAM STATISTICS**, using a 14-pt. font.

9. **Save as:** *62d worksheet1.*

Worksheet 2

1. Using *62d worksheet1*, insert the rows below after Harry Bell.

PLAYER	AT BATS	HITS	HOMERS	RBI
Pat Ortega	25	8	1	2
Brett Peterson	45	14	3	7

2. Delete the Carlos row. Make format changes as desired. Notice that the functions recalculate automatically.

3. **Save as:** *62d worksheet2.*

Worksheet 3

1. Open *df 62d worksheet3.*

2. Use the information below to key formulas or functions in the column or row indicated or perform the stated action.
   a. Col E=col C amount*2
   b. Col F=col B*col C amounts
   c. Col G=col D*col E amounts
   d. Col H=col F+col G amounts
   e. Row 13: SUM(row 4:row 12)
   f. Clear the contents in cells C13 and E13.
   g. Row 14: AVERAGE(row 4:row 12); two decimal places

3. Use the Tip at the left to display the average and sum for the employee's regular pay, over-time pay, and gross pay. Do they agree with the totals and averages you computed in rows 13 and 14?

4. Adjust column widths.

5. In cell A16, key **RADIOLOGY PAYROLL**.

6. Format worksheet as desired.

7. **Save as:** *62d worksheet3.*

★TIP SS software typically computes the average, sum, and count for numbers in a selected range of cells and displays them in the status bar below the bottom scroll bar as shown below.

Average: $49.24   Count: 9   Sum: $443.20

Career Clusters

© Laurence Gough/Shutterstock.com

Planning a Career in Science, Technology, Engineering, and Mathematics

Businesses rely on workers in the fields of science, technology, engineering, and mathematics to plan, manage, and provide scientific research as well as other services such as product testing and development, systems design and analysis, and mathematical modeling. These jobs are critical because competitive pressures and ever-changing technology force many companies and government organizations to constantly improve and update product and system designs and to optimize their manufacturing and building processes.

What's It Like?

Individuals who work in this field invent new products, do research and development, and often serve as the link between scientific discoveries and the commercial applications that meet consumer needs. For example:

- They set up, operate, and maintain laboratory instruments, monitor experiments, make observations, and formulate results.
- They perform laboratory and field tests to monitor environmental resources and determine the contaminants and sources of pollution in the environment.
- They supervise production in factories, determine the causes of a component's failure, and test manufactured products to maintain quality.
- They apply mathematical modeling and computational methods to formulate and solve practical problems such as the most efficient way to schedule airline routes between cities, the effects and safety of new drugs, or the cost-effectiveness of alternative manufacturing processes.

These professionals work in a variety of settings, from comfortable offices and high-tech laboratories to the factory floor and outdoor labs in remote locations. They are employed in all types of industries, including pharmaceuticals, agriculture, education, aeronautics, oil and gas, chemicals, and manufacturing.

Employment Outlook

Given the need for companies and governments to be on the cutting edge of technology, demand for workers is high and job possibilities abound, even during economic downturns. Employment is expected to increase much faster for these occupations than for others. Employers seek well-trained individuals with highly developed technical skills. Most require a bachelor's or master's degree while many in mathematics and science require a doctorate. In addition, many positions also require state licensure.

What About You?

The Science, Technology, Engineering, and Mathematics career cluster is covered in box 15 of the Interest Survey Activity you completed in Unit 1 of this text. If this box had one of the three highest scores on your survey, you should further explore the cluster's pathways and related occupations.

1. Why do you think a career in one of these fields could be a good choice?
2. What skills can you develop now that would be helpful to a career in one of these fields?
3. Why are these jobs important to a business and to our economy?

Functions

Examples of Frequently Used Built-in Functions

=SUM(XX:XX)

=AVERAGE(XX:XX)

=COUNT(XX:XX)

=MAX(XX:XX)

=MIN(XX:XX)

Spreadsheet software has built-in predefined formulas called **functions**. Commonly used functions are showed at the left and are accessed in the Editing group in the Home tab (see Figure 12-14). Additional functions can be accessed by choosing the More Functions option or by choosing from the many options in the Function Library group in the Formulas tab.

Functions have three parts: an equals sign to signal the beginning of the mathematical operation; the function name (SUM, COUNT, etc.) to identify the operation; and an argument (usually the cell range) that defines the numbers to be used in the calculation (see function examples at the left).

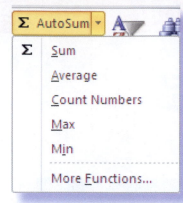

Figure 12-14 Functions

1. Open *df 62c worksheet*.
2. Use the SUM function to add the numbers in cells A1:F1 and cells A2:F2, placing the answers in column G; add the numbers in cells A1:A6 and cells B1:B6, placing the answers in row 7.
3. Use the AVERAGE function to average the numbers in cells A3:F3 and cells A4:F4, placing the answers in column G; average the numbers in cells C1:C6 and cells D1:D6, placing the answers in row 7.
4. In cell G5, use the MIN function to find the lowest number in cells A5:F5; in cell E7, display the lowest number in cells E1:E6.
5. In cell G6, use the MAX function to find the highest number in cells A6:F6; in cell F7, display the highest number in cells F1:F6.
6. Format all numbers in cell range A1:G7 as Accounting with no decimal places.
7. In cell G11, use the Count function to determine the number of cells that contain numbers in cells E1:G7.
8. Print gridlines and column/row headings.
9. **Save as:** *62c worksheet*.

Worksheets

Worksheet 1

1. Key the worksheet.

	A	B	C	D	E	F
1	PLAYER	AT BATS	HITS	HOMERS	RBI	AVG
2	Roberto Orlando	700	225	23	45	
3	Bill York	423	134	2	14	
4	Ernie Hack	590	176	15	35	
5	Joe Dimperio	805	256	33	102	
6	Jose Carlos	476	175	12	31	
7	Hector Avila	365	75	2	5	
8	George Barnes	402	99	16	45	
9	Harry Bell	575	158	17	55	
10	TOTAL					
11	MINIMUM					
12	MAXIMUM					

© Jim West/Alamy

Complete this activity to help prepare for the Word Processing I event in FBLA-PBL's Business Management and Administration division. Participants in this event demonstrate their basic word processing skills.

1. In a new word processing document, use the information you learned in this unit to write a business letter. Use the following guidelines to write your letter.

   - **Date:** Insert the current date.
   - **Letter Address:** Address the letter to Mr. Ryan Wilcrest | Youth Arts Community Foundation | 705 W. Fourth St. | Cincinnati, OH 45202.
   - **Body:** We are delighted to hear that the Youth Arts Community Foundation will sponsor a five-day summer camp for students in the Central City School District. Our staff and students are excited to be a part of this enrichment program. ¶At your convenience, please forward the necessary registration materials and information packets. We will distribute these to students who are eligible to participate in the program. ¶Thank you for choosing our school district as one of your summer camp sites. We look forward to working with you.
   - **Complimentary Close:** Use your name and title of District Arts Coordinator.

2. When you are done writing, be sure to proofread, check the spelling and grammar, and revise as necessary. Save and print the document as directed by your instructor.

For detailed information on this event, go to www.fbla-pbl.org.

Think Critically

1. Why are word processing skills important to just about any career you choose?
2. How are the tone and structure of a business letter different from those of a personal letter?
3. What activities can you participate in now that will strengthen your word processing skills?

School and Community
Whether it's vehicle emissions, landfills and dumping, or endangered wildlife, all of us are affected in some way by issues concerning the natural world—the soil, water, air, and plant and animal life—around us.

Volunteering for an organization that promotes awareness, conservation, and preservation is one way for you to learn about environmental problems and help find solutions.

1. Research to identify an environmental issue that affects your community. You can check resources such as the World Wide Web, local newspapers, or a community bulletin board. Your community's government offices might also be a helpful source.
2. Develop a list of local, regional, and national organizations that focus on the environmental issue you identified. Find out the volunteering opportunities available to individuals in your age group with each of the organizations.
3. Select one of the organizations and write a one-page summary about it. You should introduce the environmental issue and describe the organization's mission statement and objectives for dealing with the issue. Discuss the types of activities in which the organization is involved to educate people about the issue. Then explain what you can do as a volunteer in the organization to promote its cause.

Worksheets with Formulas and Functions

OUTCOME

- Use formulas and functions to perform calculations in a worksheet.

62B

Key Formulas

★TIP To show formulas in cells, follow this path:

Formulas/Formula
Auditing/Show Formulas

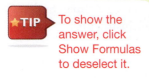

★TIP To show the answer, click Show Formulas to deselect it.

Spreadsheet software can add, subtract, multiply, and divide numbers in cells. To perform calculations, activate the cell in which the results of the calculation are to appear, and then key a **formula** in the formula bar (see Figure 12-13). Formulas typically begin with an equals sign (=). The ss software interprets the formula to calculate the answer, following this order of operations: (1) Calculations inside parentheses are performed first before those outside parentheses. (2) Multiplication and division are performed next in the order that they occur in the formula. (3) Addition and subtraction are performed last in their order of occurrence.

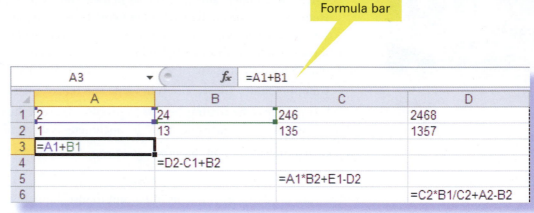

Formula bar

A3		f_x	=A1+B1	
	A	B	C	D
1	2	24	246	2468
2	1	13	135	1357
3	=A1+B1			
4		=D2-C1+B2		
5			=A1*B2+E1-D2	
6				=C2*B1/C2+A2-B2

Figure 12-13 Formulas

1. Open **df 62b worksheet** and key these formulas in the specified cells.
   a. =A1+B1 in cell A3
   b. =D2-C1+B2 in cell B4
   c. =A1*B2+E1-D2 in cell C5
   d. =C2*B1/C2+A2-B2 in cell D6
   e. =(C1+D2)+(D1/A1)+E2 in cell E7
   f. =(D1+A1*B2)-(E2/C2-B1*A1)+E1 in cell F8
   g. In cell G9, write and key a formula to add cells C2, D1, and E2; divide that answer by cell B1; and then subtract cell D2.
2. Format the answers for steps a–g above as Currency with two decimal places.
3. **Save as: 62b worksheet.**

Lesson 43	Tables—Basic Features	Lesson 46	Tables—Application and Assessment
Lesson 44	Table Layout Features		
Lesson 45	Table Design Features		

Application Guide

Tables

Tables

A **table** is an arrangement of data (words and/or numbers) in rows and columns. **Columns** are vertical lists of data that are labeled alphabetically from left to right; **rows** are horizontal lists of data that are labeled numerically from top to bottom. A **cell** is the intersection of a column and a row. Cells are identified by the column letter and row number. For example, a cell at the intersection of column B and row 3 is identified as cell B3. In this unit, you will use the Table feature to create tables.

Table Parts

Tables range in complexity from those with only two columns and a title to those with several columns and special features. The tables in this unit are limited to those with the following parts:

Rows, Columns, and Cells

Cell A1	Cell B1	Cell C1
Cell A2	Cell B2	Cell C2
Cell A3	Cell B3	Cell C3

Rows 1, 2, & 3

Columns A, B, & C

MAIN HEADING
Secondary Heading

Column A	Column B	Column C
100	200	300
400	500	600
700	800	900
1000	1100	1200
1300	1400	1500

Source note

Figure 8-1 Table parts

- **Main heading** (bold, ALL CAPS, centered in first row or placed above the gridlines of the table).
- **Secondary heading** (bold, capital and lowercase letters, centered in second row or placed on the line below the main title above the gridlines).
- **Column headings** (bold, centered over the column).
- **Body** (data entries).
- **Source note** (bottom left in last row or may be placed beneath the gridlines of the table.) If placed beneath the gridlines, use the Add Space Before Paragraph feature to place space between the gridlines and the source note (Home/Paragraph/Line Spacing/Add Space Before Paragraph) and set a tab to place the source note at the table's left edge.
- **Gridlines** (the lines around the cells). Gridlines may or may not be printed.

Refer to Figure 8-1 for an example of the table parts described above.

Worksheet 2

1. Key the worksheet.

	A	B	C	D	E
1	YEAR	MEDIAN	LOAN	MONTHLY	% OF
2		PRICE	RATE	PAYMENT	INCOME
3	2002	$158,100	6.55%	$804	18.3%
4	2003	$180,200	5.74%	$840	19.1%
5	2004	$195,200	5.73%	$909	20.2%
6	2005	$219,000	5.91%	$1,040	22.4%
	Source: *The World Almanac, 2011.*				

2. Adjust the column widths to fit the contents.
3. Center-align cells A1:E6.
4. Format using cell styles and other format options.
5. **Save as:** *61e worksheet2.*

Worksheet 3

1. Open *61e worksheet2.*
2. Insert the following rows in the proper places.

2000	$139,000	8.03%	$88	19.3%
2006	$221,990	6.58%	$1,131	23.2%
2008	$196,600	6.15%	$958	18.1%
2010	$179,300	4.76%	$749	14.9%

3. Delete the rows for 2003 and 2005.
4. Make formatting adjustments as needed.
5. Change all text to 12-pt. Times New Roman; bold and center all the headings.
6. Adjust column widths as needed.
7. Prepare notes that you can use to explain the conclusions you can draw from the data presented in this worksheet.
8. **Save as:** *61e worksheet3.*

© iStockphoto.com/Doug Berry

Table Format Features

The following features can be used to make your tables attractive and easy to read.

Vertical placement. A table may begin 2" from the top edge of the page, or it may be centered vertically (equal top and bottom margins).

Horizontal placement. Tables are most attractive when centered horizontally (side to side) on the page.

Column width. Generally, each column should be only slightly wider than the longest data entry in the column.

Vertical alignment. Within rows, data entries can be aligned at the top, center, or bottom. Most often you will use center vertical alignment for the headings and bottom vertical alignment for data rows beneath the headings. If a source note is included, it should also be bottom-aligned.

Horizontal alignment. Within columns, words are usually left-aligned or center-aligned. Whole numbers are usually center-aligned or right-aligned. If a column total is shown, numbers should be right-aligned. Decimal numbers should be decimal-aligned.

Table Styles design. The Table Styles feature may be used to quickly enhance the appearance of a table. Once a table style has been applied, changes to the format for the selected style can be made, such as bolding or removing preset bolding, changing font size, changing alignment, etc., to further enhance the appearance of the table.

Robert Kneschke/Shutterstock.com

Format Cell Content

Home/Font
or
Home/Styles/Cell Styles

The contents of cells (both numbers and text) can be formatted in much the same way as text is formatted in word processing software. The commands in the Font group (see Figure 12-11) can be selected and applied to a cell, a cell range, or one or more rows and/or columns. Use the Font dialog box launcher to access the Font tab where additional formatting features can be selected.

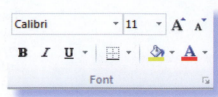

Figure 12-11 Font group

If desired, you can use the Cell Styles command in the Styles group to format cell content (see Figure 12-12). A cell style is a defined collection of formats for font, font size, font color, font attributes, numeric formats, shading, borders, etc. You can use built-in cell styles or create new ones.

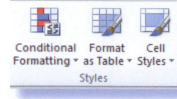

Figure 12-12 Cell styles

1. Open **df 60c worksheet**.
2. Format row 1 using Heading 1 cell style.
3. Format cells A2:A10 using Blue 60% Accent 1 cell style.
4. Format cell ranges B2:B10, D2:D10, and F2:F10 using Neutral cell style.
5. Format cell ranges C2:C10 and E2:E10 using Good cell style.
6. Bold and italicize cell range A2:A10.
7. Key **Wednesday** in cell D1; shrink the font size of all entries in row 1 to fit within the cells. Shade row 1 with a light blue color.
8. Key [(1)] in superscript position to the right of *Hector* in cell C10 (*Hint:* Use the dialog box launcher to access the Font tab.)
9. Double-underline *Bonita* in cell D7.
10. Center-align all cells.
11. **Save as:** **61d worksheet**.

Worksheets

Worksheet 1

1. Key the worksheet.

	A	B	C
1	COURSE	PERIOD	ROOM
2	Applied Mathematics I	1	134-E
3	Consumer Economics	2	114-S
4	Sophomore English	3	210-E
5	Physical Education	4	Gym-N
6	Computer Applications	6	104-S
7	Principles of Technology	7	101-W
8	World Cultures	8	205-S

2. Insert a row between rows 5 and 6; key **Lunch** in A6, **5** in B6, and **Cafeteria** in C6.
3. Adjust the column widths to fit the contents.
4. Center-align cells B2:C9.
5. Insert a row at the top, and key **TOM HALL'S SCHEDULE**, left-aligned.
6. Format the worksheet using cell styles and other format options.
7. **Save as:** **61e worksheet1**.

WP Applications

Activity 1

Insert Table

OUTCOMES

- Use the Insert Table, Insert/Delete Rows and Columns, adjust Cell Size, Merge and Split Cells features to design tables.
- Format and align cell contents, center tables, and print tables with and without gridlines and in portrait and landscape orientations.
- Use Table Styles, Borders, Shading, and Sort features.

Insert/Tables/Table

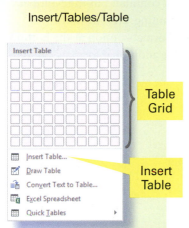

Figure 8-2 Insert Table

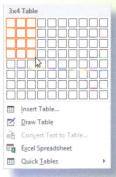

Figure 8-3 Table grid

There are several options for creating various kinds of tables. In this unit, you will use two options within the Table feature to create tables—the table grid and the Insert Table command illustrated in Figure 8-2.

When the **table grid** is used, drag on the grid to select the number of columns and rows needed for the table. The illustration in Figure 8-3 shows the selection for a table with 3 columns and 4 rows (a 3 × 4 table).

When the Insert Table feature is used, the dialog box shown in Figure 8-4 opens when Insert Table is clicked in the list of options. Key the desired number of columns and rows in the appropriate spaces and click OK to create the table.

Keying and Moving Around in a Table

When text is keyed in a cell, it wraps around in that cell instead of wrapping around to the next row. A line space is added to the cell each time the text wraps around.

To fill in cells, use the Tab key or right arrow key to move from cell to cell (left to right) in a row and from row to row. To move back a cell, tap Shift + Tab. To move around in a filled-in table, use the arrow keys, Tab, or the mouse (click the desired cell). Tapping Enter after keying text in a cell will simply insert a blank line space in the cell.

Figure 8-4 Insert Table dialog box

1. Open a new document. Position your insertion point to have a 2" top margin.
2. Use the table grid to create a table with 3 columns and 4 rows (3 × 4 table).
3. Key the information in the table below into the table grid. Use the default alignment and column widths. Tap Tab to move from cell to cell and row to row.

Student	High School Class	Position
Jimmie Warner	Junior	Third Base
Harry Killingsworth	Senior	Second Base
Jiminez Sanchez	Sophomore	Center Field

4. Click at the left on the line below the table. Tap Enter twice and use the **Insert Table** command to create a table with four columns and five rows (4 × 5 table). Select the **AutoFit Contents** option in the AutoFit options. *Note:* By selecting this option,

6. Insert three rows between 3 p.m. and 4 p.m.; key **3:15 p.m.** in A13, **3:30 p.m.** in A14, and **3:45 p.m.** in A15.

7. Delete column B.

Home/Cells/Format/
AutoFit Column Width

8. Adjust all column widths to fit the cell contents (see path at the left).

9. Key **APPOINTMENT SCHEDULE** in cell A1.

10. **Save as:** *61b worksheet*.

61C

Format Numbers

Home/Number

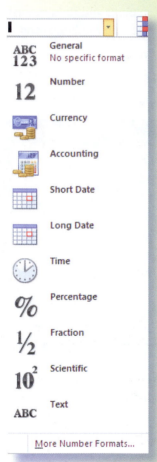

Figure 12-10 Number Format list

When numbers are keyed into a worksheet, ss software formats them as General, the default format. If another format would be more appropriate, you can use a command in the Number group (see Figure 12-9), choose a format (Number, Currency, Accounting, etc.) from the Number Format list (see Figure 12-10), or click the More Number Formats option at the bottom of the Number Format list to access a Format Cells dialog box where additional formats can be selected.

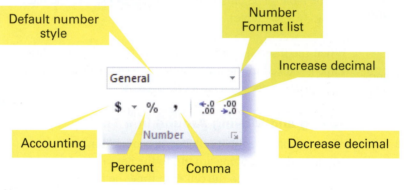

Figure 12-9 Number group

Worksheet 1

1. Open *df 61c worksheet1* and format the numbers as directed.

2. **Save as:** *61c worksheet1*.

Worksheet 2

1. Open *df 61c worksheet2*.

2. Format cells A1:A7 using Number format, two decimal places, and no comma separators.

3. Format cells B1:B7 using Currency format with two decimal places.

4. Format cells C1:C7 using Accounting format with two decimal places.

5. Format cells D1:D7 using Percentage format with no decimal places.

6. Format cells A9:D9 using Special, Type: Phone Number.

7. Format cells A10:D10 using Special, Type: Social Security Number.

8. Format cells A11:D11 using Short Date format.

9. Format cells A12:D12 using Long Date format.

10. Format cells A13:D13 using Date, Type: March 14, 2001.

11. Adjust column widths to fit longest entry.

12. **Save as:** *61c worksheet2*.

the column widths will adjust automatically to be slightly larger than the longest entry in the column as you key.

5. Key the information in the table below into the table grid. Use the default alignment. Tap Tab to move from cell to cell and row to row.

Student	Home Room Teacher	Bus Route	Parking Pass
Mary Tillitson	Ms. Henrietta Jones	18	Yes
Janet Thompson	Mr. Jack Holliday	6	No
Joseph Larrimore	Dr. Kate Newsome	15	Yes
Maurice Quinnone	Mrs. Anne Guidos	9	No

6. **Save as:** *aa8 activity 1*.

Activity 2

Selecting and Formatting Cell Content

Table Tools Layout/
Table/Select

The formatting changes (bold, italicize, alignment, etc.) that you have learned to make to text can also be made to the text within a table. You can do this prior to keying the text into the table, or it can be done after the text has been keyed. Make formatting changes by selecting the portion of the table (cell, row, column, or table) that is to be changed.

One option is to use the Select command to select the portion you want. Click in the table, click Table Tools Layout/Table/Select, and then select the desired portion (cell, column, row, or table) from the list as shown in Figure 8-5.

Figure 8-5 Using Select

Another option is to use the mouse to make your selection.

- To select a cell, double-click the cell; to select adjacent cells, click the first desired cell, drag through the desired cells, and release the mouse button. Apply the desired format changes(s).
- To select a row, move the insertion point just outside the left area of the table, and when the pointer turns into an open diagonal arrow, click the left mouse button to select the row, and then apply the desired format change(s).
- To select a column, move the insertion point to the top border of the table, and when the pointer turns to a solid down arrow, click the left mouse button to select the column, and then apply the desired format change(s).
- To select a table, move the insertion point over the table and click the Table move handle at the upper-left corner of the table; then apply the desired format change(s).

1. Open *aa activity 1* you created above.
2. Select the whole table at the top, and change the font in all cells to 12-pt. Arial.
3. Select row 1 and change it to bold, 14-pt. Arial, aligned at the center.
4. Center-align the cells in columns B and C.
5. Select the first row in the bottom table, and change the format to bold, 12-pt. Verdana, aligned at the center.
6. Select the cells C2 through C5 (C2:C5), and apply right alignment.
7. Select the cells B2:B5 and D2:D5, and apply center alignment.
8. Select the cells A2:A5, change the font to a dark red, and apply bold to the text.
9. **Save as:** *aa8 activity2*.

Worksheet 2

1. Using **60f worksheet1**, make the following changes:
   a. Edit cell A1 to read: **BUDGET AND MONTHLY EXPENSES**
   b. Move row 18 to row 3.
   c. Copy column B to column F.
   d. Clear rows 16 and 17.
   e. Edit cell E15 to **95**.
   f. Copy B3 to C3:E3 and B4 to C4:E4.
   g. Copy B10 to C10:E10.
   h. Print without gridlines or row and column headings.
2. **Save as:** *60f worksheet2*.

Worksheet 3

1. Key the worksheet below, using the Copy feature as much as possible.

	A	B	C	D	E	F	G
1	NAME	QUIZ 1	QUIZ 2	QUIZ 3	QUIZ 4	QUIZ 5	QUIZ 6
2	JOE	90	90	90	100	90	90
3	MARY	90	90	90	80	90	90
4	PAUL	100	100	100	100	100	100
5	CARL	100	80	90	100	90	90
6	SUE	90	100	100	100	100	80
7	TWILA	90	90	90	80	80	80

2. Print with gridlines and row and column headings.
3. **Save as:** *60f worksheet3*.

LESSON 61 Format Worksheets

61B

• Format cell contents, adjust column widths, and insert/delete columns and rows.

Insert and Delete Rows and Columns

Home/Cells/Insert Cells or Delete Cells

Rows and columns can be inserted and deleted. One or more rows or columns can be inserted at a time. Columns may be added at the left or within worksheets; rows may be added at the top or within worksheets. See Figure 12-8.

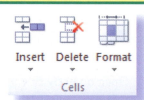

Figure 12-8 Insert and Delete

1. Open **df 60c worksheet** and insert two rows at the top.
2. Delete the Friday column. Insert one column between Monday and Tuesday, one column between Tuesday and Wednesday, and two columns between Wednesday and Thursday.
3. Key **Murphy** in cells D2 and I2; **Shandry** in cells C2, E2, and G2; and **Lawler** in cell H2.
4. Key **Monday** in C3; **Tuesday** in E3; **Wednesday** in F3:H3.
5. Insert a row between 2 p.m. and 3 p.m., and key **2:30 p.m**. in cell A11.

Activity 3

Format Painter

Home/Clipboard/
Format Painter

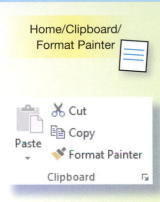

Use the Format Painter to quickly copy formatting from one place to another. In tables, this feature is particularly useful when formatting cells that are not adjacent. Click the paintbrush (as shown at the left) once to apply the formatting to one place in the table or document; double-click it to apply it to multiple places. When the Format Painter feature is activated, a paintbrush will appear to the left of the insertion point.

1. Open *df aa8 activity3*.
2. Use the Format Painter to copy the formatting used for the name in column A to the other cells in columns B to E that have the same name.

   Suggestion: Preview the entries in the table. If a name in column A appears only once in columns B to E, click the Format Painter once to copy the formatting to the cell with the same name. If a name in column A appears more than once in columns B to E, click the Format Painter twice to copy the formatting to multiple locations. When all occurrences of a name have been formatted, click the Format Painter to deactivate it, and repeat the process for the next name.

3. **Save as:** *aa8 activity 3*.

Activity 4

Centering Tables

Horizontal:

Table Tools Layout/
Table/Properties

Vertical:

Page Layout/Page Setup
dialog box launcher/
Layout tab/Page/Vertical
Alignment/Center

Use the **Table Properties** dialog box (shown in Figure 8-6) to center a table horizontally on a page. This will make the side margins (right and left margins) equal. Another method of centering a table horizontally is to select the table and click the Center button in the Paragraph group on the Home tab.

Use the Page **Vertical alignment** in the **Page Setup** dialog box (shown in Figure 8-7) to center a table vertically on the page. This will make the top and bottom margins equal.

Figure 8-6 Table Properties dialog box

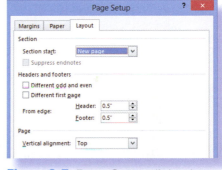

Figure 8-7 Page Setup dialog box

1. Open *aa8 activity 3* that you created above, and center the table horizontally and vertically.
2. **Save as:** *aa8 activity 4*.

Cut, Copy, and Move

Home/Clipboard/Cut,
Copy, or Paste

The contents of a cell or range of cells can be cut (moved) and copied to another cell or range of cells. Select the cell or range of cells to be cut or copied; select the operation (*Cut* or *Copy*); select the cell (or first cell in the range) where the information is to be copied or moved; and finally, click Paste to copy or move the information (see the buttons in Figure 12-7).

Figure 12-7 Cut, Copy, and Paste

1. Open *df 60c worksheet*.
2. Clear the contents of cells B6:F6.
3. Move the data in cells in B2:F3 to a range beginning in cell B11.
4. Copy the data in cells in A2:A10 to a range beginning in cell A11.
5. Copy the data in cells in A1:F1 to a range beginning in cell A20.
6. Copy C5 to C6, E5 to E6, B4 to D3, and F4 to F3.
7. Move D12 to B3, C12 to E3, B12 to D6, and F11 to B6.
8. **Save as:** *60e worksheet*.

60F

Worksheets

Worksheet 1

1. Key the worksheet and then print with gridlines and row and column headings.
2. **Save as:** *60f worksheet1*.

	A	B	C	D	E
1	BUDGET				
2	ITEM	BUDGET	JAN	FEB	MAR
3					
4	Rent	400			
5	Electric	44	46	43	42
6	Oil	110	115	90	72
7	Water	20		60	
8	Sewage	22			67
9	Telephone	35	32	38	45
10	Cable TV	35			
11	Insurance	80	120		95
12	Food	315	305	302	325
13	Clothing	75	60	90	55
14	Leisure	75	55	80	60
15	Personal	90	90	85	100
16	Auto Loan	425			
17	Auto Exp.	80	80	95	110
18	Savings	185			

Activity 5

Insert/Delete Rows & Columns

Table Tools Layout/
Rows & Columns

The **Table Tools Layout** tab can be used to edit or modify the layout of existing tables. The commands found in the **Rows & Columns** group (shown at the left) are used to insert and delete rows and columns in an existing table. A cell, row, column, or entire table can be deleted using the Delete command. Use the Insert commands to place rows above or below existing rows and columns to the right or left of existing columns.

1. Open **df aa8 activity 5**.
2. Delete the 2000 to 2002 award winners.
3. Insert this information for the 2007–2010 award winners in the appropriate cells.

2010	Josh Hamilton	Rangers
2009	Joe Mauer	Twins
2008	Dustin Pedroia	Red Sox
2007	Alex Rodriquez	Yankees

4. Delete the column showing the team for which the award winner played.
5. Undo the last change made to restore the deleted column.
6. **Save as:** *aa8 activity 5*.

Activity 6

Merge and Split Cells

Table Tools Layout/Merge/
Merge Cells or Split Cells

Merge Cells
Split Cells
Split Table
Merge

Use the **Merge Cells** feature to join two or more adjacent cells in the same row or column into one cell. This feature is useful when information in the table spans more than one column or row. The main heading, for example, spans all columns. Use the **Split Cells** feature to divide adjacent cells into multiple cells and columns. Select the cell(s) to be merged or split, and then select the command.

1. Open a new document, and create a table with four columns and five rows.
2. Use the Merge Cells and Split Cells features to make your table grid look like the one shown below. Then key the data in the table as shown, using center alignment and 8-pt. Calibri font in all cells.
3. **Save as:** *aa8 activity 6*.

All cells in row 1 were merged into one cell that spans all five columns.				
Cells A2:A5 were merged into one cell.	Cell B2 was split into two cells and cells B3:B5 were merged.		Cells C2:C3 were merged; C4:C5 were merged and then split into four cells.	Cells D2:D3 were merged.
						Cells D4:D5 were merged.

Clear and Delete Cell Content and Format

Home/Editing/Clear &
Home/Cells/Delete

Most ss software has a Clear command (see Figure 12-5) that enables you to clear the contents *or* format of a cell *or both* without shifting the surrounding cells to replace the cell you cleared.

The Delete command (see Figure 12-6) deletes the contents *and* format of the cell, and surrounding cells are shifted to replace the deleted cell.

1. Open *df 60c worksheet* and specify that gridlines and row and column headings are to be printed.
2. Make these changes without having surrounding cells shift:
   a. Clear contents in cells B2, C4, D6, E8, and F10.
   b. Clear format (bold) in cells B4, B6, D4, D8, F6, and F8.
   c. Clear contents and formats in cells B8, B10, D2, D5, F2, and F4.
3. Delete cell B3 and have cells C3 through F3 shift to the left.
4. Delete cell C5 and have cells C6 through C10 shift up.
5. Key **Susan** in cell F4.
6. **Save as:** *60c worksheet*.

Figure 12-5 Clear

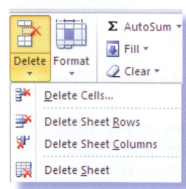

Figure 12-6 Delete

Select a Range of Cells

Page Layout/Page Setup/
Print Area/Set Print Area

A range of cells may be selected to perform an operation (move, copy, cut, clear, format, print, etc.) on more than one cell at a time. A **range** is identified by the cell in the upper-left corner and the cell in the lower-right corner, usually separated by a colon (for example, A5:C10).

To select a range of cells, highlight the cell in the top left corner. Hold down the left mouse button, and drag to the cell in the opposite corner. The number of rows and columns in the range is typically shown in the Name box as you drag the mouse. When you release the mouse button, the top left cell is the active cell, and its name appears in the Name box.

To print a specific range of cells, click the Page Layout tab and select the Set Print Area option from the Print Area command in the Page Setup group. When you print the document, only the specified cell range will print. Remember to select the Clear Print Area option when you no longer want only the selected cell range.

1. Open *df 60d worksheet*.
2. Select the range of cells B1:F1, and bold the text in the cells.
3. Select the range of cells A2:A10, and print the text in the cells.
4. **Save as:** *60d worksheet*.

Activity 7

Adjusting Column Width & Row Height

Table Tools Layout/
Cell Size

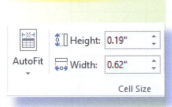

The **Cell Size** group contains several features that can be used to change column widths and row heights (see the Cell Size group shown at left). Options within **AutoFit** can be used to format the width of columns. The **AutoFit Contents** feature automatically resizes the column widths based on the text in each column. The **AutoFit Window** feature automatically resizes the table so it begins and ends evenly at the left and right margins. If you want to specify an exact height of a row or a width for a column, key or select the desired size (in inches) in the **Height** or **Width** boxes.

1. Open *aa8 activity 3* that you created in Activity 3. Apply AutoFit Contents and then center the table horizontally.
2. **Save as:** *aa8 activity 7a*.
3. Open *aa8 activity 5* that you created in Activity 5, and set column A width at 0.5", column B at 1.3", and column C at 0.7". Set row 1 to be 0.5" high, and change the font of the text in row 1 to 16 pt. Center table horizontally on the page. Center the column heads.
4. **Save as:** *aa8 activity 7b*.

Activity 8

Portrait/Landscape Orientation

Page Layout/Page Setup/
Orientation

Portrait orientation. The way text is printed on a page determines what type of orientation is used. **Portrait orientation,** sometimes referred to as vertical—8½" × 11", has the short edge of the paper at the top of the page, as shown at the top right.

Landscape orientation. **Landscape orientation,** sometimes referred to as horizontal—11" × 8½", has the wider edge of the paper at the top of the page, as shown at the bottom right. When a table is too wide to fit on the page in portrait orientation, switching to landscape orientation gives 2½ more inches to fit the table.

1. Open *df aa8 activity 8*.
2. Change the orientation to landscape.
3. Apply the AutoFit to Window command; center the table vertically.
4. **Save as:** *aa8 activity 8*.

Activity 9

Vertical Alignment

Table Tools Layout/
Alignment

Use the **Layout Alignment** commands shown at the left to change the alignment of the text in cells. The text within a cell can be aligned in any one of the nine positions shown in Figure 8-8.

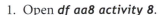

Top Left	Top Center	Top Right
Center Left	Center	Center Right
Bottom Left	Bottom Center	Bottom Right

Figure 8-8 Alignment options

1. Open *df aa8 activity 9*.
2. Change row height as follows: row 1—0.6"; row 2—0.5"; rows 3–12—0.4".
3. Change vertical alignment as follows: cells A3:A12, bottom left; cells B3:B12, bottom center; and cells C3:C12, D3:D12, and E3:E12, bottom right. Center-align rows 1 and 2.
4. **Save as:** *aa8 activity 9*.

Worksheet 2

1. Key the worksheet while viewing the gridlines and headings.
2. Print without gridlines but with headings.
3. **Save as:** *59f worksheet2.*

	A	B	C	D	E
1	PLAYER	SINGLES	DOUBLES	TRIPLES	HOMERS
2	Bosco	65	13	3	1
3	Elliot	54	14	8	4
4	Horan	58	19	10	5
5	Huang	64	22	9	14
6	Myers	52	21	4	9
7	Pasco	49	14	3	4
8	Cordero	25	7	2	2
9	Paulie	27	2	4	0

LESSON 60   Edit Worksheets

OUTCOME

- Select a range of cells and edit, clear, copy, and move information in a worksheet.

60B

Select and Edit Cell Content

To select (activate) a cell, click the cell. The Edit feature enables you to change information already keyed in a cell. To edit, double-click the desired cell and then use the mouse, navigation keys, **Font** group buttons, etc., as you would with wp software to make the changes in the cell. When finished, click outside the active cell, tap Enter, or click the Enter button (check mark) on the formula bar. Alternatively, cell contents can be edited by clicking the desired cell once and then making the changes in the formula bar.

If the entire contents of a cell are to be changed, click the desired cell once and then key the correct information. The new information will replace the old information.

1. Open *df 60b worksheet* and complete steps a–c.
   a. **Edit** existing cell content to what is given below:
      | A1: **charge** | B1: **care** | C1: **butler** | D1: **compost** |
      | A2: **whether** | B2: **flew** | C2: **except** | D2: **personal** |

   b. **Change** the cell contents to what is given below:
      | A4: **54321** | B4: **20202** | C4: **four** | D4: **shirt** |
      | A5: **98765** | B5: **stars** | C5: **herd** | D5: **college** |

   c. Edit or change the cell contents to what is given below:
      | A7: **4567** | B7: **Jeanne** | C7: **Kristine** | D7: **8614** |
      | A8: **Dormont** | B8: **Sandra** | C8: **Hutton** | D8: **Blue** |

2. **Save as:** *60b worksheet.*

Activity 10

Table Styles

Table Tools Design/Table Styles or Table Style Options

Preformatted table styles that are available in the **Tables Styles** group (shown in Figure 8-9) can be used to improve the appearance of your table. As you move the mouse over each of the styles, your table will be formatted in that style. The style name is also displayed. When you find a style you prefer, click its style box. The selected table style can be modified by selecting or deselecting features in the Table Style Options group (shown at left in Figure 8-9) to further improve its appearance.

Click the More button to access additional styles

Figure 8-9 Table Style Options and Table Styles

1. Open *aa8 activity 7b* that you created in Activity 7.
2. Use plain, grid, or list style table, no gridlines, and the color blue.
3. Deselect Header Row in the Table Style Options group.
4. Center the table horizontally.
5. **Save as:** *aa8 activity 10.*

Activity 11

Shading and Borders

Table Tools Design/Table Styles/Shading or Borders

Use the **Shading** and **Borders** features to enhance the appearance of tables when you are not using one of the preformatted table styles. The Shading feature allows you to fill in areas of the table with varying shades of color, as shown in Figure 8-10. Shading covers the selected area. It may be the entire table or a single cell, column, or row within a table.

Figure 8-10 Shading colors

TIP If you select the No Borders option before keying the text in your table, displaying gridlines that will not print may make it easier for you to move from cell to cell, merge cells, or split cells. Select the View Gridlines button in Table Tools Layout/Tables shown below.

By default, each cell in a table has thin, single-line borders around it. Features within the Borders group allow you to change the line thickness, color, and style. The Borders drop-down list (illustrated in Figure 8-11) shows many of the options available for changing the default borders.

1. Open a new document and create a 5 × 6 table.
2. Shade cell B2 in a light blue color; cell C3 in a light black color; and column D in a light purple shade.
3. Remove the shading from cell D6, and shade row 6 in a light orange.
4. Remove all borders from cell A1; format cell E1 without a top or right border.
5. Format cell C2 with a 6-pt. dark red border on all sides.
6. Delete the borders from row 6 and column D.
7. **Save as:** *aa8 activity 11.*

Figure 8-11 Borders options

59D

Key Labels and Values

Data keyed into a cell is automatically assigned either a **label** or **value** status. Data that is to be used in calculations must be keyed as a value, since labels cannot be used in calculations. When only numbers are keyed into a cell, the value status is assigned and the data is right-aligned (see Figure 12-3). When letters and/or symbols (with or without numbers) are keyed into a cell, the label status is assigned and the data are left-aligned. Numbers that *will not be used* in calculations (such as house or room numbers, years, course or invoice numbers, etc.) can be keyed as labels by preceding the cell entry with an apostrophe.

1. Open a new blank worksheet and key the following names as labels, each in a separate cell, in column A, beginning with row 1: **Mary**, **Henry**, **Pablo**, **Susan**, **Helen**, **John**, **James**, **Paul**, and **Sandy**.

2. Key the following numbers as values, each in a separate cell, in row 15, beginning with column A: **135793**, **673455**, **439321**, **93888**, **569321**, **102938**, **547612**, **102938**, and **601925**.

3. Key the following invoice numbers as labels, each in a separate cell, in column I, beginning with row 11: **514620**, **687691**, and **432987**.

4. Check that data keyed as labels are left-aligned and data keyed as values are right-aligned.

5. **Save as:** *59d worksheet*.

Figure 12-3 Labels and values

59E

View and Print Gridlines and Column and Row Headings

Page Layout/Sheet Options/Gridlines or Headings/View or Print

Gridlines (cell borders) and **Headings** (row numbers and column letters) may or may not be viewed on the screen or printed on a worksheet. Typically, the default setting is to display (view) the worksheet gridlines and headings on the monitor but not to print the gridlines and headings. The selections in Figure 12-4 will display the gridlines and headings on the monitor and print both.

Figure 12-4 Sheet Options

1. Open *df 59e worksheet* and change the settings as needed to View and Print the Gridlines and Headings, and then print the worksheet.

2. **Save as:** *59e worksheet*.

59F

Worksheets

Worksheet 1

1. Key the worksheet.
2. View and print the gridlines but not the headings.
3. **Save as:** *59f worksheet1*.

	A	B	C	D	E	F
1	MONTH	JOHN	MARY	LUIZ	PEDRO	SARA
2	January	5567	6623	7359	4986	6902
3	February	2457	7654	3569	2093	6432
4	March	6930	3096	5792	4607	7908
5	April	4783	6212	4390	5934	5402
6	May	5042	5092	4500	9453	5321
7	June	5430	6098	5781	5009	6023

Table Tools Layout/Sort

Use the **Sort** feature to arrange text in alphabetical order and numbers in numerical order. Ascending order is from A to Z and 0 to 9. Entire tables or lists can be sorted, or parts of a table or list can be selected and sorted. If the table has a header row, select that option in the Sort dialog box shown in Figure 8-12 to exclude it from the sort.

1. Open *aa8 activity 7b* that you created in Activity 7.
2. Sort the listings in the table (exclude the column headings) in ascending order by year. Your selections should be the same as shown in the above illustration.
3. **Save as:** *aa8 activity 12a.*
4. Using *aa8 activity 12a* that you just created, sort the listings in the table in descending order by team name.
5. **Save as:** *aa8 activity 12b.*
6. Using *aa8 activity 12b* that you just created, sort the listings in the table in ascending order by player name.
7. **Save as:** *aa8 activity 12c.*

Figure 8-12 Sort options

Digital Citizenship and Ethics

The Internet makes it easy to copy someone else's work and pass it off as your own. But this is unethical—and sometimes illegal. **Copyright** is a form of protection given to the authors or creators of original works, including literary, dramatic, musical, artistic, and other intellectual works. That means that only the author has the right to make or distribute copies of the work, perform the work publicly (such as songs or plays), or change it in any way. If you want to use copyrighted material, you have to get the author's permission first.

© 2011 Ingram Publishing/Jupiterimages Corporation

Plagiarism occurs when you copy another person's ideas, text, or other creative work and present it as your own, without getting permission or crediting the source. All schools take plagiarism very seriously. If you are caught plagiarizing, you will certainly receive a failing grade and you might even be suspended.

TEAMWORK

As a class, discuss the following:
1. How could you legally use a copyrighted photo of a penguin in a school report on Antarctica?
2. Provide an example of plagiarism, and suggest how it could be avoided.

LESSON 59   Worksheets

- Key data, move around in a worksheet, and print a worksheet.

59–64A

Warmup

Key each line twice at the beginning of each lesson; first for control and then for speed.

alphabet	1	Jay asked four zany questions before each good example was given.
figures	2	My mutual fund fell 4.87 points to 65.92 on Friday, May 30, 1998.
speed	3	The men may pay for a big emblem of the chapel with their profit.

| gwam | 1' | 1 | 2 | 3 | 4 | 5 | 6 | 7 | 8 | 9 | 10 | 11 | 12 | 13 |

59B

Learn About Spreadsheet Software, Workbooks, and Worksheets

1. Read about spreadsheet (ss) software on pp. 237–239.
2. Access your ss software, and learn the parts of the program window and worksheet by referring to Figure 12-2.
3. Open wp file *df 59b learn*, and complete the activity.
4. **Save as:** *59b learn*.

59C

Move Around in a Worksheet

Information is keyed in the **active cell** of a worksheet. The active cell is the one with the thick border around it (see Figure 12-2). Cells can be activated with the mouse, the arrow keys, or keyboard shortcuts.

To activate a cell with the mouse, move the pointer to the desired cell and click the mouse.

To move the active cell one or more cells to the left, right, up, or down, use the arrow keys.

To move the active cell from one spot to another quickly, use keyboard shortcuts. For example, to make the first cell in a row active, tap Home; to activate cell A1, press Ctrl + Home; to move the active cell up one page, tap PgUp, etc.

1. Open a new blank worksheet, and complete steps a–i.
   a. Use the mouse to make cell G4 active.
   b. Use the mouse to make cell B24 active.
   c. Use the mouse to make cell A12 active.
   d. Use the arrow keys to make cell D11 active.
   e. Use the arrow keys to make cell F30 active.
   f. Use the arrow keys to make cell P30 active.
   g. Use PgDn and the arrow keys to make cell J100 active.
   h. Use PgUp and the mouse to make cell L40 active.
   i. Press Ctrl + Home to make cell A1 active.

Tables—Basic Features

- Create 2-, 3-, and 4-column tables with main headings, secondary headings, column headings, and/or source notes using the Table feature.
- Use wp features to change column width and row height, align cell entries, format cells, and center tables horizontally.

43–46A

Warmup

Key each line twice at the beginning of each lesson, first for control and then for speed.

alphabet 1 Fay's bright jacket has an amazing weave and exceptional quality.

fig/sym 2 The computer (786-SX) was $2,159 and printer (Elon 340) was $259.

speed 3 If they go to the social with us, they may visit the eight girls.

gwam 1' | 1 | 2 | 3 | 4 | 5 | 6 | 7 | 8 | 9 | 10 | 11 | 12 | 13 |

43B

Table

Robert Frost

@ Everett Collection Inc/Alamy

1. Study the application guide for tables on pp. 157 and 158.
2. Use this information to key the table below.
   - Center, bold, and key the main heading in ALL CAPS at or near the 2" line. Tap Enter once after the heading, and insert a 2 × 9 table.
   - Center and bold the column headings.
   - Center the table horizontally on the page.
3. **Save as:** *43b table*.

POEMS TO IMPROVE OUR LIVES

Poem	Written By
Great Men	Ralph Waldo Emerson
Success	Henry Wadsworth Longfellow
If	Rudyard Kipling
The Road Not Taken	Robert Frost
Will	Ella Wheeler Wilcox
The Sin of Omission	Margaret E. Sangster
Good and Bad Children	Robert Louis Stevenson
Lady Clare	Alfred Tennyson

What Are the Basic Parts of a Worksheet?

Cells. A worksheet contains **cells** where information is keyed. The cells are arranged in rows and columns (see Figure 12-2).

Columns. **Columns** run vertically in a worksheet. Each column has a heading (letters from A to Z, AA to AZ, etc.) running left to right across the worksheet (see Figure 12-2).

Rows. **Rows** run horizontally in a worksheet. Each row has a heading (a number) running up and down the left side of the worksheet (see Figure 12-2).

The Excel Worksheet Window

The *Excel* worksheet window has many features that you have seen in *Word* and *PowerPoint* windows. Among these are the **title bar** that displays the worksheet filename, the **Quick Access Toolbar** used to access frequently used commands, **File tab** used to access *Office* file commands, **ribbons** that display tools and commands grouped by category, **Ribbon tabs** used to access various ribbons, **dialog box launchers** used to open dialog boxes or task panes, **List** and **Gallery** buttons used to access lists and galleries, **Zoom** controls used to zoom in and out, **View** buttons used to switch between views, and a **status bar** that displays information about the active document.

The *Excel* worksheet window also has features that are used only with spreadsheet software. They are illustrated in Figure 12.2.

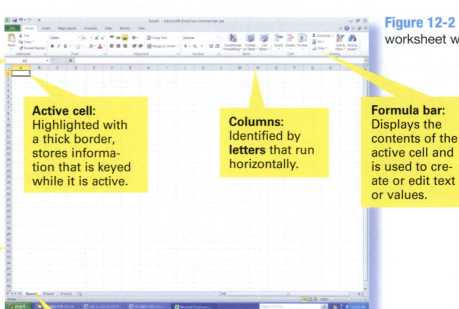

Figure 12-2 *Excel* worksheet window

Name box: Identifies the active cell(s) by a letter(s) and number(s).

Active cell: Highlighted with a thick border, stores information that is keyed while it is active.

Columns: Identified by **letters** that run horizontally.

Formula bar: Displays the contents of the active cell and is used to create or edit text or values.

Rows: Identified by **numbers** that run vertically.

Worksheet Tabs: Identify the active worksheet and the number and names of the worksheets in the workbook

1. Use the following information to key and format the table below:
   - Key the main heading on or near the 2" line; use a 16-pt. font; center and bold it.
   - Set height of row 1 at 0.5"; rows 2 to 9 at 0.3".
   - Center-align (vertically and horizontally) the column headings in bold, 14-pt. font.
   - Use bottom-left alignment for columns 1 and 3; use bottom-center alignment for column 2.
   - Use AutoFit Contents to adjust the column widths.
   - Center the table horizontally.
2. **Save as:** *43c table*.

SELECTED WORKS BY AMERICAN AUTHORS

Author	Life	Work
Robert Lee Frost	1874-1963	West-Running Brook
Henry W. Longfellow	1807-1882	Ballads
Carl Sandburg	1878-1967	Smoke and Steel
Louisa May Alcott	1832-1888	Little Women
William Faulkner	1897-1962	The Sound and the Fury
Samuel L. Clemens	1835-1910	Adventures of Tom Sawyer
F. Scott Fitzgerald	1896-1940	All the Sad Young Men

1. Use the following information to key and format the table below:
   - Key the main heading on or near the 2" line; use a 16-pt. font; center and bold it.
   - Key the secondary heading on the line below the main heading. Use bold, 14-pt. font.
   - Create a 3 x 11 table. Set column A width at 3.1", column B at 0.8", and column C at 1.1". Center the table horizontally.
   - Center the column headings in bold, 12-pt. font.
   - Center-align column B, and right-align column C.
   - Key the source note on the line below the table. Remember to set a tab to align the source note at the left edge of the table.
2. **Save as:** *43d table*.

What Are Worksheets and Workbooks?

Worksheet. A **worksheet** is one spreadsheet computer file—it is where you key information.

Workbook. A **workbook** contains one or more worksheets, usually related. When spreadsheet software is opened, a worksheet will appear on the screen. Other worksheets in the workbook appear as **sheet tabs** at the bottom of the screen (see Figure 12-1). If needed, additional worksheets can be inserted into the workbook.

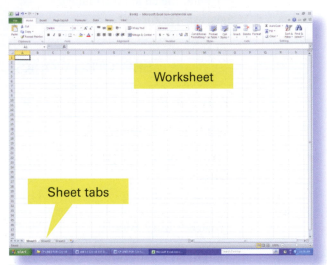

Figure 12-1 Worksheet and Sheet Tabs

Digital Citizenship and Ethics

According to recent research, 60 percent of students aged 10–14 own a cell phone, as do close to 85 percent of teens between the ages of 15 and 18. While cell phones and smartphones provide a convenient and quick way to communicate and can be invaluable in emergency situations, they are also frequently misused or used irresponsibly in social and public situations. For example, have you ever been annoyed by someone talking loudly on a cell phone? Following are some cell phone etiquette tips:

- Turn your phone off in school, theaters, libraries, places of worship, and doctor's offices.
- Do not use your cell phone while you are doing something else, such as driving, riding a bike, or simply having a conversation with others.
- Do not shout or speak loudly to compensate for a bad connection. Call back when you are in a quiet or private place.

As a class, discuss the following.

1. What benefits does a cell phone or smartphone provide as it relates to academics and your schoolwork?
2. What are some of the health risks associated with extensive cell phone usage?

ALL-TIME TOP MOVIE BOX OFFICE GROSSES

As of August 22, 2010

Movie	Year	Revenue
Avatar	2009	$749,800,000
Titanic	1997	600,800,000
The Dark Knight	2008	533,300,000
Star Wars	1977	461,000,000
Shrek 2	2004	436,700,000
E.T. The Extra-Terrestrial	1982	435,000,000
Star Wars: Episode I	1999	431,100,000
Pirates of the Caribbean: Dead Man's Chest	2006	423,300,000
Toy Story 3	2010	403,800,000
Spider-Man	2002	403,700,000

Source: *The World Almanac and Book of Facts*, 2011.

21st Century Skills: Information, Communications, and Technology (ICT) Literacy

www.avebreakmedia ttd/Shutterstock.com

Today's technology has drastically changed the way we present and exchange information. Through word processing and other types of software applications, we can quickly and easily prepare professional-looking correspondence, reports, tables, and other types of documents.

Being a proficient user of software applications, including word processing, spreadsheet, presentation, and database programs, is an important skill both in the classroom and on the job. Further, knowing how to use these tools to effectively communicate information and ideas will help you succeed in all areas of your life.

Think Critically

Open a new word processing document and create a table with the following headings. Under each heading, key the information as shown. Insert another row and list at least two types of files you could create with each type of application.

- **Word Processing:** Use to create text documents
- **Spreadsheet:** Use to create worksheets for recording and calculating data
- **Presentation:** Use to create multimedia slide shows
- **Database:** Use to organize and manage data

Save the document as *u08 21century*.

UNIT 12

Spreadsheet: Learn Spreadsheet Essentials

Lesson 59   Worksheets
Lesson 60   Edit Worksheets
Lesson 61   Format Worksheets
Lesson 62   Worksheets with Formulas and Functions

Lesson 63   Worksheets with Charts
Lesson 64   Worksheet Application and Assessment

Application Guide

What Is Spreadsheet Software?

Spreadsheet software is a computer program used to record, report, and analyze information, especially information that relates to numbers. Many different types of employees in business, education, and government use spreadsheet software in a variety of ways. Spreadsheet software is especially useful when you need to make repetitive calculations accurately, quickly, and easily. It works equally well with simple and complex calculations.

Numbers can be added, subtracted, multiplied, and divided in a worksheet, and formulas are used to perform calculations quickly and accurately. Additionally, charts can be constructed to present the worksheet information graphically.

One big advantage of spreadsheet software is that when a number is changed, all related "answers" are automatically recalculated. For example, you can use spreadsheet software to quickly calculate how money saved today will grow at various interest rates over various periods of time by changing the values for the rate and time.

SS Applications

Using *Excel* is fun once you master how to use rows, columns, and cells. In this unit you will learn how to:

- Work with worksheets
- Edit worksheets
- Format worksheets
- Use formulas and functions
- Create charts

© iStockphoto.com/Jacob Wackerhausen

Camilo Torres/Shutterstock.com

1. Use the following information to key and format the table below:
   - Key the main heading centered and bold, using 2" top margin and 16-pt. font.
   - Create a 4 × 11 table and key the table.
   - Use AutoFit Contents to adjust the column widths.
   - Set row heights to 0.3"; center-align the column headings in bold, 12-pt. font.
   - Align Center entries in rows 2 to 11; center the table horizontally on the page.
   - Key the source note on the line below the table.
2. **Save as:** *43e table*.

NOTABLE INVENTIONS

Invention	Date	Inventor(s)	Nationality
Adding Machine	1642	Pascal	French
Calculating Machine	1833	Babbage	English
Typewriter	1867	Sholes, Soule, Glidden	United States
Electronic Calculator	1942	Atanasoff, Berry	United States
Cellular Telephone	1947	Bell Labs	United States
Mini Computer	1960	Digital Corporation	United States
Floppy Disc	1970	IBM	United States
Digital Camera	1977	Lloyd, Sasson	United States
Laptop Computer	1987	Sinclair	English
Google Search Software	1996	Brin, Page	United States

Source: *The World Almanac and Book of Facts*, 2011.

The Winning Edge

Monkey Business Images/
Shutterstock.com

Complete this activity to help prepare for the **Advanced Word Processing Skills** event in BPA's Administrative Support division. Participants in this event demonstrate advanced skills in word processing and document production.

The Internet is a necessary tool for just about every type of business in operation today. Although it provides easy access to a vast array of resources, it can also have negative effects in the workplace. Many employers attribute a decline in worker productivity to Internet use on the job. They also are concerned about the security of confidential company information. Your manager wants to establish an Internet usage policy for your company. He has asked you to research Internet usage policies for the workplace and prepare a report on your findings. Your report should cover the following:

- Ways in which employees misuse the Internet, such as sending personal e-mail, reading news or sports articles, shopping, accessing and sharing websites, and entering contests
- Negative effects of Internet misuse on the company and other employees; for example, decline in productivity, loss of data security and confidentiality, and the use of offensive material to harass others
- How to design an Internet usage policy and the issues it should address
- Consequences for violating the policy

Use the Internet and other resources to gather information. Prepare a report of at least two pages on your findings. In addition, your report should include a cover page, footnotes (as needed), and a reference list, bibliography, or Works Cited page.
For detailed information on this event, go to www.bpa.org.

Think Critically

1. How can the Internet help businesses operate more efficiently?
2. List examples of web content that might be considered offensive to some people.
3. How is your school's acceptable-use policy similar to an Internet usage policy put in place for a business?

© iStockphoto.com/Lisa F. Young

School and Community
The growth of the older population (65+) in the United States is increasing at an unprecedented rate. The aging of baby boomers, better health care, and healthier lifestyles have all contributed. But even though people are living longer, the quality of life for many is dependent on the help of volunteers and non-family members. There are many ways you can volunteer to help the elderly:

- Be a friendly visitor
- Run errands
- Read a book or newspaper

- Deliver meals
- Perform seasonal yardwork
- Clean and do other basic housework

1. Contact a retirement community or organization for the elderly in your town and learn about the volunteer opportunities for people in your age group.
2. Prepare a one-page report on the organization that describes its focus, summarizes the activities for which it uses volunteers, and encourages readers to take action and volunteer their time. Share the report with your class.

LESSON 44

Table Layout Features

OUTCOMES

- Create tables with main headings, secondary headings, column headings, and/or source notes using the Table feature.
- Use Merge and Split and Insert/Delete Rows/Columns, Center Vertical Alignment, Sort, and Landscape orientation, as well as previously applied wp features.

44B

Table

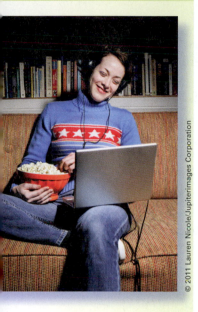

© 2011 Lauren Nicole/Jupiterimages Corporation

1. Preview the table below. Note the merged cells for the main and secondary headings and the source note.
2. Create a 3 × 14 table, and key it using AutoFit to Window. Merge cells as shown.
3. Set row 1 at 0.5", row 2 at 0.4", and remaining rows at 0.3".
4. Key heading in bold, 16-pt. font. Use Align Center.
5. Key secondary heading in bold, 14-pt. italic font. Use Align Center.
6. Key column headings in bold, 12-pt. italic font. Use Align Center.
7. Key cell entries using Align Bottom Left for rows 4–14 in column A and Align Bottom Center for rows 4–13 in columns B and C.
8. Center the table vertically on the page.
9. **Save as:** *44b table*.

TOP FILM WEBSITES		
June 2010		
Website	Unique Visitors	% Change from June 2009
Yahoo Movies	26,616,000	70.7
IMDb.com	25,091,000	14.7
Fandango Movies Network	15,713,000	76.2
Moviefone	14,378,000	13.0
MSN Movies	10,929,000	80.6
Hollywood.com Network	9,097,000	44.3
Fixster.com	6,666,000	130.0
The Movie Network	5,163,000	NA
Film.com	4,491,000	43.0
UGO Film-TV	4,230,000	20.7
Source: *The World Almanac and Book of Facts*, 2011.		

Planning a Career in Arts, Audio/Video Technology, & Communications

Have you ever dreamed of becoming a famous actor? Maybe you'd like to write the next Great American Novel. Perhaps you'd rather be an anchor for the evening news. Then again, maybe your goal is to operate a graphics and printing shop or manage audio/video operations for a local television station. If you're interested in the arts, communications, or entertainment, then this cluster field is for you.

What's It Like?

Individuals who work in this field are involved in designing, producing, exhibiting, performing, writing, and publishing multimedia content including visual and performing arts and design, journalism, and entertainment services. For example:

- They set up and operate audio and video equipment, including microphones, projectors, and recording equipment for concerts, sports, and news conferences.
- They create animated images or special effects seen in movies, television programs, and computer games.
- They serve as curators for museums and galleries, directing the acquisition, storage, and exhibition of art collections.
- They write content for radio and television broadcasts, movies, and the Web.
- They set up and maintain the sophisticated equipment used to transmit communications signals around the world and enable billions of users to connect to the Internet.

Employees in these fields work in a variety of settings, from indoor broadcast booths to concert halls to outdoor sports stadiums. They might work from home or on the road, in computer labs or in offices. They are often required to travel, and many work under strict deadlines.

Employment Outlook

Most observers expect the job growth rate within this cluster to be at about 14 percent for the foreseeable future, although in just the AV technology field, growth is expected to be closer to 20 percent. Many people are drawn to these creative fields, so the competition for jobs is tough. Employers are looking for experienced workers, preferring those with a college degree or comparable on-the-job training.

© Thor Jorgen Udvang/Shutterstock.com

What About You?

The Arts, AV Technology & Communications career cluster is covered in box 3 of the Interest Survey Activity you completed in Unit 1 of this text. If this box had one of the three highest scores on your survey, you should further explore the cluster's pathways and related occupations.

1. Why do you think a career in this field could be a good choice?
2. What skills can you develop now that would be helpful to a career in this field?
3. Why do you think so many people are attracted to these types of occupations?

Table

1. Open *df 44c table*.
2. Update the table using the following information:
   a. Place the heading, secondary heading, and source note within the grid. Merge cells as needed. Use bold 16-pt. font for the heading, bold 14-pt. font for the secondary heading, and 12-pt. font for the source note. Change the source note to *The World Almanac and Book of Facts,* **2011**.
   b. Delete the *Post/Rocky Mountain News* paper from the table.
   c. Insert **2007** before *Circulation* in the column C heading.
   d. Insert a column at the right, and title it **2010 Circulation**. Remerge the title rows and source note row as needed.
   e. Starting in cell C4 and proceeding down to C5, C6, etc., insert the following circulation numbers for 2010:

   1,908,116 | 2,011,999 | 927,851 | 657,467 | 582,844 | 465,892 | 544,167 | 361,480 | 384,419

   f. Add a row before the source note and key this information.

   Post   New York, NY   Not available   508,042

   g. Sort the table in descending order by 2010 circulation.
   h. Change orientation to landscape.
3. **Save as:** *44c table*.

LESSON 45   Table Design Features

OUTCOMES

- Create tables with main headings, secondary headings, column headings, and/or totals row using the Table feature.
- Use Table Styles, Borders, Shading, and No Borders as well as previously applied wp features.

Table

1. Open *df 45b table*.
2. Merge the cells of row 1.
3. Adjust the column widths so that the name of the sales representative fits on one line. Adjust the width of other columns as needed.
4. Bold and center the main heading and column headings.
5. Center-align column B; right-align columns C, D, and E.
6. Bold and italicize the highest sales figure for each month.
7. Sort the rows in ascending alphabetical order by territory.
8. Apply the Table Style that is a grid and uses orange coloring.
9. Center the table on the page.
10. **Save as:** *45b table*.

Academic and Career Connections

Complete the following exercises that introduce various topics that involve academic themes and careers.

Grammar and Writing: Sentence Types and Proofreading

MicroType 6

- **References/Communication Skills/Sentence Types**
- **References/Communication Skills/Proofreading**
- **CheckPro/Communication Skills 8**
- **CheckPro/Word Choice 8**

1. Go to *MicroType* 6 and use this feature path for review: References/Communication Skills/Sentence Types.
2. Click Rules and review the rules of using simple, compound, and complex sentences.
3. Then, under *Sentence Types*, click *Posttest*.
4. Follow the instructions to complete the posttest.
5. Repeat this process for *Proofreading*.

Optional Activities:

1. Go to this path: CheckPro/Communication Skills 8.
2. Complete the activities as directed.
3. Go to this path: CheckPro/Word Choice 8.
4. Key the Apply lines, and choose the correct word.

Communications: Speaking

You have been selected to introduce a speaker, Douglas H. Ruckert, to your class. You can find his resume in the data file **df u11 communications**. The introduction is to be 30 seconds to 1 minute long. The audience is your classmates.

1. Review the résumé and decide which points you will include in your introduction.
2. Open a new word processing document, and key an outline of these points. Save the document as **u11 communications**, and with permission, print a copy.
3. Practice your introduction by reading aloud. Add transitions as necessary. Pay attention to your tone of voice, facial expressions, posture, and body language. Your goal is to introduce the speaker without having to read directly from your printed document.
4. As directed by your instructor, present your introduction to the class.

Math Skills: Probability

Matt is an actor who has just moved to New York City and is trying to find work. He is 6'2" tall, has blond hair, plays the piano, and has worked as a stand-up comedian.

1. Matt auditions for the role of a piano teacher. He learns that he is one of eight actors in contention for the role. What is the probability that Matt will get the role? Express the probability as a fraction, ratio, and percent (rounded to the nearest whole percent).
2. Matt goes to an audition for a television commercial for which the advertiser is seeking four males with blond hair who are at least 6' tall. If Matt is one of 20 males who meet these qualifications, what is the probability that he will get the part? Express the probability as a fraction, ratio, and percent (rounded to the nearest whole percent).
3. Matt finds a job working as a comedian in a nightclub. Every Saturday, the club holds a competition in which the audience votes for the best comedian. The winner receives $250. If Matt is one of 12 comedy acts, what is the probability that he will win? Express the probability as a fraction, ratio, and percent (rounded to the nearest whole percent).

45C

Table with Table Style

1. Create a grid for the table below, using AutoFit Contents and default row heights.
2. Key the main heading in bold, 16-pt. font. Use Align Center.
3. Key the secondary heading in bold, 14-pt. font. Use Align Center.
4. Key the column headings in bold, 12-pt. font. Use Align Center.
5. Key the data entries using alignments shown in the table. Right align all numbers.
6. Sort the information in the rows in ascending alphabetic order by program.
7. Insert a totals row at the bottom, and calculate the total enrollments for columns B to E.
8. Apply the Table Style that is a list and uses orange coloring; then deselect *Banded Columns*. Remember to rebold and recenter headings if necessary.
9. Center the table horizontally and vertically on the page.
10. **Save as:** *45c table*.

CENTURY COLLEGE				
School of Applied Sciences				
Program	Students Enrolled			
	Last Year		This Year	
	Females	Males	Females	Males
Actuarial Sciences	10	14	12	11
Operations Management	33	28	37	30
Sports Management	56	54	50	62
Health Services Management	27	31	32	35
Logistics Engineering	12	10	14	14
Software Engineering	22	24	20	26
Applied Math	14	16	10	12

58C

Unbound Report with Footnotes

1. Open *df 58c report*. Format it as an unbound report.
2. Insert the following footnotes where indicated. The ¶s with the footnotes are long quotations.

   ¹ *Medical and Health Services Management Careers, Jobs, and Training Information*, 2011, http://www.careeroverview.com/medical-health-manager-careers.html (January 25, 2011).
   ² *Occupational Outlook Handbook*, 2010-2011, http://stats.bls.gov/oco/ocos014.htm#outlook (January 25, 2011).

3. Number the pages aligned at the top right; hide the number on p. 1.
4. Proofread and correct errors.
5. **Save as:** *58c report*.

58D

MLA Report with Textual Citations

1. Open *df 58d report*. Format it as an MLA report using 11-pt. Times New Roman font. The ¶ before *The Intranet* side heading is a long quotation.
2. Create a Works Cited page using the following sources:

   Fulton-Calkins, Patsy and Karin M. Stulz. *Procedures & Theory for Administrative Professionals*. 6th edition. Mason, OH: South-Western Cengage Learning, 2009.

   Odgers, Patti. *Administrative Office Management*. 13th edition. Mason, OH: Thomson South-Western, 2005.

   Oliverio, Mary Ellen, William E. Pasewark, and Bonnie R. White. *The Office, Procedures and Technology*. 5th edition. Mason, OH: Thomson South-Western, 2007.

3. Insert page numbers. Adjust page breaks as needed.
4. Proofread and correct errors.
5. **Save as:** *58d report*.

Letter with Table

1. Open *df 45d letter*. Read the business letter.
2. Insert *45c table* you created in 45C, placing it where indicated in the letter. Leave about 10 pts. of blank space above and below the table.
3. **Save as:** *45d letter*.

45E

Table with Borders and Shading

1. Open file *df 45e table* and revise it so it appears as shown below.
2. Increase the row height of the heading rows to enhance the appearance.
3. Bold the team names.
4. Change the orientation to landscape, and apply AutoFit Window.
5. **Save as:** *45e table*.

TIP-OFF BASKETBALL TOURNAMENT **Altoona** November 28					
Altoona Middle School Gym		Time	Altoona High School Gym		
Score	Boys		Girls		Score
	Bruce Somerset	9:00	Bruce Somerset		
	St. Croix Central St. Croix Falls		St. Croix Central St. Croix Falls		
	Menomonie Rice Lake	11:15	Menomonie Rice Lake		
	Altoona Eau Claire		Altoona Eau Claire		
	St. Croix Falls Bruce	1:30	St. Croix Falls Bruce		
	St. Croix Central Somerset		St. Croix Central Somerset		
	Rice Lake Eau Claire	3:45	Rice Lake Eau Claire		
	Menomonie Altoona		Menomonie Altoona		

45F

Table without Gridlines

1. Open *df 45f table*.
2. Remove the borders.
3. **Save as:** *45f table*.

- Create unbound and MLA reports with and without documentation using word processing features presented in this and previous units.

58B

MLA Report

1. Open a new document, and key the report below in MLA format. Use Times New Roman 11 pt. font to keep this on one page.
2. Proofread and correct errors.
3. **Save as: _58b report_.**

Student's Name
Mr. Lonnie Repack
General Science
15 April 20--

Tires, Tires, and More Tires

Have you ever stopped to think about all the tires that are sold each year? The United States has more than 140,000,000 passenger vehicles. Just think of the number of tires needed if these vehicles have tires replaced every other year. About 280,000,000 tires would be sold each year. Add to this figure the number of tires used by large trucks. Some trucks have 16 to 18 tires each. They drive hundreds of thousands of miles each year delivering products to our plants, distribution centers, and stores. What about tires for busses and bicycles? The number of tires that are no longer needed by drivers must also be considered. Have you ever thought about what happens to all these tires? Are they recycled? Are they abandoned?

The Concern

Unfortunately, far too many tires are abandoned rather than recycled. Abandoned tires often litter the sides of our rivers and creeks or the lands in our forests. Too often, worn-out tires are abandoned in tire piles that are ugly and provide breeding grounds for mosquitoes. These tire piles are fire hazards. If they catch fire, they can burn for weeks, polluting the air. The heat of the fire can cause the rubber to decompose into oil. This oil is likely to seep into and pollute nearby ground and surface water, causing damage to the environment.

What You Can Do

The next time you change tires, even on your bicycle, make sure you dispose of them appropriately. If you can, leave them with the retailer that sold you the replacement tires. The old tires can be recycled into useful products such as buckets, shoes, mouse pads for your computer, and dustpans.

Tables—Application and Assessment

- Create tables with main headings, secondary headings, column headings, and/or totals row using Table features.

46B

Table

1. Key the table below as shown.
2. Adjust column widths to fit contents.
3. Format heading in bold, 16-pt. font and column headings in bold, 14-pt. font.
4. Sort the data entries in ascending alphabetic order by painting.
5. Apply a table style to improve the appearance of the table.
6. Center the table on the page.
7. **Save as:** *46b table*.

FAMOUS PAINTINGS	
Artist	Painting
Claude Monet	The Boat Studio
Paul Cezanne	Riverbanks
Rembrandt	The Mill
Michelangelo	The Holy Family
Leonardo da Vinci	The Mona Lisa
Vincent van Gogh	The Starry Night
Raphael	The School of Athens
Berthe Morisot	Little Girl Reading
Pierre-Auguste Renoir	Girls at the Piano
Jan Vermeer	The Milkmaid

Lazar Mihai-Bogdan/Shutterstock.com

2. Insert the text from file **df 57b text** below the last line. Change the text from the Normal style to the appropriate line and ¶ spacing for a MLA report.

3 If needed, format the bulleted lists so they both have the same bullet symbol and the symbol is aligned with the indent of the first line of each ¶.

4. Format the last ¶ as a long quotation.

5. Key the following footnotes where indicated in the text; then delete the text in red.

[1] Pattie Odgers, *Administrative Office Management*, 13 edition (Cincinnati: South-Western, 2005) 74.

[2] Robert F. Russell and A. Gregory Stone, "A Review of Servant Leadership Attributes: Developing a Practical Model," *Leadership & Organizational Development Journal*, 23.3-4 (2002) 145–158.

[3] Patsy Fulton-Calkins and Karin M. Stulz, *Procedures & Theory for Administrative Professionals*, 6 edition (Cincinnati: South-Western Cengage Learning, 2009) 454.

6. Key a Works Cited page using the following sources.

Fulton-Calkins, Patsy, and Karin M. Stulz. *Procedures & Theory for Administrative Professionals*. 6 edition. Cincinnati: South-Western Cengage Learning, 2009.

Odgers, Pattie. *Administrative Office Management*. 13 edition. Cincinnati: South-Western, 2005.

Russell, Robert F., and A. Gregory Stone. "A Review of Servant Leadership Attributes: Developing a Practical Model." *Leadership & Organizational Development Journal*, 23.3-4 (2002).

7. Proofread the document carefully to find the five embedded errors. Correct errors detected.
8. **Save as: *57b report*.**

57C

MLA Report with Textual Citations

1. Open **df 57c text** and format it as an MLA report with a Works Cited page, using your name for the student, your teacher's name, your course name, and today's date. Use 11-pt. Times New Roman font, and make all formatting decisions according to the guides presented in this unit.

2. Insert the following sources on a Works Cited page.

Works Cited

Railton, Stephen. "Your Mark Twain." http://etext.lib.virginia.edu/railton /sc_as_mt/yourmt13.html (accessed January 25, 2011).

Railton, Stephen. "Sam Clemens as Mark Twain." http://etext.virginia.edu /railton/sc_as_mt/cathompg.html (accessed January 25, 2011).

Waisman, Michael. "About Mark Twain." http://www.geocities.com /swaisman/huckfinn.htm (accessed January 25, 2011).

3. Proofread and correct errors.
4. **Save as: *57c report*.**

1. Open **df 46c table**.
2. Delete all rows with players who have played four years.
3. Delete *Years Played* column.
4. Insert a column before the e-mail address, and key the telephone numbers below, starting in cell E3.

Telephone
555-678-1033
555-678-1709
555-348-0144
555-374-3056
555-678-2133
555-472-0337
555-678-1678
555-374-4585

5. Insert three rows at the bottom, and key the following information in the rows.

Bauer, Brianne	Left Back	11/04/ 98	555-374-6032	bauer.b@telstar.net
Haupt, Janet	Right Back	09/14/ 96	555-678-5502	rback.haupt@ford.net
Trianez, Dee	Left Wing	06/05/ 95	555-348-8173	trianez77@alt.com

6. Sort the data entries by last name.
7. Insert a row at the top, merge cells, and key HURRICANES TENTATIVE STARTING LINEUP as the heading for the table in bold 18-pt. font; format column headings in bold 16-pt. font; use 14-pt. font for all other rows.
8. Change orientation to landscape.
9. Center-align columns C and D; left-align all others.
10. Apply an appropriate table style.
11. Center table on the page.
12. **Save as: 46c table**.

www.cengage.com/school/ keyboarding/c21key

1. Open **df 46d table**.
2. Use the information in the table below to finish keying any columns that are incomplete. Merge, split, and align cells as needed to complete the layout as shown below.
3. Format the main heading in bold, 16-pt. font and column headings in bold, 12-pt. font.
4. Apply a double-line border around all cells, and shade the cells so they are similar to what is shown below.
5. Center the table on the page in landscape orientation.
6. **Save as: 46d table**.

Works Cited

"Great Lakes." *Encyclopaedia Britannica.* http://search.eb.com/eb/article-39973 (14 July 2007).

The World Almanac and Book of Facts. "The Great Lakes." New York: World Almanac Books, 2007.

The World Almanac and Book of Facts. "The Great Lakes." New York: World Almanac Books, 2011.

4. Insert a page number at the top, right-aligned, with **Popelas** preceding the number. Number all pages, including p. 1 and the Works Cited page.

5. Correct any page endings and beginnings that are not correct. Proofread and correct errors.

6. **Save as:** *56c report*.

LESSON 57 — MLA Reports with Documentation

OUTCOMES
- Format MLA reports with footnotes and textual citations and Works Cited pages.
- Use previously learned wp features to process MLA reports.

57B

MLA Report with Footnotes

1. Open a new document, and key the text below in MLA format. Include your last name in the page number and your name, teacher's name, your course name, and today's date in the report identification lines. Make the necessary revisions as you key. Do not insert the footnote at this time.

Leadership Seminar Progress Report

Development of the leadership seminars for supervisors *and first-line managers* is progressing on schedule. One seminar will be conducted at *each of the four* ~~our~~ Indiana plants. The primary objectives of the seminars *is* ~~are~~ to have the participants understand the following points:

change to bulleted list

1. The importance of having leaders at all levels of the corporation.
2. The definition of *effective* leadership.
3. How leadership traits are developed for use within the corporation *and the community*.
4. That various styles of leadership exist and that there is no one best leadership style.

Seminar Presenter

Three *of our* staff members observed training sessions conducted by five *professional* ~~prominent~~ training and development companies before selecting the firm to conduct these leadership seminars. Derme & Associates, Inc., a *local* consulting firm specializing in career enhancement seminars, has been selected to develop and conduct the seminars.

One *primary* reason for selecting Derme & Associates is that they will develop the content of the seminars around Odgers' definition of leadership,[1] which we want to emphasize with employees.

ACCOUNTING MAJOR

General Electives (40 credits)				Business Core (32 credits)	Accounting Requirements (28 credits)
Category I (9 Credits)	**Category II** (9 Credits)	**Category III** (11 credits)	**Category IV** (11 Credits)	Acct 201	Acct 301
CJ 202 Math 111 Math 245	Biol 102 Chem 101 Geog 104	Econ 103 Econ 104 Psyc 100 Soc 101	No specific courses required.	Acct 202 Bcom 206 Bcom 207 MIS 240 Bsad 300 Bsad 305 Fin 320 Mktg 330 Mgmt 340 Mgmt 341 Mgmt 449	Acct 302 Acct 314 Acct 315 Acct 317 Acct 321 Acct 450 Acct 460 Fin 326 Fin 327

Category I – Communications and Analytical Skills
Category II – Natural Sciences
Category III – Social Sciences
Category IV – Humanities

46E

Table

1. Key the table below.
2. Format the heading in bold 16-pt. font; secondary in bold 14-pt. font; column headings in bold 12-pt. font; and all other rows in 12-pt. font.
3. Set row 1 height at 0.6" and other rows at 0.4"; align cells as shown below.
4. Apply a List or Grid table style with green shading and Banded Rows deselected.
5. Center the table on the page.
6. **Save as:** *46e table.*

GENERATIONAL MEMORIES, 1929–1995				
Top Five Events by Age Group as of 1998				
Rank	18–35	36–54	55–64	65 and Over
1	Oklahoma City Bombing	Oklahoma City Bombing	JFK Death	JFK Death
2	Challenger	JFK Death	Moon Walk	Pearl Harbor
3	Gulf War Begins	Challenger	Oklahoma City Bombing	WWII Ends
4	Reagan Shot	Moon Walk	Challenger	Moon Walk
5	Berlin Wall Falls	Gulf War Begins	MLK Death	FDR Death
Source: The Pew Research Center, "America's Collective Memory," December 15, 2011, http://people-press.org/reports/display.php3?PageID=283				

MLA Reports with Textual Citations

- Format MLA reports without references and with textual citations and Works Cited pages.
- Use previously learned wp features to process MLA reports.

56B

MLA Report

1. Read the MLA Report format guide section on p. 215, and then read very carefully the content in the model MLA report on p. 218. This report contains guides for formatting MLA reports.
2. Open a new document. Set Line Spacing to 2.0 and Paragraph Spacing to 0 pt. Before and After. Key the model MLA report as shown on p. 218.
3. **Save as:** *56b report*.

56C

MLA Report with Textual Citations

1. Key and format the text below as an MLA report with textual citations. Use 11-pt. Times New Roman font.

Harry Popelas
Mr. Roper
Geography
22 February 20--

The Great Lakes

The five Great Lakes (Lake Erie, Lake Huron, Lake Michigan, Lake Ontario, and Lake Superior) in North America are the largest group of freshwater lakes in the world.

The present configuration of the Great Lakes basin is the result of the movement of massive glaciers through the mid-continent, a process that began about one million years ago. . . . Studies in the Lake Superior region indicate that a river system and valleys formed by water erosion existed before the Ice Age. The glaciers undoubtedly scoured these valleys, widening and deepening them and radically changing the drainage of the area. (Great Lakes, 2007)

Physical Features

The Great Lakes have a combined area of 94,510 square miles (244,780 square kilometers). Although the Great Lakes were all formed by glacial activity during the same period, they are quite different from one another. The irregular movement of the glacier created variation in the size, elevation, and depth of the lakes.

2. Insert the text in file *df 56c text* below the last ¶, and format it in MLA report style.
3. Insert a blank page at the end of the report. At the 1" line, key the title **Works Cited** as shown below. Then key the references using 2.0 line spacing and hanging indent.

(continued on next page)

© VEER.COM/STILLFX

Academic and Career Connections

Complete the following exercises that introduce various topics that involve academic themes and careers.

MicroType 6

- References/Communication Skills/Other Internal Punctuation
- References/Communication Skills/Semicolons
- CheckPro/Communication Skills 6
- CheckPro/Word Choice 6

1. Go to *MicroType 6* and use this feature path for review: References/Communication Skills/ Other Internal Punctuation.
2. Click *Rules* and review the rules of using apostrophes, colons, hyphens, dashes, and parentheses.
3. Under *Other Internal Punctuation*, click *Posttest*.
4. Follow the instructions to complete the posttest.
5. Repeat this process for Semicolons.

Optional Activities:

1. Go to this path: CheckPro/Communication Skills 6.
2. Complete the activities as directed.
3. Go to this path: CheckPro/Word Choice 6.
4. Key the Apply lines, and choose the correct word.

Communications: Listening

1. You answered a telephone call from George Steward, your father's business associate. Mr. Steward asked you to take a message for your father.
2. Open the sound file *df u08 communications*. Take notes as you listen.
3. Key the message—in complete sentences—for your father.
4. Below the message, key the following information that your father will want to share with Mr. Steward at the meeting.

Current Office Renovations

	Contractor	Architect	HVAC	Designer
105 W. Fourth Street	Bramble & Hayes	Lopez Brothers, Inc.	All Weather	Lauren Design Associates
1220 Sycamore	Rinehart Construction	To be determined	Thomas Heating & Cooling	Today's Office Environs
306 Clifton Avenue	Bramble & Hayes	William Loftus Associates	Office Comfort Systems	Grafton Design

5. Format and align the data as shown. Apply a table style of your choice.
6. **Save as:** *u08 communications*.

1. Using a cover page built-in style of your choice, create a cover page for the report you keyed in 55E. Supply appropriate information in the placeholders. Delete unused placeholders as well as the blank page following the cover sheet.
2. **Save as:** *55f cover page*.

21st Century Skills: Make Judgments and Decisions

Caroline is the manager of a customer service center for a large online retailer. She manages close to 30 service representatives whose primary responsibility is taking customer orders over the phone. She has just been told by upper management that starting the next week, the service representatives will also be responsible for selling additional products to customers who call to place orders. Caroline informs the reps of the change during a weekly department meeting. She immediately hears groans and complaints from several of the workers. Their primary complaint is that they don't want to sell anything. Sales, they claim, is not in their job description.

Caroline is concerned that morale in the department will be affected by those with negative attitudes about the change.

Think Critically

1. Evaluate the manner in which Caroline announced the added responsibility to her department. Do you think her approach was appropriate?
2. With a partner, brainstorm ideas and strategies for how Caroline could have more successfully promoted this new responsibility to the service reps. Create a new word processing document, and write a report that summarizes your strategy. Save the document as *u11 21century*.

© 2011 Digital Vision/Jupiterimages Corporation

Katelyn and Meredith run a successful dog boarding and grooming business. Although they are both involved in the day-to-day care of the dogs, Katelyn also does the accounting for the business. At the end of the year, she wants to determine the following:

1. The business had 43 customers who used both the boarding and grooming services. If this represents 40 percent of their customers, how many total customers did they have? (Round to the nearest whole number.)

2. The dog boarding service generated $73,800 in sales for the year. If this was 60 percent of total sales, what were the total sales?

3. The business's biggest expenditure is the mortgage, which totaled $19,200 for the year. If this was 48 percent of all expenses, what were the total expenses?

4. At year-end, Katelyn had paid off $5,200, or 30 percent, of the loan they received from the bank to start the business. How much is the loan?

School and Community Under federal law, every U.S. citizen 18 years of age or older has the right to vote. But in the last presidential election, only about 55 percent of the voting age population exercised that right. Voting in an election is one way to demonstrate civic responsibility. What can you do to convince the voting-age population to get out and vote?

1. Identify a group(s) in your community that focuses on voter registration and assistance. Find out how you can contribute to the group's mission.

2. Research the laws on voter registration and alternative means of voting. Contact your municipal leaders or election board for information.

3. Gather information on polling stations and resources for assisting those who may have problems getting to the polls.

4. Using the information you have gathered, prepare a handout that provides information to potential voters on how they can exercise their right to vote. Distribute the handout in your neighborhood.

"Geometry." *Encyclopaedia Britannica.* http://www.britannica.com/EBchecked/topic/229851/geometry (January 25, 2011).

"Statistics." *Encyclopaedia Britannica.* http://www.britannica.com/EBchecked/topic/564172/statistics (January 25, 2011).

4. Number the pages at the top right; hide the page number on p. 1.
5. Verify that styles have been applied correctly and that page endings and beginnings are correct. Proofread the document and correct errors.
6. **Save as:** *55c report*.

55D

Cover Page

1. Select a cover page style and create a cover page for the report you keyed in 55C. Use your school name as the company name and your name as the writer. Delete the *Year* placeholder and others not used as well as the blank page following the cover sheet.
2. **Save as:** *55d cover page*.

55E

Unbound Report with Footnotes

1. Open *df 55e report*. Verify that it is formatted using 1.0 line spacing with 0 pt. of space before and after the ¶s.
2. Select all the text, and apply the Normal style to all the text.
3. Format the text as an unbound report using styles appropriately for the title and side headings. The second ¶ in the Susan B. Anthony section is a long quotation. The second ¶ in the Abraham Lincoln section is a long quotation.
4. Number the pages at the top right, and hide the number on p. 1.
5. Insert the following footnotes where indicated in the text, and then delete the text in red. Divide the website address in footnote 2 so its first line ends nearer the right margin, if necessary.

[1] Susan Clinton, *The Story of Susan B. Anthony* (Chicago: Children's Press, 1986), p. 5.

[2] Mary Bellis, "Biography of Thomas Edison," http://inventors.about.com/od/estartinventors/a/Edison.Bio.htm, January 25, 2011.

[3] "An Overview of Abraham Lincoln's Life," http://rogerjnorton.com/Lincoln77.html, January 24, 2011.

6. Insert a separate page at the end; title it **References** and key the following sources. Divide the website address in reference 2 so its first line ends nearer the right margin, if necessary.

Clinton, Susan. *The Story of Susan B. Anthony.* Chicago: Children's Press, 1986.

Bellis, Mary. "Biography of Thomas Edison." http://inventors.about.com/od/estartinventors/a/Edison.Bio.htm (January 25, 2011).

"An Overview of Abraham Lincoln's Life." http://rogerjnorton.com/Lincoln77.html (January 24, 2011).

7. Proofread and correct all errors. Verify that all pages begin and end correctly.
8. **Save as:** *55e report*.

Hospitality & Tourism

Planning a Career in Hospitality and Tourism

Most of us interact on a regular basis with workers in the hospitality and tourism fields, whether it's ordering food at a restaurant, going to a movie, or visiting a local zoo or museum. Travel and tourism is one of the largest and fastest-growing industries in the world, with hospitality-related businesses located in communities around the globe. Employees in this field are involved in the management, marketing, and operations of restaurants and food/beverage services; lodging facilities; travel-related services; and recreation, amusements, and attractions.

What's It Like?

Individuals who work in this field are busy, energetic, and have excellent people skills. Their responsibilities often focus on catering to the needs of others. For example:

- They advise travelers about their destinations and make arrangements for transportation, hotel accommodations, car rentals, and sites to see.
- They bring people together at meetings and conventions by identifying suitable meeting sites, securing speakers, organizing lodging and meals, and arranging for support services such as audiovisual equipment, forms of electronic communication, and transportation.
- They greet diners in restaurants, take food and drink orders, and serve food and beverages. They also answer questions, explain menu items and specials, and keep tables and dining areas clean and set for new diners.
- They lead groups in activities such as arts and crafts, sports, performing arts, camping, and other special interests. Or they might manage recreation programs in parks, playgrounds, and other settings.

Employees in the hospitality and tourism fields work in a variety of settings, from offices to restaurants and movie theaters, to parks and campgrounds. They are employed by hotels, restaurants, travel agencies, cruise ships, amusement parks, museums, and other attractions and recreation facilities.

Employment Outlook

The job outlook is good for workers in the hospitality and tourism industry, with the recreation, amusements, and attractions sector experiencing the fastest growth. Most employers prefer workers with formal training in their field. Completion of post-secondary training is becoming increasingly important for advancement.

fotorobs/Shutterstock.com

What About You?

The Hospitality and Tourism career cluster is covered in box 9 of the Interest Survey Activity you completed in Unit 1 of this text. If this box had one of the three highest scores on your survey, you should further explore the cluster's pathways and related occupations.

1. Why do you think a career in this field could be a good choice?
2. What skills can you develop now that would be helpful to a career in this field?
3. Why are these jobs important to a community and to our economy?

1. Open a new document, and key and format the text below and on the next page as an unbound report with textual citations. Use the default setting for the bulleted list.

Mathematics

Most high school students study several types of mathematics. In college, they complete additional math courses, some of which prepare them to study even *more* kinds of mathematics. You may think of math as one subject; in fact, there are many types of mathematics. This report describes seven kinds.

Arithmetic

Arithmetic is the first branch of mathematics that you studied in elementary and middle school. It deals with the study of numbers and the use of the four fundamental processes:

Edyta Pawlowska/Shutterstock.com

- Addition
- Subtraction
- Multiplication
- Division

Arithmetic is everyday math. You use it daily in your personal affairs, and arithmetic is the basis for most other branches of mathematics.

Algebra

Algebra is used widely to solve problems in business, industry, and science by using symbols, such as x and y, to represent unknown values (algebra). The power of algebra is that it enables us to create, write, and rewrite problem-solving formulas. Without algebra, we would not have many of the items we use on a daily basis: television, radio, telephone, microwave oven, etc.

2. Open *df 55c text* and insert it after the algebra section. Format the last five lines (beginning with the ellipsis) as a long quotation.

3. Key the following sources on a new page at the end of the report.

References

"Calculus." *Encyclopaedia Britannica.* http://www.britannica.com/EBchecked/topic/89161/calculus (January 25, 2011).

"Elementary Algebra." *Encyclopaedia Britannica.* http://www.britannica.com/EBchecked/topic/184192/elementary-algebra (January 25, 2011).

(continued on next page)

Complete this activity to help prepare for the Word Processing II event in FBLA-PBL's Business Management and Administration division. Participants in this event demonstrate that they have acquired word processing proficiency beyond entry level.

1. You work for your community's travel and tourism office. You have been asked to write a business letter to travel agents in neighboring states inviting them to visit your community and experience its attractions. Your goal is to motivate them to share their experience with their clients. Use the following guidelines to write your letter.

   - **Date:** Insert the current date.
   - **Letter Address:** Address the letter to **Ms. Anna Ramirez** at the **Ramirez Travel Agency | 504 Montgomery Road**. Use your city, state, and ZIP Code.
   - **Body:** The body of the letter should consist of three ¶s. In the first ¶, introduce your community and state the purpose for writing the letter. In the second ¶, provide a basic description of your community, including its general location, climate, and major attractions. In the third ¶, state why your community would be a good place to visit and why the travel agent should recommend it to his or her clients.
   - **Complimentary Close:** Use your name and the title of **Communications Assistant**.

2. When you are finished writing, be sure to proofread, check the spelling and grammar, and revise the document as necessary. Apply appropriate formatting and styles (bold, italic, and underline). Save and print the document as directed by your instructor.

3. In a new word processing document, create a table in landscape orientation that lists at least three restaurants, two to three hotels, and a minimum of three attractions in your area. Organize the information logically in the table. Insert a title for the table, and apply formatting and alignment options as appropriate. Save and print the document as directed by your instructor.

For detailed information on this event, go to www.fbla-pbl.org.

Think Critically

1. How can strong word processing skills help you be a more productive employee?
2. How can you use written communications as a tool for persuading others?
3. Tables are an effective format for organizing information. What types of information do you receive in table format?

© iStockphoto.com/AlbanyPictures

1. Using a cover page of your choice, create a cover page for the report you keyed in 54C. Use your name as the writer and the current date. Delete all placeholders not used as well as the blank page following the cover sheet.
2. **Save as:** *54d cover page*.

LESSON 55 — Unbound Reports with Documentation

OUTCOMES

- Prepare unbound reports with textual citations and footnotes and reference pages.
- Use Page Break, Insert Footnote, Indentation, and Line and Paragraph Spacing as well as previously learned wp features.

55B

References Page

1. Read the Documentation Guides on p. 215–216. The references below follow the Century 21 style that is described on p. 399 at the back of the text.
2. Open a new document, and key the model references shown below. You do not need to number the page.
3. Proofread and correct errors.
4. **Save as:** *55b references*.

Figure 11-15 References page

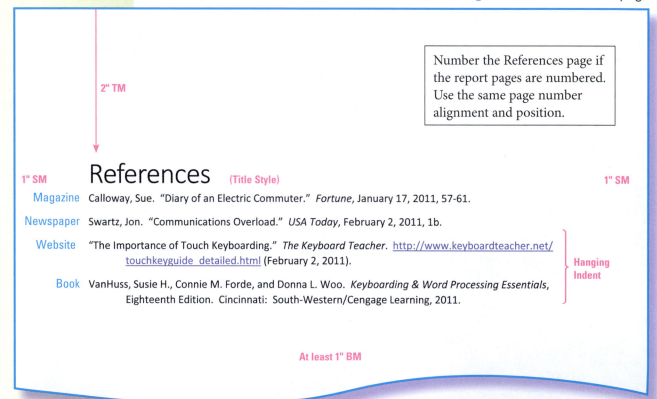

Number the References page if the report pages are numbered. Use the same page number alignment and position.

2" TM

1" SM

References *(Title Style)*

1" SM

Magazine   Calloway, Sue. "Diary of an Electric Commuter." *Fortune*, January 17, 2011, 57-61.

Newspaper   Swartz, Jon. "Communications Overload." *USA Today*, February 2, 2011, 1b.

Website   "The Importance of Touch Keyboarding." *The Keyboard Teacher*. http://www.keyboardteacher.net/touchkeyguide_detailed.html (February 2, 2011).

Hanging Indent

Book   VanHuss, Susie H., Connie M. Forde, and Donna L. Woo. *Keyboarding & Word Processing Essentials*, Eighteenth Edition. Cincinnati: South-Western/Cengage Learning, 2011.

At least 1" BM

UNIT 9

Presentations—Slide Shows

Lesson 47   Text Slides
Lesson 48   Slides with Graphics
Lesson 49   Tables, Graphs, and Charts

Lesson 50   Create and Deliver a Presentation
Lesson 51   Slide Show Assessment

Application Guide

What Is an Electronic Presentation?

Electronic presentations are computer-generated visual aids (usually slide shows) that can be used to help communicate information. Presentations can combine text, graphics, audio, video, and animation to deliver and support key points. With the powerful features of presentation software such as *Microsoft PowerPoint*, attractive and engaging presentations can be created with ease.

Presentations are an important part of communication in business. Presentations are given to inform, to persuade, and/or to entertain. Visual aids generally make a speaker more effective in delivering his/her message. That is because the speaker is using two senses (hearing and sight) rather than just one. The probability of a person understanding and retaining something seen as well as heard is much greater than if it is just heard. For example, if you had never heard of a giraffe before, you would have a better idea of what a giraffe was if the speaker talked about a giraffe and showed pictures of one than if the speaker only talked about what a giraffe was.

© 2011 Echo/Jupiterimages Corporation

With presentation software, visuals (slides) can be created that can be projected on a large screen for a large audience to view or shown on a computer for a smaller audience. Web pages, audience handouts, and speaker notes can be created using presentation software.

LESSON 54

Unbound Reports with Styles

OUTCOME

- Use the Styles, Page Numbering, and Insert Cover Page and previously learned wp features to format one- and two-page unbound reports and cover pages.

54–58A

Warmup

Key each line twice at the beginning of each lesson, first for control and then for speed.

alphabet 1 We moved quickly to pack an extra dozen lanyards Bif just bought.

fig/sym 2 I sold 22 at $45 less 13%, 8 at $69 less 5%, & 16 at $70 less 8%.

speed 3 Both of the men risk a big penalty if they dismantle their autos.

gwam 1' | 1 | 2 | 3 | 4 | 5 | 6 | 7 | 8 | 9 | 10 | 11 | 12 | 13 |

54B

One-Page Unbound Report

1. Read the Unbound Report format guide section on p. 215, and then read very carefully the content in the model unbound report on p. 217. This report contains guidelines for formatting unbound reports.
2. Open a new document and key the model unbound report on p. 217, using appropriate styles and spacing; proofread and correct errors.
3. **Save as:** *54b report*.

54C

Two-Page Unbound Report

1. Open a new document, and key the report below as shown.
2. Insert the text from *df 54c text* after the last line of the report.
3. Adjust the width of the table so it extends to the left and right margins; center the column headings.
4. Change formatting as needed to create an unbound report.
5. Insert page numbers that are right-aligned at the top; hide the page number on p. 1.
6. Proofread and correct any errors.
7. **Save as:** *54c report*.

The Importance of Saving Money

Most professional planners advise school-aged children to open a savings account and then make regular deposits whenever they receive money for doing chores or as gifts on birthdays and holidays. The primary advantage of doing this is to get into the habit of saving and having your money grow by earning interest. When you are in your teens, you may also choose to make higher-yielding and higher-risk investments in stocks and bonds to help you save for your future education; however, opening a savings account and making regular deposits is a critical first step to a secure financial future.

Financial Plan

A good financial plan is one that makes you feel good now in anticipation of what you will be able to do with your savings in the future. How much do you need to save now and in the near future to attend the college or technical school of your choice, to purchase your first automobile, or to purchase furniture when you decide to move into your own apartment? Experts agree that saving is simpler when you set financial goals that are important to you.

What Are the Key Features of Presentation Software?

Learning how to use *PowerPoint* is quite easy for individuals who have had experience with *Word*. *PowerPoint* has many of the same features as *Word* and is set up the same way, using ribbons, groups, and tabs (see Figure 9-1). However, you will learn new features unique to *PowerPoint*. In this unit, you will learn how to:

- choose an appropriate slide layout
- create text slides
- insert illustrations and images
- create tables, charts, and graphs
- create and deliver a presentation

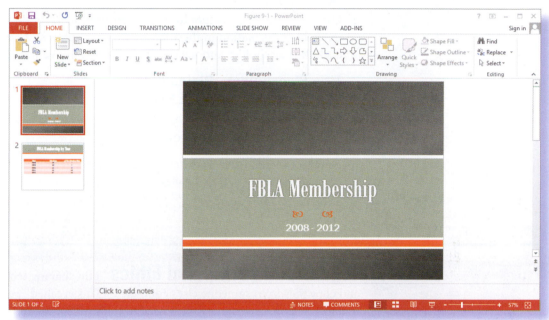

Figure 9-1 *PowerPoint* main screen

What Is a Design Theme?

PowerPoint comes with files containing design themes (see examples in Figures 9-2 through 9-5). A **design theme** provides a consistent, attractive look. All the person creating the presentation has to do is select the slide layout, key the information, and insert appropriate graphics. The fonts and font sizes, places for keying information, background design, and color schemes are preset for each design theme. Even though these themes are preset, they can be changed to better fit the needs of the user. Using design themes gives your presentations a professional appearance.

Figure 9-2 Sketchbook design theme (Office 2010)

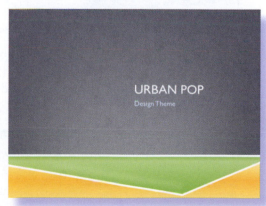

Figure 9-3 Urban Pop design theme (Office 2010)

The **Cover Page** feature (see Figure 11-14) inserts a fully formatted cover page. The file contains placeholders for keying the title, author, date, etc. In this unit, you will create cover pages as new documents and delete the blank page that is automatically inserted following the cover page. To delete the blank page, use the Show/Hide ¶ feature, and delete the page break if it is visible. If it is not, go to the beginning of the blank page, and tap Backspace until the blank page is deleted.

📄 Cover Page ▾
📄 Blank Page
📰 Page Break
Pages

Figure 11-14

1. Open a new document.
2. Use the Cover Page feature to create a cover page using the **Sideline** style. Key the following information in the appropriate placeholders. *Note:* For placeholders not used, click the placeholder and tap the Space Bar to remove the placeholder from the page.

    Title Placeholder: Plains Indians
    Subtitle Placeholder: A Brief History
    Author Placeholder: Your Name
    Date Placeholder: Current Date

3. Apply a different style to the cover page you created.
4. Change the style back to Sideline style, and delete the blank page.
5. **Save as:** *aa11 activity 9.*

Digital Citizenship and Ethics   **File-sharing** technology lets you search for and copy files from someone else's computer. (This is called "peer-to-peer" or P2P technology.) File sharing is most often used to trade MP3s, but movies, games, and software programs can also be shared. BitTorrent, uTorrent, Kazaa, FrostWire, and Shareaza are popular file-sharing programs. They give you direct access to other computers without having to go through a central server.

File-sharing programs are a convenient way to share public domain files (material that isn't owned by anybody). But file sharing can quickly turn into piracy. **Piracy** is sharing or downloading copyrighted material without paying for it. It is another form of stealing, and it is illegal. Burning copies of CDs or DVDs and even swapping MP3 files with your friends are forms of piracy.

As a class, discuss the following.

1. "Borrowing" someone's copy of the latest computer game and installing it on your own PC is piracy. Why do you think this is considered stealing?
2. How could illegal file sharing cause harm or damage to the holders of copyrighted materials?

TEAMWORK

Figure 9-4 Faucet design theme (Office 2013)

Figure 9-5 Integral design theme (Office 2013)

What Is a Slide Layout?

Layout refers to the way text and graphics are arranged on the slide. Presentation software allows the user to select a slide layout for each slide from a menu, as shown in Figure 9-6. Some of the more common layouts include:

- Title Slide layout
- Title and Content layout
- Section Header layout
- Two Content layout
- Comparison layout
- Title Only layout
- Blank layout
- Content with Caption layout
- Picture with Caption layout

Note in Figures 9-7 through 9-14 how different the same slide layout appears when shown in a different design theme.

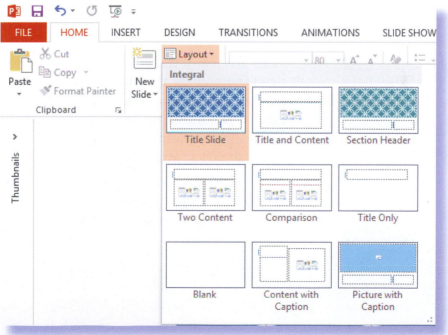

Figure 9-6 Slide layout

One way to identify sources cited in your text is to add footnotes. The **Insert Footnote** feature (see Figure 11-12) can be used to automatically insert the footnote at the bottom of the same page as its reference. As you edit, add, or delete footnotes, changes in numbering and formatting are automatically made. *Note:* The **Insert Endnote** feature works in a similar way, except that endnotes appear at the end of the document. In this unit, you will use footnotes as a method to document sources.

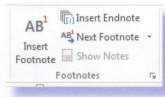

Figure 11-12

1. Open file *df aa11 activity 7*. Insert the three footnotes shown below where indicated in the file. Tap Enter between footnotes. Delete *(Insert footnote No. x)* from the copy.

   [1] David J. Rachman and Michael H. Mescon, *Business Today* (New York: Random House,1987), p. 529.

   [2] Greg Anrig, Jr., "Making the Most of 1988's Low Tax Rate," *Money*, February 1988, pp. 56–57.

   [3] Andrew Chamberlain, "Twenty Years Later: The Tax Reform Act of 1986," http://www.taxfoundation.org/blog/show/1951.html (accessed January 26, 2011).

2. **Save as:** *aa11 activity 7*.

To insert text from an existing file into a file that is open, use the **Text from File** feature shown in Figure 11-13.

1. Open a new document.
2. Leaving a 2" top margin, key the copy below (except the words printed in color). Use the Title style for the heading.

   Table Exams

   Here is a list of the software features you will need to know for the first exam on tables.
   <Insert df aa11 activity 8a file.>
   For the second exam on tables, you will need to know the following table formatting software features.
   <Insert df aa11 activity 8b file.>

3. Insert the *df aa11 activity 8a* and *df aa11 activity 8b* files where indicated in the text. Add space above paragraph 2.
4. **Save as:** *aa11 activity8*.

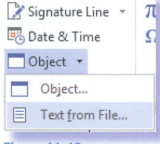

Figure 11-13

Figure 9-7 Title Slide layout—Apothecary design theme

Figure 9-8 Title Slide layout—Thatch design theme

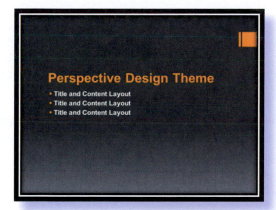

Figure 9-9 Title and Content layout—Perspective design theme

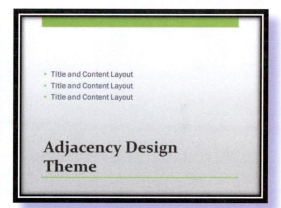

Figure 9-10 Title and Content layout—Adjacency design theme

Photo Courtesy of the Author

Figure 9-11 Two Content layout—Grid design theme

Photo Courtesy of the Author

Figure 9-12 Two Content layout—Kilter design theme

Left (paragraph) indent 0.5"

    This example shows text that is indented from the left margin. Notice that each line begins at the indentation point.

Hanging indent 0.5"

This example shows hanging indent. Notice that the first line begins at the left margin, but the remaining lines begin at the indentation point.

1. Open a new document. Set margins at Wide and use Century Gothic 14-pt. font.
2. Key the two ¶s shown above, indenting them as indicated. Tap Enter once between ¶s. Clear the indent that was inserted in the first paragraph before keying the second one.
3. **Save as:** *aa11 activity 5*.

Activity 6

Styles

Home/Styles/select style

A **style** is a collection of format settings for font, font size, color, ¶ spacing, alignment, and so on that are named and stored together in a style set (see Figure 11-11). The default style set is named *Word 2013,* and the default style is named *Normal.* The Normal style uses Calibri 11-pt. black font, 1.08 line spacing, 8-pt. spacing after ¶s, and left alignment.

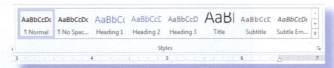

Figure 11-11

As shown in Figure 11-11, each style set contains styles for titles, subtitles, and various headings that can be quickly applied to text to make it attractive and easy to read. To format text using the Styles feature, select the style set of your choice. Then select the text to be formatted, and click on the style with the desired formatting. The text will be automatically formatted, as shown in sample below.

Before·Style·Applied¤	After·Style·is·Applied·(Word·2013·Style·Set)¤
Title¶ Subtitle¶ Heading·1¶ Heading·2¶ Intense·Quotation¶ Intense·Reference¤	Title¶ Subtitle¶ Heading·1¶ Heading·2¶ *Intense·Quotation¶* INTENSE·REFERENCE¤

1. Open *df aa11 activity 6*.
2. Select the text for the first line (Title).
3. Click the Title style button.
4. Select the next line of text, and click on the corresponding style (Subtitle).
5. Repeat for each of the remaining lines of text.
6. **Save as:** *aa11 activity 6*.

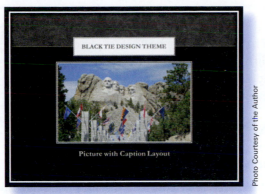

Figure 9-13 Picture with Caption layout—Black Tie design theme

Figure 9-14 Picture with Caption layout—Angles design theme

View/Presentation Views/
select desired view

What View Options Are Available to View Slides?

As you are working in presentation software, there are different view options available. Each view serves a distinct purpose for creating, editing, and viewing slides. These views are explained and illustrated below.

- **Normal View.** The Normal View with slides is used for creating and editing individual slides, viewing miniatures of slides that have already been created, and creating notes.
- **Outline View.** The Outline View is used for creating and editing individual slides, outlining, and creating notes. This view shows the text on your slides in outline form. To see Outline View in Office 2010, select Normal View and then select the Outline tab in the left pane (see Figure 9-18).
- **Notes Page View.** The Notes Page View can be used to create and edit speaker notes. Use the Notes Page View to see how the notes will look prior to printing to avoid unnecessary printing if changes need to be made.
- **Reading View.** The Reading View presents each slide one at a time, filling up most of the screen. In Reading View, the status bar stays active, allowing you to see which slide number you are viewing and to view the previous slide or the next slide by clicking the arrows on the status bar.
- **Slide Sorter View.** The Slide Sorter View shows all the slides in miniature. This is helpful for rearranging slides and for applying features to several slides at a time.
- **Slide Show View.** The Slide Show View is used to see how the slides will look during a presentation. This view is helpful for rehearsing and presenting your slide show.

These views can be accessed through the View tab as shown in Figure 9-15 or by clicking the icons at the bottom of the screen on the status bar as shown in Figure 9-16. Each of the five views are shown on the next page in Figures 9-17 through 9-21.

View/Presentation Views

Figure 9-16 View icons

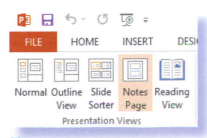

Figure 9-15 View tab

Activity 3

Line and Page Breaks

Page Layout/Paragraph
Dialog Box/Line and
Page Breaks

In multiple-page documents, the first line of a ¶ should not appear at the bottom of a page by itself (**orphan line**), and the last line of a ¶ should not appear by itself at the top of a page (**widow line**). The **Widow/Orphan** feature prevents ¶s from splitting incorrectly.

Figure 11-8

The **Keep with Next** feature prevents a page break from occurring between two ¶s. (See Figure 11-8.) Select this feature when a side heading appears as the last line at the bottom of a page and the text that relates to it begins on the next page.

1. Open *df aa11 activity 3*. An orphan line appears at the top of page 2.
2. Select all the text in the document, and turn on the Widow/Orphan feature. The ¶ is automatically reformatted to prevent an orphan line.
3. **Save as:** *aa11 activity 3a*.
4. Tap Enter twice on p. 1 before the title. Verify that a side heading appears as the last line on p. 1, separated from the text to which it relates.
5. Place your insertion point on the side heading, and select the Keep with Next feature to move the side heading to the top of p. 2. Verify that the side heading moved to p. 2.
6. **Save as:** *aa11 activity 3b*.

Activity 4

Page Numbers

Insert/Header & Footer/
Page Number

Use the **Page Number** feature (see Figure 11-9) to place page numbers in specific locations on the printed page. Most software allows you to select the style of number (Arabic numerals—1, 2, 3; lowercase Roman numerals—i, ii, iii; uppercase Roman numerals—I, II, III). You can place numbers at the top or bottom of the page, aligned at the left margin, center, or right margin. Check the **Different First Page** box (Headers & Footers Tools/Design/Options) to keep the page number from appearing on the first page.

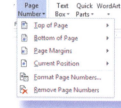

Figure 11-9

1. Open *df aa11 activity 4*.
2. Number all five pages with the page number at the bottom center of the page. Hide the number on p. 1.
3. Use Print Preview to verify that the page numbers have been added (pp. 2–5) or hidden (p. 1).
4. **Save as:** *aa11 activity 4a*. Close the file.
5. Open *df aa11 activity 4* again. This time, number all five pages with the page number at the top right of the page. Key your name followed by a space before the page number. Do not hide your name and page number on p. 1.
6. **Save as:** *aa11 activity 4b*.

Activity 5

Indentations

Home/Paragraph Dialog
Box/Indents and Spacing

Use the **Indent** feature to move text away from the margin. A **left indent** (**paragraph indent**) moves the text one tab stop to the right, away from the left margin, as shown below. A **hanging indent**, also shown below, moves all but the first line of a ¶ one tab stop to the right. Refer to Figure 11-10. Set the left indent under General/Alignment and the hanging indent under Indentation/Special in the Paragraph dialog box.

Figure 11-10

Figure 9-17 Normal View

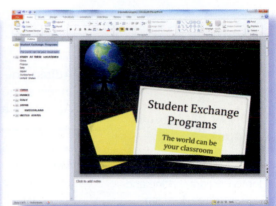

Figure 9-18 Outline View

Figure 9-19 Full Screen Reading View

Figure 9-20 Slide Sorter View

Photo Courtesy of the Author

Figure 9-21 Slide Show View

WP Applications

Activity 1

Line and Paragraph Spacing

Home/Paragraph/Line and Paragraph Spacing

Page Layout/Paragraph/ Spacing Before or After

For each activity, read and learn about the feature described; then complete the activity as directed.

OUTCOMES

- Adjust line and ¶ spacing, page endings, and indentations.
- Insert page numbers and text from another file.
- Apply styles and create cover pages.

Use the **Line Spacing** feature to change the amount of white space between lines of text. The default line spacing for *Word 2013* is 1.08. If another line spacing is desired, 1.0, 1.15, 1.5, 2.0, and 3.0 can be selected (see Figure 11-5).

You can use the **Spacing Before** and **Spacing After** options to customize the amount of white space that appears before the first line of a ¶ and after the last line of a ¶. *Word 2013* default spacing is 0 pt. (point) before a ¶ and 8 pt. after a ¶ (see Figure 11-6).

1. Open *df aa11 activity 1*.
2. Select the text and change line spacing to 2.0 and spacing before and after ¶s to 0 pt.
3. **Save as:** *aa11 activity 1*.

Figure 11-5

Figure 11-6

Activity 2

Page Break

Insert/Pages/Page Break

Word processing software has two types of page breaks: **soft** and **hard**. Both kinds signal the end of a page and the beginning of a new page. The software inserts a soft page break automatically when the current page is full (when the bottom margin is reached). You insert hard page breaks manually when you want a new page to begin before the current one is full (see Figure 11-7). When a hard page break is inserted, the wp software adjusts any following soft page breaks so that those pages will be full before a new one is started. Hard page breaks do not move unless you move them. To move a hard page break, you can delete it and (1) let the software insert soft page breaks, or (2) insert a new hard page break where you want it.

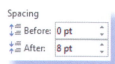

Figure 11-7

1. Open a new document.
2. Key the roster sign-up sheet for the Red Sox shown below. Leave a 2" top margin on each page. Use 14-pt. Comic Sans for the font; 1.15" line spacing below the title and between the numbers; 12 players will be signing up for the team.
3. Insert a hard page break at the end of the Red Sox Roster page. Create sign-up sheets for the Mets, the Dodgers, and the Cubs, beginning each on a new page.
4. **Save as:** *aa11 activity 2*.

RED SOX ROSTER

1.

2.

11.

12.

LESSON 47   Text Slides

- Navigate through an existing presentation.
- Create a title slide.
- Create a bulleted list slide.

47A–51A

Warmup

Key each line twice.

alphabet 1 Jake Lopez may give a few more racquetball exhibitions in Dallas.

figures 2 Ray quickly found the total of 8.16, 9.43, and 10.25 to be 27.84.

speed 3 Bob's neighbor may dismantle the ancient shanty in the big field.

`gwam` 1' | 1 | 2 | 3 | 4 | 5 | 6 | 7 | 8 | 9 | 10 | 11 | 12 |

47B

View Presentation

1. Open *df 47b pp* in your presentation software program. The file will open in Normal View (Slides).
2. Click the Slide Show View button at the bottom of the screen (see Figure 9-22) and view the slide show, noting the different design themes and layout options. Tap the Enter key or the down arrow key, or click the mouse, to advance to the next slide.
3. When you are done viewing the slide show, click Slide Sorter View. Left-click and hold on slide 4 and drag it to the space between slides 2 and 3. Notice how slide 4 becomes slide 3 and Slide 3 becomes slide 4.
4. Click on slide 1 and then click Normal View; notice the notes beneath each slide. Read each note and then use the down arrow key to go to the next slide.
5. Close the presentation without saving.

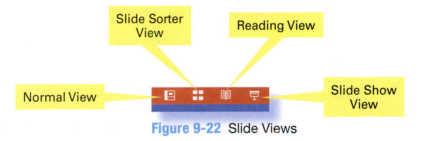

Figure 9-22 Slide Views

Figure 11-4 MLA report

Report is formatted in 11-pt. Calibri with 2.0 Line Spacing and 0 pt. Space Before and After Paragraphs for all text in the report, including headings.

Fuentes 1 Writer's name and page number

1" TM

Report Identification Lines

Maria N. Fuentes

Mrs. Kostelik

English

17 September 20--

Title → Formatting MLA Report Guides

Body → School reports are often formatted using a simple form of the MLA (Modern Language Association) style guidelines.

Margins and Spacing

The top, bottom, left, and right margins on all pages of the report are 1". All lines of the report, including long quotations, bulleted and numbered lists, and tables, use 2.0 line spacing (double spacing) with 0 pt. of space before and after paragraphs.

Report Parts

1" LM

A page number right-aligned at the top appears on every page, including the first page. The writer's last name may precede the page number. A space separates the name and page number.

1" RM

The report identification lines begin 1" from the top at the left margin and are double spaced. They include the writer's name, teacher's name, subject name, and date (day/month/year style).

The report title is a double space below the date. The title is center aligned and is keyed following the rules for capitalizing and punctuating titles.

The body of the report follows the title. The first line of each paragraph is indented 0.5". If headings are used within the body, they are formatted the same as the report title. Long quotations (four or more lines) are indented 1" from the left margin.

If the report contains references, a works cited page is keyed on a separate page. You will learn to format a works cited page in an upcoming lesson.

At Least 1" BM

Create Title Slide

Design/Themes/Thatch
Home/Slides/Layout/
Title Slide

Title slide. A presentation should begin with a title slide. Include the presentation title, presenter name, and other relevant information.

1. Start a new presentation.
2. Open *df 47c thatch pp.*
3. Select the Title Slide layout.
4. Create the title slide as shown in Figure 9-23.
5. Increase the font size of the title of the presentation to 40 pt. and the name of the presenter and the company name to 24 pt.
6. **Save as:** *47c pp.*

Figure 9-23 Slide 1—Title slide

Create Title and Content Slide

Home/Slides/New Slide/
Title and Content

Title and Content (bulleted lists). Use the Title and Content layout for lists to guide discussion and help the audience follow a speaker's ideas (see Figure 9-24). If too much information is placed on a single slide, the text becomes difficult to read. Keep the information on the slide brief—do not write complete sentences. Be concise.

When creating lists, be sure to:

- focus on one main idea.
- add several supporting items.
- limit the number of lines on one slide to six.
- limit long wraparound lines of text.

1. Open *47c pp* and insert three new slides with the Title and Content (bulleted list) layout after the slide you created in 47C.

Figure 9-24 Title and Content layout

Figure 11-3 Unbound report

2" TM

> Report is formatted in Word 2013 Normal Style (11-pt. Calibri with 1.08 Line Spacing and 8 pt. Space After Paragraph). The title is formatted in Title style, and side headings are formatted in Heading 1 style.

Title

1" SM

Unbound Report Guides

Short reports are often prepared without binders. If they consist of more than one page, the pages are usually fastened together in the upper-left corner by a staple or paper clip. Such reports are called unbound reports.

Side heading

Margins and Spacing

The side and bottom margins on all pages are 1", the top margin on the first page is 2" and 1" on the second and subsequent pages. Use the default line spacing and spacing after paragraph for the paragraphs within the body of the report (1.08 line spacing and 8 pt. spacing after paragraph for Word 2013). Do not indent the first line of each paragraph.

Side heading

Titles and Headings

For the report title, use the default Title style (Calibri Light 28 pt. for Word 2013). For the side headings, use the default Heading 1 style (Calibri Light 16 pt. with Blue, Accent 1 for Word 2013). Capitalize the first letters of all words except prepositions in titles and side headings.

Side heading

Page Numbers

The first page of an unbound report may or may not include a page number. *The reports keyed for this unit will not include a page number on the first page.* On page 2 and subsequent pages, right-align the page number at the top of the page.

Side heading

Long Quotations, and Lists

Long quotations (four or more lines) are indented 0.5" (or at the first default tab setting) from the left margin. When bulleted or numbered lists are included in the body, use the default 0.25" indentation for the lists.

Side heading

Documentation

Textual citations, footnotes, or endnotes may be used to document the sources cited in the report. In this unit you will use the textual citations and footnotes methods. You will learn how to format the citations and the reference pages in an upcoming lesson.

2. Create the slides shown in Figures 9-25, 9-26, and 9-27.

3. **Save as:** *47d pp*.

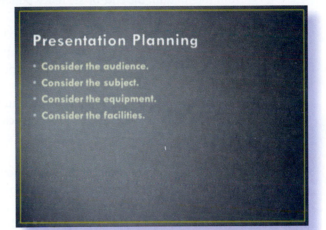

Figure 9-25 Slide 2—Bulleted list 1

Figure 9-26 Slide 3—Bulleted list 2

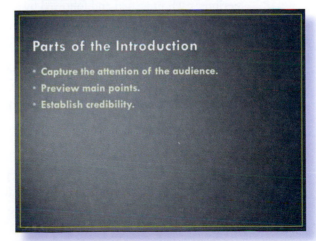

Figure 9-27 Slide 4—Bulleted list 3

When a textual citation appears at the end of a sentence, the end-of-sentence punctuation follows the textual citation. However, if a textual citation follows a long quote that is indented from the margin, the end-of-sentence punctuation precedes the textual citation.

When the author's name is used in the text introducing the quotation, only the year of publication and the page number(s) appear in parentheses. For example, **McWilliams (2009, 138) said that . . .** would be inserted at the appropriate place.

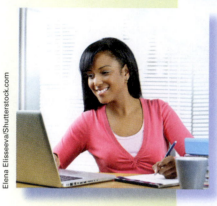

For electronic references, include the author's name and the year. When there are two articles by the same author, the title of the article will also be included.

Footnotes

The **footnote** method of documentation identifies the reference with a superscript number . . . .[1] The complete documentation for the reference appears at the bottom of the same page and is identified with the same superscript number. Footnotes should be numbered consecutively throughout the report and should use the default settings of the Footnote feature of the software. Following is an example of a footnote for a journal article.

[1]**Richard G. Harris, "Globalization, Trade, and Income,"** *Canadian Journal of Economics,* **November 1993, p. 755.**

Reference List, Bibliography, or Works Cited Page

All references used in a report are listed alphabetically by author's last name at the end of the report on a separate page under the title *References* (or *Bibliography* or *Works Cited*), formatted with the same margins and line and ¶ spacing as the first page of the report. *References, Bibliography,* or *Works Cited* is formatted with the same style that was used for the report title.

Begin the first line of each reference at the left margin; indent subsequent lines 0.5" (hanging indent; see Activity 5 below).

Other Report Guides

Ellipsis

An **ellipsis** (. . .) is used to indicate material omitted from a quotation. An ellipsis is three periods, each preceded and followed by a space. If the omitted material occurs at the end of a sentence, include the period or other punctuation before the ellipsis as shown in the example below.

> In ancient Greece, plays were performed only a few times a year. . . . The festivals were held to honor Dionysius in the hope that he would bless the Greeks. . . . (Prince and Jackson, 1997, 35)

Cover Page

The Cover Page feature of the software can also be used to create professional-looking cover pages for your reports. Normally, a cover page is not required with an MLA-style report, since the report identification lines contain the information that usually appears on the title page.

Change Template Design

Design/Themes/Macro
(Adjacency, Newsprint)

1. Open **47d pp**; change the template design to three other designs (such as those shown in Figures 9-28, 9-29, and 9-30), and see how the appearance of the different layouts changes with each template. Compose a brief ¶ explaining which of the template designs you prefer and why.

2. Close the file with the Dividend design theme if you are using Office 2013; close the file with the Newsprint design theme if you are using Office 2010.

3. **Save as:** **47e pp.**

Figure 9-28 Dividend design theme (Office 2013)

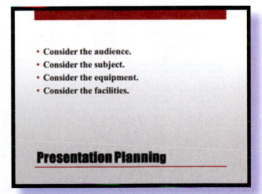

Figure 9-29 Wisp design theme (Office 2013)

Figure 9-30 Newsprint design theme (Office 2010)

UNIT 11

Word Processing: Reports

Lesson 54   Unbound Reports with Styles
Lesson 55   Unbound Reports with Documentation
Lesson 56   MLA Reports with Textual Citations

Lesson 57   MLA Reports with Documentation
Lesson 58   Report Application and Assessment

Application Guide

Reports

Unbound Report Guides

When a printed report is very long, it is usually presented in a folder or binder. However, short reports are often prepared without binders. If they consist of more than one page, the pages are usually fastened together in the upper-left corner by a staple or paper clip. Such reports are called **unbound reports** (see an example in Figure 11-1). The guides for formatting unbound reports are shown in the Unbound Report model copy in Figure 11-3. Read and study the information presented in the model copy.

MLA Report Guides

The **Modern Language Association (MLA)** style is often used to document and format students' papers (see an example in Figure 11-2). The guides for formatting MLA reports are given in the MLA Report model copy in Figure 11-4. Read and study the information presented in the model copy.

Report Documentation Guides

Documentation is used to give credit for published material (electronic as well as printed) that is quoted or closely paraphrased (slightly changed). Two types of documentation will be used in this unit: textual citations and footnotes.

Textual (Within Text) Citations

The **textual citation** method of documentation inserts the author name(s), the date of the referenced publication, and the page number(s) of the material within parentheses at the appropriate point in the text. For example, **(McWilliams, 2009, 138)** would be inserted in the text.

Figure 11-1   Unbound report

Figure 11-2   MLA report

LESSON 48   Slides with Graphics

- Describe how to use appropriate graphic images, lines, and shapes.
- Insert, position, and size graphic images, photos, lines, and shapes.
- Create and enhance slides with graphics.

48B

Insert Clip Art

Insert/Online Pictures

Graphics. **Graphics** can enhance a message and help convey ideas. Graphic images might include clip art from your software collection or other sources such as the Internet (see Figure 9-31). Graphic images could also include photos or even original artwork scanned and converted to a digitized image. Recall from Unit 1 that Web content such as photography, clip art, video, and music is protected by copyright law, and you may need permission from the owner or author of the content.

Use graphics only when they are relevant to your topic and contribute to your presentation. Choose graphics that will not distract the audience. Clip art can often be used to add humor. Be creative, but use images in good taste. An image isn't necessary on every slide in a presentation.

1. Learn how to insert clip art on a slide and how to size and position graphics.
2. Open **df 48b insert photos pp**. Insert an appropriate piece of clip art from your software or from Office.com Clip art on slide 1 (see Figure 9-32) and slide 2 (see Figure 9-33). Size and position the clip art attractively.
3. **Save as: 48b pp.**

Figure 9-31 Sample clip art

Figure 9-32 Slide 1—Title slide with clip art

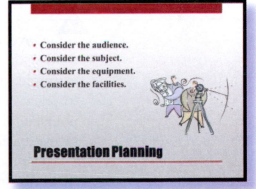

Figure 9-33 Slide 2—Bulleted list with clip art

53E

Technique: Number Keys/Tab

Set tabs at 2" and 4". Key the copy below.

Concentrate on finger location; quick tab spacing; eyes on copy.

331 Summit St.	589 Gabriel Ave.	364 Topaz Ave.
2490 Tucker Ave.	981 Toweridge Rd.	72 Viking Rd.
587 Telemark Ct.	207 Maplewood Trl.	481 Osceola Ave.
6021 Mission Hills	365 Westover St.	2963 Hunt St.
9987 Park Pl.	224 Norton Way	745 Sinclair Ct.

gwam 1' | 1 | 2 | 3 | 4 | 5 | 6 | 7 | 8 | 9 | 10 |

53F

Technique: Response Patterns

Key each line twice.

letter response

1 be you as him cat ill get ink was oil tax pop set pin ads joy car
2 as you set up | after you bat | look at Jim | as you stated | better pony
3 John created a great dessert treat: stewed plum in a sweet tart.

word response

4 big air all the wig sir lay own for iris odor rush auto bush city
5 my neighbor | make a sign | their firm | half the problem | kept the rock
6 Pamela may go with us to the city to do the work for the auditor.

combination response

7 base city draw them star soap pink sign debt odor milk lend dates
8 up to | was he | if you | you did hop | up to my dock | see the cat | my goal
9 Reese is as aware as they are that the state tree is the buckeye.

53G

Timed Writings

1. Key a 1' timing on ¶ 1; key four more 1' timings on ¶ 1, trying to go faster each time.
2. Repeat the procedure for ¶ 2.

www.cengage.com/school/keyboarding/c21key

LA   **all letters used**   gwam 1'

Government is the structure by which public laws are	11
made for a group of people. It can take many forms. For	22
example, in one type of structure, the populace has the right	34
to elect citizens to govern for them and make the laws and	46
policies. This way of making the laws is called a represen-	58
tative government.	62
Democracy or republic form of government are two names	12
that are quite often used to refer to this type of governance	24
by the people. This type of a structure is in direct contrast	37
to a dictatorship, in which all the decisions are made by just	49
one person.	52

gwam 1' | 1 | 2 | 3 | 4 | 5 | 6 | 7 | 8 | 9 | 10 | 11 | 12 |

Insert Photos

1. Learn how to insert photos in a slide and how to size and position the picture.
2. Open **48b pp**.
3. Open **df 48c pp**. Copy photo 1 and insert on slide 3 as shown in Figure 9-34. Copy photo 2 and insert on slide 4. Size and position the picture attractively.
4. **Save as:** **48c pp**.

Photo 1 for slide 3

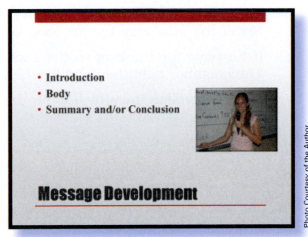

Photo Courtesy of the Author

Figure 9-34 Slide 3—Bulleted list with photo

48D

Insert Shapes

Insert/Shapes/Click
on shape

Shapes. Ready-made shapes can be inserted into your presentation. Some examples are shown in Figure 9-35. Arrow shapes can be used to focus an audience's attention on key points. Lines can be used to separate sections of a visual, to emphasize key words, or to connect elements. Boxes, too, can separate elements and provide a distinctive background for text.

These shapes include:

- Lines
- Rectangles
- Basic shapes
- Block arrows
- Equation shapes
- Flowchart shapes
- Stars and banners
- Callouts
- Action buttons

1. Learn how to use the Shapes features of your software.
2. Open **48c pp**. Create a simple logo for Multimedia Design Services. You can base it on the clip art you inserted in 48B or create something new. Use a circle, box, or other shape and add a fill to it. Put clip art or text on or around the shape. Place your logo attractively on the title slide.
3. **Save as:** **48d pp**.

53C

Speed-Forcing Drill

Key each line once at top speed; then try to complete each sentence on the 15", 12", or 10" call as directed by your instructor. Force speed to higher levels as you move from sentence to sentence.

Emphasis: high-frequency balanced-hand words

	gwam	15"	12"	10"
Glen and I may key the forms for the city auditor.		40	50	60
He may make a sign to hang by the door of the bus.		40	50	60
They may make a profit if they do all of the busy work.		44	55	66
Six of the men may bid for good land on the big island.		44	55	66
If he pays for the bus to the social, the girls may also go.		48	60	72
The neighbor paid the maid for the work she did on the dock.		48	60	72
It is their civic duty to handle their problems with proficiency.		52	65	78
Helen is to pay the firm for all the work they do on the autobus.		52	65	78

53D

Timed Writings

1. Key a 1' timing on ¶ 1; determine *gwam*. Set new goal by adding 2–4 *gwam* to the rate attained; determine quarter-minute checkpoints from the chart at the left.
2. Key two 1' guided timings on ¶ 1 to increase speed. Practice ¶ 2 in the same way.
3. Key two 3' timings on ¶s 1 and 2 combined; determine *gwam* and the number of errors.

A   **all letters used**

Quarter-Minute Checkpoints				
gwam	1/4'	1/2'	3/4'	Time
16	4	8	12	16
20	5	10	15	20
24	6	12	18	24
28	7	14	21	28
32	8	16	24	32
36	9	18	27	36
40	10	20	30	40

	gwam	3'
Extraordinary would be an appropriate word to use to describe Michelangelo. It would be a good word to express how an individual may feel about the statue of David. It would also be an excellent choice of words for describing the exquisite works of art on the ceiling of the Sistine Chapel. It would be just as fine a word to use to describe the dome of St. Peter's Basilica. Each of these outstanding works of art was completed by Michelangelo, quite an extraordinary person.		4 71 / 8 75 / 12 79 / 16 84 / 20 88 / 24 92 / 28 96 / 32 100
The paintings, sculptures, and architecture of this man are recognized throughout the world. Michelangelo was born in Caprese, Italy, but spent much of his early life in the city of Florence. Here he spent a great deal of time in the workshops of artists. His father did not approve of his doing so, because artists were considered to be manual laborers. His father considered this to be beneath the dignity of his family members. This did not stop the young artist, who would eventually become one of the greatest of all times.		36 104 / 40 108 / 44 112 / 48 116 / 52 120 / 56 124 / 61 128 / 65 132 / 68 135

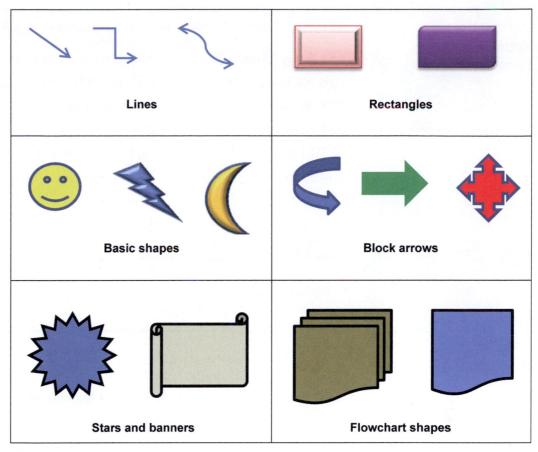

Figure 9-35 Sample Shapes

48E

Create Slides with Shapes

1. Open **48d pp**. Insert a fifth slide with a Title Only layout.
2. Use the Draw Shapes feature to create the slide shown in Figure 9-36. Use the Arial font (24-pt. bold and 18-pt. bold) for the text boxes.
3. **Save as:** **48e pp**.

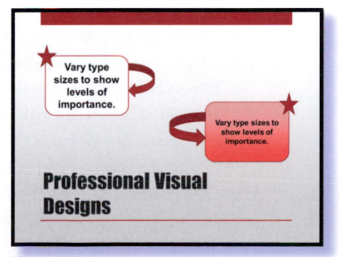

Figure 9-36 Slide 5

**Technique:
Number Keys/Tab**

Set tabs at 2" and 4". Key the copy below; concentrate on finger location and quick tab spacing.

451 Rose Thorn Pl.	892 Santa Maria Ln.	630 Sinclair St.
728 Richland Dr.	829 Scotch Pine Ct.	88 Redcoat Dr.
307 Sheldon St.	65 Shiloh Rd.	656 Regina Cr.
521 Shoshone Dr.	23 Rhone Ter.	147 Powell St.
3769 Prague Rd.	861 Rainbow Ln.	410 Beech Ave.
154 Foxhill St.	901 Kirby Ln.	72 Gwendolyn Dr.

gwam 1' | 1 | 2 | 3 | 4 | 5 | 6 | 7 | 8 | 9 | 10 |

LESSON 53   Input Skill Development

OUTCOMES

- Build speed and accuracy.
- Enhance keying technique.

53A

Warmup

Key each line twice.

alphabet 1 Wang B. Vazquez quickly forced the board to combine six projects.

figures 2 He gave me $365 on May 29 for the items ordered on Invoice 40187.

speed 3 Orlando paid them for their work on the city chapel by the docks.

gwam 1' | 1 | 2 | 3 | 4 | 5 | 6 | 7 | 8 | 9 | 10 | 11 | 12 |

53B

**Technique:
Letter Keys**

Key each line twice. Focus on limiting keystroking movement to the fingers.

N 1 Nancy knew she would win the nomination at their next convention.

O 2 Roberto opposed opening the store on Monday mornings before noon.

P 3 Pam wrapped the peppermints in purple paper for the photographer.

Q 4 Qwin quietly queried Quincy on the quantity and quality of quail.

R 5 Raindrops bore down upon three robbers during the February storm.

S 6 The Mets, Astros, Reds, Twins, Jays, and Cubs sold season passes.

T 7 Trent bought the teal teakettle on the stove in downtown Seattle.

U 8 Ursula usually rushes to the music museum on Tuesday, not Sunday.

V 9 Vivacious Eve viewed seven vivid violets in the vases in the van.

W 10 We swore we would work with the two wonderful kids for two weeks.

X 11 Rex Baxter explained the extra excise tax to excited expatriates.

Y 12 Yes, Ky is very busy trying to justify buying the yellow bicycle.

Z 13 Dazed, Zelda zigzagged to a plaza by the zoo to see a lazy zebra.

gwam 1' | 1 | 2 | 3 | 4 | 5 | 6 | 7 | 8 | 9 | 10 | 11 | 12 | 13 |

Create Slides with Clip Art

1. Open **48e pp**.
2. Insert two slides with Two Content layout after slide 5.
3. Create the slides as shown in Figures 9-37 and 9-38. Insert an appropriate piece of clip art from your software, or use Clip Art from Office Online.
4. **Save as: 48f pp**.

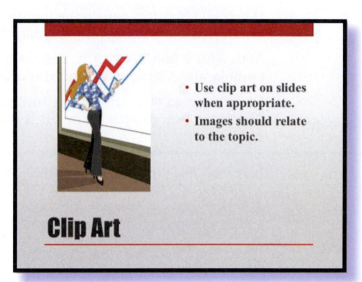

Figure 9-37 Slide 6

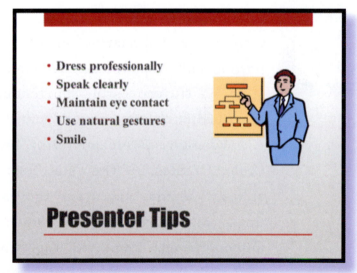

Figure 9-38 Slide 7

Speed-Forcing Drill

Key each line once at top speed; then try to complete each sentence on the 15", 12", or 10" call as directed by your instructor. Force speed to higher levels as you move from sentence to sentence.

Emphasis: high-frequency balanced-hand words

	gwam	15"	12"	10"
Hal paid the men for the work they did on the rig.		40	50	60
Orlando and I did the work for the eight busy men.		40	50	60
Helen and Rodney may do the handiwork for the neighbor.		44	55	66
When I visit the neighbor, Jan may go down to the dock.		44	55	66
Alan and I laid six of the eight signs by the antique chair.		48	60	72
Pamela and Vivian may sign the proxy if they audit the firm.		48	60	72
Chris may go with the widow to visit the city and see the chapel.		52	65	78
The maid may go with them when they go to the city for the gowns.		52	65	78

52D

Timed Writings

1. Key a 1' timing on ¶ 1; determine *gwam*. Set new goal by adding 2–4 *gwam* to the rate attained; determine quarter-minute checkpoints from the chart at the left.
2. Key two 1' guided timings on ¶ 1 to increase speed. Practice ¶ 2 in the same way.
3. Key two 3' timings on ¶s 1 and 2 combined; determine *gwam* and the number of errors.

Quarter-Minute Checkpoints				
gwam	1/4'	1/2'	3/4'	Time
16	4	8	12	16
20	5	10	15	20
24	6	12	18	24
28	7	14	21	28
32	8	16	24	32
36	9	18	27	36
40	10	20	30	40

A all letters used

	gwam	1'	3'
Which of the states has the least number of people?		10	3
Few people realize that this state ranks first in coal,		21	7
fifth in natural gas, and seventh in oil production. Quite		33	11
a significant number of deer, antelope, and buffalo dwell		44	15
within the boundaries of this exquisite state. A major		55	18
portion of Yellowstone National Park is located in the		66	22
state. If you still don't know which state is being		77	26
described, it is Wyoming.		82	27
Wyoming is located in the western portion of the		92	31
United States. The state is bordered by six different		103	34
states. Plains, mountain ranges, and national parks make		114	38
up a vast portion of the landscape of the state. Several		126	42
million people come to the state each year to view the		137	46
beautiful landscape of this unique state. Visitors and		148	49
the extraction of natural resources make up a major portion		159	53
of the economy of the state.		165	55

gwam	1'	1	2	3	4	5	6	7	8	9	10	11	12
	3'		1			2			3			4	

Create Slides with SmartArt

Insert/Illustrations/
SmartArt

SmartArt. You have probably heard a picture is worth a thousand words. **SmartArt** can be used to present your ideas in graphic form with text (see below) and pictures (see 50B, slide 4 on p. 200) to more effectively communicate your message.

1. Learn how to insert SmartArt.
2. Open *df 48g pp.*
3. Key your name and current date on the title slide.
4. Complete the slide presentation by inserting SmartArt and keying the information on slides 2, 4, 9, and 11 as shown below.
5. Use Slide Show View to view the presentation.
6. **Save as:** *48g pp.*

Figure 9-39 Slide 2

Figure 9-40 Slide 4

Figure 9-41 Slide 9

Figure 9-42 Slide 11

UNIT 10   Enhance Input Skills

| Lesson 52 | Input Skill Development |
| Lesson 53 | Input Skill Development |

LESSON 52   Input Skill Development

OUTCOMES
- Build speed and accuracy.
- Enhance keying technique.

52A
Warmup

Key each line twice.

alphabet   1   Extensive painting of the gazebo was quickly completed by Jerome.

figures   2   At least 456 of the 3,987 jobs were cut before November 18, 2005.

speed   3   Keith and I may go to the island to dismantle the bicycle shanty.

gwam   1' | 1 | 2 | 3 | 4 | 5 | 6 | 7 | 8 | 9 | 10 | 11 | 12 | 13 |

52B
Technique: Letter Keys

Key each line twice. Focus on limiting keystroking movement to the fingers; keep the fingers curved and upright.

A   1   Katrina baked Marsha a loaf of bread to take to the Alameda fair.

B   2   Barbara and Bob Babbitt both saw the two blackbirds in the lobby.

C   3   Carl, the eccentric character with a classic crew cut, may catch.

D   4   David and Eddie dodged the duck as it waddled down the dark road.

E   5   Ellen needed Steven to help her complete the spreadsheet on time.

F   6   Before I left, Faye found forty to fifty feet of flowered fabric.

G   7   George and Greg thought the good-looking neighbor was gregarious.

H   8   John, Hank, and Sarah helped her haul the huge bush to the trash.

I   9   Michigan, Illinois, Indiana, and Missouri are all in the Midwest.

J   10   Jeff juggled jobs to join Jane for juice with the judge and jury.

K   11   Katie knocked the knickknacks off the kiosk with her knobby knee.

L   12   Please allow me to be a little late with all legal illustrations.

M   13   Mary is immensely immature; her mannerisms make me extremely mad.

gwam   1' | 1 | 2 | 3 | 4 | 5 | 6 | 7 | 8 | 9 | 10 | 11 | 12 | 13 |

LESSON 49   Tables, Graphs, and Charts

OUTCOMES
- Create tables, graphics, and charts to convey information in a presentation.
- Recognize which graph or chart to use for particular situations.
- Describe the key elements of graphs and charts.

49B

Create a Table

Home/Slides/New Slide/
Layout/Title and Content/
Insert Table

Tables. Tables can be used to organize information in presentations to compare and contrast facts or figures and to list data. Tables can be created in *PowerPoint*, or they can be created in *Word* or *Excel* and inserted into *PowerPoint*.

1. Open **df 49b decatur pp.**
2. Create a title slide using **FBLA Membership** for the main heading and **2008–2012** for the secondary heading, as shown in Figure 9-43.
3. Create a second slide titled **FBLA Membership by Year** using the Title and Content layout. Insert a table to include the information, as shown in Figure 9-44.
4. **Save as: 49b pp.**

Figure 9-43 Slide 1

Year	Members	+/- from Previous Year
2008	25	-
2009	32	7
2010	41	9
2011	53	12
2012	67	14

FBLA Membership by Year

Figure 9-44 Slide 2

49C

Learn Graph Elements

Graph Elements. Numeric information can be easier to understand when shown as a **graph** or **chart** rather than in text. The relationship between data sets or trends can be compared using bar graphs, line graphs, area graphs, or pie charts. Each type of graph or chart is best suited for a particular situation.

- **Bar and Column graph**—comparison of item quantities
- **Line graph**—quantity changes over time or distance
- **Pie chart**—parts of a whole

Elements common to most graphs are identified on the bar graph shown in Figure 9-45. They include:

- **X-axis**—the horizontal axis; usually for categories
- **Y-axis**—the vertical axis; usually for values
- **Scale**—numbers on the Y- or X-axis representing quantities
- **Tick marks**—coordinate marks on the graph to help guide the reader
- **Grids**—lines that extend from tick marks to make it easier to see data values

Complete this activity to help prepare for the **Business Presentation** event in FBLA-PBL's Marketing division. Participants in this event demonstrate their ability to deliver an effective business presentation while using presentation technology.

You will prepare a presentation of five to seven minutes on how businesses use social media to communicate with customers. The presentation should cover the following:

- Information on social media tools, such as social networks, blogs, and video sharing sites.
- Listing of specific social media sites. The listing should include the name and type of site, a brief description of the site and its users, the costs (if any) for using it, and the advantages and disadvantages of using the site.
  - Issues regarding privacy of the business's financial and other sensitive information.
  - Ways in which a business can use social media tools to communicate with customers.
  - Basics on how to implement a social media plan.

Gather information on the topics above. Start a new word processing document, and prepare a report on your findings. Note that one-and-a-half to two pages of single-spaced, 12-pt. type translates into about four minutes of speaking.

After you have written your report, create a slide show highlighting the main points. You should have at least three slides to support each of the topics in your report. Apply a design theme and other formatting. Add graphics, tables, and charts to enhance the slide information. Using the information you learned in this unit, practice the delivery of your presentation. As directed by your instructor, share the presentation with your class.

For detailed information on this event, go to www.fbla-pbl.org.

Think Critically

1. Why is thorough research so important to a successful presentation?
2. How can strong verbal communications and public speaking skills contribute to your academic as well as your career success?
3. What can you do while you are in school to develop your public speaking skills?

School and Community
Homelessness in America continues to be an issue of deep concern for many people. Some estimates indicate that there are more than 3 million people who do not have a place to call home, and close to half of them are children.

Many government agencies and nonprofit groups are working to address the issues of inadequate housing, poverty, and unemployment, which are the major causes of homelessness.

1. Research homelessness in your community. What is the estimated homeless population?
2. Identify the government offices and other organizations that exist to address the problem of homelessness.
3. Contact a homeless shelter or organization for helping the homeless in your community, and learn about the opportunities for volunteers in your age group.

- **Labels**—names used to identity parts of the graph
- **Legend**—the key that identifies the shading, coloring, or patterns used for the information shown in the graph

To change the design of the graph, click on the graph to select it. This activates the Chart Tools. The Chart Styles under the Design tab allow you to select from a variety of preset designs. Notice the difference between the appearances of the two graphs shown in Figure 9-45 when different designs are applied.

Locate the various graph elements in the bar chart below.

49D

Create Bar and Column Graphs

Design/Chart Style/ Style 34

Same slide with Chart Style 4 (Office 2013)

Same slide with Chart Style 42 (Office 2010)

Bar and Column Graphs. Bar and Column graphs compare one or more sets of data that are plotted on the horizontal X-axis and the vertical Y-axis. One axis usually contains category information (such as years or months); the other axis usually contains measured quantity values (numbers).

Vertical bars (columns) and horizontal bars (bars) are easy to interpret; the baseline scale should begin at zero for consistent comparisons when several graphs are used. Special effects can be added, but a simple graph is effective for showing relationships.

1. Learn how to create a column graph.
2. Open **49b pp** and add slide 3 with a Title and Content layout. Create the column graph as shown below for slide 3. Use the data from the table in 49b to create the column graph.
3. Change the Chart Style design.
4. **Save as:** **49d pp**.

Figure 9-45 Slide 3—Graph Elements

© iStockphoto.com/Neustockimages

Planning a Career in Health Science

When you hear about a career in "health science," you probably think of doctors, dentists, and nurses. But this field provides opportunities in many other occupations that focus on health, wellness, diagnosis, treatment, and research and development. In fact, health care is now the largest and fastest-growing industry in the United States.

What's It Like?

Individuals who work in this field are involved in planning, managing, and providing therapeutic services, diagnostic services, health information, support services, and biotechnology research and development. They might work directly with people, or they might be in a lab researching disease or collecting and analyzing data. In addition:

- They work with patients to rehabilitate muscle or bone injuries or educate them on how to reduce their risk for injuries.
- They examine and analyze body fluids and cells to help detect, diagnose, and treat diseases.
- They organize and manage patients' health information including medical history, symptoms, examination results, diagnostic tests, treatment methods, and all other health-care provider services.
- They combine their knowledge of biology and medicine with engineering principles and practices to design and develop devices, procedures, and systems that solve medical and health-related problems.
- They dispense prescription medicines, advise physicians about medication therapy, and counsel patients on the use of medications as well as general health topics such as diet, exercise, and stress management.

Employees in the health science field work in a variety of settings, from hospitals and doctor's offices to schools and research labs to sports arenas and cruise ships.

Employment Outlook

Employment in the health-care industry is projected to grow by almost 20 percent by 2014. And, according to the Bureau of Labor Statistics' *Occupational Outlook Handbook*, more than half of the top fastest-growing occupations will be in the health science area. Most employers prefer a four-year or advanced degree, although in some occupations, a two-year degree is acceptable. Many occupations have state and/or national licensure requirements.

What About You?

The Health Science career cluster is covered in box 8 of the Interest Survey Activity you completed in Unit 1 of this text. If this box had one of the three highest scores on your survey, you should further explore the cluster's pathways and related occupations.

Why do you think a career in this field could be a good choice? What skills can you develop now that would be helpful to a career in this field? Why do you think employment in this career cluster is growing so quickly?

Create Line Graph

Line graphs. Line graphs display changes in quantities over time or distance. Usually the X-axis shows a particular period of time or distance. The Y-axis shows measurements of quantity at different times or distances. The baseline of the Y-axis should be zero to provide a consistent reference point when several graphs are used in a presentation.

When the numbers for the X-axis are keyed, lines appear connecting the values on the graph to reflect the changes in amounts. A grid with vertical lines helps the viewer interpret quantities. Several sets of data can be displayed by using lines in different colors. Various options are available for placing titles, legends, and labels on line graphs.

1. Learn how to create a line graph.
2. Open **49d pp** and create the line graph shown in Figure 9-46 for slide 4, using Title and Content layout.

   - 2008   23
   - 2009   32
   - 2010   41
   - 2011   53
   - 2012   67

3. Change the Design Chart Style to Style 7 (Office 2013) or Style 42 (Office 2010).
4. **Save as:** *49e pp.*

Same slide with Chart
Style 42 (Office 2010)

Figure 9-46 Slide 4—Line graph with
Chart Style 7 (Office 2013)

Create Pie Chart

To create pie chart:

Home/New Slide/Title and
Content/Insert Chart/Pie

To change chart style:

Chart Tools/Design/Style 42

Pie Charts. Pie charts are best used to display parts of a whole. They show clearly the proportional relationship of only one set of values. The set of values cannot include negative numbers. Without any numbers displayed, the chart shows only general relationships. In the examples shown below, the different colors used for the pie slices are identified in a legend. Colors used on the pie chart should provide adequate contrast between the slices. Consider also the color scheme of your entire presentation so that the pie chart will coordinate with other visuals.

Pie Chart 1

1. Open **49e pp**.
2. Create the pie chart shown in Figure 9-47 as slide 5. Use Design Chart Style 42 and Centered Data Labels.

© VEER.COM/STILLFX

Academic and Career Connections

Complete the following exercises that introduce various topics that involve academic themes and careers.

Grammar and Writing: Abbreviations and Word Usage

MicroType 6

- References/Communication Skills/Abbreviations
- References/Communication Skills/Word Usage
- CheckPro/Communication Skills 7
- CheckPro/Word Choice 7

1. Go to *MicroType 6* and use this feature path for review: References/Communication Skills/Abbreviations.
2. Click *Rules* and review the rules of using abbreviations.
3. Then, under *Abbreviations*, click *Posttest*.
4. Follow the instructions to complete the posttest.
5. Repeat this process for Word Usage.

Optional Activities:

1. Go to this path: CheckPro/Communication Skills 7.
2. Complete the activities as directed.
3. Go to this path: CheckPro/Word Choice 7.
4. Key the Apply lines, and choose the correct word.

Communications: Reading

Open the document **df u09 communications**. Read the document carefully, and then close the file. Create a new presentation and apply a design theme of your choice. Insert a title slide and key the title **Habitat for Humanity**. Key your name as the subtitle. Insert a slide for each of the following questions. Key the question on the slide. Below the question, key your answer in a complete sentence. Select an appropriate slide layout, and apply formatting of your choice.

1. Who founded the organization Habitat for Humanity International?
2. What motivated the founder to start the organization?
3. What is the basic mission of Habitat for Humanity?
4. Habitat is not a giveaway program. When Habitat works on a home, what are the partner family's financial obligations? What other obligation does the family have?
5. Habitat for Humanity operates at the grassroots level. What does this mean?
6. Save the presentation as **u09 communications**.

Math Skills: Markups and Discounts

1. Will is a pharmacist who operates a small drugstore. In order to achieve a targeted level of gross profits (sales revenue minus product costs) to cover his fixed expenses—such as rent, utilities, and payroll—he needs to determine how much he should mark up his products. For example, if he expects to sell $2.5 million of products (based on cost) and he needs to produce gross profits of $500,000 to cover fixed expenses, how much does he have to mark up his products, on average, to achieve that target?
2. Will's drugstore has just signed up to participate in a health-care discount program. Although he does not know yet exactly how many customers will sign up to be club members, he expects that purchases on average will earn a 4 percent discount. How much will that reduce the store's projected sales revenue?
3. If he wanted to make up for the discounts, how much would Will now have to mark up his products to achieve his target of $500,000 in gross profits?

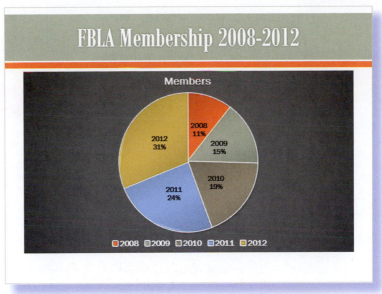

Figure 9-47 Slide 5—Pie Chart, Style 7 (Office 2013)

Pie Chart 2

1. In Normal View, copy the small slide 5 in the left pane and paste it beneath slide 5.
2. With slide 6 active, click on the pie chart and change the chart to 3-D Pie format with Chart Style 7 (Office 2013) or *Exploded pie in 3-D* format with Chart Style 42 (Office 2010). Use the commands shown at the left.
3. **Save as:** *49f pp.*

Figure 9-48 Slide 6—3-D Pie (Office 2013)

Slide 5

Slide 6

Slide 7

Slide 8

www.cengage.com/school
/keyboarding/c21key

Figure 9-51 Slides for Lesson 51B presentation

21st Century Skills: Media Literacy

Think about the various ways you receive information. In addition to classroom lectures and studies, you might watch a television show, listen to a radio broadcast, browse the Web, or read a magazine. As you process the information you receive daily, you form impressions and make interpretations and judgments. Consciously—or subconsciously—the many messages you process every day influence the decisions you make and have a significant impact on the way you live your life.

Think Critically

1. Think of an advertisement you have recently seen or heard. Where did you see or hear the ad? What was being advertised? How did the ad influence your opinion of the advertiser? Would you make a purchase based on the ad?

2. Create a presentation about one of your favorite products (e.g., a brand of clothing or shoes or a favorite food or drink). Include at least five slides that identify the product, who makes it, the target market, the format in which you saw it advertised (print, broadcast, Web, etc.), and the key features of the product that convinced you to buy it. Save the presentation as *u09 21century*.

3. Present the slide show to your class as directed by your instructor. As a class, discuss the appeal of the product and why consumers with different demographic characteristics (such as age, gender, race, income level, etc.) would or would not buy it.

Create and Deliver a Presentation

• Create a presentation.
• Deliver a presentation.

50B

Create a Presentation

A slide presentation has been started on the student exchange programs available through your school. Open *df 50a pp* and finish the slide presentation by creating the slides that have not already been created (see slides 1 through 16 in Figure 9-49 below). The additional photos that you will need to complete the slides are in *df 50b pp*.

The flag clip art can be copied and pasted from the already-completed slides. To get the picture effect for the photos, click the photo to activate the Picture Tools feature. Then, in the Picture Styles group, click the down arrow to the right of the photos and select Rotated White. Paste a copy of the beginning slide at the end of the presentation so that slide will appear rather than a black screen when you finish delivering the presentation.

Save as: *50b pp*.

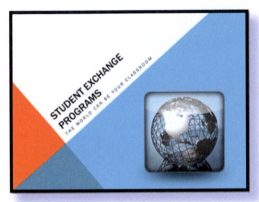

Slide 1—Title slide

Slide 2—Title and content with SmartArt

Slide 3—Title and content (table) with clip art

Slide 4—Title and content (SmartArt) with clip art and pictures

Slide Show Assessment

- Assess slide show creation skills.

1. Open *df 51b apothecary pp*. Create the slides shown below. Choose other appropriate clip are if the art shown isn't available with your software.

   Slide 1: Title slide

   Slide 2: Section header

   Slides 3–8: Title and content slides

2. **Save as:** *51b pp*.

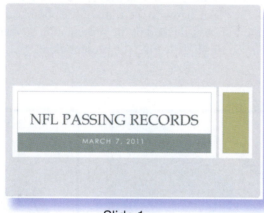

Slide 1

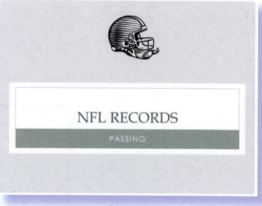

Slide 2

CAREER PASSING RECORDS FOR:

- Highest Passer Rating (1,500 attempts)
- Most Touchdown Passes
- Most Passing Yards
- Most Interceptions Thrown
- Most Passes Attempted

Slide 3

HIGHEST PASSER RATING

Aaron Rodgers 98.4%	• Green Bay
Philip Rivers 97.2%	• San Diego
Steve Young 96.8%	• Tampa Bay • San Francisco

Slide 4

Slide 5—Title Only with pictures

Slide 6—Title Only with pictures

Slide 7—Title Only with pictures

Slide 8—Title Only with pictures

Slide 9—Title Only with pictures

Slide 10—Title Only with pictures

	Excellent	Good	Need(s) Improvement	Comments
The introduction to the topic is				
The body of the presentation is				
The visual aids are				
The speaker's ability to use the visual aids is				
The speaker's enthusiasm is				
The speaker's eye contact is				
The speaker's gestures are				
The speaker's confidence is				
The speaker's vocal variation is				
The speaker's facial expressions are				
The closing is				

Figure 9-50 Presentation evaluation form

© iStockphoto.com/Sean Locke

Digital Citizenship and Ethics
The rules governing appropriate and courteous behavior while you are online are called **netiquette**. Think of netiquette as online manners—the way you should behave as you surf the Web or correspond via e-mail, text messaging, and chats.

You might already know some netiquette rules. For example, you should not send e-mails or text messages in all caps because it implies shouting. Long and wordy postings on discussion groups and forums are another no-no. Sarcasm should be avoided because readers may not pick up on it without the benefit of hearing the tone of your voice or seeing your facial expressions. Don't flood your friends' mailboxes with "funny" messages or cute pictures you've found online. And don't start **flame wars**—hostile, insulting arguments meant to cause trouble rather than discuss issues.

You can find out more about netiquette rules online. Go to your favorite search engine and key *netiquette*.

As a class, discuss the following.

1. People commonly use online slang as well as emoticons in personal messages they exchange with friends. Do you think it is appropriate to use slang and emoticons in professional correspondence? Why or why not?
2. Why is it important to avoid using sarcasm, cynicism, or a joking, flippant tone in electronic messages?

Slide 11—Title Only with pictures

Photo Courtesy of the Author

Slide 12—Title Only with pictures

Photo Courtesy of the Author

Slide 13—Title Only with pictures

Photo Courtesy of the Author

Slide 14—Title Only with pictures

Photo Courtesy of the Author

Slide 15—Title Only with pictures

Photo Courtesy of the Author

Slide 16—Title Only with pictures

Photo Courtesy of the Author

Figure 9-49 Slides for Lesson 50b presentation

50C

Create a Presentation

TEAMWORK

Work with two other students to plan a presentation based on the slides you created in 50B. Each student will be responsible for gathering information about two of the following countries:

- China
- France
- Italy
- Japan
- Switzerland
- United States

Use the Internet or reference books to learn more about each of the countries. Gather information about culture differences among the countries as well as significant sites to visit in each country. Write speaker notes based on your research.

Decide which group member's slides from 50B your group will use for the presentation. Add speaker notes to the presentation after you gather information about the countries by clicking beneath each slide in the *Click to add notes* box.

Divide the presentation among the group members so that each member has an equal part of the presentation. Then read the information below about presentation delivery, and study the evaluation form.

50D

Deliver a Presentation

Planning and preparing a presentation is only half the task of giving a good presentation. The other half is the delivery. Positive thinking is a must for a good presenter. Prepare and practice before the presentation. This will help you be confident that you can do a good job. Don't worry that the presentation will not be perfect. Set a goal of being a better speaker each time you present, not of being a perfect speaker each time. Practice these tips to improve your presentation skills.

- **Know your message.** Knowing the message well allows you to talk with the audience rather than read to them.
- **Look at the audience.** Make eye contact with one person briefly (for two to three seconds). Then move on to another person.
- **Look confident.** Stand erect and show that you want to communicate with the audience. Avoid unnecessary movement.
- **Let your personality come through.** Be natural; let the audience know who you are. Show your enthusiasm for the topic you are presenting.
- **Vary the volume and rate at which you speak.** Slow down to emphasize points. Speed up on points that you are sure your audience is familiar with. Don't be afraid to pause. It gives greater impact to your message and allows your audience time to think about what you have said.
- **Use gestures and facial expressions.** A smile, frown, or puzzled look, when appropriate, can help communicate your message. Make sure your gestures are natural.
- **Know how to use the visuals.** Practice using the visual aids you have chosen for the presentation. Glance briefly at each visual as you display it; then focus back on the audience.

Practice your presentation with your group members. After the first person presents his or her part, the other two members should offer suggestions on how the first presenter can improve. Suggestions should include comments based on the evaluation form (shown in Figure 9-50 and also provided in the file *df 50d eval form*). After providing feedback to the first presenter, the other group members should present their parts and receive feedback. Your instructor may ask you to present to the class.

GLOSSARY

A

active cell the selected cell in a worksheet; it has a thick border

active window window the user can work in

agenda a list of topics to be discussed or actions to be taken, usually at a meeting

antivirus software commercial software that protects a computer system from viruses and malware

application letter a one-page personal-business letter that always accompanies a résumé

application programs software that provides instructions for accomplishing a specific type of task, such as creating a word processing document, sending e-mail, or finding information on the Web

Attachment/Enclosure notation if another document is attached to a letter, the word *Attachment* is keyed at the left margin; if the additional document is not attached, the word *Enclosure* is used

AutoCorrect software feature that detects and corrects *some* typing, spelling, and capitalization errors automatically

AutoFit Contents software feature that automatically resizes table column widths based on the text in each column

AutoFit Window software feature that automatically resizes a table so it begins and ends evenly at the left and right margins

B

bar and column graph type of graph that compares item quantities

bit the most basic unit of data stored or processed by a computer, and it must be either a 1 or a 0, which basically correspond to an On or Off state in the computer's electronic circuits

block letter format commonly used format in which all letter parts begin at the left margin

blog a type of Web page dedicated to the owner's frequent updates on a particular topic

body message of a letter

Bold software feature that prints text darker than regular copy

browser a software application that allows a computer user to view online documents and graphical content on websites created with HTML

bullet special character used to add visual interest or emphasis to text in a list

business letter letter typically printed on letterhead stationery (stationery that has a preprinted return address)

byte a unit of data typically composed of a group of 8 bits

C

Calendar PIMS feature for keeping track of schedules

cell intersection of a column and a row

chart sheet chart that appears on a separate worksheet

chart titles headings that identify chart contents and the X-axis and/or Y-axis

click tap the left mouse button once and let go

Close button closes a window and shuts down the open application

cloud computing software and files are stored on remote computers and accessed through the Internet rather than residing on an individual user's computer

columns vertical lists of data in a table that are labeled alphabetically from left to right; also, vertical sections in a worksheet; each column has a heading (letters from A to Z, AA to AZ, etc.) running left to right across the worksheet

communications programs software used to communicate on the Web

complimentary close the farewell portion of a letter

computer virus damaging computer code or program sent to computers via a downloaded file that the receiver opens; other types of attacks include Trojan horses and malware

confidentiality maintaining the privacy of business information pertaining to a project, service, or product

Contacts PIMS feature for maintaining information needed to contact others

Copy software feature that copies the selected text so it can be placed in another location (pasted), leaving the original text unchanged

Copy notation indicates that a copy of the letter is being sent to someone other than the addressee

copyright the laws that govern the use of other people's original work; a user must seek permission from the owner or author of the content before reusing it on a website or for a personal or school project

Cut software feature that removes selected text from the current location

cyber predator someone who uses the Internet to hunt for victims whom they take advantage of in many ways, such as sexually, emotionally, psychologically, or financially

cyberbullying using online communications to harass or upset someone by sending hateful, humiliating, or threatening messages or photos

D

data labels numbers or words that identify values displayed in the chart

data type determines the kinds of values that can be displayed in a database field

database an organized collection of facts and figures (information)

Decimal tabs align all text at the decimal point or any other specified character

design theme software feature that provides a consistent, attractive look to a presentation

desktop primary screen and main work area of an operating system

distribution enables the computer to share information with computers and other users, typically across a network

documentation notes used to give credit for published material (electronic as well as printed) that is quoted or closely paraphrased

domain last portion (after the period) of the website address or URL, such as .com, .org, or .edu

double-click tap the left mouse button twice quickly and let go

drag press and hold down the left mouse button and move the pointer to another location

E

e-commerce conducting business online

e-learning a popular and accessible way for learners at all levels to take classes and further their academic pursuits; also called online education

electronic presentations computer-generated visual aids (usually slide shows) that can be used to help communicate information

electronic résumés résumés that are attached to e-mail or posted to a company Web page or Internet job search site

ellipsis set of three periods, each preceded and followed by a space, that is used to indicate material omitted from a quotation

e-mail electronic mail

e-mail attachments documents and files that can be sent with e-mail

e-mail tags reminders that can be placed on e-mail messages in an inbox to mark them as unread, to categorize them, or to mark them for follow-up

embedded chart chart that appears as an object in the worksheet along with the chart data

employment documents provide applicants an opportunity to present their best qualities to prospective employers

ergonomics using proper posture and well-designed office furniture to avoid repetitive stress injuries such as carpal tunnel syndrome or pain in your back, shoulders, or neck when using the computer

extension part of a file name after the period that indicates what kind of a file it is

F

fair use the law that allows some material to be used without permission if the user is quoting only a small amount of content for a purpose such as research or criticism, not for profit

fields the columns in a database; in a database form, the blanks in which information is entered are called fields

file-sharing technology that allows users to search for and copy files from someone else's computer (also called "peer-to-peer" or P2P technology)

Filter database feature used to display specific records in a table instead of all the records

follow-up letter a thank-you to each person that had a significant role in your interview

footnote method of documentation in which the reference is identified with a superscript number in the text and the complete documentation for the reference appears at the bottom of the page with the same superscript

Format Painter software feature that quickly copies formatting from one place to another

forms used to enter and display database information

formulas perform calculations on the numbers in spreadsheet cells; formulas typically begin with an equals sign (=)

freeware commercial or privately developed software that can be downloaded from the Internet and used for free

functions built-in predefined formulas

G

gigabyte just over a billion bytes

graphics images that can enhance a message and help convey ideas; can include clip art, photos, or scanned original artwork

gridlines borders around cells in a table; they may or may not be printed; also, lines through a chart that identify intervals on the axes

grids lines that extend from tick marks to make it easier to see data values

gwam gross words a minute; the number of standard words keyed in one minute

H

hanging indent moves all but the first line of a paragraph one tab stop to the right

hard page break the end of a page and the beginning of a new page; inserted manually at any point where a new page must begin before the current one is full

hard return tapping Enter to return the insertion point to the left margin and move it down to the next line

headings row numbers and column letters

Help software component that provides a user's manual on how to use the application

home keys the keys where you place your fingers to begin keying: f d s a for the left hand and j k l ; for the right hand

Hyphenation software feature that automatically divides (hyphenates) words that would normally wrap to the next line; this evens the right margin, making the text more attractive

I

icons small picture symbols that identify computer programs, features, and documents

identity theft malicious attack in which someone obtains personal information such as Social Security number, bank account information, personal data, and job information for the purpose of stealing or impersonating the victim online

input the raw data you enter into the computer

insert default insertion method for keying text in a document; newly keyed text appears at the position of the insertion point and existing text moves to the right

Insert Date & Time software feature that inserts the date and/or time in a document

instant messaging (chat) a Web service that allows users to communicate in real time

Internet the global network of computers that connects millions of networks and computers around the world

Internet service provider (ISP) company that provides a connection to the Internet on a user's computer

Italic software feature that prints letters that slope up toward the right

K

keyword search techniques used in a search engine to quickly find information

L

labels letters and/or symbols (with or without numbers) that are keyed into a spreadsheet cell; the label status is assigned automatically and the data is left-aligned; also, the names used to identity parts of a graph

landscape orientation text is printed on a page with the wider edge of the paper at the top

layout the way text and graphics are arranged

leadership the ability to motivate other people to follow you toward a common goal

left indent moves the first line of a paragraph one tab stop to the right, away from the left margin

left tabs align all text evenly at the left by placing it to the right of the tab setting

legend a key (usually with different colors or patterns) used to identify the categories and information in a chart or graph

line graph type of graph that shows changes in quantity over time or distance

Line Spacing software feature that changes the amount of vertical white space between lines of text

local area network (LAN) relatively small network of computers, such as in a home or at a school

M

margin the amount of blank space at the top, bottom, right, and left edges of the paper

Maximize button enlarges a window to take up the entire screen

meeting minutes written records of what was discussed and decided at a meeting

megabyte approximately one million bytes

menu bar bar that typically appears at the top of an application window and provides software functions and commands

Merge software feature that is often used to merge a letter file (main document) with a name and address file (data source) to create a personalized letter (merged file) to each person in the data source file

Merge Cells software feature that joins two or more adjacent table cells in the same row or column into one cell

Minimize button reduces a window to a button on the taskbar; useful for multitasking (performing more than one task at a time)

mixed punctuation a colon after the salutation and a comma after the complimentary close

Modern Language Association (MLA)style report style often used to document and format student papers

mouse a peripheral device for getting around the desktop and operating the computer via a pointer on the screen

N

netiquette simple rules of common courtesy for communicating online

network two or more computers connected by either a cable or a wireless connection

Normal View—Outline used for creating and editing individual slides, outlining, and creating notes

Normal View—Slides used for creating and editing individual slides, viewing miniatures of slides that have already been created, and creating notes

Notes Page View used to create and edit speaker notes and to see how the notes will look prior to printing

Notes PIMS feature for recording reminders

O

online applications (online apps) software that resides online rather than on a user's computer; used to accomplish specific tasks such as finding directions, browsing multimedia content, sending e-mail, or creating office documents such as presentations and spreadsheets

online scams bogus financial offers or sweepstakes designed to obtain personal information, persuade the victim to give money, or sell something illegal

open punctuation no punctuation after the salutation or complimentary close

open-source software the software code is available for users to develop their own applications for it and to distribute it according to the terms of a license

operating system the software program that provides the interface between the user and the computer and manages the various devices and data used by the computer

orphan line the first line of a paragraph that appears at the bottom of a page by itself

output results of a computer process, which may be displayed on a screen, printed on a report, played over speakers as sound, or sent via a network link to another computer

overtype insertion method that allows you to replace (type over) current text with newly keyed text

P

Paste software feature that places cut or copied text at another location

peripheral the various external hardware parts and components of a computer system, such as the monitor, printer, scanner, speakers, disk drives, etc.

personal information manager software (PIMS) provides a way for individuals to manage their information and to be personally and professionally organized

personal-business letter letter written by an individual to deal with business of a personal nature; typically printed on personal stationery that does not have a preprinted return address

phishing computer scam in which the victim receives an official-looking e-mail that appears to be from a bank or other financial institution; the e-mail says there is a problem with an account and asks the user to provide an account number, Social Security number, password, or some other personal information

pie chart type of graph that shows parts of a whole; the proportional relationship of one set of values

pinned programs programs that you use regularly, so they have a shortcut icon on the Start menu

piracy sharing or downloading copyrighted material without paying for it

plagiarism using someone else's work without credit or portraying it as your own

point move the mouse (roll it on the work surface) so that the pointer (the arrow that represents the mouse's position on the screen) points to an item

portrait orientation text is printed on a page with the short edge of the paper at the top

primary key used to identify each record in the database table with a number

primary sort the first sort

Print Preview software feature that shows what a document will look like when it is printed

print résumés résumés that are printed on paper and mailed to prospective employers

process computer is performing some action to manipulate data

public domain some published content may be used without permission if it is part of the public domain—generally content that is more than 75 years old

Q

queries questions used for drawing information from one or more database tables

R

RAM (random-access memory) memory used for temporary storage while the computer is processing data

range a set of spreadsheet cells identified by the cell in the upper-left corner and the cell in the lower-right corner, usually separated by a colon

Reading View presents each slide one at a time; the status bar stays active, allowing you to see which slide number you are viewing and to view the previous slide or the next slide by clicking the arrows on the status bar

records the rows in a database

Redo software feature that reverses the last Undo action

reference initials if someone other than the originator of the letter keys it, his/her initials are keyed in lowercase letters at the left margin below the writer's name and/or title

reference list document provided to a prospective employer that gives the name, address, telephone number, and e-mail address (if the person uses e-mail) of three to six people (not relatives) who know you well

reports used to summarize and present database information

Restore Down button replaces the Maximize button when the window is maximized; clicking this button restores the window to a smaller size

résumé document that presents information to a prospective employer

Ribbon part of an application interface that provides a convenient way to organize toolbar icons according to the type of task the user is currently doing

Ribbon tab the Ribbon is organized by tabs that include icons for commands relating to a particular feature or task

right tabs align all text evenly at the right by placing it to the left of the tab setting

right-click tap the right mouse button once and let go

ROM (read-only memory) long-term memory that resides in the computer and is used for programs that run when the computer is started up; it cannot be easily accessed or changed

router hardware that directs information in a network

rows horizontal lists of data that are labeled numerically from top to bottom; also, horizontal sections in a worksheet; each row has a heading (a number) running from top to bottom at the left side of the worksheet

S

salutation the greeting portion of a letter

scale numbers on the Y- or X-axis representing quantities

scroll bar allows the user to display more material than the monitor can show at once by moving vertically or horizontally

secondary sort the second sort

selecting clicking with a mouse to make something active

server hardware that houses vast databases of information in a network

shareware copyrighted commercial software that you can use on a trial basis before deciding to purchase it; downloaded from the Internet

Slide Show View used to see how the slides will look during a presentation; helpful for rehearsing and presenting a slide show

Slide Sorter View shows all the slides in miniature; helpful for rearranging slides and for applying features to several slides at a time

SmartArt software feature that is used to present ideas in graphic form with text

social network a Web application such as Facebook or Twitter that allows a user to connect with friends, family, and colleagues

soft page break the end of a page and the beginning of a new page; automatically inserted by the software when the current page is full (when the bottom margin is reached)

software instructions that tell the computer what to do with data; a general term used to describe computer programs such as applications and operating systems

Sort software feature that arranges text in alphabetical order and numbers in numerical order

source document a paper form from which data is keyed

spam unwanted, unsolicited e-mail messages such as promotions for businesses or chain letters

special documents a variety of documents other than letters, tables, and reports that are created using word processing software

Spelling & Grammar Check software feature that checks a document for misspellings and grammar errors

Split Cells software feature that divides adjacent table cells into multiple cells and columns

spreadsheet software computer program used to record, report, and analyze information, especially information that relates to numbers

standard word in keyboarding, five characters or any combination of five characters and spaces

Start menu Windows menu on the desktop where programs and documents can be easily found and opened

style collection of format settings for font, font size, color, paragraph spacing, alignment, and so on that are named and stored together in a style set

system utilities (utility software) software that keeps the computer running well and performs routine tasks associated with file maintenance

T

table an arrangement of data (words and/or numbers) in rows and columns; also, format used to enter and store database information

Tasks PIMS feature for recording items that need to be done

template a master file with a set of predefined styles for a particular type of document; it may contain text and formatting for margins, line spacing, colors, borders, styles, themes, etc.

textual citation method of documentation in which the name(s) of the author(s), the date of the referenced publication, and the page number(s) of the material are placed in parentheses at the appropriate point in the text

Thesaurus software feature that finds synonyms or antonyms for a selected word

tick marks coordinate marks on the graph to help guide the reader

toolbar part of an application interface that lets the user choose commands quickly and easily by tapping icons or buttons

U

unbound reports short reports that are prepared without binders; if they consist of more than one page, the pages are usually fastened together in the upper-left corner by a staple or paper clip

Underline software feature that underlines text as it is keyed

Undo software feature that reverses the last change made

uniform resource locator (URL) unique website address

V

value numerical data that is to be used in calculations in a spreadsheet; when only numbers are keyed into a cell, the value status is assigned automatically and the data is right-aligned

W

wide area network (WAN) large network of computers, such as a whole city

widow line the last line of a paragraph that appears by itself at the top of a page

Windows Explorer application that shows a computer's files and folders in a hierarchical or tree view

workbook a workbook contains one or more worksheets, usually related

worksheet one spreadsheet file; all worksheets in a workbook appear as tabs at the bottom of the screen

World Wide Web the system of sites, documents, and graphical content hosted on Internet servers

X

X-axis the horizontal axis; usually for categories

Y

Y-axis the vertical axis; usually for values

Z

Zoom software feature that increases or decreases the amount of the page appearing on the screen

INDEX

A key, control of, 34

Abbreviations, state and territory, 396

Academic and career connections: abbreviations and word usage, 207; capitalization, 30; central tendency, measures, 324; commas, 101; composition, 30, 154, 256; internal punctuation and semicolons, other, 177; listening, 84, 177, 288; math skills, 31, 84, 101, 119, 154, 178, 207, 234; mental math, 288; modifiers, 324; number expression, 119; probability, 234; pronoun agreement/case, 288; proofreading, 234; punctuations, terminal, 84; quotation marks/italics, 154; reading, 101, 207, 324; semicolons, 177; sentence types, 234; simple interest, 256; speaking, 119, 234; spelling, 324; subject-verb agreement, 256; word usage, 207

Active cell, spreadsheets, 240

Address block, mail merge, 283

Addresses: block style, 128; on envelopes, 396; international, 396

Adjacency design theme, in electronic presentations, 184

Adjacent keys, 68

Advanced WP skills, 236

Agenda: template, 260, 400

Alphanumeric keys, 402

ALT key, 402

Angles design theme, in electronic presentations, 185

Apostrophe (') key, 80

Apostrophes, 389; appearance on computer, 80

Apothecary design theme, in electronic presentations, 184

Application: forms, 279–280, 401; letters, 278–279, 287, 401; software, 6

Attachment/enclosure notations, 130; in interoffice memo, 259; in personal-business letter, 130

AutoFit contents, 159, 163

AutoFit window, 163

B key, control of, 60

Backspace key, 76, 402

Balanced-hand: phrases, 88; sentences, 73, 123; words, 65, 73, 88

Banners, in electronic presentations, 192

Bar graph, in electronic presentations, 196–197

Black tie design theme, in electronic presentations, 185

Blind copy notation (Bcc), e-mail messages, 393

Block arrows, in electronic presentations, 192

Blog, 25

Body: of e-mail messages, 105, 393; of interoffice memo, 259; in personal-business letter, 130

Bound reports, 397

Bulleted list: with clip art in electronic presentations, 191; with photo in electronic presentations, 192

Bullets, 134

Business card, special documents, 271

Business letter: arranged copy, 144; block style, 146; envelope, 149–153; model copy, 142; revised copy, 147; unarranged copy, 145

Business letters, block style: assessment, 354; with specialized features, 394; two page, 395

Business letters, modified block format: with list, 395; with postscript, 395; second-page heading, 395

Business Professionals of America (BPA), 32

C key, control of, 55

Calculator, accessing, 375

Calendar, for personal information management, 107

Callouts in electronic presentations, 192

Capitalization, 388; first word of a complete sentence following a colon, 71

Caps lock, 74, 402; release of, 74

Career clusters, 31; agriculture, food, and natural resources, 289; audio/video technology and communications, 235; business management and administration, 85; finance, 257; government and public administration, 325; health science, 208; hospitality and tourism, 179; information technology, 102; marketing, 120; science, technology, engineering, and mathematics, 155

Carpel tunnel syndrome (CTS), 403

CD-ROM drive, 402

Cells: column, 157; content in spreadsheets, 247; range selection, 243; row, 157; select and edit cell content, 242; in spreadsheets, 239

Central processing unit (CPU), 402

Century 21 skills: access information, 96; communicate clearly, 110; creativity and innovation, 287; entrepreneurial literacy, 148; ICT literacy, 168; judgments and decisions, 228; leadership, 29; media literacy, 206; productivity and accountability, 255; use and manage information, 303

Century 21 style report documentation, 399

Certificates, 260; template, 269

Charts, spreadsheets, 252–253; assessment, 361; layout and styles, 253; type, 252

Clear and delete cell content and format, spreadsheets, 243

Clip art: in electronic presentations, 191

Cloud computing, 25

Colon (:) key, control of, 71

Colons, 389; space twice after colon when used as punctuation, 71

Columns: in spreadsheets, 239, 241, 245–246; in tables, 157

Comma (,) key, control of, 67

Commas, 389

Communications programs, 6–7

Complimentary close, 129

Computer basics: charm bar, 10–11; hardware basics, 4–5; importance of, 1–2; process information, 2–3; search engines, 26; software basics, 5–7; technology, choosing, 8–9

Computer ethics and safety: antivirus software, 28; backup, 27; browser, 24; computer virus, 28; copyright law, 27; cyberbullying, 27; ergonomics, 29; identity theft, 28; internet, 24; plagiarism, 28; routers, 24; spam, 27

Computer, keyboard arrangement, 402

Confusing words, 392

Contacts feature, for personal information management, 108–109

Copy: in spreadsheets, 244

Copy notation (Cc): e-mail messages, 130, 393

Copyright, 165

Cover page: assessment, 360; WP, 223

Credit line, 27

CTRL key, in document navigation, 402

Cyber predator, 139

D   key, control of, 34

Dash, 389

Database: adding new fields to table, 314–316, 321; add records to existing, 301–307; add records to form, 304; add records to table, 303, 309; add records to update, 311–312; assessment, 319–323, 364; autonumber, 294; components, 292; create filters/queries, 318, 319; create new database and table, 308–310, 319–320; datasheet/design view, 293; data type, 294; date and time, 294; defined, 291; description field, 294; design/applications, 326; edit records, 314, 322; fields, 292, 295; filter, 300; forms, 292, 295, 304, 313; multiple sort, 299; navigate within tables and forms, 313; new, creation, 308–310, 319–320; number, 294; preview, 300; primary sort, 299; queries, 292, 295–296; records, 292, 295, 301–302; reports, 292, 297; secondary sort, 299; sort, 298; sort information, 317–318, 323; tables, 292–295, 298

Database design/applications, 326

Data source: mail merge, 282–284

Date: block style, 128; in personal-business letter, 128

Decimal tabs, 135

Delivery address, for envelopes, 396

Del key, 402

Design themes: in electronic presentations, 182, 190

Desktop publishing, 290

Diagram, special documents, 271, 285

Digital citizenship/ethics, 19, 82, 94, 118, 139, 165, 204; cell phone etiquette, 238; e-learning, 300; file-sharing, 223; Internet activities, 270; piracy, 223

Documentation in reports: Century 21 style, 399; Modern Language Association style, 399

Double letters, 68, 91, 125–126

E   key, control of, 41

Electronic presentations, 181–209; adjacency/angles/apothecary design theme, 184; assessment, 205–206, 356–357; bar graph, 196–197; basic shapes, 192; block arrows, 192; bulleted list with photo/clip art, 191–192; clip art, 191; defined, 181; deliver a slide presentation, 200, 203; design theme, 182; equation shapes, 192; features of, 181; flowchart shapes, 192; graphs and charts, 196–199; grid/kilter design theme, 184; layouts, 183; line and area graph, 196; lines, 192; normal view, 199; perspective design theme, 184; photos, 192; pie chart, 196–199; section header layout, 183; shapes, 192; slide layouts, 183; slide presentation, 200; slide presentation, evaluation, 200; slide show/sorter view, 185; slide with shapes/clip art, 194; stars, banners, and callouts, 192; tables, 196; template design, 190; thatch design theme, 184; title and content bulleted list, 188; title and content layout, 183; title slide, 188; title slide layout, 183; view options/presentation, 185, 188

Electronic resumes, 274, 276, 286, 401

E-mail messages, 105, 393–394; address list, 393; attachments, 105; blind copy notation (Bcc), 393; body, 105, 393; copy notation (Cc), 393; formatting, 111–114; heading, 105, 393; inbox, 106; in personal information management, 104; review, 350; sent copies, 105; signature, 393; special features, 393; tags, 106

Employment application form/letter, 401

Employment documents, 260, 274–281, 401

Enter key, 35, 36, 44, 50, 52, 59, 66, 87, 402

Envelopes, 396; delivery address, 396; in personal-business letter, block style, 130; return address, 128, 396; size of, 396

Equation shapes, in electronic presentations, 192

Esc key, 402

Exclamation point, 390

F   key, control of, 34

Fields: adding new to table, 314–316, 321; database, 292, 295

Files and folders, managing: grouping, 22; quick access toolbar, 21

File-sharing, 223

Files, in mail merge, 283

Filter, database, 300

Flowchart shapes, in electronic presentations, 192

Flyers, special documents, 272–273, 285, 363

Format painter, 161

Format references, 394–401; agenda, 400; bound report, 397; business letter in block format with specialized features, 394; business letter in modified block format with list, 395; business letter in modified block format with postscript, 395; business letter showing second-page heading, 395; electronic resume, 401; employment application form/letter, 401; envelope guides, 396; interoffice memo, 394; interoffice memo with special features, 395; itinerary, 400; meeting minutes, 400; MLA report, 398; MLA report with works cited page, 398; news release, 400; personal business letter with open punctuation, 394; print resume, 401; reference pages, 397; report documentation, 399; with special features, 395; title page, 398; unbound reports, 397

Forms, database, 292, 295, 304, 313
Formula bar, spreadsheets, 239
Function keys, 402
Functions, spreadsheets, 250
Future Business Leaders of America-Phi Beta Lambda
    (FBLA-PBL), 32

G **key,** control of, 49
Grammar Check, 131
Grammar guides, 391
Graphics, in electronic presentations, 191
Graphs/charts, 196–199; bar, 196–197; in electronic presentations,
    196; grids, 196; labels, 197; legend, 197; line and area graphs,
    196; pie, 198–199; scale, 196; tick marks, 196; X-axis, 196;
    Y-axis, 196
Greeting line, mail merge, 284
Grid design theme, in electronic presentations, 184
Gridlines: spreadsheets, 241
Grids, graphs and charts, 196
Guided timings, 91, 123–124

H **key,** control of, 41
Hanging indent, WP, 220–221
Hard page break, WP, 219
Hard return, 35
Headings: in e-mail messages, 105, 393; in interoffice memo, 259
Help, 93; assessment, 352; contents, table, 93; manufacturer's
    website, 93; menu in, 93; online training, 99; pop-up description
    feature, 97; screen tips, 97, 98; size and location of Help box, 94
HJP Communications Specialists, 332–349
Home keys (fdsa jkl;) position, 33–34, 38
Horizontal alignment: tables, 158
Hyphenation, 131
Hyphen (-) key, 80
Hyphens, 390

I **key,** control of, 43
Identity theft, 28
Inbox, e-mail messages, 106
Information, communications, and technology (ICT), 168
Input skills, 210–214, 327–331; assessment, 353, 358; keying
    technique, 87, 125, 210–214, 327–331; speed and accuracy,
    building, 87, 125
Insert endnote/footnote, WP, 222
Ins key, 402
International addresses, 396
Internet service provider (ISP), 25
Interoffice memo, 259; assessment, 362, 394; body, 129; template,
    265–266
Interview follow-up letter, 281
Invitations, 260; template, 269

Italics: for play titles, 390
Itinerary, 400

J **key,** control of, 34

K **key,** control of, 34
Keyboard arrangement on computer, 402
Keyboards, ergonomic, 404
Keyboard technique, 41
Key formulas, spreadsheets, 249
Keying position/speed, 34, 126
Keying technique, 87, 122, 210–214, 327–331, 368–369
Keystroking, 35
Keyword search, 26
Kilter design theme, in electronic presentations, 184

L **key,** control of, 34
Labels: in graphs and charts, 197; spreadsheets, 241
Landscape orientation: tables, 163
Layouts: in electronic presentations, 183
Leadership development, 382–387; characteristics, leadership,
    382–384; opportunities, leadership, 384–387
Left (paragraph) indent, 220–221
Left shift key, control of, 51, 56
Legend, in graphs and charts, 197
Letterhead: special documents, 271
Letter keys, 122, 125
Letter keys review, 44, 53
Letter parts, 128–129, 142
Letters: interview follow-up, 281
Line and area graph, 196
Lines, 192
Line spacing, WP, 219
Local area networks (LAN), 24
Long direct reaches, 68

M **key,** control of, 63
Mail merge: address block, 283; data source, 282–284; greeting
    line, 284; main document, 282; merged file, 282; records and
    files, 283
Main document, mail merge, 282
Manufacturer's website, in Help, 93
Math skills, 31, 84, 101, 119, 154, 178; central tendency, measures,
    324; markups and discounts, 207; mental math, 288; probability,
    234; simple interest, 256
Meeting minutes, 260, 400; template, 260, 268–270
Menu, in Help, 93
Merge cells, 162
MLA-style reports, 215–218, 359–361, 398–399; assessment,
    360–361; cover page, 216; documentation, 215, 230–231;

Modern Language Association (MLA) style of report documentation, 399; ellipsis, 216; footnote, 216, 230; formatting, 229–231; header and page number, 216; indentations and long quotations, 216; line spacing, 216; margins, 216; model, 216; report identification, 215; report title, 216; textual citations, 215–216, 229–230, 233; title page, 216; unbound, 216; works cited (references), 216, 398
Monitor, 402
Mouse, 402

N key, control of, 49
Name box, 239
Name of writer in personal-business letter, block style, 129
Negative forms, verbs, 391
Netiquette, 27
News release, 400
Normal view, electronic presentations, 199
Notes: in personal information management, 110
Number expressions, 388
Numbers, database, 294
Numbers, spreadsheets, 246
Numeric keypad, 374–381, 402; addition, 375–379; division, 381; math calculations, 381; multiplication, 380; subtraction, 380
Numeric keys, 365–374
Num (number) lock, 375
Num Lock key, 402

O key, control of, 47
One-hand words, 65, 73, 88
Online training, in Help, 99
Orientation, 98
Orphan line, WP, 220

P key, control of, 65
Page numbers, WP, 220
Page setup, 161
Paragraphs, block, 72, 75
Parentheses, 390
Period key, control of, 51
Periods: spacing after, 51
Personal-business letter, block style: arranged copy, 137; assessment, 354; attachment/enclosure notations, 130; body, 129; complimentary close, 129; date, 128; envelopes, 133, 148; formatting, 137–139; letter mailing address, 129; with mixed punctuation, 140; model copy, 137; open punctuation, 137, 394; return address, 128; unarranged copy, 139; writer name, 129
Personal information management, 104–107; calendar, 107; contacts feature in, 108; E-mail feature, 104; notes, 110; tasks, 104, 109
Personal information manager software (PIMS), 104; assessment, 351
Perspective design theme, in electronic presentations, 184

Photos, in electronic presentations, 192
Pie charts: in electronic presentations, 198–199; spreadsheets, 254
Piracy, 223
Plagiarism, 28, 165
Plural verbs, 391
Pop-up description feature, in Help, 97
Portrait orientation, 163
Print resumes, 274, 277, 401
Pronoun agreement, 391
Pronouns, commonly confused, 391
Proofreaders' marks, 76, 92, 127, 366, 393
Public domain, 28
Punctuation marks, 389–390; spacing with, 51

Q key, control of, 67
Queries, database, 292, 295–296, 319
Question mark (?) key, 74
Question marks, 74, 390
Quotation marks, 390
Quotation marks (") key, 77

R key, control of, 43
Reach technique, 40, 42, 47, 49, 55, 57, 63, 65, 67, 71, 74, 365
Reading view, in electronic presentations, 185
Records: adding to existing database, 301–307; adding to form, 304; adding to table, 303, 309; adding to update database, 311–312; database, 292, 295, 301–302; edit, 314, 322; in mail merge, 283
Reference initials, 130; interoffice memo, 259; in personal-business letter, block style, 130
References: in bound reports, 278; in MLA-style reports, 225, 360
Remove space after paragraph, 133
Repetitive stress injury (RSI), 403–404; carpel tunnel syndrome (CTS), 403; causes of, 403; ergonomic keyboards, 404; reducing risk of, 403; symptoms of, 403
Reports: assessment, 359–361; database, 292, 297; documentation for, 399 See also MLA-style reports; Unbound reports
Response patterns, 89
Resumes, 274–277, 401; electronic, 274, 276, 286, 401; print, 274, 277, 401; scanning, 274
Return address, envelopes, 396
Ribbons, 239
Right shift key, control of, 57
Rough draft (edited copy), 92, 127, 366
Rows: headings on spreadsheets, 241; height in tables, 163; spreadsheets, 239, 245–246

S key, control of, 34
Salutation, in personal-business letter, block style, 129
Scale, in graphs and charts, 196

School and community, 32, 86, 103, 121, 156, 178, 209, 236, 258, 290, 326

Screen tips, in Help, 97

Script copy, 368

Section header layout, in electronic presentations, 183

Semicolon, 390

Sentences: capitalization of first word, 71; spacing after periods ending sentences, 58

Shapes: in electronic presentations, 192

Shifting, 123

Shift keys, 77, 91, 402

Signature, e-mail messages, 393

Singular verbs, 391

Slides: with clip art in electronic presentations, 191; layouts in electronic presentations, 183; presentation in electronic presentations, 200; shapes in electronic presentations, 192; show view in electronic presentations, 185; sorter view in electronic presentations, 185; title layout in electronic presentations, 183

SmartArt, 195

Social network: blog, 25; instant messaging, 25

Soft page break, WP, 219

Software application, using, 15

Software basics, application: active/application windows, 14; toolbars, working with, 13

Sorts: database, 298; information, 317–318, 323; multiple, 299; primary/secondary, 299; tables, 165

Space bar, 35, 50, 52, 56, 59, 125, 402

Spacing, 35, 52, 64, 123; after colons, 71; after commas, 67; double, 70; after an internal, 64; after periods at end of sentence, 58; after periods following initials, 58; after periods in abbreviations, 58; after question marks, 74; single, 70

Spam, 27

Special documents, 259–290; application letter, 287; assessment, 285–287, 362–364; business card, 271; diagram, 271, 285; electronic résumé, 286; flyers, 272–273, 285, 363; letterhead, 271; online pictures, 264; shapes, 263; template, 261, 264; text boxes, 262

Special features, e-mail messages, 393

Spelling Check, 131

Split cells table feature, 162

Spreadsheet applications, 258

Spreadsheets, 237–258; active cell, 240; applications, 258; assessment, 361; cells, 239; change chart layout and styles, 253; change chart type, 252; charts, 252–253; chart sheet, 252; clear and delete cell content and format, 243; column chart, 254; column headings, 241; columns, 239; copy, cut, and move, 244; dialog box launchers, 239; embedded chart, 252; file tab, 239; format cell content, 247; format numbers, 246; formatting worksheets, 241–242, 244–248, 250–251, 254; formula bar, 239; functions, 250;

gridlines, 241; insert and delete rows and columns, 245–246; key formulas, 249; labels and values, 241; list and gallery, 239; move around in a worksheet, 240; name box, 239; numbers, 246; pie charts, 254; quick access toolbar, 239; ribbons, 239; row headings, 241; rows, 239; select and edit cell content, 242; select a range of cells, 243; status/title bar, 239; view buttons, 239; workbook, 238; worksheet, 238; zoom controls, 239

Spreadsheet software, 237

Stars in electronic presentations, 192

Styles: tables, 158; WP, 221

System utilities, 7

T key, control of, 47

Tab key, control of, 76, 78, 402

Table grid, 159

Table of contents, in Help, 93

Tables, 157–176; application and assessment, 174–176; assessment, 355; basic features, 166–169; columns, 157; column width, 158; create new, database, 308–310, 319–320; in database, 292–295, 298; design features, 171–173; in electronic presentations, 196; formatting tables, 159–165; grid, 159; horizontal alignment/placement, 158; layout features, 170–171; navigation, 313; parts, 157; properties, 161; row height, 163; shading and borders, 164; table styles design, 158; update in database, 311–312; vertical placement, 158

Table styles, 164

Tabs: spreadsheets, 239

Tasks, in personal information management, 104, 109

Templates, 190, 259, 265–270

Text boxes, 262

Text from file, WP, 222

Text wrapping break, 133

Thatch design theme, in electronic presentations, 184

Thesaurus, 98, 132

Tick marks, in graphs and charts, 196

Timed writings, 123

Title and content bulleted list, in electronic presentations, 188

Title and content layout, in electronic presentations, 183

Title slide, in electronic presentations, 188

Tools layout tab, tables, 162

U key, control of, 55

Unbound reports, 397; assessment, 359–360; cover page, 227; documentation, 217, 225–228; footnotes, 227, 233, 359; formatting, 215, 217; headings, 217; long quotations, 217; margins and spacing, 217; page numbers, 217; reference lists, 225, 360; styles, 224–225; textual citations, 226–227; titles, 217

Underline, 390

Uniform resource locator (URL), 25

V key, control of, 65
Values, spreadsheets, 241
Verbs: negative forms of, 391; plural, 391; singular, 391
Vertical alignment and placement, tables, 158
View buttons, spreadsheets, 239
View options, in electronic presentations, 185
View presentation, in electronic presentations, 188

W key, control of, 57
Wide area network (WAN), 24
Widow line, WP, 220
Winning edge, 103, 121, 156, 180, 209, BPA, 32; business letter, 86; database design/applications, 326; desktop publishing, 290; FBLA-PBL, 32; interoffice memo, 86; report, 86; spreadsheet applications, 258; WP advanced skills, 236
Word choice, 392
Word Processing (WP) applications: advanced skills, 236; AutoCorrect, 45; bold, 46; bullets, 134; cell content, formatting, 160; cover page, 223; cut, copy, and paste, 54; decimal tabs, 135; envelopes, 133; font group, 130; Grammar Check, 131; hanging indent, 220–221; hard page break, 219; hyphenation, 131; insert, 45; insert endnote/footnote, 159; insert table, 159; layout alignment, 163; left (paragraph) indent, 220–221; line spacing, 70, 219, margins, 70; merge cells, 162; orphan line, 220; overtype, 45; page numbers, 220; portrait orientation, 163; print preview, 62; select text, 54; shading and borders, 164; soft page break, 219; styles, 221; table properties, 160; table styles, 164; tabs, 79; text from file, 222; thesaurus, 132; underline, 46; undo and redo, 62; widow line, 220; zoom, 62.
Work area arrangement, 33
Workbooks, spreadsheets, 238
Workplace simulations: H|P Communications Specialists, 332–349
Worksheets and spreadsheets, 238, 241–242, 244–248, 250–251, 254; tabs, 239
Writer name in personal-business letter, block style, 129

X key, control of, 63
X-axis, in graphs and charts, 196

Y key, control of, 60
Y-axis, in graphs and charts, 196

Z key, control of, 71
Zoom controls, spreadsheets, 239